THE HOUSEHOLD OF EDWARD IV

THE HOUSEHOLD
OF EDWARD IV

THE BLACK BOOK
AND THE
ORDINANCE OF 1478

edited
with Introduction, Notes and Glossary, by
A. R. MYERS
Senior Lecturer in Medieval History
in the University of Liverpool

MANCHESTER UNIVERSITY PRESS

Published by the University of Manchester at
THE UNIVERSITY PRESS
316–324, Oxford Road, Manchester 13

Printed in Great Britain by Butler & Tanner Ltd., Frome and London

To
MY WIFE

PREFACE

This volume is a modified form of a thesis approved by the University of London in 1956 for the award of the degree of Doctor of Philosophy. Its publication was made possible by a prompt and generous grant from the Marc Fitch Fund, to whose founder, committee, and secretary, Mr. F. W. Steer, I am deeply grateful. In the making of this book I was much encouraged by the interest shown by Sir Frank Stenton in the Ordinance of 1478 when I first discovered it, and by the willingness of other scholars to help when asked about particular problems. Wherever possible, this assistance has been acknowledged at the relevant point; but I should like to record here especial gratitude to Dr. R. W. Hunt and Dr. H. Liebeschütz. I also wish to thank Professor J. G. Edwards, Mr. K. B. McFarlane, and Professor J. S. Roskell, who scrutinized the whole work, and Professor G. Barraclough, who read the Introduction, for their suggestions for emendation. I have been heartened by the advice and encouragement of Professor E. F. Jacob, to whom my debts are too great to be ever repaid. I have been greatly aided in the final stages by Professor C. N. L. Brooke, whose unstinted help and wise counsel have been most valuable in the hard task of reducing the bulk of the work for publication. I have also greatly appreciated his generous assistance in the dull but important task of proof-correction. I should like to thank Mr. T. L. Jones, the Secretary of the Manchester University Press, for his help. Finally, I am indebted to the Trustees of the British Museum for permission to reproduce the two drawings in Harleian MS. 642; to the Editor of the Bulletin of the John Rylands Library, Manchester, for permission to reprint the Ordinance of 1445; to the Society of Antiquaries of London for allowing photostats to be made of MS. 211; and to the Librarian of the Queen's College, Oxford, for kindly consenting that MS. 134 be deposited for my use in the University Library, Liverpool.

A. R. MYERS

Liverpool, 1958

TABLE OF CONTENTS

	PAGE
TABLE OF CONTENTS OF THE BLACK BOOK OF THE HOUSEHOLD OF EDWARD IV	ix
INTRODUCTION	I
1. The Importance of Royal and Noble Households in the Fifteenth Century	I
2. The Financing of the Household of Henry VI . .	5
3. The Ordinance of 1445	8
(a) The Character of the Ordinance of 1445 . .	8
(b) The Effects of the Ordinance of 1445 . . .	9
4. Edward IV and the Royal Household . . .	10
5. The Black Book of the Household of Edward IV .	13
(a) The Character of the Black Book . . .	13
(b) The Date and Authorship of the Black Book . .	29
6. The Continued Financial Difficulties of the Royal Household	35
7. The Ordinance of 1478	39
(a) Its Character	39
(b) The Effects of the Ordinance	44
8. Manuscripts.	50
(a) The Ordinance of 1445	50
(b) The Black Book of the Household of Edward IV .	51
(c) The Ordinance of 1478	56
(d) Notes on the Editing of the Manuscripts . . .	60
THE ORDINANCE OF 1445	63
THE BLACK BOOK OF THE HOUSEHOLD OF EDWARD IV .	76
THE BEGINNING OF THE ORDINANCE OF 1478, FOLLOWED BY PROVISIONS OF 1471	198
THE DRAFT OF THE ORDINANCE OF 1478. . . .	203
WARRANT UNDER THE SIGNET FOR THE ENGROSSMENT AND SEALING UNDER THE GREAT SEAL OF THE ORDINANCE OF 1478	211

PAGE

THE ROYAL HOUSEHOLD ORDINANCE OF 1478 . . . 211

ESTIMATE OF THE YEARLY EXPENSES OF THE ROYAL HOUSE-
 HOLD IN THE TIME OF KING HENRY VII . 229

ABBREVIATIONS USED IN THE NOTES TO THE TEXTS . . 231
NOTES TO THE FOREGOING TEXTS 232

 1. The Ordinance of 1445 232
 2. The Black Book of the Household of Edward IV . 233
 3. The Ordinance of 1471 262
 4. The Draft of the Ordinance of 1478 264
 5. The Ordinance of 1478 266

SELECT GLOSSARY 270

 1. English 270
 2. Latin 281
 3. French 284

APPENDIX I: LISTS OF PRINCIPAL OFFICIALS OF THE ROYAL
 HOUSEHOLD DURING THE REIGNS OF THE YORKIST
 KINGS OF ENGLAND 286

 A. Stewards of the Household 286
 B. Chamberlains of the Household 287
 C. Treasurers of the Household 288
 D. Controllers of the Household 289
 E. Cofferers of the Household 290
 F. Treasurers of the Chamber 291
 G. Deans of the Chapel Royal 291
 H. King's Almoners 292
 I. King's Secretaries 293
 J. Keepers of the Great Wardrobe 294
 K. Clerks of the Greencloth 295
 L. Clerks of Controlment 295
 M. King's Physicians 296
 N. King's Surgeons 297

APPENDIX II: THE LOST ORDINANCE OF EDWARD III . . 298
BIBLIOGRAPHY 300
INDEX 309

PLATES

I. DOMUS REGIE MAGNIFICENCIE . . . *facing page* 76
II. DOMUS PROVIDENCIE. . . . . *facing page* 142

TABLE OF CONTENTS OF
THE BLACK BOOK OF THE HOUSEHOLD OF EDWARD IV

SECTION	PAGE	SECTION	PAGE
Tabula	76	30. Secretary: duties, allowances and service . . .	110
1. Domus regis magni . .	79	31. Chaplains: duties, allowances and service . . .	111
2. Domus regis Salamonis .	81		
3. Domus regis Lud . . .	82	32. Squires of the body: duties, allowances and service	111
4. Domus regis Cassibellanj .	83		
5. Domus regis Hardknout . .	83	33. Sewer: duties, allowances and service	112
6. Domus regis Henrici primi	83		
7. Domus regis Edwardi tertii	84	34. Surveyor: duties, allowances and service . . .	113
8. Domus regie magnificencie	86		
9. The present royal household	86	35. Wardrober: duties and livery	114
10. Visus status domus regis .	87		
11. Memorandum on the choice of nine smaller households	89	36. Gentlemen ushers of the chamber: duties, service and allowances	114
12. The king's order to his household officers to apply all the regulations in this book and the reasons for this	89	37. Yeomen of the Crown: duties, service and allowances	116
13. The king's diet and livery	90	38. Yeomen of the chamber: duties and allowances . .	117
14. The king's offerings . .	90		
15. The ordering of the king's chamber	91	39. Wardrobe of robes: duties, service and allowances .	117
16. The queen's service and expenses	92	40. Wardrobe of beds: duties, service and allowances .	119
17. A prince's service, allowances and expenses . .	93	41. Grooms of the chamber: duties, service and allowances	120
18. A duke's allowances, service and expenses	94	42. Pages of the chamber: duties, service and allowances	121
19. A marquis's allowances, service and expenses . . .	96		
20. An earl's allowances, service and expenses . . .	98	43. The jewel-house: duties, service and allowances .	121
21. A bishop confessor's service, allowance and expenses .	100	44. Physician: duties, service and allowances	123
22. The chancellor's fees . .	100	45. Surgeon: duties, service and allowances	124
23. The chamberlain of England's fees	101	46. Apothecary: duties, service and allowances	125
24. The fees of the chief justice of common pleas . . .	101	47. Barber: duties and allowances	125
25. A viscount's allowances and expenses	101	48. Henchmen: service and allowances	126
26. A baron's allowances, service and expenses . .	103	49. Master of henchmen: duties, service and allowances .	126
27. The chamberlain's duties, allowances and service .	104	50. Squires of the household: duties, allowances and expenses	127
28. Bannerets: their duties, allowances and service .	106		
29. Knights of Household: duties, allowances and expenses	108	51. Kings at arms, heralds and pursuivants: duties, service and allowances	130

xi

SECTION	PAGE
52. Sergeants at arms: duties, service and allowances	131
53. Minstrels: duties, service and allowances	131
54. A wait: duties and allowances	132
55. Messengers: duties, service and allowances	133
56. Dean of the Chapel: duties, service and allowances	133
57. Chaplains and Clerks of the Chapel: duties, service and allowances	135
58. Yeomen of the Chapel: duties, service and allowances	136
59. Children of the Chapel: allowances and nurture	136
60. Clerk of the closet: duties, service and allowances	137
61. Master of grammar: duties, service and allowances	137
62. Office of vestiary: duties, service and allowances	138
63. Clerk of the Crown: fees	139
64. Clerk of the market: duties and fees	140
65. Clerk of the works: livery	141
66. Wards' marriages: expenses	141
67. Domus providencie	141
68. Steward of the household: rights, duties and allowances	142
69. Treasurer of the household: rights, duties and allowances	144
70. The treasurer's oath	146
71. Controller of the household: duties, service and allowances	147
72. The controller's oath	149
73. Cofferer of the household: duties, service and allowances	150

SECTION	PAGE
74. Clerks of the greencloth: duties, service and allowances	152
75. Clerk of controlment: duties, service and allowances	154
76. The counting house: duties and powers	156
77. The counting house: staff and allowances	158
78. The regulations of the counting house	160
79. The bakehouse: staff, duties and allowances	165
80. The pantry: staff, duties and allowances	169
81. The wafer: staff, duties and allowances	172
82. The butler of England: duties, servants and fees	174
83. The purveyors of wine: duties and allowances	176
84. The cellar: staff, duties and allowances	177
85. The buttery of ale: staff, duties and allowances	181
86. The pitcher-house and cup-house: staff, duties and allowances	183
87. The office of ale-takers: staff, duties and allowances	184
88. The great spicery: staff, duties and allowances	186
89. The office of confectionary: staff, duties and allowances	188
90. The office of chandlery: staff, duties and allowances	190
91. The office of ewery and napery: staff, duties and allowances	192
92. The office of laundry: staff, duties and allowances	195

INTRODUCTION

1. The Importance of Royal and Noble Households in the Fifteenth Century

A hundred years ago the great household was still a most potent force in every aspect of English life. Despite Radical and Chartist agitations it was still in full vigour; indeed, it was just entering the Indian summer of the Victorian age. Its ancestry and importance stretched back in unbroken succession through the centuries, from the households of a Marquis of Salisbury, an Earl of Derby, or a Duke of Newcastle, to those of Godwin, Brihtnoth, or Alfred. Now, however, apart from those of the Crown, the great houses are fast becoming museums, public institutions, hotels, or ruins—anything but the social units and important centres of power which, under the great variations that themselves attest the vitality of the institution, they had been for over a thousand years. This means that now, as never before, there is a danger of underestimating the importance of aristocratic and hierarchical principles in English history. It is very natural that in the present century there should have been a growth of investigation into the history of peasants and town workers, a shift of interest from the architecture of mansions to the development of middle-class villas and worker's cottages. But it should not unwittingly draw us into underestimating the importance of aristocratic leadership and the great household before the twentieth century. To-day, with the withering of the noble households and the gathering of their records into county record offices, more information is available about their life than ever before. But already there are some for whom attention to the organization of a great household seems irrelevant. For them it is only a matter for indignation that in 1587 Henry, Earl of Derby, should have had 118 persons in daily attendance upon him,[1] or that in 1512 the Earl of Northumberland had twenty servants on duty in the Great Chamber in the morning, eighteen in the afternoon and thirty in the evening;[2] a matter of indifference what were the duties of a Comptroller or a Gentleman-Usher and whether they took precedence over a Treasurer or a Carver. Yet if we fail to realize that at the time these things seemed both natural and momentous, we shall miss an important element in the spirit of the age and the dynamic forces of its society.

[1] *Derby Household Books*, pp. 23–37.
[2] *Northumberland Household Book*, p. 45

I

This is especially true of the fifteenth century. When it opened, developments of the fourteenth century such as its prolonged warfare, the rise of indentured retinues, and the growing political and financial weakness of the Crown, had not only made the aristocracy more powerful in the realm; the fluidity of the social order, and in particular of the 'affinity' [1] on which the strength of a noble was essentially based, meant that the power of the magnates was increasingly competitive. If a lord did not ceaselessly strive to maintain and to enlarge his affinity, he might find himself in the position of a modern bank if the rumour should begin to spread that its finances were no longer sound. No more than a bank could a magnate afford to look shabby and poverty-stricken; on the contrary, in this lethally competitive society he must impress men by his ostentation and attract them by his hospitality. It is not uncharitable to see other motives besides unlimited generosity in the princely bounty of 'Warwick the Kingmaker' [2] or in the gargantuan feast of his brother George Neville at his installation as Archbishop of York in 1467. Six thousand guests are said to have been present, including dukes, duchesses, earls, countesses, bishops, abbots, deans, lords, ladies, mayors, and judges; and the kitchen provided, amongst other items, 300 quarters of wheat, 300 tuns of ale, 100 tuns of wine, 104 oxen, 6 bulls, 1,000 sheep, 2,000 geese, 2,000 pigs, 2,000 chickens, 4,000 pigeons, 4,000 rabbits, 2,000 hot custards, 3,000 baked cold custards, 3,000 dishes of jelly, and 4,000 cold tarts. [3]

This description is characteristic of the time in two other important respects. It states with care just what grades of guests were seated together and to which rooms they were assigned—great chamber, gallery, or hall; and it gives a meticulous description of the complicated ritual of serving the archbishop, a solemn rite involving gentleman usher, yeoman of the ewry, pantler, carver, sewer, cupbearer, marshal, and chaplain, not to mention many lowlier ministers. Such magnificence, grading and formality were the product of many causes. In part they were due to the tensions between the craving for stability and the fact of change. Fifteenth-century society was competitive and fluid, yet wished to maintain respect for order and degree. It is no accident that this century, when the number of 'bourgeois gentilhommes' was quickly increasing, saw the appearance of more books on etiquette than ever before, telling one how to behave in courtly circles and devoting special attention to

---

[1] Much has recently been written to illustrate this point; specially illuminating is K. B. McFarlane's article 'Bastard Feudalism', *B.I.H.R.*, XX (1945), 161–80.

[2] Cf. *Great Chronicle*, p. 207.

[3] Leland, *Collectanea*, ed. T. Hearne (1744), VI. 2 ff.

subtle differences and equivalences of rank.[1] Feudal tenures had lost their *raison d'être*; but the trappings of chivalry grew more splendid, orders of knighthood increased in numbers, pomp and pretensions, the rules of courtesy became more artificially strict. The use of symbolism and allegory grew more elaborate and far-fetched. The old tradition of aristocratic patronage and generosity was transmuted into seignorial control and ostentation. Here were factors to urge great households forward to ever greater magnificence and to a formalism of arrangement which in its more important aspects had the air of a solemn ritual,[2] with symbolical interpretations of its moral or theological significance.

The eighteenth-century historian Vico gave a salutary warning against exaggerating the grandeur of past ages; but we must not underestimate the importance of magnificence as a social ideal in the fifteenth century, merely because our time is apt to prefer comfort and convenience in its way of living. Our modern attempts at an easy informality in social intercourse may prevent us from understanding the importance attached in the fifteenth century to order and degree. There is a kernel of truth in the view of the nobility of this time that 'as they gradually emerged from this barbarity (which happened as soon as the feudal institutions began to relax) they found it necessary to establish very minute domestic regulations, to keep their turbulent followers in peace and order. And from living in a state of disorderly grandeur, void of all system, they naturally enough ran into the opposite extreme, of reducing every thing, even the most trifling disbursements, to stated rule.'[3]

All these tendencies of the age found their fullest expression in the Court of Burgundy, which not only in art and in dress but in household management set the fashions for Western Europe. In the later fifteenth century the ruling classes were eager to know what was the latest Burgundian fashion of jerkin or doublet, to have their portraits painted by a Memling or a Van der Goes, to see their churches decorated by Flemish wall painters and glaziers, to possess Flemish manuscripts as sumptuously illuminated as those of the Burgundian

---

[1] See, for example, the fifteenth-century books on etiquette collected in *The Babees Book*, ed. F. J. Furnivall (E.E.T.S., London, 1868, Orig. Series, No. 32). Cf. the elaborate sumptuary laws of 1463 and 1483 (*R.P.*, V. 504–6, VI. 220–1), prescribing the degree of magnificence in clothing which each rank in society was to be allowed to wear.

[2] Cf. for example, the very detailed and intricate rite for serving a lord at meals, as described in *A Fifteenth Century Courtesy Book*, ed. R. W. Chambers (E.E.T.S., Orig. Series, Vol. 148, 1914), pp. 11–15. Much of this tradition of symbolical formality in the serving of meals still survived in the seventeenth century, as may be seen in *Some rules and orders for the government of the House of an Earle set downe by Richard Braithwait* (London, 1821), pp. 22–5.

[3] *Antiquitates Culinariae*, by Rev. Richard Warner (London, 1791), p. xlvi.

dukes and nobility. So it was with the conduct of the household. The example of the Burgundian court was potent, from the duties of its resplendent officials to its rules of etiquette, which regulated precisely how many paces nobles of varying ranks should advance to welcome a guest or the numbers of times a superior should, out of politeness, offer precedence to those of lower rank before himself leading the way. We find the Burgundian master of ceremonies, Olivier de la Marche, recognized throughout Western Europe as the greatest authority of the age on court ceremonials and rules, responding to an English request for information on the question of household management, especially the immensely complicated ritual of regulating a banquet, by writing in 1473–4 his *L'État de la Maison du Duc Charles de Bourgongne dict le Hardy*.[1] Something of the influence exerted by Burgundian culture on Edward IV may be seen in his collection of sumptuously illuminated Flemish manuscripts,[2] begun after his exile in 1470–1 when he had been so impressed by the Seigneur de la Gruthuyse's great library at Bruges. Burgundian standards of opulence probably affected, too, the elaborate entertainment provided for Louis de Gruthuyse when he came to England in 1472 to be created Earl of Winchester by his former guest.[3]

The desire to vie with the court of Burgundy, or at any rate the need for the English court to achieve a certain degree of magnificence and order, may well have been one of the reasons which prompted the compilation of the Black Book of the Household of Edward IV. The widespread feeling that these qualities were not only fitting but necessary for the king's court can be seen in the preamble to Henry VII's Act of Resumption in 1485. '. . . your Honorable Houshold . . . must be kept and borne Worshipfully and Honorably, as it accordeth to the Honour of your Estate and your said Realme, by the whiche your Adversaries and Enemyes shall fall into the drede wherin heretofore they have byne'.[4] But it was not only a matter of impressing foreign observers; it was necessary to present an effective counter

[1] See bibliography and cf. O. Cartellieri, *The Court of Burgundy*, esp. pp. 135–63.

[2] These and other volumes acquired by Edward IV form, of course, the nucleus of the Old Royal Library in the British Museum; cf. Harleian MS. 4780, f. 21b, for the payments of Pier Curteys, Keeper of the Great Wardrobe, in 1480, for binding, gilding, and dressing various books, and (f. 40b) for the expense of binding six books in velvet, blue and black silk, with laces and tassels of silk, 'buttons' of blue silk and gold, and clasps of copper and gilt adorned with roses and the royal arms.

[3] C. L. Kingsford, *English Historical Literature in the Fifteenth Century*, pp. 379–88.

[4] *R.P.*, VI. 336.

attraction to the splendours of seignorial establishments. If an earl of Warwick could enter London in 1458 with a train of 600 men, all in red jackets adorned with his badge of the ragged staff,[1] if, after nearly 25 years of Tudor subjugation of the old nobility, the Duke of Buckingham could celebrate Epiphany with 319 guests at dinner and 279 at supper at Thornbury Castle,[2] then it was essential for the Crown to ensure an impressive and well-ordered court.[3] A king who failed to keep up the state expected of royalty would forfeit support, as did Henry VI at his re-adeption in 1470. Observers were repelled not only by his mental incapacity but by his poverty; his progress, it was said, was 'more lyker a play than the shewyng of a prynce to wynne mennys hertys, ffor by this mean he lost many and wan noon or Rygth ffewe, and evyr he was shewid In a long blew goune of velvet as thowth he hadd noo moo to chaunge with'.[4] Abbot Whethamstede pityingly records[5] how Henry, after spending Easter at St. Albans in 1459, gave his best robe to the prior and how the treasurer of the realm had to redeem it, much against the king's wishes, for the sum of 50 marks, because it was the only presentable gown which the king possessed for state occasions.

2. The Financing of the Household of Henry VI

But if it was necessary to avoid the shabby indigence of the household of Henry VI, it was also essential to shun its expensive inefficiency. Financial stability was an aim which neither Henry IV nor his son and grandson were able to achieve; the Crown's financial position grew steadily worse, and by the time that Henry VI came of age, it was already very grave.[6] The normal revenue had suffered a further heavy fall during his minority, owing in part to the corruption

---

[1] *Great Chronicle*, p. 207. We are told on pp. 206–7 that in January Warwick had brought 400 men to London, Salisbury 500, the Dukes of Exeter and Somerset 800, Northumberland, Egremont and Clifford 1,500 men.

[2] *Archaeologia*, XXV (1834), 325.

[3] When the brother of the queen of Bohemia visited England in 1466 Edward IV welcomed his party with a feast of 50 courses; but during their visit they were entertained by two earls (of whom one was presumably Warwick) with a feast of 60 courses and were impressed accordingly (*Des böhmischen Herrn Leos von Rozmittal Ritter-, Hof- und Pilger-Reise durch die Abendlande, 1465–67* (Stuttgart, 1844), pp. 155–8.

[4] *Great Chronicle*, p. 215.

[5] *Registrum Abbatiae Johannis Whethamstede Abbatis Monasterii Sancti Albani*, ed. H. T. Riley (Rolls Series, 1872), I. 323.

[6] As the statement of the Treasurer, Lord Cromwell, in 1433 strikingly showed, *R.P.*, IV. 433–8. Mr. J. L. Kirby's attempt to lessen the seriousness of the position, in his 'The Issues of the Lancastrian Exchequer and Lord Cromwell's Estimates of 1433' in *B.I.H.R.*, XXIV (1951), pp. 121–51, does not

B

and incompetence of the council and the growing strain of the
French war; and the increasing inability of the government to pay
its way was reflected in a large and mounting debt—from £168,000 in
1433 to £372,000 in 1449.[1] This in turn made it more difficult to raise
loans and drove up the rate of interest which had to be paid for them
—to between 25 and 33⅓ per cent according to Sir John Fortescue.[2]
The deepening financial insolvency and confusion was reflected in
the increasing debts of the household, which added to the growing
dissatisfaction in the country against the government. For the reign
of Henry V[3] and the early years of Henry VI[4] it could be pleaded that
the household had to help to finance the war; but the fact remains
that by 1432 fifteen accountants of the household were having to ask
in a parliamentary petition for pardon for arrears of accounts as far
back as the beginning of the reign,[5] and by 1433 the debts of the
household totalled approximately £11,000.[6] And as the burden of
the French war on the household was lightened, the position grew,
not better, but worse. In 1433 the expenses of the household had
been estimated at about £13,000; by 1449 they were reckoned
at £24,000, as against a total basic royal revenue (lyvelode) of
only £5,000.[7] By 1449 the serjeants, gentlemen, yeomen, priests,
and clerks of the household were forced to petition parliament for
arrears of wages, overdue by several years and amounting to over
£3,800.[8]

Attempts were made to remedy this position. Assignments of
specified items of revenue were repeatedly made for the expenses of

appear altogether convincing, though his article is useful for its analysis of
Lord Cromwell's statement and of the contemporary receipt and issue rolls of
the Exchequer.

[1] *R.P.*, IV. 43, 463.

[2] Sir John Fortescue, *The Governance of England*, p. 118; K. B. McFarlane,
'Loans to the Lancastrian Kings; The Problem of Inducement', *Cambridge
Historical Journal*, IX (1947), pp. 51–68.

[3] Cf. the summary of Miss Eileen de L. Fagan's M.A. thesis entitled 'Some
Aspects of the King's Household in the Reign of Henry V' in *B.I.H.R.*, XIV
(1937), 194–5; Tout, *Chapters*, IV. 225.

[4] The household accounts of the earlier years of Henry VI deal with amounts
far higher than those for his later years, and it is clear that much if not all of
these extra sums were for war expenditure. In the accounts of John Hotoft for
8–9 Henry VI and of John Tirell for 9–15 Hy. VI they are described as 'custos
garderobe hospicij regis nunc Henrici Sexti ac Thesaurarij guerre eiusdem
regis' (E 101/408/9, 13).

[5] *R.P.*, IV. 397.

[6] *Ibid.*, IV. 436.

[7] *Ibid.*, IV. 435, V. 183. The total expenditure of the household had been
estimated in 1433 at £13,678 12s. 11d.; but of this sum £733 6s. 8d. was for royal
works and the repair of Windsor Castle.

[8] *Ibid.*, V. 157–9.

the household,[1] as had been done in the days of Henry IV;[2] but as these items had often been allocated to other purposes or granted away to other persons, this device did not solve the problem of chronic deficits.[3] As in the reign of Henry IV, the weakness of the monarchy and the widespread discontent with the management of the royal household resulted in repeated demands for its reform. In 1442 the king granted a petition of the commons in parliament that 'as many of your Lordes as it pleasith your Highnesse, to have suffisaunt power and autorite to se establish, apoynte and ordeign, that good and sadde ruele be hadde in and of your seid Houshold, and that redy paiement in hand be hadde for the dispenses of the same Houshold, in the fourme above seid'.[4] Perhaps it was partly as a result of this commission's labours that an Ordinance[5] for the reform of the household was introduced in parliament in 1445 and apparently received the royal assent:[6] perhaps it was partly due to the necessity of making provision for the newly-wedded Queen Margaret, who arrived in England in April 1445, and for whom revenues of nearly £6,700 were assigned in the parliament of this year.[7] The financial problems of the household may have been made all the more pressing by the diversion of revenues to pay for the expenses of her coming to England, expenses which amounted to over £5,560.[8]

[1] E.g. *R.P.*, IV. 7, 32, 62, 474; V. 7, 58, 63, 70-2, 174-6, 183-99, 217-24, 229, 246-7, 293, 300, 320-1.   [2] *Ibid.*, III. 528, 548, 579, 586.

[3] Only a minority of the household accounts are now available, and of these only the smaller part is complete; but where a balance can be struck, the result is either a plain excess of expenditure over receipts (e.g. in the account book of Sir John Stourton, keeper of the wardrobe for 30-31 Hy. VI the total receipts are £13,248 13s. 2½d. against total expenses of £15,976 3s. 0d.; E 101/410/9) or a small credit balance, achieved only with the help of subventions from the queen's income (e.g. the account of William Fallan, keeper of the wardrobe, for the period 3rd December, 33 Hy. VI, to 11th May, 34 Hy. VI, shows a credit balance of just over £1,273, but the queen's receiver had contributed £3,668; E 101/410/15).

[4] *Ibid.*, V. 63.   [5] See below for the text.   [6] Cf. below, p. 50, n. 4; p. 51.

[7] She was able at times to dispose of a larger revenue than this. In the only account of hers still preserved in the Public Record Office (D.L. 28/5/8, published by the present writer in *B.J.R.L.*, Vol. XL (1957-8), her total income for the year 31-32 Henry VI amounted to over £7,560. In his thesis on 'The royal household, 1437-60', awarded the Oxford D.Phil. degree in 1953, Dr. G. L. Harriss has shown that the king's marriage was one of the factors upsetting the royal household's finances which had until 1445 enjoyed a comparative stability but thereafter sank into chronic insolvency. I have not seen the thesis, but its conclusions on this point were communicated to me by Professor E. F. Jacob, and Dr. Harriss has kindly allowed me to quote them.

[8] Add. MS. 23, 938. Only £5,129 2s. 0d. had been assigned from real income; and the account closed with a debit balance of £434 15s. 5d. due to the accountants, John Brekenoke and John Everdon.

3. THE ORDINANCE OF 1445

(a) The Character of the Ordinance of 1445

Unlike the ordinance of Henry VII[1] this is not concerned with the regulation of the details of elaborate ceremonial but it resembles in many ways the household ordinances of both past and future reigns —for example, of Edward II or of Edward IV and Henry VIII.[2] Like the ordinance of 1478, which resembles it in general form and repeats many of its provisions, it is concerned with promoting economy in the running of the household. It ends with lists of permitted personnel and their proper allowances. It tries to check expenditure by detailed regulations of the consumption of food, light, and fuel, the ordering of supplies, and the numbers and categories of approved personnel; and the instrument for seeing that these regulations were observed was to be the countinghouse. Such provisions can be found in rules for the government of the royal household from the twelfth century to the seventeenth.[3]

But there are also significant differences. We are given a glimpse of the weak kindliness of Henry VI in the concession that all the king's squires and officials[4] who were not on the establishment should have the right to come to the king's court at the five principal feasts of the year, during sessions of parliament and great councils, or even at the 'coming of strangers', if they could persuade one of the chief officials of the household to authorize it (§19). The royal improvidence necessitated a provision that if the king should order any additional charges for his household, he should also find the money for them, and that if any privy seal or other warrant were directed to the officers of the household, telling them to undertake any charge not allowed by the establishment, they should disregard such a warrant (§24).[5] Nevertheless, in fairness it must be noted that most of the provisions were sufficiently wise and commendable to be re-enacted in 1478. Both ordinances give prominence to the

---

[1] *Household Ordinances*, pp. 109–33. The editors were mistaken in ascribing this ordinance to 1494. As the regnal years of Henry VII dated from 22 August, 31 December 9 Hy. VII was 31 December 1493.

[2] *Edward II*, pp. 244–84; O 1478 (printed below); *Household Ordinances*, pp. 137–240.

[3] Cf. 'The Constitutio Domus Regis' of Henry I, in *Dialogus de Scaccario*, ed. C. Johnson, pp. 129–35, and 'The Establishment of the Household of King William and Queen Mary, A.D. 1689' in *Household Ordinances*, pp. 380–422.

[4] For the year 25–26 Hy. VI as many as 247 squires received money for robes (E 101/409/16, f. 34a).

[5] The weakness and confusion of Henry's government are further reflected in §§13 and 31 of the ordinance.

perennial question of abuse of purveyance, against which the commons petitioned in this parliament of 1445.[1]

(b) The Effects of the Ordinance of 1445

If this ordinance came into force, it was not effective in solving the financial difficulties of the household, nor, indeed, did it have a very long life. As already mentioned, by 1449 the chancellor and treasurer felt it necessary to give a very alarming picture of the expenses of the household in relation to the revenue, and many classes of household servants were having to petition for arrears of wages, overdue by several years and amounting to more than £3,800. One result of these financial predicaments was that in 1450 for the benefit of the creditors of the household special assignments of the Lancaster revenues and the customs to the amount of £5,677 a year were made for seven years, the unappropriated balance of the duchy of Lancaster revenues to be applied to the current expenses of the household. Perhaps this act was largely vitiated, like the act of resumption of the same year, by the exceptions to its operation; at any rate in 1454 it was repealed and a new act was passed authorizing the treasurer of England to assign to the treasurer of the household for three years revenues amounting to nearly £5,200 a year, towards the payment of the household expenses; but the effect of this act, too, was lessened by provisos appended to it.[2]

Already in 1453 the king's first attack of madness had begun, and in consequence a Great Council was held in the autumn of 1454. One of its measures was to make a new ordinance for the household reducing the size of the royal household to 424 officials and servants for the king, 120 for the queen, and 38 for the prince;[3] nevertheless the numbers appear to be greater than were contemplated by the Ordinance of 1445. But as the king recovered his wits about Christmas

---

[1] R.P., V. 103.

[2] Ibid., 183a, 157–9, 174a–6a, 246b–7b, 237a–8a. The schedules of provisos to the Act of 1454, said to have been signed and delivered into parliament by the king himself, are obviously in the wrong place as they follow an article proroguing parliament, and precede the act they qualify.

[3] Ascribed by the Society of Antiquaries' edition of 1790 (Household Ordinances, pp. *15–*24) to the year 1455, this ordinance was correctly dated and more accurately printed by Sir N. H. Nicolas in Proceedings, VI. 220–33. The Black Book of the Household of Edward IV allows a smaller number of servants to the queen but a larger number to the prince—100 and 50 respectively. The household authorized for Henry VI remained about the same in size as that allowed in 1445, but the queen's household was doubled by 1454, and the prince's staff was, of course, additional. It is of interest to note that the staff of 120 authorized by the ordinance of 1454 represented a reduction for the queen, who had in fact paid wages to 151 servants for the year Michaelmas 1452–Michaelmas 1453 (D.L. 28/5/8, ff. 12a–14b).

1454, and Margaret loathed the regime of York's Protectorship, the Ordinance of November 1454 probably remained effective for a far briefer span than its predecessor. In July 1455, after the first battle of St. Albans, the chancellor, Archbishop Bourchier, in declaring to parliament the reasons for its summons, stated that its prime purpose was 'to establish an ordinate and a substantiall rule for the Kynges honourable Houshold, and to ordeign where redy paiement shall growe for the expenses of the same'. A committee of lords was therefore appointed to consider its management; and perhaps it was responsible for the act passed in this parliament, applying the revenues of the principality of Wales and the duchy of Cornwall to the expenses of the king's household until the prince was 14 years old, certain sums being reserved for the upkeep of the prince's household.[1] The committee was unsuccessful in solving the problem of ensuring the solvency of the royal household; for soon afterwards we find a chronicler complaining that the king was still in debt, although he 'helde no householde ne meyntened no warres.'[2] Indeed, the household treasurer's account for the period 3 December 1455 to 11 May 1456 was presented to the Exchequer only in the following reign.[3]

4. EDWARD IV AND THE ROYAL HOUSEHOLD

These, then, were the problems to which Edward IV succeeded in the administration of the royal household: to make it pay its way and yet contrive that its appearance and mode of life should be impressive. The king's subjects had had enough of unpaid household bills and wages, and purveyance without adequate recompense; yet Sir John Fortescue was probably only voicing a general sentiment when he declared: 'Item it shall nede that the kyng haue such tresour, as he mey make new bildynges whan he woll, ffor his pleasure and magnificence; and as he mey bie hym riche clothes, riche furres, . . . rich stones . . . and other juels and ornamentes conuenyent to his estate roiall. And often tymes he woll bie riche hangynges and other apparell ffor his howses . . . and do other suche nobell and grete costes, as bi sitith is roiall mageste . . . Ffor yff a king did not so, nor myght do, he lyved then not like his estate, but rather in miseire, and in more subgeccion than doth a priuate person.'[4]

---

[1] *R.P.*, V. 279a and b, 293b.
[2] *An English Chronicle, 1377–1461*, ed. J. S. Davies (Camden Society, 1856), p. 79. 'His dettes encreased dayly but payment was there none.'
[3] E 101/410/15. Henry and Margaret are referred to as 'nuper rex' and 'nuper regina'. Characteristically there would have been a deficit (of nearly £1,400) but for a grant of nearly £3,700 from the queen's receiver-general.
[4] Fortescue, *op. cit.*, p. 125.

A generation of growing disorder, culminating in a bloody civil war, had aroused in many influential elements of society a deep longing for a strong government, with financial solvency and restored prestige.

In this situation the throne was occupied by a man who not only knew the importance of charming beholders[1] and impressed both home and foreign observers by the magnificence of his court,[2] but was the first king since Henry II to die, not in debt, but worth a fortune.[3] The king who could show his powers of initiative and determination in tackling disorder in the realm[4] and display his acumen and success in merchantry[5] was unlikely to neglect so pressing a problem as restoring the credit of the household[6] and putting the establishment of the royal household on a satisfactory footing. The members of the house of York were alive to the need for well-regulated households; apart from Edward IV's ordinances for his own household, and that of his heir at Ludlow,[7] we have a household ordinance of his mother Cecily, Duchess of York,[8] his

---

[1] Cf., for example, Sir Thomas More's *Life of Richard III* (ed. J. R. Lumby' Cambridge, 1883), p. 2; Polydore Vergil's *English History* (ed. Sir Henry Ellis, Camden Society, 1844), p. 116; *Great Chronicle*, pp. 223, 228–9.

[2] *Continuator of the Croyland Chronicle*, ed. W. Fulman, apud Gale's *Scriptores* (1684), p. 563; 'The Record of Bluemantle Pursuivant, 1471–2', in Kingsford, *op. cit.*, pp. 379–388; *Ritter-, Hof-, und Pilger-Reise*, etc., pp. 155–8.

[3] *Croyland Chronicle Cont.*, pp. 559–60, D. Mancini, *The Usurpation of Richard III*, ed. C. B. J. Armstrong (Oxford, 1936), pp. 81, 87, 99.

[4] Cf., for example, *R.P.*, V. 487; *The Coventry Leet Book* (E.E.T.S., Part II, 1908), pp. 373–4; *The Paston Letters* (ed. J. Gairdner, Edinburgh, 1910), II. 76; Gloucester Annals, s.a. 1463, in Kingsford, *op. cit.*, p. 356; *Great Chronicle*, pp. 220–1; *Croyland Chron. Cont.*, p. 559.

[5] Scofield, *Edward the Fourth*, II. 404–16.

[6] Cf. B. P. Wolffe, 'The Management of the English Royal Estates under the Yorkist Kings', *E.H.R.*, LXXI (1956), 1–27, for an analysis of the determined and successful efforts made by Edward IV and his officials to reorganize the administration of the royal estates under the king's chamber, partly to help the finances of the royal household. Cf. also J. R. Lander, 'Edward IV; The Modern Legend and a Revision', *History*, XLI (1956), 38–52.

[7] The ordinance of Prince Edward's household made in 1473 is printed in *Household Ordinances*, pp. *27–*33 (where it is wrongly dated as 1474). One copy is to be found in Lord Steward's Dept. Misc. Bks. 280, ff. 277a–9b, where the word omitted on p. *30, line 8, is quite clear; it is 'man'. In 1483 a slight revision of the ordinance was made, chiefly owing to the prince's increasing years (e.g. bedtime at 9 p.m. instead of 8); this revised version is to be found in Sloane MS. 3479, ff. 53b–8a.

[8] *Household Ordinances*, pp. *37–9. It is said to be printed 'From a Collection of Papers, which formerly belonged to Sir Julius Caesar; now at the Board of Greencloth'. It was therefore in all likelihood taken from what is now Lord Steward's Dept. Misc. Book 280, ff. 284a–6a, for this was formerly part of the papers of Sir Julius Caesar. Folio 285b has material which was printed in the

brother George, Duke of Clarence,[1] and his brother Richard, who when king issued a brief ordinance touching the governance of his household in the north.[2] Moreover, apart from the urgent necessity of marrying economy with regal splendour, the revival in the strength of the monarchy gave the royal household increased importance in the work of government. It has, for example, been said that 'the importance of this reign in the development of the secretaryship can hardly be overemphasized';[3] and the secretary was still a resident member of the royal household, as the *Liber Niger* reminds us.[4] A great deal of work remains to be done on Edward IV's use of the royal household and its personnel in the task of reviving a strong rule; but even reading a list of the principal officials of the household[5] will remind us of the number of extremely influential men of Yorkist England who held some appointment there. Hence considerations of administrative efficiency probably strengthened other motives in rendering particularly desirable a well-ordered household.

Yet in the early years of the new reign the state of the household was such as to cause uneasiness. The government of Edward IV tried to establish its credit, even to the extent of honouring bad debts of the household of Henry VI;[6] but in the first years of the new reign there were considerable deficits on the working of the household.[7] In the year 6–7 Edward IV, he had for the first time a surplus;[8] but the settlement of accounts apparently remained in such arrears

---

wrong place—after the Ordinance of the household of Prince Edward (pp. *32–*33)—namely, a list of perquisites of the various household offices and a statement of more rules of the house. Probably the ordinance of Prince Edward was taken from the same manuscript; though we are in this case given no indication about the provenance.

[1] *Household Ordinances*, pp. 89–105. Taken from the Society of Antiquaries MS. 211.

[2] Harleian MS. 433, ff. 269a–b. This ordinance was made before 24 July 1484, and applied to the household of the Council of the North. For a modernized text of this ordinance see C. A. Halsted, *Life of Richard III*, II (1844), 524–5. Miss Halsted gave the year as 1 Richard III instead of 2 Richard III.

[3] J. Otway-Ruthven, *The King's Secretary and the Signet Office in the XVth Century* (Cambridge, 1939), p. 17.

[4] See below, Black Book, §30.   [5] See below, App. I.

[6] A. Steel, *The Receipt of the Exchequer, 1377–1485* (Cambridge, 1954), p. 285.

[7] Deficits of £2,384 1s. 5¼d. on the first seven months (E 101/411/11) and £1,894 10s. 1¾d. for the year Michaelmas 3 Ed. IV to Michaelmas 4 Ed. IV (E 101/411/13). Though the treasurer's account for 5–6 Ed. IV is incomplete, there is plainly a deficit, for the total receipts are £6,630 16s. 0¾d., whereas the incomplete list of expenses totals £10,210 18s. 10d. (E 101/411/15); and for the three years 3–6 Ed. IV the receipts of the household treasurer had been £23,978 0s. 3¼d., whereas his outgoings had been £37,643 11s. 3d. (E 101/411/14).

[8] A surplus of £656 17s. 8¼d. (E 101/412/2).

during this decade that in the eleventh year of Edward IV the controlment books for the year 3–8 Edward IV had still not been delivered to the exchequer.[1] Part of the difficulty was the inadequacy of the income of the household; but the continued insecurity of the king throughout this decade made it difficult for the king to give his attention to household reform. His expenses were so heavy and his income so depleted that he had to have frequent resort to loans.[2]

After the king's return from exile in 1471 and the crushing victories of Barnet and Tewkesbury, it became at once more possible and more desirable for Edward and his councillors to turn their attention to the administration of the household. More possible, now that he was securely in the saddle; more desirable, in that he must have been aware of the widespread disappointment that in the first decade of his reign his government had failed to 'amende alle manere of thynges that was amysse'[3] and that as he grew older 'he began to slyde by lyttle and lyttle into avarice'.[4] This decade therefore saw attempts at the reform of the household and finally the publication of the Ordinance of 1478. But before considering these matters it is necessary to discuss the nature of much the biggest document of this reign dealing with the royal household, the *Liber Niger Domus Regis Anglie Edwardi Quarti*, or Black Book of the Household of Edward IV.[5]

5. THE BLACK BOOK OF THE HOUSEHOLD OF EDWARD IV

(a) The Character of the Black Book

After some suitable quotations from recognized authorities, ranging from Aristotle and the Bible to St. Bernard, and a picture of the king seated in state at table,[6] the book opens with a grandi-loquent introduction.[7] This discourses on the bounty of the Divine Steward, and asserts that it is the duty of kings to copy this divine example, especially the king of England who rules such a fertile realm. These sentiments are buttressed by quotations from Scripture, Aristotle, Cassiodorus, and Augustine, and the warning is added that royal magnificence must be regulated by a sense of

[1] King's Remembrancer's Memoranda Roll, Easter Term, 12 Ed. IV (E 159/249); privy seal dated 22 February, 11 Ed. IV.

[2] Cf., for example, Scofield, *op. cit.*, I. 195 and Steel, *op. cit.*, pp. 284–96.

[3] J. Warkworth, *Chronicle* (Camden Society, 1839), p. 12.

[4] Polydore Vergil, *op. cit.*, p. 172.

[5] Presumably so called from the colour of the covers in which it was bound, as were the Black Book and the Red Book of the Exchequer (*The Red Book of the Exchequer* (ed. Hubert Hall, Rolls Series, 1896), I. iv–vi).

[6] Below, p. 76, and Plate I facing it.

[7] B.B., §§1–9; and see notes to these sections.

moderation. Examples are then given of famous kings who had kept truly magnificent households—Solomon, Lud, Cassivellaunus, Harthacnut, Henry I, and Edward III. The last-named is especially praised for his household statutes, to which the Black Book looks back as its model. The authors list the six qualities needed for a household of regal magnificence and conclude the introduction by asserting that this book which follows has been made after much deliberation among the king's councillors and careful consideration of the expenses and conduct of royal houses. Liveries, wages, clothing, fees, rewards, and other dues are to be defined so that every officer shall be able to serve the king honourably. Ecclesiastes provides a fitting conclusion: 'Domus regis edificabitur sapientia.'

The next page or two carry us to the more practical plane of an estimate of annual expenditure of the royal household, which is business-like in character and reasonable in estimate.[1] This is followed by a paragraph which says, rather surprisingly, that the book will include estimates of the costs of nine smaller households, ranging from that of a prince to that of a squire, so that the king may choose such as shall please him best (§11); then we go forward to the chamber.

Far back in Anglo-Saxon times the king had acquired a chamber to which he could withdraw from the noise and publicity of the hall; and with him to the chamber went not only all the greater courtiers but all those officials whose service was necessary to the king's person. So many guests and officials now thronged the king's chamber that a second withdrawal of the king had taken place—to a more private room, where he was attended by his more intimate servants. The chamber was, in a physical sense, becoming a series of state apartments—great chamber, privy chamber, bed-chamber. The formal distinction, so far as household organization is concerned, does not appear until Tudor times; but the distinction in fact is already to be seen in the Black Book.[2] Among this large and increasing throng of officials[3] serving in a household constantly on the move and frequented by numerous visitors of all ranks, there were innumerable opportunies for peculation and waste.[4] But the difficult

---

[1] Cf. B.B., §10 and notes to this section.   [2] See B.B., note 48.

[3] Over 400 were attached to the chamber, according to the Black Book.

[4] The problem of ensuring order and economy in the royal household was, of course, not peculiar to that age. See, for example, T. Martin, *Life of His Royal Highness the Prince Consort* (London, 1875), I. 156–61; *Memoirs of Baron Stockmar*, by E. Von Stockmar, ed. F. Max Muller (London, 1872), II. 118–25; and Vera Watson, *A Queen at Home* (London, 1952), pp. 238–40, for letters in the records of the Lord Chamberlain's Department written by the Master of the Household and others in 1881 on the great losses of towels and dusters owing to the pilfering and carelessness of the housemaids.

yet desirable aim, expounded in the introduction to the Black
Book, of wedding magnificence to order and economy, might be
furthered by a precise statement of the duties and allowances of
all the members of the royal household. Particular attention is paid
to allowances where waste was especially likely. Not much is said
about the scale of meals served for persons of quality in the
great chamber or for their servants in the hall; for economy there
ought to be ensured by various officials, and in any case the king
could not be too niggardly at public meals to important guests or
the aim of magnificence would be lost. But with the allowances of
light and fuel to private chambers, and of food,[1] there were obvious
possibilities of waste, either through fear or favour, on a large scale;
so here the amounts to be provided are carefully specified.

The first part of the book is concerned especially with the 'Domus
Regie Magnificencie', the maintenance of the household 'above
stairs', which must be able to impress the outside world by its
magnificence. The second part deals with the 'Domus Providencie',
the household 'below stairs', which by its providence or prudence
must make possible the magnificence of the chamber. This part of
the book opens with a description of the duties and allowances of
four of the chief officers of the household—steward, treasurer, controller, and cofferer—and continues with a lengthy exposition of
the functions of the countinghouse and its staff, and a series of
enactments for the conduct of the countinghouse. Then the book
deals with the workaday departments which laboured behind the
scenes to make possible the dazzling show upon the stage. Such
departments were the bakehouse, and its associated departments, the
pantry and wafery; the offices of chief butler, purveyor of wines,
cellar, buttery, pitcher-house, cup-house, and ale-takers; the great
spicery and the confectionary; the chandlery; the ewry and napery;
and the laundry. After describing the office of the laundry the text
ends abruptly.

What are we to make of this book? It claims official inspiration,
for it is said to have been made 'by the greate counsayll of lordez
spirituall and temporall, the Cardinal of Canterbury, George, Duke
of Clarence, Richard, Duke of Gloucester, the wise and discrete
jugez, and other sad, advised, and well lerned men of Inglond in all
aprowmentes' (§9). Moreover, it has various mandatory passages
which might seem to confirm its official character. Yet as we read
through the book we shall probably have increasing doubts whether
it is an official book. Is the grandiloquence of the introduction,
breaking out freely into verse, likely to be an official document of

---

[1] See note 47 to B.B., §13, and repeated references thereafter to allowances
of food for 'all-night'.

the English monarchy, whose official acts had long been character-
ized by language of terse and business-like efficiency? And even if it
should be admitted that an official document could indulge in such
a verbose introduction and pepper it with quotations ranging from
the Bible to Aquinas, would it be likely to give inaccurate citations
or wrong attributions?[1] And it appears strange that if the ordinance
of Edward III was so admirable and detailed as the Black Book
represents, not a single copy is known to have survived.

In the section on the chamber the treatment is disorderly. For
example, the squires of the household are dealt with much later
than we might expect; in view both of their dignity in the household
hierarchy and their rank in society (§50), they would certainly have
been regarded as superior, both in rank and function, to grooms of
the chamber, surgeons, and apothecaries.[2] Moreover, one might
suppose that the treatment of any one group would be all in one
place; whereas the four chaplains who are to give personal service
to the king and be at his particular disposal are treated earlier (§31)
than the twenty-six chaplains and clerks who are for the general
service of the whole household (§57). This unsystematic treatment
might be explained by the habits of the fifteenth century, which
was often disorderly in its treatment of subjects, in spite of its
reverence for formal logic. It might also be conceded that if figures
were to be given for the expense of households of varying grades and
sizes, they might conveniently, even if illogically, be inserted after
the section on the allowances in court of the rank in question. Yet
even so difficulties would remain. Why are officials included who no
longer form part of the royal household—such as the chancellor, the
great chamberlain, the chief justice of the common pleas, the clerk
of the crown, and the clerk of works? Why is so little said about the
duties of the various officials of the chamber, and so much about
their dining rights, allowances, and servants? If this is a document
of practical application, why does it speak of 'knights of chamber'
and 'knights of household' when the contemporary chancery
enrolments speak of 'knights of the body' and 'king's knights'? The
figures given sometimes appear to be lower or higher than the
number of those known to have been employed in the post in
question.[3] The specified wages are sometimes lower than what the

---

[1] See, for example, B.B., notes 1, 4, 29.

[2] The description of the staff of the chapel also comes later than we should
expect. The dean and chaplains were, contemporaries would have agreed, of
higher rank and greater consequence than grooms, pages, barber, minstrels,
and waits, who are described before them.

[3] For example, the number of squires of the household authorized according
to the Black Book (forty) is much higher than the actual number at any one
time in this reign, so far as the names can now be traced, whereas the number

officials are known to have received in practice.[1] And this section ends with a paragraph not concerned with an official of any kind, but with royal wards (§66).

In the following section on the 'Domus Providencie', queries also arise. For example, the book apparently goes out of its way (§70) to insert a paragraph on John Buckingham, actually a treasurer of the household under Edward III who died in March 1399, but here made to appear as though he had still been flourishing in the reign of Henry VI. The Black Book confuses (by modern standards) the household treasurer and the keeper of the great wardrobe, calling the former 'Custos magne garderobe hospicij domini regis' and the latter 'wardrober' (§§69, 35). This section omits to deal with other departments of the household 'below stairs', such as the kitchen, larder, acatry (which looked after the provision of meat and fish for the household), poultry, boiling-house and scalding-house (which prepared and cooked meat and poultry), pastry, scullery, marshalls and ushers of the hall, harbingers, almoners, porters, woodyard, and stable.[2] And why does the book end so abruptly after describing the duties of the office of the laundry?

Yet the discrepancy between the abruptness of the ending, on the one hand, and the elaborateness of the introduction and the detailed treatment of the household offices, on the other hand, provides on closer inspection a key to the solution of some of the problems; for it suggests that the book as we have it is unfinished. That the book was meant to treat of all departments of the household is indicated by a statement in the section on the office of wardrobe of robes. In dealing with the responsibility for the expenses of the cart attached to this office we are told that the matter is explained further in the section on the stable, 'as hit is expressed after in the office of the stable' (§39); but no such section now exists. It is unlikely that the book was ever completed; for the oldest extant manuscript ends here and yet it was copied before the close of the fifteenth century. None of the numerous manuscripts of the Black Book goes any further; and Sir Simonds d'Ewes claimed repeatedly that his copy (Harleian MS. 642), which also ends with the office of laundry, was transcribed

of serjeant-at-arms stated (four) is much smaller than the ascertainable number in practice. (See notes to §§50, 52.)

[1] For example, the wage of the yeomen of the crown is stated to be 3d. a day (§37), whereas many received 6d. a day (*R.P.*, V. 536, 594; VI. 87); and the daily wage of squires of the body is said to be 7½d. (§32), whereas most received more than this (e.g. Harleian MS. 433, ff. 77b, 88a).

[2] For descriptions of the functions of the various departments in the previous and following centuries, see J. H. Johnson, 'The King's Wardrobe and Household', in *The English Government at Work, 1327–36*, I. 207–21, and *Household Ordinances*, pp. 140–4, 232–40.

faithfully from the original as he found it among the records of the household. It is likely that what we possess are copies, not of a final version, but of a draft (or drafts) of this book. This would help to explain some of the small but numerous divergences in the texts of the principal manuscripts.[1] It would also throw light on some of the difficulties mentioned above, such as the sometimes unsystematic arrangement of the book and passages which, so far from being rules of the household, appear to be information slipped in for the king's benefit. The estimates of various sizes of household may be somewhat extraneous material which could be omitted in a more closely-knit final version. It is possible that in a revised and completed edition of the book the introductory exordium would have been more sober, compact, and accurate in quotation.

There are other points to be made in explanation of the introduction. It is true that it is strangely florid compared with the business-like brevity of the opening clauses of a contemporary charter or letters patent; but the comparison is not really apt. A household book was free from the restraints of tradition, for nothing on this scale had, so far as we know, been attempted before. Edward may well have wished to emulate, if only in grandiloquence, the brilliant court of Burgundy, where scriptural texts and divine comparisons were freely invoked in support of the Duke and his Court.[2] The authors quoted by the Black Book and the kings cited are all obvious choices for the late fifteenth century; even a belief in the historical credibility of tales about the magnificent households of King Lud or King Cassibellan was not absurd in an age which still accepted Geoffrey of Monmouth's *History* as true.[3] The apparent inaccuracies in citation may be either due to the indifference of busy men of affairs, who in their citations were concerned, not to compose a work of scholarship, but simply to embellish a text, or the result of the sources on which the authors of the book relied.[4] As for the

[1] Below, p. 56.

[2] Cf. Cartellieri, *op. cit.*, pp. 53–4: 'With that strange sanctification of daily life which was one of the features of the age, the Bible was invoked for the glorification of the Sovereign, and texts which spoke of God the Father and of Christ were freely applied to the Duke', and note the examples thereafter given of texts so used. Cf. also Alienore de Poitiers 'Les honneurs de la cour', in *Memoires sur l'ancienne chevalerie*, ed. J. B. de La Curne de Sainte-Palaye (Paris, new edn. 1781), II. 183–267.

[3] Cf. T. D. Kendrick, *British Antiquity* (London, 1950).

[4] For example, it was generally accepted that it was Seneca and St. Bernard of Clairvaux who had uttered the dicta 'Minor est quam servus dominus qui servos timet' and 'Famulum alti cordis repelle ut inimicum'; see B.B., notes 4 and 7.

It may be that some of the quotations were not taken direct from the alleged author but from one of the collections of reputed sayings which were popular

seemingly more damaging case of alleged quotations from the Bible which are not in fact to be found in the Vulgate, it is possible that these may be taken directly or indirectly, from the liturgy, in various parts of which non-Vulgate texts from the Scriptures were embedded.[1] The theme of the introduction, with its two-fold insistence on magnificence and order, is paralleled by that of the preamble to the Ordinance of 1478, which insisted on the need to marry liberality with economy, avoiding both prodigality and avarice. As for the fact that not a single copy of the Ordinance of Edward III can now be found,[2] this may be because, to judge from the frequent quotations made from it throughout the Black Book, it mostly reproduced provisions from the Ordinances of 1318 and 1323.[3] If the Ordinance of Edward III was in the main a re-enactment of those of Edward II, it may not have been worth preserving in later years; and other household ordinances are known to have existed which cannot now be found.[4]

The frequency of the references to the Ordinance of Edward III and other household regulations is understandable; for the book aims not only to describe and regulate the expenses of the household but, as is clearly indicated, to find out and state what earlier rules there had been on these matters, and which rules were still valid.[5]

at this time. Examples of such collections are (a) the 'Compendium Morale de virtuosis dictis et factis exemplaribus antiquorum', by Roger of Waltham (Canon of St. Paul's and Keeper of the Wardrobe to Edward II), of which copies still exist in the Bodleian Library (MS. Laud 616, MS. Bodley 805, and MS. Fairfax 4), the British Museum (Royal MSS. 7 E VII and 8 G VI), Caius College Library (MS. 294/688), and elsewhere, and (b) the 'Auctoritates Aristotelis Senece Boecii Platonis Apuleii Affricani Porphirii et Gilberti Porritani', which was so popular that at least ten editions of it were printed before the end of the fifteenth century.

[1] See below, B.B., note 9.

[2] The so-called 'Household of Edward III in Peace and War' printed in the 1790 *Household Ordinances*, pp. 3–12, is 'clearly not a household ordinance at all, but a series of extracts made by a Tudor antiquary from various household accounts' (Tout, *Chapters*, IV. 350, n. 1, and pp. 407–9). The 1790 text seems to be taken from Harleian MS. 782; but various extracts of this kind were made in Tudor and Stuart times; cf. B.M. MSS. Stow 570 and 574 and Bodleian MS. Rawlinson C 846. The latter was made by Samuel Pepys from a book of naval collections compiled by James Humfrey in 1558.

[3] See Appendix II, The Lost Ordinance of Edward III.

[4] E.g. the Statute of St. Albans, 1300, and the Ordinance of Woodstock, 1310 (Tout, *Chapters*, II. 49–51, 248–9).

[5] Thus in §7 the household of Edward III is said to be the example 'we take to bylde vpon a more perfit new house'; but immediately afterwards a restatement of the laws of the household is deemed necessary 'bycause this noble king Edward the iijd his household varyethe gretely fro this householde that kinges haue kept syn that tym, and yit in thies dayes' and particular examples are given of this change.

The book is conservative enough to include terms and rules which had not been definitely abrogated;[1] but it is not safe to suppose that it is so antiquarian as to repeat rules which have become plainly inoperative. Even the few apparently outstanding discrepancies prove on inspection to be much smaller than at first sight appears. If one examines the notes to the text, where comparisons are given for as many departments as possible, it will be seen that the figures stated in the Black Book for numbers of personnel are not greatly at variance with what are known or calculated to be the number of persons actually holding a particular post in this reign.[2]

In other matters the Black Book is not so out of date as it might at first appear. The modern reader, subconsciously influenced by living in an age of almost uninterrupted inflation, may find it at first sight incredible that the wages of squires and yeomen could be the same as they had been 150 years earlier, in 1318;[3] and when we learn that both household squires and yeomen were in practice usually paid more than these rates,[4] we may be tempted to conclude that the discrepancy is due to the antiquarian and unpractical nature of the Black Book. Not only, however, does the Ordinance of 1478 repeat these rates, but they are found in royal accounts of this generation.[5] It is therefore clear that the reason for these figures lies in the accepted methods of payment. Like the modern French soldier, the ordinary household officials received a small basic rate of pay, to which were added various allowances and supplements;[6] and those who were lucky enough to gain the king's favour might receive considerable grants on top of these.[7]

[1] Thus, cf. B.B., notes 95, 214.

[2] E.g. for explanations of the apparent discrepancies between the numbers of squires of the household and serjeants-at-arms specified in the Black Book and the numbers actually appointed to these grades under Edward IV, see below, notes to B.B., §§50, 52.

[3] *Edward II*, pp. 253, 272.   [4] Notes to B.B., §§32, 37.

[5] By this time the accounts of the treasurer and controller of the king's household no longer state ordinary wages, which are consolidated into a lump sum for each day in the Diets section of the account; but an account of Queen Margaret's household for 31–32 Hy. VI (D.L. 28/5/8 printed by the present writer in *B.J.R.L.*, Vol. XL (1957–8)) explicitly states the wages of squires and yeomen to be 7½d. and 3d. a day (ff. 12b, 13b), as the Black Book was to do. Moreover, the rates in the Duke of Clarence's household were almost as low as this—7½d. a day for each squire, 4d. for each yeoman, and 2d. for each groom (*Household Ordinances*, p. 94).

[6] E.g. allowances for clothing, a kind of bonus (regardum), and a great variety of grants of land, cash, and offices.

[7] An unusually dazzling example of this was soon to occur when John Russell began his rise to great fortune and an earldom from his appointment as gentleman usher to Henry VII (G. S. Thomson, *Two Centuries of Family History*, p. 130).

The suggestion that the king might wish to keep a smaller household may at first appear very strange; but there is evidence that, for one reason or another, it was not at all unusual for royal and noble households to be reduced for a time to a much smaller scale. The Northumberland establishment of 1512 was at times reduced to a third or even less than a quarter of its normal complement.[1] We find drastic reductions in royal households when they were travelling. When the Duke of Clarence journeyed, he took with him a riding household of 188 servants instead of a standing household of 299.[2] We also read of a contrast in numbers between the 'abyding household' of Edward IV and 'the kinges ryding household'.[3] Sometimes the king travelled with a very small household for choice, as, for example, when he married Elizabeth Woodville.[4] Sometimes he might consider the possibility of accepting a smaller household for a while to save money. The Earl of Warwick is said to have advised Henry VI in 1470 to reduce his household drastically for this purpose.[5]

The book's concern for economy and financial order explains the mention of outsiders such as the chancellor, the great chamberlain, or chief justice of the common pleas. They might still come to court, in which case the days of their arrival and departure are to be carefully noted in the countinghouse, as a check on the expenses of their stay in court (§22); and in any case they were still entitled to annual allowances from the royal household which therefore must appear in the household account books.[6] This overriding concern with financial order also helps us to understand the insertion of paragraphs such as the one on royal wards which closes the section on the chamber (§66). The king's duty of caring for royal wards until the right of custody had been sold to someone else or until they were put in possession of their lands meant that they and their servants would have to be given wages and other payments from the royal household. The concern for economy affected the whole description of the royal household. In contrast to the fullness with which matters

---

[1] This household normally had an establishment of 166 persons; but when the earl was travelling his riding household numbered only 57. At Michaelmas each year the audit was held and it was desirable for as many officials and servants as possible to give undivided attention to the tasks of stock-taking and accounting. Hence at this season the earl kept a 'secret house' of no more than 38 attendants (*Northumberland Household Book*, pp. 39, 366).

[2] *Household Ordinances*, pp. 99, 105.

[3] Harleian MS. 642, f. 196a (N).   [4] Scofield, *op. cit.*, I. 332–3.

[5] Fortescue, *op. cit.*, pp. 352–3. Cf. B.B., note 43.

[6] A tun of wine for the chancellor, fees for the great chamberlain, two tuns of wine for the chief justice of the common pleas. These allowances are in fact to be found in the household accounts of this reign, as the Black Book had stated. (See §§22, 23, 24, and notes to these sections.)

C.

of finance were treated, the duties of officials were described only
briefly—so briefly in many cases that the only useful purpose must
have been to let the accountants of the household know what was
the proper sphere of the official concerned and to keep a better
check on expenditure.[1] A good deal could have been written about
the duties of the secretary, especially at this time of his growing
importance; but all that we glean of his functions is of those which
have financial consequences, especially for the countinghouse (§30).
In short, the Black Book is not primarily concerned with the ceremonial of the household or the duties of its officials,[2] but with the
control of expenditure, like the Ordinances of 1445 and 1478.

There were at this time two departments in the household
concerned with this function—the jewelhouse or treasury of the
chamber, and the countinghouse.[3] Under Henry VII the treasurer
of the chamber was to become a financial official of first-rate importance and his department a treasury overshadowing the exchequer.[4]
It may be that the treasury of the chamber was already beginning
its rise to importance in the reign of Edward IV.[5] From 1465 the
treasurer of the chamber was Sir Thomas Vaughan, one of Edward
IV's most trusted personal followers.[6] The issue rolls of the exchequer
record large payments to the king's chamber right from the early
years of Edward's reign, and many items of known revenue, such as
benevolences, do not appear on the receipt rolls as paid into the
exchequer at all.[7] The Black Book gives a few hints of the growing
importance of the jewelhouse. It was evidently being used already
to finance missions in which the king was personally interested; for
we are told that if a yeoman of the crown, yeoman of the chamber,
or messengers were sent out of court by the king's chamberlain or
the ushers of the chamber or the secretary, they were to take their
wages from the jewelhouse till they returned.[8] This may foreshadow
the early Tudor practice of paying the expenses of all ambassadors
out of the chamber.[9] But, taken as a whole, the treasurer of the

---

[1] Cf., for example, §27 on the chamberlain.

[2] As were, for example, the Ordinance of Henry VII in 1493 (*Household
Ordinances*, pp. 109–33), 'A Book of Orders and Rules of Anthony, Viscount
Montague' made in 1595 (*Sussex Arch. Collections*, VII, 173–212), or 'A
Breviate touching the Order and Governmente of a Nobleman's House, with
the Officers, theire places and chardge, as particularly apearethe' (*Archaeologia*,
XIII (1809), 315–89.

[3] B.B., §§43, 76, 77.

[4] See Richardson, *Tudor Chamber Administration*.   [5] Cf. Wolffe, *op. cit.*

[6] Appointed 29 June 1465 (*C.P.R., 1461–7*, p. 459).

[7] Ramsay, *Lancaster and York*, II. 464–5; Steel, *op. cit.*, p. 354.

[8] See below, §§37, 38, 55.

[9] A. P. Newton, 'The King's Chamber under the Early Tudors' in *E.H.R.*,
XXXII (1917), p. 366.

chamber and his department occupy only a small place in the Black Book. It is made overwhelmingly clear that, whatever might be the case with the king's privy coffers, the great accounting office for the household is the countinghouse. The jewelhouse is given much the same treatment as any other office—details of its permitted personnel, allowances of food, fuel, clothing, lodging, and carriage; and the department is viewed from an external standpoint—that of the countinghouse. Thus it is noted that payments are sometimes made by the jewelhouse, revenue received by it from the chamberlain and not from the treasurer of the household, and audits held by the chamberlain there; but only in order to make it clear that the countinghouse is relieved of responsibility in such cases.[1]

The countinghouse, on the contrary, is given much the longest treatment of any department, it is accorded a special prominence in various ways,[2] and the duties of its officials, even its clerks, are stated in much greater detail than those of any other department. The great importance of the countinghouse by this time, both in control of expenditure and in the discipline of the household, is in striking contrast to the prominence of the wardrobe and the marshalsea in the royal household of 150 years earlier;[3] and this is evident, not only in the pages specially devoted to the countinghouse and its officials, but throughout the book. Apart from a few special cases,[4] it is made abundantly clear that for the great majority of the household

---

[1] E.g. B.B., §§37, 38, 43, 45, 46, 59, 62, 66, 77.

[2] As, for instance, by prefacing the last section of the book with a picture of the countinghouse in session (Plate II).

[3] Cf. Tout, *Chapters*, passim, esp. Vol. II; *Edward II*, pp. 244–84; Johnson, 'The King's Wardrobe and Household', in Willard and Morris, *op. cit.*, pp. 221–237, 211–12.

[4] As everyone in the household (except boys riding pillion) would need a horse to ride when the court made one of its frequent moves, and all officials of any consequence needed pack-horses to carry the effects of their department, it would have been possible for the office of the stable to keep a roll which would check attendances in court and so serve as a basis for payment of wages. This arrangement was in force in the household of George, Duke of Clarence, according to the Ordinance of 1468 (*Household Ordinances*, p. 94). In the royal household a roll kept in the office of the stable was evidently used to check the attendance of at least some of the staff; a 'male man' (i.e. a man who carried the mails or packs, a porter) attached to the wardrobe of beds was paid 'at iiijd. a day by the stable roll' (§40. Cf. Ordinance of 1526, *Household Ordinances*, p. 144). The groom labourers of the bakehouse were paid their 2d. a day by the record of the pantry roll (§79)—perhaps because they were not allowed to have meals in the hall, so that the clerks of the kitchen could not report their presence or absence to the countinghouse (O 1445, §8, O 1478, §34). When the groom of the ale-takers was out of court in the king's service, he was to receive 1½d. a day 'allowed in the buttrye roll' (B.B., §87); and we have already seen that a few persons were paid by the treasurer of the chamber.

staff the record of their attendances was kept in the counting-house, that their absences from court were noted there, and that their wages were paid in the countinghouse.[1] The clerk of the con-trolment would be a suitable person to keep such check-rolls,[2] for he supervised the making of the daily 'diets' of the household, which included the sum allowed for wages each day.[3] However this may be, it was certainly another official of the countinghouse, the cofferer, who paid the wages.[4]

The control of the countinghouse over the check-roll and the pay-ment of wages, and the constant reiteration throughout the Black Book for the officials of almost every department that wages are to be paid only in accordance with the testimony of the check-roll, emphasize the importance of the countinghouse in the accountancy of the household. It is natural that the section of the book on the 'Domus Providencie' should deal with the countinghouse first, and should begin by treating of its officials in order of precedence. First comes the steward, the head of the countinghouse and, indeed, of the whole household 'below stairs'; and the opening sentence emphasizes how even in matters of jurisdiction the countinghouse had gained at the expense of the marshalsea since the Ordinances of Edward II.[5] But though in an age of respect for rank and degree it was necessary to treat first of the steward and the treasurer and the controller, they were engaged in all sorts of important activities which drew them away from their household duties;[6] so most of the

[1] E.g. B.B., §§23, 27, 37, 43, 62, 71.

[2] We are not told whose task it was to keep this main check-roll. In 1540 it was to be laid down that the clerk controllers were to keep check-rolls for every quarter of the year (*Household Ordinances*, p. 230). Probably quarterly check-rolls were already used to calculate wages, as appears to have been the case in Queen Margaret's household (D.L. 28/5/8, ff. 12b, 13b, printed in *B.J.R.L.*, Vol. XL (1957–8). The earliest surviving check-roll among the Lord Steward's records dates only from James I's reign (L.S. 13/6). It appears to cover a period of several years, and notes only the dates of admission to office or death of the official in question—not days of service. It may well be that there was more than one check-roll, as there was in the Northumberland household in 1512 (*Northumberland Household Book*, pp. 34, 37, 43, 50, 55). It was the quarterly check-roll from which the wages were calculated (*ibid.*, p. 50).

[3] B.B., §75. Cf. O 1478, §§38, 65.   [4] B.B., §73.

[5] Cf. B.B., §§68 and 78 (xvii); and *Edward II*, pp. 266–7, 275, 279–81, 282, Tout, *Chapters*, II. 252–3, Johnson, *op. cit.*, pp. 211–12.

[6] See below, B.B., §§68, 70, 71. The Black Book adheres to its conservative principles by asserting the need for their presence, and recalls a statute of Edward III (drawn, like nearly all the rest, from the ordinances of Edward II, *Edward II*, p. 274) that the steward and treasurer, or one of them, are bound to be present in the countinghouse at the audit of the daily accounts and diets of the household. But it adds that the controller, cofferer, clerks of the greencloth, clerk controller, or any one of them, may act on behalf of the steward and treasurer in their absence (B.B., §78 (ii)).

actual day-to-day work of supervision of household expenditure fell on the cofferer, the clerks of the greencloth, and the clerk of control-ment. The cofferer took charge, we are told, of all the receipts on behalf of the treasurer of the household, and delivered to all officers who purveyed for the household their prests or advances. He reimbursed in the countinghouse the people of the neighbourhood from whom goods had been bought for the use of the household. He paid fees, wages, and rewards and settled the bills for all other necessities purchased for the household and sanctioned in the count-inghouse; and he had to see that all these purveyances, expenses and payments were engrossed in the great account of the whole house-hold. Well might he be described as 'a greate offycer and key-berer of thys noble court' (§73). The clerks of the greencloth were even more hard-worked. Under the steward, treasurer, controller, and next after the cofferer, they had power committed to them to regulate the accounts and diets in the household, to undertake the examina-tion of accountants and their correction, to supervise all allowances, and even to give judgement 'in small, accustomede and cotydyan thynges and questyons'.[1] The chief clerk of the controlment was expected to be equally assiduous in the service of the household; indeed he was expected to be so ubiquitous, sharp-eyed, and diligent[2] that one wonders how he managed to fulfill all his obliga-tions, even with the help of under-clerks.

After these descriptions of the administrative officials of the countinghouse, we are given long accounts of the allowances due to this supremely important department, and the duties and allowances of its lesser staff. The twenty-eight regulations which follow[3] show how wide was the authority entrusted to the officers of the counting-house, from control of expenditure or purveyance to permission for leave of absence from court or dealing with accusations of misbehaviour by members of the household; and the first two of these regulations bring out very well what seems to be the spirit of the Black Book. The desire to investigate what earlier rules are still valid, and to try to enforce them, explains the preamble to these regulations, confirming all those acts of Henry I and Edward III for the household which are still applicable.[4] But the Black Book also

---

[1] For these and other numerous responsibilities of the clerks of the green-cloth, see B.B., §74, and notes to this section.

[2] B.B., §75, and notes to this section.   [3] B.B., §78 (ix).

[4] It also explains the effort to find out previous statements of the law and customs of the household affecting expenditure, as, for example, Buckingham's book. As will be seen from note 286 to B.B., §70, the Black Book was justified in referring to such a survey, in spite of the anachronism, which may not have been evident from the survey itself.

As for the supposed confusion in describing the countinghouse as the great

tries to reconcile what ought to be the rule, in terms of the past, with the situation as it actually is. Thus a paragraph which states that, according to statutes made in former times, the steward and treasurer ought to be present daily in the countinghouse or be punished for absence, nevertheless goes on to explain how the business shall be transacted if they are in fact away. The aim of controlling the expenditure of the household more effectively is evident throughout the remainder of the book. In its treatment of the supply departments, as in its description of the officials of the chamber, the Black Book concentrates on those duties which have an obvious bearing on finance, and explains in detail the precise allowances due to the officials of those various departments; it also dwells on the methods of checking use of materials by the different offices, and the issue by them of food, fuel, and candles to other members of the household.

In the light of this survey of the contents and aims of the Black Book, what are we to say of its character and origin? Sir Edmund Chambers thought that it was 'less an ordinance than an unfinished literary treatise by a household clerk'.[1] He was certainly right in concluding that the Black Book is not a household ordinance. In style, form, and general content it is unlike any other household ordinance we have, and the editors of the 1790 edition were mistaken in treating it as such. The introductory section of the book does read like a literary exercise, with its grandiloquent, didactic manner. Much of the rest of the book might be explained as a 'literary treatise', if by this were meant a household official's *vade mecum*, written in a flamboyant style.

But this explanation fails to account for all the facts. There are three different kinds of entry; the book has not only hortatory and descriptive passages, but mandatory sections as well. The treatment of the countinghouse includes, as we have seen, twenty-seven apparently newly-made regulations for its better conduct; and these regulations open with a royal order for their observance by all the officials of the countinghouse 'as the soveraynes do and shall appoynt by the kinges counsayle and as hit ys after wryten' (§78 (i)). This is not the only royal order in the book; the section on the chamber begins with the royal command (§12) that the king has given his instructions to his principle household officials and all other household personnel to follow and carry out all the acts, statutes, and appointments

---

wardrobe of the household and the household treasurer as the 'custos magne garderobe hospicij', this is only confusion by the test of modern nomenclature: both contemporary household accounts and contemporary exchequer records used these terms. (Cf. note 32 to B.B., §7.)

[1] E. K. Chambers, *The Elizabethan Stage*, I. 29.

assigned in this book. Moreover, as we go through it we encounter statements such as 'no sergeaunt of office nor squyer nor yomen or grome, but as be apoynted in this boke, to dyne or sope out of hall or kinges chambre, nor do withdraw ony service . . . vppon such payn as the soueraynes of householde woll awarde' (§50); and the book is said (§9) to have been compiled at the instigation and with the assent of the king's council, three of whom are named. It would be an extraordinary literary conceit for a book to claim royal authority for the enforcement of its rules in this elaborate and detailed manner if the volume were only a 'literary treatise', having no official inspiration or use. A 'literary treatise' could have described the working of the royal household quite well without resorting to unnecessary lies about the participation of the king's councillors in the making of the book and royal authority for the enforcement of its rules. There is, moreover, external evidence that it had an official currency in the organization which it describes and was designed to serve. Sir Simonds d'Ewes claims repeatedly that his copy (Harleian MS. 642) was transcribed faithfully from the original manuscript as he found it among the records of the household; and an inventory made in the seventh year of James I[1] tells us that it was kept among the records of the countinghouse at that period. It seems likely that the book was kept there from the start. Not only is it, as we have seen, essentially a book of the countinghouse, but in a draft of the Ordinance of 1478 we are told: 'Item, that such liueries as shalbe giuen to any person at night be deliuered in manner and forme folloueing, that is to say, to a duke, to a bishop, etc., which appeareth yn a booke made remaineing in the countinghouse.' [2] We are aware of no other book, written before 1478, which supplies such information as the Black Book does.[3] Moreover, the preamble to the Ordinance of 1478 resembles in theme the introduction to the Black Book and, like it, recalls the teachings of Aristotle's Nichomachean Ethics. How, then, could a book to be kept in the countinghouse claim to have been made at the direction of the king's council, and repeatedly cite the royal authority for the enforcement of its rules if the officials who used the book knew that these claims were without foundation, that it was only a 'literary treatise'?

Taking the three different kinds of entry—hortatory, descriptive,

---

[1] *E.H.R.*, XXIV (1919), 237; the list is P.R.O. Lord Steward's Miscellaneous Books No. 226.

[2] Below, draft ordinance, §4.

[3] B.B., §§18, 21. The Ordinance of 1445 states the liveries at night for a duke and a bishop-confessor; but the original copy of this ordinance was a small roll, not a book, and was not kept in the countinghouse. The Ordinance of 1454 makes no mention of any livery for a duke (O 1445, f. 90a; Nicolas, *op. cit.*, VI. 222).

mandatory—together with the external evidence that the book was preserved in official custody and treated as at least a semi-official document, and also with the clear indications that it is unfinished and its own claim to conciliar inspiration, it seems that it can only be a draft intended to be turned later into a formal statement of how the household was and ought to be run, an officially sponsored custumal. It is hard to imagine what it would have been like if it had been completed, but it does seem that one can make a guess about the stage at which this draft was made. The historical references in the introduction and elsewhere suggest a preliminary investigation (like the evidence submitted to a royal commission). The terse directions which occur from time to time suggest a draft for immediate approval, or at least as the basis for formal discussion. Other passages are more hesitant in tone, and suggest by their language that they are tentative proposals for the king's consideration. For example, §11 runs: 'Memorandum that if the kinges hyghnesse plese to kepe a lesse household than the foresayde grete summe sheweth of here, in this boke are deuysed IX other smaller houses, . . . whereof the king may cheese suche as shall please hym best.' Sometimes a contrast of tone appears in the treatment of similar subjects. In dealing, for example, with the service of the king's person the language is concise and confident (§13): 'THE KING for his brekefast ij loues made into iiij maunchettes, and ij payne demayne, one messe of kychyn grosse, demi a gallon ale, etc.' The section describing the service of the queen's person, which follows almost immediately, is much more roundabout and tentative in style. 'A QUENE, ita quod sit regina regnans and endowed with liuelode sufficient, than if hit please the king and hur highness, hit hath byn used by quenez to pay a certen dayly for theyre dietes, etc.' Perhaps the haughty Queen Elizabeth Woodville had to be won by fair words! If a household official was directed by the council to collect material for a formal consuetudinary, with the idea of achieving economy by a detailed control of all expenditure, this mixture of draft regulation for uncontroversial matters (or points which he thought he could carry without open discussion) and historical support for more doubtful or difficult cases would be quite natural. Only by some hypothesis such as this can we reconcile the divergent elements of which it is composed. (See p. 60.)

Yet incomplete and provisional as the existing forms of the Black Book may be, it remains of extraordinary value; for not only is it much the most detailed description of the royal household which had yet been made, so far as is known, but a close examination of it shows, as may be seen from the notes to the text, that the author had a very good working knowledge of the household, from the point of view of the countinghouse.

In compiling such a long and detailed book the role of the king's council can scarcely have been more than that of general direction, and the actual drafting must have been entrusted to a household official. It has already been observed that a primary aim of the book seems to be to ensure the maximum degree of magnificence by the careful control of expenditure; and the instrument for maintaining this control was, above all, the countinghouse. More space is devoted to this department and its officials than to any other, and the household is surveyed primarily from the point of view of the countinghouse and the control it was to exercise. It seems likely, therefore, that its officials would have been entrusted with the drafting of the book, or at the very least with supplying the material on which it was based.[1] Of these officials it was, as we have seen, the cofferer, clerks of the greencloth, and chief clerk of controlment, rather than the steward, treasurer, and controller, who were familiar with the detailed control of expenditure with which the Black Book is so largely concerned. What persons held these offices when the Black Book was composed we cannot tell until we have determined the date of its composition; and to this problem we must now turn.

(b) The Date and Authorship of the Black Book

The councillors named in the book are the Cardinal of Canterbury, George, Duke of Clarence, and Richard, Duke of Gloucester. It is well known that council records are lacking for the reign of Edward IV; and a careful search of the chancery warrants, both signet and privy seal, has failed to reveal any evidence, such as is provided by a warrant under the signet for the Ordinance of 1478.[2] If, however, the Black Book in its present form is, as suggested above, only a draft, it is not surprising that there is no warrant for its engrossment. But much can be deduced from these three names. Archbishop Bourchier was not named a cardinal until 18 September 1467.[3] The red hat did not reach England until 1472 and so there was some delay before the title was used in England by royal officials.[4] He is not

---

[1] The book gives no certain internal evidence of its authorship, and we lack the informative reference in contemporary correspondence which we have in the case of the Ordinance of 1540 (G. R. Elton, *The Tudor Revolution in Government*, pp. 383–4).

[2] Below, p. 211.

[3] William of Worcester, Annales Rerum Anglicarum, in *Letters and Papers Illustrative of the Wars of the English in France during the Reign of Henry the Sixth*, ed. J. Stevenson, Vol. II (Rolls Series, 1864), p. 789.

[4] In archiepiscopal documents the use of the title naturally appears earlier. It first occurs in his register in a letter from the Pope to Bourchier dated 22 December 1468, where the archbishop is addressed 'Dilecto filio nostro Thome tituli sancti Ciriaci S R E presbitero cardinali Cantuarien' . . .' (f. 7v). The title is to be found even earlier in the Court Rolls, where those of Michaelmas

described on the Patent Rolls as 'cardinal archbishop of Canterbury' until 23 April 1469.[1] But for some time before that date the disaffection of Warwick and Clarence had provided more urgent matters to occupy Edward's attention than the reform of his household; and not long afterwards Clarence openly defied him. Early in July 1469 Clarence crossed to Calais, and, contrary to Edward's wishes, married the elder daughter of the Earl of Warwick, with whom he then joined in the manifesto denouncing Edward's rule. After this, one rising succeeded another until in September 1470 Edward had to flee to Holland; and although the main Lancastrian forces were crushed at Tewkesbury on 4 May 1471 the assault of the Bastard of Fauconberge on London had still to be dealt with. It cannot have been until June 1471 at the earliest that Edward and his counsellors were free to consider the reform of the household.

Clarence's name also helps us with the *terminus ad quem* of the Black Book. It cannot have been put together later than May 1477, since by that date he was already in disgrace and probably arrested. The estrangement between him and the king had been widening for some years before this; as early as the close of 1473 Edward had been irritated by Clarence's overweening desire for the Warwick estates,[2] and there is a suspicion that the duke was mixed up in the Earl of Oxford's landing in Essex in May 1473.[3] Moreover, we are told that because the Resumption Act of 1473[4] contained an exemption clause in favour of Gloucester[5] but none for Clarence's honour of Tutbury and several other lands which he had formerly obtained by royal grant, George foolishly sulked, although he had gained much more from the division of the Warwick estates. Henceforward he was reluctant to come to court and hardly ever uttered a word in council.[6] It therefore seems likely that the Black Book was compiled between the completion of Edward's victory in the summer of 1471 and Clarence's renewed estrangement from Edward in the autumn of 1473.[7] Not only was this a period when Clarence's reconciliation

1467–8 (Lambeth Court Rolls Nos. 1229, 1267) refer to the accounts of the receivers, bailiffs, etc., as of 'reverendissimi Thome Bourchier miseracione divina Sacrosancte Romane ecclesie Presbiteri Cardinalis Cantuariensis Archiepiscopi'. I owe these references to the kindness of Mr. F. R. H. Du Boulay.

[1] *C.P.R.*, *1467–77*, p. 177; cf. the use of the form of address 'To my moste honorabyl Lord Cadenall and Archbishop of Caunterbury' in a letter dated 10 October 1468 (*Paston Letters*, II. 322).

[2] E.g. *Paston Letters*, III. 98, 102 (Nos. 731 and 732).

[3] *Ibid.*, III. 92 (No. 725).

[4] Officially of 1473 but finally settled in 1474.

[5] *R.P.*, VI. 75.

[6] *Cont. Croyland Chronicle*, p. 561.

[7] The clash between Clarence and Gloucester in the autumn and winter of

with his brother was still unbroken but his recollection of the ordinance which he had made for his own household in December 1468,[1] must have been comparatively fresh and possibly useful. And within this period it seems likely that the Black Book was composed before October 1472.[2] In that month a parliament was opened at Westminster and the Bishop of Rochester announced the king's intention to resume the war against 'oure auncien and mortall ennemyes' of France and large sums of money were asked for in consequence. To increase the chances of getting them, it may well have been thought politic to show that the king had set his own house in order by the making of the Black Book, especially in view of his declaration of 1467. If so, the compilation of the Black Book would belong to the period between June 1471 and September 1472.[3]

The theory that Edward was engaged in household reform in 1471–2 is supported by the second of two groups of provisions for the household given in Harleian MS. 642, after transcripts of the Black Book and the Ordinance of Eltham.[4] The first section is an extract from the Ordinance of 1478. The introductory sentence of the second section runs: 'We will that these articles following by us ordained and ordered for the guiding and directions of our chamber be duely and surely kept by all our seruantes, as theire desire is to continue in our seruice and as they will auoyd our greuious

1471–2 over Richard's wish to marry Anne Neville did not as yet lead to any cleavage between George and the king.

[1] *Household Ordinances*, pp. 89–105.

[2] There is a long tradition that the *Liber Niger* was compiled in 1472, though the evidence adduced was inadequate. The statement, repeated by authors such as the Rev. Samuel Pegge (*Curialia* (London, 1791), p. 25), goes back to Sir Robert Cotton; in his essay on 'How the Kings of England have supported and repaired their estates', he states: 'Anno 12 Edw. 4. The King promiseth to abate his household and hereafter to live upon his own (Ex. rot. Parl. an. 12 Edw. 4) so settling a new form of his Court, which is extant in many hands, intituled Ordinations for the King's house' (*Cottoni Posthuma* (London, 1651), p. 168). But there is no such promise on the parliament roll of this year; the undertaking of this kind nearest in time was that of 6 June 1467 when the king 'ore suo proprio' told the commons that he purposed to live of his own except for great and urgent causes such as the defence of the realm (*R.P.*, V. 572). A. P. Newton asserted, in *Tudor Studies*, p. 235: 'In the Parliament of 1472 the King made formal promise to sustain all his ordinary charges without appeal for special grants and subsidies'; but he gives no reference. Perhaps he, too, was relying on Sir Robert Cotton.

[3] A slight indication in favour of assigning the later stages of compilation to the year beginning 25 March 1472, may be the calculation, in two of the oldest manuscripts, in the section on the king's oblations, of a year of 366 days (B.B., §14); but the compilers may just have been taking account of the expense of any leap year.

[4] Below, pp. 198–202.

displeasure.' This is followed by lists of the attendances of knights of the body, squires of the body, sewers, surveyor, cupbearers and carvers, gentlemen ushers, and yeomen ushers, for two periods of eight weeks, beginning 'the last day of October, the eleauenth yeare of our raigne'.[1] This would be for the period 31 October 1471 to 20 February 1471–2. All that is known of these men fits the year 1471–2,[2] whereas several of them (Sir Roger Ree, Sir Maurice Berkeley, and John Hervey) were dead before 1478.[3] The subsequent provisions for the chamber appear to follow on naturally from these lists of attendances for the chamber, and there is no reason to suppose that they are not part of 'the articles . . . for the guiding and directions of our chamber' which the king had made before 31 October 1471. Although some of these provisions have financial consequences, and the last two are related to rules later included in the Ordinance of 1478,[4] the centre of gravity of these provisions is different from that of the Ordinance of 1478 or from the Black Book. These provisions are primarily concerned with due order and decorum, and the efficient service of the king's person, rather than with the control of expenditure. This view of their intention is strengthened if we compare them with what appears to be a draft of them in Add. MS. 46, 354 and Harleian MS. 642.[5]

[1] Below, O 1471, §6. There is no question of 'the eleventh year' being a mistake for 'the eighteenth year'.

[2] Below, O 1471, notes 3–12.

[3] These lists show us what the Black Book, concerned with the control of expenditure, only hints at—that one of the ushers of the chamber—here Sir Roger Ree—acted as deputy to the chamberlain in the latter's frequent absences from his household duties.

[4] O 1478, §§18, 21, 22.

[5] Add. MS. 46, 354 is part of a mainly heraldic collection made by Sir John Writh (died 1504) and his son, Sir Thomas Wriothesley (died 1534), successively Garter king-of-arms. These provisions occupy ff. 56a and b, and may have been copied soon after they were made, for Sir John Writh became Norroy king-of-arms in 1477 and Garter king-of-arms in 1479 (*Dictionary of National Biography*, XXI, 1061). The provisions are followed by ordinances made by John Tiptoft, Earl of Worcester and Constable of England on 29 May 1467, for a joust to be held at Smithfield on 6 July before Edward and his queen and brothers, Earl Rivers, Lord Hastings, etc. I owe my introduction to this manuscript to the kindness of Professor Francis Wormald. The copy in Harleian MS. 642, ff. 204b–5a (new foliation) (which may have been copied from Add. MS. 46, 354 by Sir Simonds d'Ewes) is followed by ordinances on some nice points of precedence, such as whether a duke's eldest son and heir being of the blood royal shall go or be set before a marquis. These, too, may have been made for the court of Edward IV.

In these two manuscripts, after the heading: 'This is the king's commandement that thes articles followinge be dulie observed and kept in pain of the king's great displeasure', most of the same provisions are given, but in a more repetitive and inchoate fashion, and in a less logical order. A few are omitted, and one or two are added which are even more concerned with ceremonial.

It seems therefore that the king turned his attention to the ordering of the royal household soon after his return from exile; perhaps he had been fired by his experiences in January of the splendours of the Burgundian Court.[1] The deliberations on the maintenance of due order and decorum in the king's chamber resulted in the articles just discussed, and the investigations into the more important and difficult problem of how to combine magnificence with providence were very likely followed by the compilation of the Black Book. We can only be sure that the Black Book was composed some time during the decade 1467–77; but during that period some date during 1471 and 1472 seems most likely.

In these detailed investigations on the expenditure of the various household departments and the role of the countinghouse in controlling it, the chief clerk of controlment, the clerks of the greencloth, and the cofferer must necessarily have played a considerable part. The name of the chief clerk of controlment at this time is not known to us; but the advice of the former clerks of controlment, Richard Bindewyn and Richard Jeny,[2] would doubtless be useful. One of the clerks of the greencloth at this time was Peter Beaupie, who had formerly been chief clerk of controlment.[3] The cofferer was John Elrington whom we find receiving robes as one of the clerks and serjeants of the household for 6–7 Edward IV.[4] An account of his which seems to cover his tenure of the office and describes him as 'nuper coferarius hospicij domini regis Edwardi quarti' covers the period May 1471 to September 1474.[5] It seems to have been as true at this time as it was a century later that the coffership was 'the highest office in the household obtainable by promotion'.[6] Not only did John Elrington have, as cofferer, sufficient status to be admitted

---

[1] Philippe de Commines, *Mémoires*, ed. J. Calmette (Paris, 1924), I. 139, 211; T. Basin, *Histoire des Règnes de Charles VII et de Louis XI* (Paris, 1856), II. 252; J. de Waurin, *Recueil des Chroniques et Anciennes Istories de la Grant Bretaigne*, ed. W. & E.L.C.P. Hardy (Rolls Series, 1891), V. 614. Edward met Charles the Bold at Aire and St. Pol from January 2nd to 8th, in order to ask for aid in recovering his kingdom.

[2] E 159/249, Brevia directa Baronibus, Michaelmas Term, 12 Ed. IV, m. 4a. Richard Jeny was later to be cofferer (E 101/412/10, f. 2a) and had in 6–7 Ed. IV been a buyer for the kitchen (E 101/412/2, f. 40a).

[3] See the wording of the pardon of 1471/2 quoted in Wedgwood, *Biographies*, p. 59: 'late chief clerk of the controller of our Household alias a clerk of the account of our Household'.

[4] E 101/412/2, f. 36a.

[5] E 101/412/3. This fits in with the heading of a journal of his, which reads: 'Jornale de anno iij, viz., a primo die Nouembris anno xiij° domini regis Edwardi quarti vsque vltimum diem septembris proxime sequentis anno xiiij° domini regis' (E 101/412/5).

[6] A. P. Newton in *Tudor Studies*, p. 255.

to the deliberations of the king's household on the household but he was therefore the only one of the head officers of the household who had experienced its working at lower levels—the levels of accounting with which the Black Book was mainly concerned. Moreover, Elrington seems to have won the royal confidence in his work as an administrator in the household; for he had the distinction, very unusual at his period, of being promoted from the cofferership to the treasurership of the household, probably at Michaelmas 1474.[1] Further marks of confidence are the grant to him on 29 July 1473[2] of the office of clerk of the hanaper of chancery,[3] the bestowal of the honour of knighthood in January 1478,[4] his appointment as Constable of Windsor Castle in 1474,[5] and as Treasurer of War for the French campaign of 1475 and the Scottish campaign of 1482.[6] John Elrington was thus not only a man with intimate experience of the working of the household, but an official in whom the king had shown confidence and was to show more. Moreover, the other financial head officers of household in the years immediately after Edward's return from exile—the treasurer, Lord Howard, and the controller, Sir William Parr—seem to have been too busy with other matters in 1471 and 1472 to supervise a detailed survey of the accounting and expenditure of the royal household;[7] though no doubt they would be consulted, especially as Lord Howard had been one of the king's carvers from 1461[8] until his appointment as treasurer of the household in 1467 or 1468.[9] It therefore looks as though the share of John Elrington in the compilation of the Black Book must have been considerable.[10]

[1] E 101/412/3; C.P.R., 1467–77, p. 477.

[2] Ibid., p. 396.

[3] Ibid, p. 396. Like a kind of Pooh-Bah, he would as clerk of the hanaper receive each year the new household roll (B.B., §22), which as cofferer, and then as treasurer, he would have had a share in drawing up. As clerk of the hanaper he was paid £40 a year (ibid., p. 441).

[4] W. A. Shaw, The Knights of England (London, 1906), I. 138. He was made a banneret by the Duke of Gloucester in Scotland in July 1482 (ibid., II. 17).

[5] Archaeologia Cantiana, Vol. XLI (1929), p. 33.

[6] Rymer, V. iii. 56, 121.

[7] See below, notes to B.B., §§70, 71.

[8] E 101/411/13, f. 36a.

[9] See below, App. I, List C.

[10] Probably the clerks of the various household offices were called upon to furnish reports; for this was done in preparation for the Ordinance of 1478 (§1). Perhaps the dean, William Say, was called in for the composition of the introduction, to ensure that it had the appropriate quotations, erudite references, and fitting allusions to Scripture, the Fathers, Aristotle, and the Divine Household; for his work seems to have been used in later sections of the Black Book. He had between 1445 and 1449 written at the request of a Portuguese noble-

6. THE CONTINUED FINANCIAL DIFFICULTIES OF THE ROYAL HOUSEHOLD

The Black Book doubtless served a useful purpose in setting down so precisely the customary expenditure and the usual methods of accounting in the light of former statutes on these matters. Nevertheless, it had not succeeded in its purpose of combining magnificence with providence; for providence must, in the circumstances, include solvency. After 1471 Edward was in a much stronger position than before, financially as well as politically. His secure hold on the throne after Tewkesbury meant that his resources were not drained away in fighting constant risings and conspiracies; and he was relieved of the Lancastrian millstone of the war in France. Even though a good deal of income was probably now being diverted to the king's chamber, the improved position is reflected in the receipt rolls.[1] The royal revenues were fed by many streams, including fresh confiscations, the recovery of trade, the pressing of royal financial rights over the king's subjects, and, after 1475, the pension from Louis XI. Nevertheless, the king continued to find it difficult to pay his way, and outstanding debts of the household remained a problem. The problem could be, and was, tackled from two sides.

One was to assign revenues in advance for the payment of the household expenses, so that the accountants of the household might know in advance what they could expect, and not have to pile up debts to disgruntled creditors. In December 1474, the treasurer of the household, John Elrington, was granted £4,966 6s. 8d. a year for ten years towards the expenses of the household, mainly from customs, ulnage, wardships, and marriages.[2] When the Duke of Clarence was attainted in 1478, part of the revenues of his valuable estates was used for the support of the royal household, and[3] the revenues diverted to the king's chamber[4] may also have been drawn on to meet the household expenses. Such a policy was popular in the country, for it supported the old notion that the king should live of his own and helped to reduce the oppressive purveyance and bad debts from which the

man, Count Alvaro Vaz d'Almada, for presentation to the king of Portugal, a description of the royal chapel in Henry VI's time which still exists in the public library of Evora, Portugal. This manuscript, the only account of the English royal chapel in medieval times, is being edited by Dr. W. Ullmann; and in a letter to the present writer Dr. Ullmann suggests that the author of the Black Book summarized the rather long account which Say gives of the duties and functions of the dean and the royal chapel.

[1] Steel, *op. cit.*, pp. 297 following.
[2] *C.P.R., 1467-77*, p. 477.
[3] Cf. Steel, *op. cit.*, pp. 313, 315, 318.
[4] *Ibid.*, p. 326.

king's subjects would otherwise suffer. So we find, for example, the commons in parliament suggesting that part or the whole of the proceeds of various penalties should be applied to the expenses of the king's household.[1] Indeed, Edward's last parliament, anxious to ensure proper payment for goods taken from people by royal purveyors, secured the king's consent to an act which earmarked £11,180 a year for five years for the expenses of the royal household. The act showed publicly, however, the weakness which usually beset such assignments—that of conflicting assignments; in this case a schedule attached to the act listed some forty provisos of exemption, some of them apparently very considerable in effect, so that the net income from the sources listed may have fallen considerably short of £11,180.[2]

The second approach to the problem was to try to catch up with the outstanding debts of the household. If achieved, this would not only give satisfaction in the country, but improve the credit of the household in future transactions. So we find an enactment by parliament in 1473 that all persons holding tallies or bills against the king issued before 1 December 1470, for the expenses of the royal household, should bring them to the exchequer before the quinzaine of Easter 1475, so that arrangements could be made for paying off the debts in twenty annual instalments.[3] In January 1475, a supplementary act extended until 26 May 1475 the day for bringing such assignments to the exchequer.[4] By this time, however, there were fresh household debts to be met; in June 1475 letters patent were issued arranging for the payment of nearly £3,730 to various creditors for debts outstanding from the years 11–14 Edward IV.[5]

---

[1] *R.P.*, VI. 183b, 221a. One of these was the fines for breaches of a sumptuary law; it is interesting to note that Sir John Elrington was one of the few to be exempted from the operation of this law.

[2] It is hard to tell what was the effect of these provisos on the income actually received by the royal household. The Act repeatedly gave priority to the royal household, but we lack the household accounts to verify this. In 1484 Richard III assigned revenues from crown lands to the value of £10,574 6s. 8d. annually for the royal household (Harl. MS. 433, f. 290a, b).

[3] *R.P.*, VI. 71b.

[4] *Ibid.*, VI. 161a.

[5] *C.P.R.*, 1467–77, p. 537. Assignments were made on various Duchy of Lancaster receipts on 8 June 1475 to clear off £2,466 13s. 4d. of this sum (Accounts Various 37/44/9 & 14, cited by *Somerville*, p. 234) and an account of John Elrington, 'nuper coferarij hospicij domini regis Edwardi quarti' records his receipt of portions of this assignment from William Kerver, receiver-general of the Duchy, and lists the creditors of the household, from 10 May 1471 to 30 September 1474, to whom this money was paid (E 101/412/3). The existence of debts did not prevent the display of magnificence when this was thought desirable. After dealing with the payment of debts of the household for the years 11–14 Ed. IV, the same account goes on to record the payment of

By 1478 it was possible to think of clearing off outstanding debts. The pension from France was coming in regularly, there was additional income from the confiscated Clarence estates, the various measures which the king had been taking since 1475 to increase his revenues were beginning to bear fruit,[1] the revenues from the customs were showing an upward surge with the marked revival in the export trade,[2] and in 1478 both convocations of Canterbury and York made grants to the crown.[3] In April 1478 the king's outstanding debt of £12,923 9s. 8d. owing to the city of London was paid off,[4] and in July he sent word to the exchequer that he had given full power to John Morton, keeper of the rolls, and William Essex, remembrancer of the exchequer, to make a settlement with his creditors and that he wished these debts to be settled without delay out of 'our treasure' and the tenths last granted by the province of Canterbury.[5] There was need to settle the old debts of the household, for considerable new ones were accumulating. In the period 16–18 Edward IV the debts to various creditors for wages, victuals, and other things amounted to nearly £3,120, the net deficit to over £2,230.[6] To meet such debts the exchequer methods of auditing and payment were felt to be too slow and cumbrous, and instances had already occurred of appointing special auditors, especially members of the royal household, for certain revenues.[7] Now, in 1478, the examining of the accounts of the auditors, receivers, and bailiffs of the important Clarence estates, recently confiscated, was entrusted to a special commission composed in the main of household officials.[8] The Clarence estates would be made to serve more than one need of the household; not only could revenue be derived from them, but members of the king's household could be appointed to posts within them, as stewards of manors, bailiffs of towns and hundreds, marshals of

£330 1s. 1½d. for the sumptuous re-interment of Richard, Duke of York, and his son Edmund, killed at Wakefield in 1460, in Fotheringay church. Cf. Harl. MS. 48, ff. 78–91, and Scofield, *op. cit.*, II. 167–8.

[1] *Cont. Croyland Chronicle*, p. 559.

[2] *Studies in English Trade in the Fifteenth Century*, ed. E. E. Power & M. M. Postan (London, 1933), pp. 2, 38, 401, 406.

[3] *Concilia Magnae Britanniae et Hiberniae*, ed. D. Wilkins (London, 1737), III. 612.

[4] Scofield, *op. cit.*, II. 215.

[5] *Ibid.*, II. 216, citing Warrants for Issues, 18 Ed. IV, 20 July.

[6] E 101/412/6. Roll of Sir John Elrington, treasurer of the household.

[7] E.g. the appointment of Sir Thomas Vaughan in 1476 as surveyor and demiser of the revenues of the Norfolk inheritance (*C.P.R., 1476–85*, p. 10).

[8] *Ibid.*, p. 64. The commission was composed of Sir Thomas Vaughan, treasurer of the chamber, Sir John Elrington, treasurer of the household, Sir Robert Wingfield, controller of the household, together with Sir John Say, under-treasurer of England, and Henry Boteler or Butler, recorder of Coventry.

D

studs of horses, farmers, warreners, wardens, and so on.[1] These posts could be granted to household officials not only to ensure royal control of newly acquired estates, but also as rewards, as the Black Book had said.[2]

Such opportunities for rewarding household officials cheaply were probably very welcome, for the expense of the royal household, or households, seems to have been increasing, possibly on account of Edward's growing family.[3] The Queen's household account for the year 1466–7 shows that her household was then smaller than those of her predecessors more than a century earlier[4] and cheaper than that of Queen Margaret.[5] But the queen's household must have been more expensive to run in most years of the 1470's, when she and her husband were parted for considerable periods,[6] than it had been in 1466–7 when the king and queen were mostly together. The king's own household had to make provision for more and more children,

---

[1] See *Minister's Accounts of the Warwickshire Estates of the Duke of Clarence, 1479–80*, ed. R. H. Hilton (Dugdale Society, Publications XXI, 1952), pp. xxviii–xxix.

[2] B.B., §19.

[3] As early as October 1468 Edward had had to grant an extra £400 a year to Queen Elizabeth for the maintenance of his daughters Elizabeth and Mary (then only two years and one year old) 'in consideration of the great charge and cost she has hitherto borne for their needful expenses' (*Cal. Close Rolls, 1468–76*, p. 5). Resources had to be diverted to the upkeep of the household of his heir, who in 1473 was sent to Ludlow with an imposing and correspondingly expensive council (*Household Ordinances*, pp. *27, *29). By the time that the Ordinance of 1483 was made (Sloane MS. 3479, ff. 53b–8a) Sir Thomas Vaughan had become the prince's chamberlain in place of Earl Rivers while still remaining, apparently, treasurer of the king's chamber.

[4] The scale of the household revealed in this account (Exchequer, Treasury of the Receipt Books, Vol. 207) is very modest compared with the large size of the households of Isabella and Philippa, the queens of Edward II and Edward III (Tout, *Chapters*, V. 231–89).

[5] The total expenses of Queen Margaret's household for the year Michaelmas 1452 to Michaelmas 1453 were £7,539 15s. 4¾d. (Duchy of Lancaster Accounts Various, 5/8, f. 21b); the expenses of Elizabeth Woodville's account are not totalled; but in an unpublished thesis of Liverpool University, entitled 'A Household Account of Queen Elizabeth Woodville', Mr. D. H. Jones computed her expenses for the year 6–7 Ed. IV at £4,610.

[6] When Edward was preparing in the spring of 1475 for the invasion of France, he made arrangements for Queen Elizabeth to be allowed £2,200 a year for the expenses of the royal household during his absence (Vespasian C XIV, f. 272b). The wages and rewards of the queen's servants for four months were to be £161 0s. 9½d., or at the rate of £483 2s. 4½d. a year, whereas the fees and wages to the queen's servants in her household in 6–7 Ed. IV had been only £308 6s. 8d. (Jones, *op. cit.*, p. 13). The allowance for the Prince of Wales in 1475 was to be £2,200 a year; whereas the Black Book had allowed for a prince's household only £1,460 a year. (Cf. Vespasian C XIV, f. 272b; below, p. 47.)

who by 1478 numbered six, excluding Edward, Prince of Wales.[1] Whether from this or other causes, the household expenditure increased, although alms and gifts were dwindling.[2] A king who was already troubled by debts on the household and was in 1478 evidently making a great effort to put the royal finances on a sound basis was therefore faced by the necessity of trying to reduce the expenses of the household by paring away the 'diets'—i.e. the sums spent on food, fuel, and ordinary wages. The result was the Ordinance of 1478.

7. THE ORDINANCE OF 1478

(a) Its Character

The preamble to the Ordinance shows that its provisions were drawn up only after the interrogation of the chief officers of the household,[3] and all the clerks of the various offices of the household.[4] The purpose of the Ordinance is shown at once by the reports which the clerks were required to give, on the expenses of their offices and how they were administered from the financial point of view. The defects revealed were said to be of two kinds: the expenses needed attention, for some were too great and some were too small, and the methods of accounting were not as efficient as they should have been. Then, like the introduction to the Black Book, the preamble recalls the teachings of Aristotle's Nicomachean Ethics, to say that liberality

[1] I.e. Elizabeth, Mary, Cecily, Richard, Anne, and George (Ramsay, *Lancaster and York*, II. 469).

[2] The following figures, drawn from E 101/411/13 & 15; E 101/412/2 & 6 will illustrate the point (sums are given to the nearest pound).

Nature of outlay	1463–4	1465–6	1466–7	1476–7	1477–8
Cost of food and other provisions .	£8,187	£9,502	£9,897	£11,034	£11,940
Alms	£152	£124	£133	£32	£42
Gifts	£169	£168	£209	£25	£27

The £11,364 spent on 'dieta' in 1464–5 (E 101/411/14) seems to have been unusual for that decade.

[3] Presumably this would include the chamberlain, steward, treasurer, and controller; but whether it included a cofferer as distinct from the treasurer is doubtful, for we have no cofferer's name for the period between 1474 and 1478 (below, App. I, List E) and the very first provision of the Ordinance takes the trouble to lay down that the treasurer and cofferer be two several persons.

[4] Presumably these included, besides the cofferer's clerk, the clerks of the greencloth, and the chief clerk of controlment, the three senior clerks of the supply departments, the clerks of the kitchen, the avery, and the spicery. There may also have been interviews with lesser clerks such as those of the jewelhouse, the closet, the bakehouse, the larder, the poultry, the acatry, the scullery, the saucery, and the hall. See below, B.B., §§43, 116, O 1478, §68 (xii)–(xliii); and cf. Newton, *Tudor Studies*, pp. 254–5.

is the due mean between avarice and prodigality, and to proclaim that both these vices are to be avoided by establishing a better order for the financial administration of the household.

The emphasis of this Ordinance is very much on economy. In the overwhelming majority of cases a comparison of the Ordinance and the Black Book reveals that in 1478 the permitted number of officials was somewhat reduced, and the allowances of food, fuel and light were pared down.[1] Significant of the spirit of this Ordinance are the differences between one of its clauses and a provision of the Ordinance of 1445 from which it was evidently taken.[2] In 1478 Edward IV was not prepared to leave permitted fees to what was 'of old time accustomed'; he would have them taken only in accordance with an up-to-date list which should specify the number of authorized persons and the precise amount of food, fuel and lighting allowed. The number of persons thus authorized was sometimes smaller than in either the Black Book or the Ordinance of 1445.[3]

Not only did the Ordinance of 1478 thus try to reduce the number of authorized persons and the liveries which they were allowed; it also sought to achieve economy, as the preamble had forecast, by decreeing greater strictness in accountancy and the supervision of expenditure. To attempt this it did not need to describe, *seriatim*, the arrangements of department after department; for the Black Book had already done most of this work. The Ordinance of 1478 could therefore concentrate on those points where reform was felt to be necessary; and so the Ordinance could be much shorter than the Black Book, more peremptory and less explanatory in form, bent much more directly and briefly on the aim of efficiency. The Ordinance could concentrate on making more explicit what was merely implied or stated less emphatically in the Black Book,[4] or on repeating, often in more decided language and with specified penalties for non-observance of the rule, orders already made in the Black Book but nevertheless inadequately observed.[5] Sometimes the regulations for accounting are made stricter than they had been in the Black Book. Thus whereas the Black Book had allowed the treasurer two years in which to present his account to the exchequer after the end of the financial year, the Ordinance reduces this time to six months.[6]

---

[1] Cf. below, notes to B.B., department by department. For exceptions, cf. notes 416, 425, 458.

[2] O 1478, §34 and O 1445, §8.

[3] E.g. see B.B. notes 363, 380, 414.

[4] Cf., for example, notes to O 1478, §§6, 22, and 50.

[5] Cf., for example, notes to O 1478, §§7, 45 and 53; O 1478, §5 may be a reference to B.B., §§56–62.

[6] See note to O 1478, §50; see also note to O 1478, §47.

But in its efforts to promote greater efficiency in the household, the king's council did not limit itself to picking out items from the Black Book and underlining or revising them, nor to composing new rules based purely on the result of its investigations among the chief officers and clerks of the household. As in the case of the Black Book, the Ordinance of 1478 looks to precedent and rules of the past. The makers of the Ordinance may have found some guidance in Clarence's Ordinance of 1468;[1] but the main source of inspiration was the Ordinance of 1445. Of thirty-four paragraphs of orders in the Ordinance of 1445, twenty-one were drawn on for the Ordinance of 1478, often being transferred almost verbatim or with only small alterations.[2] These paragraphs form one third of the regulations of 1478, which shows how strong was the conservative tendency; and the general plan of the Ordinance of 1478 seems to owe much to that of 1445. It is not surprising that the makers of the Ordinance of 1478 should thus have pressed into service the Ordinance of 1445, for it was the nearest to their own both in time and purpose.[3]

Considerable, however, as are the similarities between the two ordinances, the differences are also striking. The strength of the government of Edward IV is shown in the omission of those clauses of the Ordinance of 1445 which had especially revealed the weakness of the Lancastrian government.[4] So far, for example, from any concession that all the king's squires and officials who were not on the establishment should have the right to come to the king's court at the five principal feasts of the year, during sessions of parliament and great councils, or even at the 'coming of strangers', if they could persuade one of the chief officials of the household to authorize it, the Ordinance of 1478 sharply decrees that all knights for the body, cupbearers, and knights carvers, squires for the body, chaplains, gentlemen ushers, and squires of the household are to be made to attend when required.[5] It characteristically provides a piece of machinery designed to ensure this—the delivery by the king to the countinghouse at the beginning of each quarter of the year of a book containing the names of these officials who were supposed to be in attendance during the coming quarter; the countinghouse could from this book make a check-roll of attendances. And even in the provisions which are taken from the Ordinance of 1445 into that of 1478,

[1] See notes to O 1478, §§8, 10, 14, 40, 41.
[2] See notes to O 1445, §§1–34 and O 1478, §§1–67.
[3] The Black Book aimed at a much more systematic survey and description of the household, office by office; and the Ordinance of 1445, besides being composed for the altogether exceptional circumstance of a mad king, was really only a list of authorized personnel and nothing more.
[4] See above, p. 8.
[5] Cf. O 1445, §19 and O 1478, §15.

there are sometimes significant changes. Usually these are in the direction of greater stringency. Thus the Ordinance of 1478 repeats a long order of 1445 on the subject of purveyance, but then adds that any such provisions taken for the use of the household shall be acquired at least a fortnight in advance, so that if the goods seem unsuitable, or the prices unreasonable (from the king's point of view), other goods may be obtained instead.[1]

The talk in the preamble about some expenses being too small and about avarice being a specially odious vice was not, however, merely face-saving verbiage. Occasionally the Ordinance allowed more officials or greater liveries than the Black Book.[2] This spirit of combining stricter administration with public generosity, is well seen in a rule, mostly drawn from the Ordinance of 1445, forbidding vessels of wine or ale to be taken out of the palace gates. The regulation about food or other royal property not being taken out of the gates without due permission is more stringent than in the Ordinance of 1445; the rule about the admission of poor men to receive alms is more generous.[3]

The Ordinance of 1478 also continued the tendency of the Black Book to place actual responsibility for the detailed financial administration of the household on the cofferer, the clerks of the greencloth, and the clerk controller. Both the Black Book and the Ordinance of 1478 stress the great importance of the countinghouse in controlling expenditure. But whereas the Black Book was concerned to investigate what former enactments affecting the countinghouse might still be deemed formally valid, the Ordinance of 1478 was concerned with the actual situation only.[4] As in other matters, the two documents are not contradictory but complementary.[5]

The importance of the cofferer in the day-to-day administration of the household is probably responsible for the provision that the treasurer and cofferer are to be two separate persons.[6] As was shown above, Sir John Elrington was a very trusted servant of the king and was indeed knighted in this year of 1478; and it looks as though he continued to act as cofferer after he had become treasurer at

---

[1] Cf. O 1445, §31 and O 1478, §§62, 63 and 64. Cf. also O 1445, §8 with O 1478, §34 and O 1445, §17 with O 1478, §§48 and 49.

[2] See, for example, notes 416 and 457 to B.B.

[3] Cf. O 1445, §10 and O 1478, §39.

[4] Thus the Black Book, investigating the formal responsibilities of the chamberlain, enacted that he was to assign carvers, cupbearers, sewers and squires for the body (§27); the Ordinance of 1478 recognized that he was in fact too busy to do this, and gave the duty to the ushers of the chamber (§27).

[5] Thus, cf. B.B., §78 (ii) and O 1478, §§18, 19.

[6] O 1478, §2.

Michaelmas 1474. We have no record of any other man as cofferer during those years; and the wording of some documents suggests that Elrington's appointment as treasurer was not felt to constitute a break from his tenure of the office of cofferer.[1] For the financial year 1478–9 we have the names of two cofferers—Richard Jeny, a former clerk of controlment who seems to have held the office only for a few months, and James or Jacques Bloundell or Blundell who retained the office until at least 1481.[2] Perhaps it had been found that Sir John Elrington had become too important and busy a person to give adequate time to the exacting functions of a cofferer. If the cofferership was now being separated from the treasurership, it would explain the need to place at the beginning of the Ordinance of 1478 precautions for seeing that money allocated for the expenses of the household was properly applied, principally by the checking of payments from the treasurer to the cofferer by indentures and the entering into a ledger, to be kept in the countinghouse by the cofferer, of all moneys received by him or other officers for the use of the household.[3]

The Ordinance of 1478 lays greater stress than hitherto on the role of the clerk of controlment.[4] Perhaps the most striking illustration of this is to be found in an adaptation of a provision from the Ordinance of 1445. The earlier Ordinance had provided that no payment should be made either by cash or by tally by the treasurer, or cofferer, or clerks of the greencloth, except in the countinghouse, in the presence of the steward or the controller. The Ordinance of 1478 repeated this rule, but added the clerk controller as an alternative to the steward or controller.[5] This would mean that in practice it would be the clerk

[1] A book of creditors of the household for the years 15–20 Ed. IV is described as a book of creditors 'de annis quinto sexto septimo octauo et nono Johannis Elryngton Thesaurarii dicti hospicij'; whereas if he had started his numbering from the time that he became treasurer, he ought to have called these his 1st to 5th years as treasurer. Several times his tenure of the two offices seems to be closely associated. For example, a privy seal letter of 23 March, 22 Ed. IV, speaks of the time that 'the seid John Elryngton was coferer and treasurer of our seid houshold, that is for to sey, of the xjth, xijth, xiijth, xiiijth, xvth, xvjth, xvijth, and xviijth yeres of our reigne' (K.R. Memoranda Roll (E 159/259), Easter Term, 22 Ed. IV, Brevia directa Baronibus, m. 10a. This exchequer style of dating is used by Elrington in his statement of receipts and payments in respect of debts dating from his period as cofferer, where, for example, the 14th year of Edward IV means the year Michaelmas 1473 to Michaelmas 1474, the date at which he became treasurer of the household (E 101/412/3).

[2] App. I, List E.

[3] O 1478, §§2, 3. An example of such an indenture is to be found in E 101/412/12, for assignments on the customs of Southampton and the staple of Calais.

[4] Cf. B.B., §75, and O 1478, §§4, 34, 47.

[5] O 1445, §27, and O 1478, §58.

controller who supervised all payments in the countinghouse, and we find in the next clause that he must supervise the cancelling of all debentures paid by the cofferer or the clerks of the greencloth. As the Black Book had shown,[1] the clerk controller had great powers of supervision over the quality and volume of goods delivered for the use of the household; it was therefore fitting that his concurrence should be necessary for the payment of recognitions of debt by the cofferer and the clerks of the greencloth.[2]

(b) The Effects of the Ordinance

Whether this Ordinance achieved all that was hoped of it, it is impossible to say. Certainly it did not at once free the household from deficits. A statement of the creditors of the household to Michaelmas 1479 shows that for the previous five years debts amounting to £2,501 9s. 1½d. were still outstanding, of which £975 12s. 5d. dated from the last year, 1478–9.[3] But these debts were less than those which had been usual in the reign of Henry VI or, indeed, in the earlier years of Edward IV;[4] and the continued deficit may reflect the inadequacy of income rather than the inefficiency of household administration. Considerable efforts were made at this time to increase the income of the royal household[5] and there seems to have been a reduction in household expenditure in the years immediately following the making of the Ordinance of 1478.[6]

The expenditure in the years 18–19 and 19–20 Ed. IV was £11,292 and £11,193. This helps to explain why Edward's last Parliament, anxious to ensure proper payment for goods taken from people by royal purveyors, secured the king's consent to an act which was intended to earmark £11,180 a year for the expenses of the royal

[1] B.B., §75.

[2] For a further extension of the clerk controller's supervision of payments, see also O 1478, §38.

[3] E 101/412/1.

[4] See above, pp. 6, 12.

[5] E.g. issues were assigned for this purpose in 1479 from the Duchy of Lancaster estates in Lancashire, Tickhill, Tutbury, Pontefract, Knaresborough, and Bolingbroke (*Somerville*, p. 234); and there were big assignments to the household recorded in the exchequer in 1479–80 and 1480–1 (Steel, *op. cit.*, p. 313).

[6] A comparison can be made from four accounts; E 101/412/6 (a roll of the treasurer of the household for the years 16–18 Ed. IV); E 101/412/9 (an incomplete account for 18 January 1478 to 16 January 1479); E 101/412/10 and 11 (accounts for the exchequer years 1478–9 and 1479–80). The comparison is as follows: the fourth column of the table gives the total value of prests, or advances to officers of the household, and stocks remaining in the various

household.[1] But what is of relevance here is not the result achieved but the goal attempted. It was evidently supposed at this time that a sum of £11,180 would provide for nearly all the annual expenditure of the household. It may well be that such an allocation was too parsimonious; the Black Book had estimated the annual cost of the household at £13,000.[2] But even the actual expenditures of the household in these closing years of the reign of Edward IV seem to have been moderate compared with what had gone before and what was to follow. To judge from the extant household accounts, the cost of the royal household in these years seems to have been lower than it had ever been in the days of Henry VI or than it was to be in the reign of Henry VII.[3] If one takes the account books of Henry VI's

departments at the end of the year, and these values, deducted from the total expenditure, give the true annual expenditures.

Exchequer year	Costs of diets (to nearest £)	Total expenses (to nearest £)	Praestita et remanencia (£)	True expenditure (£)
1476–7	11,034	24,339	964	23,375
1477–8	11,940			
18 Jan. 1478– 16 Jan. 1479	11,944	—	—	—
1478–9	10,853	11,671	379	11,292
1479–80	10,752	11,671	478	11,193

These sums, though not the lowest rates of household expenditure for this reign, were not the highest. For the first few months the rate was much higher; but the calls on household finances were probably unusually heavy, and included, for example, some military expenditure. From 3 March 1461 to Michaelmas 1461 the total expenditure reached £10,964 (E 101/411/11), which corresponds to an annual expenditure of over £18,000. (The expenses less 'praestita et remanencia' totalled £10,106.) For the exchequer years 1463–4 and 1466–7 the accounts E 101/411/3, E 101/412/2 give us the following particulars:

Exchequer year	Cost of diets (£)	Total expenses (£)	Praestita et remanencia (£)	True expenditure (£)
1463–4	8,907	10,801	1,062	9,739
1466–7	9,897	12,248	704	11,544

[1] R.F., VI. 198a–202b. Cf. above, p. 36.
[2] B.B., §10.
[3] Such a comparison necessarily leaves out of account the expenses of the great wardrobe for clothes, linen, furs, etc., in these reigns. The enrolled accounts for the reigns of Henry VI and Edward IV are perished and almost unusable; but it is just possible to ascertain that for the period 13 November, 37 Hy. VI to 31 August, 38 Hy. VI, the keeper of the great wardrobe, John Wode, received £1,370 3s. 4¼d.; for the period 17 April, 1 Ed. IV to 28 September, 2 Ed. IV, George Darell, the keeper, received £3,302 6s. 4¾d.; and for

household which apply clearly to whole years, it is evident that the gross expenditure was never less than £13,000 and might, even in apparently quiet years, exceed £14,000 or £15,000.[1] When there were military preparations to pay for, the cost might be greater; thus in 1429–30, when the royal household was helping to organize and finance the war in France, the receipts were as much as nearly £47,098.[2] And if we turn to the extant household accounts for whole years of the reign of Henry VII we find that the total expenditure was never less than £12,000 and was more usually well over £13,000 or £14,000.[3] In 1485 various revenues were assigned by act of parliament to pay the expenses of the king's household: but now, instead of an assignment of only £11,000, as in 1483, the total was over £14,000,

the period from Michaelmas, 2 Ed. IV, to 4 April, 5 Ed. IV, he received £5,393 6s. 10d.—an average of a little over £2,000 a year (E 361/6). The original accounts are almost all lost. The account of Robert Rolleston, keeper of the great wardrobe, for 1434–5 (Add. MS. 17, 721) shows receipts of £1,387 1s. 5d. and expenses of £1,413 17s. 7½d.; and the account of Piers Curteys for the period from 18 April to Michaelmas, 20 Ed. IV, in Harleian MS. 4780, edited by Sir Harris Nicolas in 1830 in his *Wardrobe Account of Edward IV* shows that for this period Curteys received £1,174 5s. 2d.

[1] The following tabulation may be of help (sums are given to the nearest pound):

P.R.O. reference	Year	Total expenses (£)	Praestita et remanencia (£)
E 101/409/8 } E 101/409/9 }	20–21 Hy. VI	13,513	1,020
E 101/409/11	22–23	14,446	1,689
E 101/409/16	25–26	14,275	1,321
E 101/410/6	29–30	13,205	716
E 101/410/9	30–31	15,976	4,323

For the seventeen months 3 December 1454–11 May 1456, the expenditure amounted to £17,685, which is at the rate of about £12,500 for twelve months (E 101/410/15).

[2] E 101/408/9. No total of expenditure is given.

[3] The following table may help:

P.R.O. reference	Year	Total expenses (£)	Praestita et remanencia (£)
E 101/413/8	8–9 Hy. VII	12,107	1,039
E 101/414/3	10–11	13,842	1,440
E 101/414/14	13–14	14,510	1,188
E 101/415/12	19–20	13,625	1,721

The account for 2–3 Hy. VII (E 101/412/19) does not provide us with a total, but it is probably £14,717. The 'dieta' amount to £13,705 for this year, and the 'prests and stock' to £912. For the year 15–16 Hy. VII the account (E 101/415/2) is too incomplete to enable one even to estimate the total expenditure; but it must have been well over £11,500, as the 'dieta' cost £11,450. The receipts totalled £14,814.

with an extra £2,100 for the expenses of the great wardrobe.[1] Later
in the reign a detailed estimate was made of the yearly cost of the
royal household 'aswell the dayly dyettes as all other fforen charges
belongyng to the kynges housholde', and the sum total came to
nearly £14,366.[2]

Not only does the annual household expenditure of substantially
less than £12,000 appear moderate compared with the corresponding
sums spent by Henry VI and Henry VII[3] but the 'prests and stocks'
of less than £500 a year in these last years of Edward IV are in contrast with the much higher 'prests and stocks' of the extant accounts
of Henry VI and Henry VII, which were usually over £1,000, sometimes substantially so. It may be that in the first years after the
Ordinance of 1478, with its detailed injunctions for supervision and
economy and accounting, the various departments of the household
were driven to work to a comparatively small margin of advances of
money and stocks of food and utensils.

Yet moderation in expenditure was not accompanied by a pinch-
beck and down-at-heel appearance at the court of Edward IV. In
1468 the considerable sums of £397 and £984 were spent for the
furnishing and adornment of the royal palace, including four pieces
of arras representing the stories of Nebuchadnezzar, Alexander, the
Passion, and the Judgement.[4] The great wardrobe accounts of Piers
Curteys in 1480 record the purchase of quantities of costly garments
and fine furnishings, from a gown of cloth of gold and blue upon
'enamelled satin', lined with green satin, or a gown of tawny velvet,
lined with black damask, to pillows stuffed with down or feather
beds and bolsters. Besides all this there was buying of large amounts
of velvets, satins, silks, and precious furs, and binding of books in
figured velvet or blue silk, with much gilding and tassels of silk, not
to speak of the purchase of various pieces of arras, such as two de-
picting the story of Paris and Helen.[5] The party of Bohemians who
visited England in 1466 had been impressed by the royal splendour,
as they were meant to be. Gabriel Tetzel, the narrator, who accompanied Leo, Lord of Rozmittal, brother of the Queen of Bohemia, in

---

[1] *R.P.*, 299a–303b; 303b–304b. This allocation of £14,000 was reduced by
provisos in favour of various persons; indeed in 1495 so many of the sums
assigned could not in fact be obtained that fresh assignments were made to the
value of £13,059 for the upkeep of the royal household, no provisos being
allowed, except for Edward, Duke of Buckingham, *R.P.*, VI, 497b–502a.

[2] See below, pp. 229–30, for the text of this estimate.

[3] The household expenditure of Henry VIII was much higher, but it is
difficult to compare because of the marked rise in prices during his reign.

[4] F. Devon, *Issues of the Exchequer* (London, 1837), p. 491.

[5] *The Privy Purse Expenses of Elizabeth of York; Wardrobe Account of
Edward the Fourth*, pp. 146, 144, 143, 134, 152, 132.

his journeys through Europe, commented enthusiastically 'Der Kunig . . . hat des allerhubst hofgesind als man in aller cristenheit mag finden'. He recounts with respect all his experiences of the ostentatious magnificence of the English court, as, for example, the way in which the king distributed largess in a very conspicuous manner to the trumpeter, pipers, and other players, the forty-two singing men, and the twenty-four heralds and pursuivants, who then told everyone how much they had been given, or how, at the queen's churching feast, when the lord of Rozmittal had finished his meal, he was led into a very impressive-looking room, where the queen was to dine, and seated in a corner so that he might watch all the sumptuous arrangements.[1] And this splendour did not disappear— at any rate on great occasions—in Edward's later years, when his avarice had grown and he was striving for economy. During his last Christmas the king appeared frequently (so we are told by a con- temporary who usually deserves to be heeded), 'clad in a great variety of most costly garments, of quite a different cut to those which had been usually seen hitherto in our kingdom . . . You might have seen, in those days, the royal court presenting no other appearance than such as fully befits a most mighty kingdom, filled with riches and with people of almost all nations.' [2] To impress the beholder with a display of magnificence, based on strict supervision of expenditure; this seems to have been the example set by Edward IV to his successors.

Of his work in the Duchy of Lancaster its historian has written: 'The impression left by all this is of an active and competent ad- ministration and of an enterprising and reforming spirit. It is no disrespect to Henry VII's great qualities as a shrewd and careful administrator to say that he carried on and extended the work that had been developed under Edward IV'.[3] It may be that the work of Edward IV in the royal household exerted an influence beyond the reign of Henry VII. When in the last years of his life Thomas Crom- well sought to provide the detailed machinery which could render the good intentions of the Ordinance of 1526 more effective, he was con- cerned, so Dr. Elton tells us, to make the countinghouse supreme in the management of the household. It was hard to get the chief officers of the household to attend the board of greencloth, however, because they were well on the way to becoming leading ministers of state. Cromwell tried to deal with the problem by ordering the clerks of the greencloth and the clerks controllers to take over the duties if none of the great men attended. Detailed rules were laid down for

[1] *Ritter- Hof- und Pilger-Reise*, pp. 155–8.
[2] *Cont. Croyland Chronicle*, p. 563.
[3] *Somerville*, p. 255.

the active officials of the board; and these regulations show that the
clerks controllers 'were in a way the linchpin of the whole system—
they were simply to provide the check on the activities of all other
officers which their designation implied'.[1] An attempt was made to
transfer the payment of most of the regular chamber officers to the
cofferer of the household and to establish the board of greencloth as
the proper administrative organ over the whole court.[2] To anyone
who has studied the Black Book and the Ordinance of 1478 these
features of the reforms of 1539–40 have a familiar ring; and the detailed rules for the conduct of the countinghouse and the supply
departments which, says Dr. Elton, formed 'the core of Cromwell's
reforms'[3] do not appear altogether novel. Some features of the reforms
of 1539–40 were quite new, such as the institution of the lord great
master of household; and doubtless Cromwell's work was, as Dr. Elton
holds, more thoroughgoing and more lasting than previous attempts
at household reforms. Yet Cromwell was painstaking in his reforms;
and since he aimed to establish the supremacy of the countinghouse
in the government of the household, as the chamber administration
established by Henry VII was breaking down, it would have been
very strange if he had not consulted the last considerable survey
and ordinance which had tried to stress the predominance of the
countinghouse in household finance. These books should have been
accessible to him; the Black Book was still kept in the countinghouse,
and the Ordinance of 1478 ought to have been there.[4] The point is of
interest since the Ordinance of 1539-40 lasted in the main as the
constitution for the household 'below stairs' until the reforms of
Edmund Burke.[5] It is no detraction from the importance and ability
of Thomas Cromwell to suggest that his work on the household, and
the character of the household in and after his day, owes more to the
past than Dr. Elton seems to allow, and that the effects of the Black
Book and the Ordinance of 1478 were not limited to the reign in
which they were made.[6]

[1] Elton, op. cit., pp. 380, 389, 391.

[2] Ibid., pp. 393, 404. It is true that Cromwell was dealing with a very different situation from that of Yorkist days, for during the reign of Henry VII the
chamber and its treasurer had become very important in the household, overshadowing the countinghouse; but for that very reason is he not likely to have
turned for guidance to books which had also tried to assert the predominance
of the countinghouse, as the Black Book and the Ordinance of 1478 had done?

[3] Ibid., p. 389.

[4] Some of the provisions of 1539–40 have antecedents in the Ordinance of
1478, others have precursors in the Black Book. Thus compare O 1540, §1 and
O 1478, §2; O 1540, §§6, 8 and O 1478, §47, B.B., §88.

[5] Newton, Tudor Studies, p. 247, note 42.

[6] For example, it has been said of the Black Book's statement on the diet
and allowances of the king's secretary and the clerks of the signet that 'this

8. MANUSCRIPTS

(a) *The Ordinance of 1445*

The only full copy which has so far been found is in Lansdowne MS.
1, ff. 86a–93b;[1] but when an article[2] containing this text was in the
press Mr. H. C. Johnson of the Public Record Office kindly drew the
attention of the present writer to some household provisions of
Henry VI to be found in Chancery Miscellanea 3/36.[3] On inspection this
document proved to be an incomplete version, if not of the original,
at least of a contemporary copy of this ordinance of 23 Henry VI.[4] It
is now in a fragmentary state. Only four membranes of the roll are
left, the opening and concluding ones having been lost, and the
writing of what remains has had in many places to be revived by
chemicals. Enough still exists, however, to show the very dependable
character of the copy in L. C starts only with what in L is §4 and ends
with what in L is §34, thus omitting all the lists of personnel entitled
to bouche of court.

The extant parts of the fifteenth-century copy correspond closely
to the correlated paragraphs in L, except for minor variations of
spelling. The only important difference is the order of five paragraphs.[5] But this does not seem to be a discrepancy of any significance,
for in C these five paragraphs are written on a separate membrane
(No. 2), shorter than the others. In the course of centuries the membranes had come apart, and some of them are lost. When the document reached the care of the Public Record Office and the staff came
to fasten together the four membranes which remained, there was
nothing in the text to show what the order should be; and it looks
as though the membrane with the five paragraphs in question was
inserted at the wrong place.

It may, perhaps, at first sight seem curious that there should be

formed the foundation for all later rulings on the subject' (F. M. G. Evans,
The Principal Secretary of State; A Survey of the Office from 1558 to 1680, Man-
chester, 1923, p. 218); and as late as the eighteenth century some of the
'Ordinances to be observed for regulating accompts and for the well governing
of our house' in the Establishment of the Household of George II, 1727
(Bodleian Library MS. Eng. hist. b. 136, pp. 56–9) wear a familiar look to
anyone who has read the Black Book of the Household of Edward IV and the
Ordinance of 1478.

[1] For a description of this manuscript (hereafter referred to as L), see the
present writer's article in *B.J.R.L.,* XXXVI (1954), 449.

[2] *Ibid.,* pp. 456–66.

[3] Hereafter referred to as C.

[4] At the top of membrane 4, before the heading 'prouisions which be semene
necessarie for the kynges household' (below, p. 67) are the letters R.H., in a
different hand, which may be the sign manual.

[5] §§22–6 of L are placed earlier in C, after the paragraph which in L is no. 13.

two headings in the Ordinance almost duplicating one another—
'Prouisions made for the kynges houshold' and 'Prouisions which be
semene necessarie for the kynges houshold', each accompanied by the
letters 'R H' and each followed by the word 'First' at the beginning
of the next paragraph, as though starting a new enactment. It may
be that this betokens separate proposals for the reform of the royal
household. If so, they were entirely complementary, for nothing in
the first set is repeated in the second; and the latter set is justified by
its character in having a separate heading, for it is distinctively concerned with payments for purchases and purveyances on behalf of the
household. Moreover, the Ordinance of 1478, which is certainly one
unit, follows a parallel arrangement.[1] It therefore looks as though
the provisions for the government of the household preserved in L
were also meant to form a unit.

At the top of f. 86a in L are the incompatible headings: 'Amongst
the peticions offered in parlement in the XXIIIth yere of K.
Henry the sixt is found as followeth' and 'Prouisions made for the
kynges houshold. 1458'. The Ordinance refers in §32 to 'this present
parlement'[2] and no parliament was held in 1458. Moreover, the
Ordinance does not mention Prince Edward, who was, of course, alive
in 1458 and for whom provision was made in the Ordinance of 1454.[3]
Moreover, the situation had deteriorated too much by 1458 for the
Lancastrian government to have either the authority or the leisure
to make ordinances for the reform of the household. In the twenty-
third year of Henry VI, on the other hand, a parliament assembled
on 25 February 1445 and Prince Edward was not yet born. In the
list of authorized household staff at the end of the Ordinance provision is made for the attendants of a queen, and the newly wedded
Queen Margaret arrived in England in April 1445. Furthermore, on
the dorse of C are the words 'Peticio parliamenti aº 23 H.VI'; and
though these are written in a later hand, they give additional weight
to the view that this Ordinance belongs to the year 1445 and not to
1458. The evidence of C therefore not only supports the authenticity
of the Ordinance and confirms the accuracy of L but also clarifies its
date.

(b) The Black Book of the Household of Edward IV

Though the original is now lost, numerous copies were made, most
of them in the seventeenth century; and with the revival of interest
in medieval life in the late eighteenth century it is not surprising

---

[1] See below, pp. 211–28.
[2] The same paragraph, by its reference to 'the parliament holden atte Westminster the xviii yere of the kyng . . . that nowe is' makes it certain that the
ordinance is at any rate later than 1439. [3] Nicolas, *Proceedings*, VI. 233.

that this remarkable book attracted the attention of the Society of Antiquaries. On 29 June 1787, the Council of the Society resolved that the Black Book (of which there was a manuscript in the Society's Library) should be printed at the Society's expense, and that the Rev. Dr. Lort, Mr. Gough, Mr. Topham, and Mr. Brand should superintend 'the collating that Copy with such other Transcripts as they shall think necessary, and the printing thereof when collated'.[1] We must be grateful to the Fellows of the Society of that generation for making the Black Book available in print so long ago; but a new edition is nevertheless called for. Various historians have commented on curious readings in the 1790 edition, and a detailed examination of it makes one wonder, indeed, whence many of the spellings and readings were derived. The title-page would lead one to believe that the text is a straightforward printing of a version to be found in Harleian MS. 642 (H); whereas, as will be described more fully later, the edition is based on the manuscript preserved by the Society of Antiquaries (A) collated with H. But no indication is given in print of the provenance of the various sections of the text.

It seems clear that the only original copy of the Black Book was by 1790 already lost. The original was probably still preserved among the records of the Board of Greencloth in 1610. A list of the records extant in that year begins with the Black Book,[2] and it seems likely

[1] *Ordinances*, p. iii. Michael Lort (1725–90), elected F.S.A. in 1755, was probably appointed because in 1787 he was a vice-president of the Society, as well as having been Regius professor of Greek at Cambridge from 1759 to 1771. Richard Gough (1735–1809) elected F.S.A. in 1767, was not only director of the Society from 1771 to 1797 but had in 1786 published Vol. I. of his great work, *Sepulchral Monuments of Great Britain to illustrate the History of Families, Manners, Habits, and Arts from the Norman Conquest.* John Brand (1744–1806), elected F.S.A. in 1777, had been appointed resident secretary of the Society in 1784. John Topham (1746–1803), elected F.S.A. in 1767, and soon to be appointed treasurer of the Society, in November 1787, was probably the member of the Committee most interested in the project. He had contributed 'Observations on the Wardrobe Accounts of the twenty-eighth year of King Edward I (1299–1300)' to the *Liber Quotidianus Contrarotulatoris Garderobae* published by the same Society in 1787 under his direction. In 1771 he had obtained a place in the State Paper Office, had worked there with Sir Joseph Ayloffe and Thomas Astle, and had helped to publish the Rolls of Parliament.

[2] Although nearly all the early records of the Board of Greencloth were probably lost in a fire in the palace of Whitehall in the middle of the eighteenth century, some may before this have found their way into private hands. (*Second Report of Commission on Public Records*, II. iii, Evidence, Questions 6900–3, quoted by A. P. Newton in his article 'A List of the Records of the Greencloth extant in 1610', in *English Historical Review*, XXXIV (1919), 237.) The list is in the Lord Steward's Miscellaneous Books No. 226, which is marked on the back in the hand of William Bray, clerk of the Board of Greencloth to George III, 'Records No. 1, 1598–1630'. Hence it was probably in his day the earliest book preserved in the department.

that this was an original and not just a copy. The industrious antiquary Sir Simonds d'Ewes (1602–50), made a transcript of the Black Book which he claimed more than once was copied from the original.[1] A version which is given in Harleian MS. 610 and dated 1623 has (in a different hand and ink) the statement at the top of folio 1a: 'The coppye of the Blacke booke of the orders of the kinges household kepte in the Custodye of the Comptroler.'

Most of the transcripts were made in Stuart times, partly doubtless because of the reforms of the household then made, especially that of James I in 1604, partly owing to the antiquarian curiosity, inextricably mingled with political considerations, of the men of the seventeenth century. Of seven extant manuscripts of this period, all but two date from the first half of the century; three were made in the sixteenth century, and one in the fifteenth. The extant manuscripts of the Black Book are as follows:

(i) *Fifteenth century. Society of Antiquaries MS. 211, hereafter referred to as A.*

This contains not only a transcript of the Black Book but part of the only known text of the ordinance made for the household of George, Duke of Clarence, in 1468; it is in a hand of the late fifteenth century.[2] It is a workaday copy of the Black Book, of which the cursive writing and the occasional mistakes or repetitions indicate haste in execution, and it lacks the illustrations or other possible embellishments of the original. It has suffered much at the hands of those who prepared the 1790 edition. In the absence of an original text it was laudable that the editors should wish to collate this manuscript with d'Ewes's copy in Harleian MS. 642; but modern canons of respect for medieval documents would not permit of methods of editing which used a fifteenth-century manuscript as a working draft for the publishers. Words are struck out, abbreviations are expanded, and spellings are altered on every page, and, indeed, on every line, to such an extent that the original transcript is often hard to decipher beneath the late eighteenth-century hand. Since then the

---

[1] His transcript is in Harleian MS. 642, discussed more fully below in this introduction. He copied many documents kept amongst the public records (*The Autobiography and Correspondence of Sir Simonds d'Ewes*, ed. J. O. Halliwell, I (London, 1845), 235 sqq.).

[2] It may be as early as 1480–5 and is unlikely to be later than the very early sixteenth century, as it quite lacks the inverted r which came into fashion in the secretary hand of Henry VIII's day. Miss Kathleen Major has kindly examined the manuscript and agrees with these conclusions. The watermark, consisting of an outstretched hand, with a star surmounting the second finger, is one that can be dated to the late fifteenth or early sixteenth century; it is to be found in many leaves of the book.

E

manuscript has undergone further deterioration. On 21 May 1888 the late W. H. St. John Hope noted[1] that pages 239 to 274 (containing the final section of the Black Book as known to us and most of Clarence's household ordinance) were missing; presumably the rest of the manuscript was still intact or so careful an antiquary would surely have noted the fact. At the present day, however, pages 187 to 230 are lacking as well.

(ii) *Sixteenth century*

There are three manuscripts of this century, all written in hands of the reign of Henry VIII.

(*a*) The fullest copy is *P.R.O., Exchequer, Treasury of Receipt, Misc. Book, No. 230 (E 36/230), hereafter referred to as E.* It omits the entire section of the cost of a squire's household and the whole paragraph beginning 'Domus Prouidencie' which should open the last great section of the book; but it is more complete than any other copy, except that in Harleian MS. 642. It bears a strong resemblance to A and may have been copied from it or from the same archetype.

(*b*) *College of Arms, Arundel MS. XVII.* It continues to the office of laundry, like the fullest versions, but has many omissions, especially at the ends of sections, and in the estimate of the cost of various types of household.

(*c*) *B.M., Harleian MS. 369.* This copy ends abruptly in the middle of the section on the office of bakehouse, and has numerous omissions, sometimes of whole paragraphs.

(iii) *Seventeenth century*

(*a*) *B.M. Harleian MS. 642, hereafter referred to as H.* Compiled by Sir Simonds d'Ewes, this is a volume of royal household documents, from the Black Book of Edward IV to the book signed by Prince Henry in 1610 for the authorized personnel of his household and the allowance of diets, wages, rewards, and liveries within it. Apart from being a fuller version of the Black Book than any other, this copy claims in several places to be taken from the original. Moreover, this copy is unique in providing two drawings, both of which claim to be taken from illustrations in the original book.[2] A marginal note on f. 13b[3] states that 'this last clause is not in the black booke, but I found it in a copie of it written in an hande of about H. 7th time'. The care with which d'Ewes copied the book is illustrated by a marginal note on f. 71 which runs: 'these words had a line drawn through them as if they

---

[1] On a sheet of notepaper preserved in the manuscript.

[2] See the reproduction of these below, Plates I and II.

[3] The folios of the manuscript have been numbered twice: all references are to the second foliation.

had bin to be rased out'; and checking is indicated by the marginal note on f. 80a that 'all this is to bee added and was part of the booke', followed by a passage which had been omitted from the text.

(b) *B.M. Harleian MS. 610, dated 1623.* This is the second fullest of the seventeenth-century copies, but some of the readings suggest either a careless or an uncomprehending reading of the text.[1]

(c) *B.M. Add. MS. 21,993.* It follows a translation of the household ordinances of Edward II 'translated out of an old French Coppy, 13th Martij 1603'. It has more omissions than Harl. MS. 610; for example all the estimates for the cost of the diets of the various types of house-hold—king, prince, duke, bishop, etc.—are left out.

(d) *B.M. Harleian MS. 293.* A note on f. 1a states that 'This booke as Mr. Robert Hare informed me, was made in the tyme of Edward the 4th', and as the antiquary Robert Hare died in 1611, the manu-script must belong to the first half of the century. The handwriting is that of the first quarter. This version is not as full as that of (c).

(e) *Bodleian Library MS. Ashmole 1147.* Written in a secretary hand of about 1600,[2] it has omissions on almost every page, some-times leaving out whole sections, and, like (c) and (d), breaks off in the course of the chapter on the office of the bakehouse.

(f) *Bodleian Library, MS. Dugdale 8* also ends suddenly in the middle of the office of the bakehouse and has numerous omissions. It is said to have been transcribed by William Dugdale between 1668 and 1677.

(g) *P.R.O., Lord Steward's Department, Misc. Books, No. 278 (L13/278).* Written in a secretary hand of the late seventeenth century, it has not been from the outset in official custody. According to a note on f. 2a, it was bought at a sale of the manuscripts of John Anstis, Esquire, sometime Garter King of Arms, on 14 December 1768, for fourteen shillings on behalf of the Board of Greencloth by its clerk, William Bray.[3] Like MS. Dugdale 8, however, it contributes no part of the text which cannot be obtained from earlier copies, and has numerous omissions as compared with the best extant versions.

The claim of adherence to the original by a noted and reputable antiquarian earns H a place as a basic text; but as it was copied a century and a half after the Black Book was written, it is very

---

[1] E.g. f. 7 'rushes for his Chamber on the serjeant and usher of the hall' instead of 'of the serjeant usher of the hall'; or f. 24, 'without presentacion or confirmacion yf any Bishopp' instead of 'of any'.

[2] The remainder of the manuscript was written by the antiquary Francis Tate in 1601.

[3] He was, of course, a noted antiquary, who was elected a Fellow of the Society of Antiquaries in 1771, became its treasurer in 1803, and published various antiquarian writings. He seems to have been one of the more worthy office-holders of this century.

desirable to compare it with earlier copies. In spite of its imperfections
A must also be used to establish the text of the Black Book, for it is a
close second to H in fullness and is the oldest manuscript now extant.
The third manuscript of fundamental value is E, which is so similar
to A that it can be used to fill the gaps in the latter. It therefore seemed
best to collate the text of the Black Book from these three copies, A,
E, and H. H was more carefully written than either A or E, and,
moreover, claims repeatedly to be following the original version. A
has, nevertheless, been taken as the basis of the text rather than H;
for not only is the orthography of A nearer to the original, but so,
it would seem, was its understanding of the text in many cases. Sir
Simonds d'Ewes did not always understand his text, and made
what he doubtless regarded as amendments but are, in fact, corruptions. Hence, for example, H turns 'grooms for the kings' mouth'
into 'groom for the king's month' and 'maynie' (retinue) into 'men';
and its readings are not always the most lucid.[1] Moreover, a text of
this kind is of interest to the philologist as well as the historian; and,
indeed, the Black Book, as given in the 1790 edition, was one of the
books on which the *New English Dictionary* relied for fifteenth-
century spellings.[2] However, throughout the book all the variants
in E and H are noted, except for mere differences in spellings; and if
a reading from H is preferred, it is incorporated into the text accordingly. Where, in spite of collations and study, the text seems
awkward or obscure, as it occasionally does, the present writer has
tried to heed the advice of Cassiodorus[3] on the copying of manuscripts and to be on his guard against plausible emendations. This is
the more necessary as the work appears to exist only in a draft stage,
and may therefore easily display obscure and awkward phraseology,
apart from any corruptions that may have occurred in transcription.
It will be seen that though all three manuscripts are basically the
same in order and content, there is considerable divergence of detail
between A and E on the one hand and H on the other. This suggests that
there was more than one draft; the first draft may have been revised.

(c) The Ordinance of 1478

In marked contrast to the Black Book we are told in the first
sentence that the Ordinance was made in the month of June the year
of Our Lord 1478; and we still have the warrant under the signet,

---

[1] See, for example, p. 185 note (a).

[2] If the editors of the 1790 edition had adhered wherever possible to the
fifteenth-century spellings of A, instead of drawing extremely freely on the
text of H, the *New English Dictionary* would not have included words, such as
'pelter' and 'garquince', which never existed.

[3] In his *De Institutione Divinarum Litterarum* (Migne, *op. cit.*, LXX. 1129–30).

dated 9 July 1478, telling the chancellor that 'we by thaduis of oure counsell have made certain ordinaunces for the stablysshing of oure howshold which by oure commaundement shal be deliuered vnto you by oure trusty and righte welbeloued clerc and counsellor, Maister Thomas Langtone' and directing the chancellor to 'put alle the ordinaunces in writing seled vnder oure great sele, and the same so seled send vnto vs by oure said counsellor without delay'.[1] And instead of having to reconstruct a text from transcripts, some made long afterwards, we have a very early copy to inform us. This is valuable, as the official copy of the Ordinance which the king ordered the chancellor to seal with the great seal and return to him has disappeared. The copy of the Ordinance which has been generally known and quoted is that in the P.R.O., Exchequer, Treasury of Receipt, Miscellaneous Book No. 206. This has the heading on f. 1a: 'Orders in his Majesties household. Being a copy of a faire MS. Booke given me by Dr. Barlow, Provost of Queens Coll, Oxon. 1671/2. J. W.'[2] Sir Joseph Williamson must have meant 'lent' rather than 'given', for the manuscript from which he made his transcript is still in the library of the Queen's College, Oxford, where it is MS. 134; on f. 7b of the fourteen leaves of paper which protect the manuscript at the front and the back (seven at each end) is the note: 'Mem. This MS, was given me by my worthy friend Dr. Barlow Provost of Queens Colledge in Oxon. 1671. Joseph Williamson.' The manuscript is bound in vellum, and, except for the seven leaves of paper at either end of the book, consists of twenty folios of good parchment. The text is written very carefully in a fair 'bastard' hand of the late fifteenth century; there are no 'secretary' hand features. Space was left at the beginning for an illuminated initial I, which was never made. The text is set out (on lines ruled with mauve ink, a very unusual procedure at this period)[3] and written with great care. All this suggests that the manuscript is a very fair and very early copy.[4]

---

[1] Below, p. 211. Dr. Thomas Langton, later successively Bishop of St. Davids, Salisbury, and Winchester, was one of the chaplains to Edward IV. He was in high favour with the king and was much used by him as a messenger and ambassador (Scofield, *op. cit.*, II. *passim*).

[2] Sir Joseph Williamson (1633–1701) was keeper of the state paper office from 1661; Dr. Barlow (1607–91) was Provost of the Queen's College from 1657 to 1675 when he became Bishop of Lincoln. It is quite natural that Sir Joseph Williamson should have had this book from the head of Queen's College; for he had been an undergraduate of Queen's (1650–4), and then a Fellow of the College (1657), and always remained a great friend of the College and its members (as his detractor Anthony Wood was forced to admit), even when he became immersed in the duties of a secretary of state (1674).

[3] I am indebted to Dr. R. W. Hunt, Keeper of Western MSS. in the Bodleian Library, Oxford, for this information.

[4] If the book was kept in the countinghouse, it might have been removed by

Included in the great collection of royal household documents compiled by Sir Simonds d'Ewes, in Harleian MS. 642, are thirty-nine paragraphs of provisions for the government of the household.[1] A comparison of these provisions with the Ordinance of 1478 shows that of the thirty-nine paragraphs twenty-seven are included in the Ordinance verbatim or with only comparatively small changes in the published version; and five more clearly correspond to provisions in the Ordinance. It looks as though these thirty-nine provisions form a draft of the Ordinance. They begin abruptly instead of having a preamble, like the Ordinances of 1478 or 1526, they are often less neatly worded than the corresponding passage in the Ordinance of 1478, and they are sometimes less logically arranged.[2] There seem to be reasons for the omission of the seven draft provisions left out of the Ordinance.[3] The last rule not included in the Ordinance of 1478 comes at the end of the provisions and may have been added in Henry VII's time, according to one interpretation of the marginal note, which was probably the work of Sir Simonds d'Ewes;[4] certainly, the concern which this last rule shows with precedence is more akin to the spirit of Henry VII's Ordinance of 1493, with its precise

one of the officers of the department, as so often happened with official documents. It is well known that Sir Joseph Williamson made considerable efforts to recover for the state paper office documents which had thus strayed from official custody.

At the top of f. 1a of the paper leaves at the front of the manuscript is the following remark: 'This MSS [*sic*] would form a valuable edition to what has been already printed respecting the Royal Household. J. Hunter, June 20, 1832'. This celebrated antiquarian became sub-commissioner of public records in 1833 and assistant keeper in 1838.

[1] See below, Draft of the Ordinance of 1478. The similarity of the phrase 'ordinance made for the stablishment of the king's house' in the heading to the phrase 'ordinaunces for the stablysshing of oure howshold' in the warrant under the signet cited above, will be noted.

[2] Cf. notes to Draft.

[3] (a) Rule §4 which appears to refer to B.B. is superseded in O 1478 by §34 there; (b) rule §5 would not help directly towards the objective of promoting economy, and might be thought to overlap a rule already given in B.B., §78 (xxii); (c) rule §20 was perhaps considered sufficiently covered by §§14, 75 in B.B.; (d) rule §29 was covered by the list of allowances at the end of O 1478, and §58 in O 1478; (e) perhaps §31 was felt too much of a slight to the household treasurer, Sir John Elrington; (f) rule §35 probably seemed on reflection to be too impracticable, in view of their necessary absences, and O 1478 has instead merely §7; (g) rule §36 was unsuitable for a public enactment and inappropriate to an ordinance concerned with promoting economy. Moreover, B.B. has spoken of the daily service of wafers and of fruit to be served in season (B.B., §§81, 89).

[4] Below, provisions, §39. The marginal summaries were probably his work, for his copy of the Black Book, in the same manuscript, Harleian 642, has the same kind of marginalia, which are to be found in none other of the numerous manuscripts of the Black Book.

regulations of ceremonial[1] than to the aim of the Ordinance of 1478 to further economy. So it seems that the provisions transcribed by d'Ewes are a preliminary draft for the Ordinance of 1478; if so, the heading to them shows, what the published Ordinance does not, that they were prepared, as was the Black Book, by the advice of the king's council.

The provisions are followed in Harleian MS. 642[2] by a section which is headed 'Remembrance vntill another tyme to be made of thinges that are after written'. This introduces a miscellany of matters, much concerned with weights, measures, and prices, to be observed by various departments, for example, the spicery, acatry, scullery, and stable, and often set down in note form.[3] The first paragraph echoes the Black Book; it explains that the steward and treasurer of the household must each Michaelmas make a warrant to the chief butler of England, assigning how much wine will be needed for the royal household during the coming year, and where it shall be lodged. It adds that with good oversight 300 tuns should suffice; 'and for other things looke the statutes of noble Edward'.[4]

This section continues with attempts to estimate the wages and numbers of personnel of the household, and ends with some articles concerning the bakehouse. It alludes to wages which by estimation 'may be ghessed after this booke, making monethely one hundred poundes', and to 'The number of the persons eating in the Kinges chamber and hall, as the booke appointeth . . . is after three hundred persons.'[5] That the book referred to is the Ordinance of 1478 rather than the Black Book seems to be indicated by the next paragraph, which runs: 'Not comprised in the same number noe manner of liueries heerein appointed, which eate neither in the kinges hall nor in his chamber, as pages, chamberlains, and other laborers'; categories of persons of whom the Black Book takes cognisance and the list of authorized personnel appended to the Ordinance of 1478 generally does not. It therefore appears that the investigations of 1478 were wider and more detailed than would be suggested by the contents of the published Ordinance, which concentrated on the more important and public financial aspects.

---

[1] Especially 'The sitting of all dukes, earles, and barons' (*Household Ordinances*, p. 112).

[2] ff. 190a (N) sqq.

[3] E.g. 'A last of white herring is twelve barrells; a barrell shall hold one thowsand herringes, Dutch man's herringes; salting and packeing of a barrell, nyne shillingez' (f. 191b (N)).

[4] f. 190b (N).

[5] ff. 194a, 195b (N). The Black Book had described a total staff of over 400 attached to the chamber.

(d) Notes on the Editing of the Manuscripts

In the left-hand margin of H are often summaries or catch-sentences to indicate the contents of the paragraphs against which they stand. It is likely that they are the work of Sir Simonds d'Ewes, as they do not occur in any other manuscript of the Black Book. In transcribing the provisions given on pages 198–210, below, these marginalia have, however, been included, since H is our only source of knowledge of these provisions.

As is well known, fifteenth-century scribes used capitals and punctuation in an extremely erratic manner, judged by modern standards. Hence the punctuation and use of capitals have been modernized in these transcripts. The original spelling has, of course, been retained, except in the case of the letters u and v. Here the strong tendency of the scribes has been carried into a consistent usage; v always stands for either u or v to begin a word and u represents either u or v in medial positions, except for a few compound words, such as gardeviande, where the manuscript clearly means a v to be used.

The divisions of the documents into numbered sections do not appear in the manuscripts; these numbers have been added by the editor to facilitate reference.

The notes to the texts are abbreviated to save space.

It will be seen that of the seven documents which follow, the first and the last are not concerned with the household of Edward IV. The Ordinance of 1445 has been included because, as is explained briefly above, and in more detail in the notes to the Ordinance below, twenty-one of the thirty-four paragraphs of orders in the Ordinance of 1445 were drawn on often verbatim, for the Ordinance of 1478. The hitherto unpublished estimate of the yearly expenses of the royal household in the time of Henry VII has been printed here for comparison; it is of help in forming a judgement on the cost of the household of Edward IV.

ADDENDUM

Since this volume went to press Dr. J. M. W. Bean has published *The Estates of the Percy Family, 1416–1437* (O.U.P., 1958). In this book Dr. Bean says of the *Northumberland Household Book* that 'it gave the Earl and his officials a standard with which they could compare actual expenditure' (*ibid.*, p. 138). There are obviously important differences of form and purpose between the *Northumberland Household Book* and the Black Book; but Dr. Bean's observation suggests an interesting comparison between them.

THE TEXTS

THE ORDINANCE OF 1445

Lansdowne MS. 1

Document no. 37

[f. 86a] Amongst the peticions offered in Parlement in the xxiiith yere of K. Henry the Sixt is found as followeth.

Prouisions made for the kynges houshold. 1458 [sic].[1]

§1. First, that al the lordes, knyghtys, squiers and other yeue into the countynghous the names of the nombre of her seruants after the appointement, and that they leue no men behinde hem for keepyng of her chambre after there departinge fro courte and that they haue no dyners out of meles ayenst the old rule of courte.[2]

§2. Also, that the usshers of the chambre come dayly with her recordes to the countynghous of the expens of the kynges chambre, and that he that recordith sette his name in his recorde for this intent, that yf so be that they doo any excesse that it may be seen who is most wastfull. And whatsoeuer be fette for the kynge, that to sey, in the offices of the pantrie, buterie, celer, picherhouse, spicerie, and chaunderie, or in any other office, that it be fette by the usshers and that they recorde it. And that they recorde no thing in her recordes but such as is spendid in the kynges chambre.[3]

§3. Also, that the officers of the wardrobe and of the vestiarie[4] trusse noon other mannys harneys in ther offices undir colour of the kinges but the kynges owne.

§4. Also, that the marshall of the halle suffre no lord ne other persone that haue men syttynge in the halle by appointment to haue mo sittinge therein but after the appointement. And that they dayly set no straunger in the haulle but suche as they thenken by there discrecions ben for the kynges worship.[5] And that they come in there owne persones dayly to the countynghous with there recordes and that they sette nothing in her recordes but such as is spendid within the halle, and that they sette there names in ther recordes to the entent that it may be seen hoo doth best his deuer. And that they comaunde nothinge out of the halle to no man, but to straungers if any come to court out of melys and that in the absence of the soueraignes, and that it be set in her recordes, and that the ordre of sittynge in the halle be kept aftir the old custume.[5]

§5. Also, that the usshers of the halle kepe out of the halle dore all men at mele tymes but suche as shoulde come in of deute and strangers such as they thynken by there discrecions ben for the kynges worship. And yf eny be sette at mete without the marshall that they take hem up, and that they kepe the halle that no persone bere out noone almes.[6]

[f. 86b] §6. Also, that the offices of the panetrie, buterie, seller, and alle other offices, bene kept that no man come not in hem, nouthir to mete ne soper ne at non othir tyme, but such as bene ordeyned therto. And that the officers of the seid panetrie, buterie, and seller deliuer to no man nether breade, ale, ne wyne by the comaundement of the usher of the chambre and marshall of the halle, but if it be to straungers out of mele tymes in the absence of souueraignes, and that noon of thise said officers deliuere neither breue upon no man more than they deliueren after the forme of appointement and that is truly spendid to the kynges worship. And that the butiller abrooche non ale into the tyme that it be seyne by the countrolloures clerke and the prise made.[7]

§7. Also, that the clerk of the spicerie deliuer nothinge that longeth unto his office unto no man but after the forme of appointe- ment, and that he spend nothinge that longith to his purueance unto the tyme that the countrollour or oon of his clerkys haue seene yt and the prises, to wite whethir the prises bene resonable or noone.[8]

§8. Also, that the clerk of the cechyne and the maister cokes taken hede that ther be no waste do by them in there offices ne by noon othir undir hem, and that euery man of the seid office go to the halle at her meles but such as ben ordeyned the contrarie. And that the countrollour or on of his clerkys with the seid clerk of cechynne se that non of the seid officers haue no fees in ther offices but suche as haue bene of old tyme acustumed, and that noon of them take no mete out of the cechynne neither for hem self ne for noon othir, but by deliueraunce by suche as haue the gouernaunce. Also, that the clerk of cechyne sette the nombir of messes both of the chambre, the halle, and the liueres dayly in the panetrie rolle, and the ussher of the cechynne suffre no mannys man ne other persone to come into the cechynne but such as ben of the office self.[9]

§9. [10]Also, that the sergeantes of the squillerie, saucerie and picher- house deliuer no vesselle, pottes, ne cuppes to no man, but liuere vesselle to such as shuld haue of deute, as they shulden haue warnynge out of the countinghous.

§10. Also, that the porters of the yate ne suffre no vessell, pottes, cuppes, torches, ne botell of wyne passe the yate, ne fees of the [f. 87a] cechynne ne of the panetrie unserched; ne that they suffre no straung man come in at the yate, but such as they thenken by there discressions be for the kynges worship, and also pore men for to come in for hir paymentis at the kynges remeuinge.[10] And also that they lette euery squier and sergeant haue in a man at the yate, and euery two yemen a man, and euery foure gromes of the chamber a child and no mo without speciall comaundement of the stuard by aduyse made in the countynghous; and that they comen dayly, summe at oon mete summe at an othir, into the halle to mete.

§11. Also, that there be no hors logged withinne the kynges yates but the kynges owne, and that soiourne be logged fro the kynges court v mile at the leste; and that there be no man kepe mo horse at the kynges cost then be appointed ne that noon othir officer haue no hors standing amonges the kynges.[11]

§12. Also, that no manner of man that longen to the kynges courte kepe neither children, dogges, ne ferettys withinne the kynges court, but aftir the forme of appointement.[12]

§13. Also, that no lord, knyghte, no squier, no noon othir persone, labour neither to the kynge ne to the stiward ne to noon officer of the kynges for chargyng of non officer in non office unto the tyme that thappointement be seine in the countynghous, to the extent that no mo such inconuenient of excedinge of officers be not founde in the kynges house her after, and that it may be sene by good aduys what personnes shallen so come into office, there good rule and abylite.

§14. Also, that no maner lord, knyghte, ne squier, ne noone othir persone, haue no cariage of the kynges carriage ne of the countre, but of her owne, ne that no maner of officer trusse no mannys harneys in ther offices among the kynges cariage but the kynges owne.[13]

§15. Also, that all the wyne the which is graunted as wel by the kynge our souueraigne lord that nowe is as by his noble progenitours to diuers houses of religioses in perpetuall almesse, and to diuers persones terme of there liues, and to diuers officers by cause of there offices and the wages of the mwes [mews], with such othir foreyne expenses, be sett in thaccompt of the tresorer of houshold in [f. 87b] a parcel by it self, so that it may clerly appere what is expended withynne the houshold.[14]

§16. Also, that all purueiours and yemen of the stable lese her wages and here horsmete when they be out of court, but yf so be that they be in the kynges seruice, and that the auenar recorde yt truly in his dayly accompt; and that noon of hem ete in the halle dayly but such as be appointed.[15]

§17. Also, that the porter of the kinges chambre kepe the light and the wode that he fecchith for the kynges chambre, and that he yeue away noon to no man; but yef any leue in his keepinge that it be kept and splendid to the kinges vse.[16]

§18. Also, that the aumener se that euery man haue his seruice, that is to sey, euery messe in the halle haue a lof, euery two messe a gallon of ale at mete, and euery iij messe a gallon of ale at soper, and euery iij messe of gentilmen dim'. pitcher of wyne, and euery v messe of yemen dim' pitcher of wyne at both meles, and that the gromes and chamberleyns haue none. And that he bring into the countynghouse a recorde of the seid seruice, and also of what rewardes the mareshall setith in the halle. And also that he se the pottys both of wyne and ale ben fylled as the mesure woll, and that he suffre no maner of man to giue away his mete that should go to the kinges almesse.[17]

§19. Also, that all maner of the kynges squiers and surpluse of officers excedinge the nombre of appointemente mowen resorte to the kynges courte at the v festes of the yere, at parlamentes, grete counsell, or for comynge of straungers, and at othir tymes necessarie after the case requireth, by the discrecion of the stiward or of sume of the soueraignes of the kynges house.

§20. Also, that the styward or on of the soueraignes seen that these persones that shullen go to her houses excedinge the nombre of appointment shullen be such personnes as hauen owthir fees or offices of the kinges yeft, and tho that shullen abide bene such as hauen lest or nought of the kynges yeft.

§21. Also, that all the huntys that noon of hem be in court but euerith of hem aftir ther sesons, and as son as their sesons be do [f. 88a] that they go fro court. And as for the tyme that they be in court, that her wages for bouch of court be rebatid in the certificate made by the tresorer of houshold by the aduyce of the controller of [sic] unto the priue seale for her warantes for her payment as the statutys of houshould wollen.[18]

§22. Also, that in all the places that the kynge resortith unto that ther be parker, keper of beddys, gardiners, ne such other foreine officers haue no liuere of the court ne bouche of courte but only the keepers of the placys. And in cas be that any such keepers be of the kynges hous and haue bouch of court, that they haue no such liuere.[19]

§23. Item, that all maner of prystes auaunced to the summe of xl li. be yer,[20] euery squier hauinge xl li. yerly of the kynges yefte, and eche yeman that hath xx marc yerly of the kinges yefte, shullen haue no dayly wages in his chekerrolle.[21]

§24. Item, that no sergeant of the kinges house put into his office be his owne auctorie no page without the aduyce of the stuard or of oon of the soueraignes of the kynges house for the tyme beinge.[22]

§25. Item, if the kyng comande any owteward chargis into his household mo than ben appointed, that than hit shall plese him of his noble grace for to ordeyne money for all such charges; or ellis yf there be any priue seall or other warrant direct vnto the officers of the seid houshold comaundyng them with ony maner of chargis in the houshold ouir the appointemente, that than the said officers for the tyme beinge shullen haue auctorite by these present ordinance not for to obey hem.

§26. Item, be it ordayned for the kynges profitte that all his grete horse ordayned for to be at soiourne mowe from hens forward soiourne to gidre yn a certayne place, to be limited after aduys and discrecion of the styward and tresorer of the houshould, and not in diuers places as it hath ben vsed before this tyme.[23]

R.H.[a] Prouisions which be semene necessarie for the kynges houshold.

§27. First, that no payment be made in payment nor in taille by the tresorer or cofrer or clercks of the grene cloth but openly in the countynghouse beinge present the stuard or countroller.[24]

§28. Item, that euery quarter of the yere the stuard sitte in the countynghouse and se the estate of the houshold, that is to say, all that is owinge that [f. 88b] tyme, to thentent that of such goode as there is in honde in money, taylles, or assignementis, payement maye be made to the creditours in the sergeantries be thauise and discrecion of the stuard and the officers.[25]

§29. Item, that none officer of the kynges house, of what estate or condicions that he be, nor officer's clercke nor seruant, from the hyest to the lowest, by him or any mesne persone to his behoue any taille, obligacion, or assignement of any creditour, vpon peyne of to be putte oute of his office and the kynges seruice for euer.[26]

§30. Item, that at euery yeres end the tresorer of the kynges houshold delyuer the names of all the creditours to whom any goode is oweinge in his office and the summes due vnto hem, and wherfore, to the stuard or the countrollour of the kynges house, to thentent that the kynge mowe yerly knowe his estate and by the auise of his consaille ordeine for contentinge of the same creditours.[27]

§31. Item, that all the purueours and acatours for the kynges housholde be made in the presence of the stuard, tresorer, and countrollour of the kynges houshold, and be thaire aduys; and that such as shall be named or taken thereto be sobre and peisible men, and men of good sufficeance and power, such as wyll se that the purueance and acate to be made by thayme be duely made for the kynges worship and profite, and in such wyse that the grete clamour had afore tymes vpon purueances and acates made for the kynges household mowe cesse. And that such purueours be not chaunged withoute grete and notable cause, and that in the presence abouesaid, and that euery such purueoure and acatour afore his admyttinge to such office make his othe in manere and fourme folowinge:—That he shal truly, justely and egally, withoute oppression of the poore

[a] C has here what is apparently a royal sign manual R.H.

or fauor of the riche, obserue and vse his commission and occupie his said office, to the most profite and behoue of the kyng and eschuyng of the hurt of his people, and yn especiall that he shall obserue and keepe thynges that folwene. That is to say, that he shall nothinge take vppon him to do be any depute in any place there as he shall make any achate or purueiance be force of his commission or office. And that he shall before thenne he any such achate or purueiance make or any good take of any persone, before the constable or other officer hauing rule or auctorite [f. 89a] there, and before the people there openly shewe and make to be redde his commission. And that neither for affection nor fauour of any persone ne for receyuinge of any reward or good, ne for hope to resceyue any good, he shall forbere to take yn due manere mesure for the kynges [sic] there as shall mowe take, ne for euyll wyll or hate of any persone, nor to thentent to hurte or to compelle any persone to doe any thynge to the assiethyng or to the fulfillinge of his owne or of any other persons pleisir, nor to auenge his owen or any other persons displeisir, take stufe or vitaille belonginge to his achate or purueiance of any of the kynges subiectes nor vndre colour of his office anythynges take to the behoue of himself or of any other persone, saue only of the kynge and his houshold. And that the prouision, swich as he shall make or take yn any manere of thinges, he shall withoute any sale thereof or chaungyng or applyinge to his owen or to any othir persones profite truly withoute fraude or male engyne or lessinge therof bryng hit or make it to be brought to the vse of the kynge and of his houshould, and make a treue and full certification thereof to the kynges countynghous by writyng, describinge clerly all the parcels of his achates and purueiaunces, and the pris, and the persones names that the said parcels be taken of.[28]

§32. Also, that all pardons to be graunted to any of the sergeantes of the kynges houshold for any thinge wherof they shall stand chargeable yn theire said offices be examined by the stuard and the hede officers of the kynges houshold before any suyte to be made therfore to the kyng, to thentent that the kyng mowe be clerely enformed of the causes which shulde moeue hym to graunte hem or not graunte hem. And yf any thynge be done in the contrarie hereof, that it be of non effect but stand for naughte and void and of none auaile.[29]

§33. Also, that the tresorer of Inglond for the tyme beinge first pay and preferre in payment the payment and contenting of thexpenses of the kynges household of the reuenues of the roialme as well as of wardes, mariages, voydance of byshopryckes, abbes, prioures, forfaitures, eschetes, and all other casuelties, commodities and profitz of the roialme afore any payment to be made to any

other persone. Alwey forseyne that be the strength of this ordin-
auance or act no preiudice be done to the kynges justices of the oone
benche nor of that other, nor to none other justice of assise, nor to
the kynges seriantz of lawe, nor to his atourne in his courtez, nor
to non acte[30] or ordinaunce touchyng them made in the parliament
holden [f. 89b] atte Westminster the xviij yere of the kyng our
soueraigne lord that nowe is or to any other of the kynges justices,
or to any graunte or assignement made to any persone afore this
present parlement, nor that any persone be hurte nor preiudiced in
any wise of his right, his freehold, his inheritance, office or fee,
wages or rewardes, for his entendances to the kynges counseiles,
nor of any other fee be the strength of this act or ordinance.

§34. And if any officer abouesaid do the contrarie of the said
article or any of hem, he to lese his office and to be putte out of the
kynges hous foreuer.

[f. 90a] §35 (i). R H

Une duke { j chapellein, iiij escuiers, iij valetz { mangeant en le sale, ij liueres pur sa chambre { et pur la nuyt { ij pains, j pitchere de vine, ij gallons de seruoise[31]

(ii)

Le confessour du roy { j chapellein, j escuier, j vallet { mangeant en la sale, j liuere pur sa chambre { et pur la nuyt { j pain, j pitchere de vine, j gallon de seruoise[32]

(iii)

Chapelleins pur la roy { Oue le confessour et son chapellein soient deux auters chapelleins seculers assignez, et prendrent pur tout la nuyt demi pitcher de vine, j gallon de seruoise[33]

(iv)

Le chamberlain del hostelle { toutz ces gentz mangeant en la sale, et liueres pur sa chambre se doyt bien gouerner pur doner as autres ensample de soy contenter de moderatz costagez en lostielle[34]

(v)

iiij cheualiers, keruers, et cupberers { chescun une escuier et j vallet mangeant en la sale. j liuere pur sa chambre { et pur la nuyt { j pain, j pitcher de vine, j gallon de seruoise[35]

(vi)

Le secretarie { j escuier, ij clerkes { mangeant en la sale. j liuere pur sa chambre { et pur la nuyt { j pain, j pitcher de vin, j gallon de seruoise[36]

F

(vii)

   iij phisiciens et surgeons[37]

(viii)

Lasmoigner
{ sous asmoigner
  j vallet
  ij clerkes pur
    garder lasmoigne }
mangeant en
  la sale et
  pur la
  nuyt
{ j pain
  j pitcher de vine
  j gallon de seruoise[38]

(ix)

Le dean de la
  chapell
{ j escuier mangeant
  en la sale, et
  j liuere pur sa
  chambre }
et pur
  la nuyt
{ j pain
  demi pitcher de vine
  j gallon de seruoise[39]

(x)

Les autres chapelleins
  de la chapell entre
  eux toutz a nuyt
{ j pain
  j pitcher de vine
  j gallon de
    seruoise }
et soient chapelleins et
  clerks xx en nombre,
  enfantz pur la chapell vij,
  valletz du vestiaire ij[40]

(xi)

Pur la chambre du roy soient
assignez xij cheualiers dont
soient vj ouert les officers
continuelment demurantz en
la court, qe tantsoulement
prendront liuere desquex
  chescun auera un
  chambre mangeant
  en la sale; pur la
  nuyt
{ j pain
  demi pitcher
  de vine
  j gallon de
  seruoise

[f. 90b]

  Et sil ne soit as iours de festez, ne serront en la court plousours qe vj
  dez xij cheualiers susdictz[41]

(xii)

  iiij escuiers pur la corps[41] soient habergez ensemble,
    et preignent a nuyt . . .
  et sils soient autrement
  habergez, chescun preigne
  solonc lafferant
{ j pain
  demi pitcher de
  vine, j gallon
  de seruoise

(xiii)

  iiij vsshers pur la chambre, preignantz liueres
  come les escuiers pur le corps, desquex
  vsshers soient deux en la court continuelment

(xiv)

  j assewer et
  j surueour } preignent liuere come lez escuiers de la corps.
  viij escuiers pur la chambre   et prendrent iiij pains, et
    dont j assewer pur la chambre } iiij gallons de seruoise
  iiij herlautz
  iij messagers
  ij valletz vsshers pur la chambre
  xxiiij valletz pur la chambre, des queux soient xij continuelment en

la court qe continuelment soient entendantz a la persone de nostre
dit seigneur le roy quant il doit chiuacher[42]
ij valletz pur les robes de queux lun pelter, j page, j grome
j vallet pur les lectes, ij gromes, j page
vj garcons pur la chambre, des queux j pur lez arcus[43]
iij pages pur le chambre
vj henxmen pur le roy[44]
xij memstrealx oue le gaite
j sergeant, j vallet, j grome pur larmorie
Le gardein dez mewes
v valletz fauconers, chescun a vjd.,[45] des queux vn contrebener
vj porteurs, chescun a ijd.
xx faucons, chescun a jd.
ij cheens, chescun a ob.

[f. 91a] (xv)

Pur le Countynghous

Le seneschall ⎧ toutz lour gentz mangeant en la sale, et liuerez pur
Tresorer ⎪ lour chambre, se doient ben gouerner pur doner a
Counproller ⎨ autres ensample de soy contenter de moderatz cos-
⎩ tagez en lostiell[46]

Le coffrere
ij clerckes dez accomptz
j clerk countrollour
j clerke de souz luy
j sergeant
j messager
j grome
j page[47]

(xvi)

Pur la sale

j cheualier vssher
Le cheualier mareschall
Le cheualier herberciour
iij mareschalx
j sergeant vssher
ij assewers
ij surueours
xij escuiers pur la sale
iij valletz vsshers
iiij garcons
iij pagez

(xvii)

Pur ma dame la royne[48]

Countesse ⎧ ij dauncelles ⎫ mangeant en la salle ⎧ et pur la nuyt
⎪ j chambrere ⎬ j liuere pur sa ⎨ come pur un
⎨ ij escuiers ⎭ chambre ⎩ conte
⎩ ij valletz

Baronesse $\begin{cases} \text{ij dauncelles} \\ \text{j escuier} \\ \text{j chambrer} \\ \text{j vallet} \end{cases}$ $\left.\begin{array}{l} \text{mangeant en la sale} \\ \text{j liuere pur sa} \\ \quad\text{chambre} \end{array}\right\}$ $\begin{cases} \text{et pur la nuyt} \\ \text{come pur un} \\ \text{barone} \end{cases}$

[f. 91b]

ij dames, chescun $\begin{cases} \text{j dauncell'} \\ \text{j vallet} \end{cases}$ $\begin{cases} \text{mangeant en la} \\ \text{sale, et j liuere} \\ \text{pur sa chambre} \end{cases}$ $\left.\begin{array}{l} \text{et pur la nuyt} \\ \text{come pur un} \\ \text{bachilier} \end{array}\right\}$

vj dauncelles pur ma dame $\left.\begin{array}{l}\\\\\end{array}\right\}$ j seruant mangeant en la sale sanz autre
le [sic] royne de lesqueles $\quad$ liuere
eiant trois chescun
ij chambrers
ij lauenders

Le chamberleyn $\begin{cases} \text{j escuier} \\ \text{j vallet} \end{cases}$ $\begin{cases} \text{mangeant en la} \\ \text{sale, j liuere} \\ \text{pur sa chambre} \end{cases}$ $\left.\begin{array}{l} \text{et pur la nuyt come} \\ \text{pur un dez keruers} \end{array}\right\}$
de la royne

Chapelleins pur la royne $\begin{cases} \text{j confessor} \\ \text{j chapellein seculer} \\ \text{j clerk du closet} \end{cases}$ mangeant en la sale

Keruers et cupberers pur la royne . . . . . iiij
Secretarie pur la royne . . . . j
Vssher pur la royne . . . . ij
Asshewers pur la royne et sa chambre . . ij
Escuiers pur sa chambre . . . . iiij
Mestre de chiualx . . . . j et liuere come un dez
                                      escuiers pur la corps

Henxmen . . . . ij
Vssher vallet . . . . j
Valletz de la chambre . . . . viij dont vn pur lez robez
                                      et j pur lez litez
Garcions pur la chambre . . . . iiij dont vn pur lez robez
                                      et j pur les litez
Page pur la chambre . . . . ij

(xviii)
Paneterie[49] $\begin{cases} \text{j sergeant} \\ \text{iiij valletz} \\ \text{iiij gromez} \\ \text{ij pagez} \end{cases}$

[f. 92a] (xix)
Wafrere[49] $\begin{cases} \text{ij wafreres} \\ \text{j gromes} \end{cases}$

(xx)

Le pistrine[50] $\begin{cases} \text{j sergeant} \\ \text{ij valletz pistours} \\ \text{ij valletz purueiours} \\ \text{j clerk} \\ \text{j vallet pur la bouch du roy} \\ \text{iiij boulters} \\ \text{j gryndere} \\ \text{ij pagez} \end{cases}$

(xxi)

Le seller[51] et le botillerie $\begin{cases} \text{j sergeant} \\ \text{j vallet pur la royne} \\ \text{ix valletz} \\ \text{viij garceons} \\ \text{iiij pages} \end{cases}$

(xxii)

Le spicerie[51] $\begin{cases} \text{j chief clerk} \\ \text{iiij valletz, dez queux soit vn clerc} \\ \text{ij garceons} \\ \text{ij pagez} \end{cases}$

(xxiii)

La chaunderie[51] $\begin{cases} \text{j sergeant} \\ \text{ij valletz} \\ \text{iiij garcions} \\ \text{ij pagez} \end{cases}$

(xxiv)

La cusine[52] $\begin{cases} \text{j cheif clerk} \\ \text{iiij sergeant pur la cusyne} \\ \text{ij soubz clerces} \\ \text{x valletz, dez queux ij pur le bouche du roy et j pur le} \\ \quad \text{bouch du royne } [sic] \\ \text{viij garcons, dez queux j pur le bouche du roy et j pur le} \\ \quad \text{bouch du royne } [sic] \\ \text{viij pagez, dez queux j pur le bouch du roy et j pur le} \\ \quad \text{royne} \end{cases}$

[f. 92b] (xxv)

La larderie[52] $\begin{cases} \text{j sergeant} \\ \text{iiij valletz} \\ \text{j clerk} \\ \text{iiij garceons} \\ \text{iiij pagez} \end{cases}$

(xxvi)

La caterie[52] $\begin{cases} \text{j sergeant} \\ \text{iiij valletz} \\ \text{j clerk} \\ \text{iiij bouchours} \\ \text{ij portours de la bocherie} \\ \text{j pastour et son seruant} \\ \text{j cariour dez pik} \end{cases}$

(xxvii)

Fyshers $\begin{cases} \text{j vallet} \\ \text{j garcion} \end{cases}$

(xxviii)

Fureters $\begin{cases} \text{j vallet} \\ \text{j garcion} \end{cases}$

(xxix)

La pultrie[53] {
j sergeant
j clerk
j vallet
j garceon
iiij purueours
iij soutremen
ij pagez
}

(xxx)

La squillerie[53] {
vne sergeant
iiij valletz
v garceons
iiij pagez
iiij portones
}

(xxxi)

La salcerie[53] {
j sergeant
j vallet
j clerk
iij garceons
iij pagez
}

[f. 93a] (xxxii)

Napperie et eawerie[54] {
j sergeant
iiij valletz
iiij garceons
ij pagez
}

(xxxiii)

Lauenders[54] {
j vallet
j garcion
ij pagez
}

(xxxiv)

La porte {
j sergeant
iiij valletz
ij garceons
j page
}

(xxxv)

Herberiours {
j sergeant
ij valletz
j clerk
}

(xxxvi)

Scalding-house[55] {
j vallet
j garceon
j page
}

(xxxvii)

Pur le stable du roy {
iiij dextrers
vj bastardz
xij coursours
xij trotters
viij palfreys
} pur le celler du roy

vj pur le chariot

xij pur somers pur le chambre

[f. 93b]

Pur les chariotz	cxxvj chiualx
pur le mestre dez chiualx	ij chiualx
pur le aueigner	ij chiualx
pur le sergeant du cariage	ij chiualx
pur le ferour	ij chiualx
pur ij clerk del aueignerie........	ij chiualx
pur le garnere...................	ij chiualx
pur le vj purueours	vj chiualx
pur iiij ferours	iiij chiualx
pur vn palfrey et vn purueour....	ij chiualx
pur vn seller	j chivalx
pur vn wheller	j chiuall

Someres
{
pur le closet.................. j
pur le panetrie .... j
pur le seller et botillerie ....ij
pur le spicerie et chaunderie....ij
pur le larder .... j
pur la squillerie...............ij
pur le saucerie................. j
pur lesmoignerie .... j
pur les liueres du roy..........ij
pur le countinghous .... j
pur lewerie et napperie ....ij
}

THE BLACK BOOK OF THE
HOUSEHOLD OF EDWARD IV

H, f. 2a[a]   LIBER NIGER DOMUS REGIS ANGLIAE, ID EST,
DOMUS REGIAE SIUE AULAE ANGLIAE REGIS.
Transcriptum verissimum et accuratius comparatum
ex ipsissimo MS⁰ originali sumptum, quod in ipsa aula
regia curiose et diligenter sub custodia reconditur.

H, ff. 2b   (Blank)
& 3a

H, f. 3b   Domus regis edificatur sapientia—Eccles.[1]
Qualis est rector domus tales in ea habitantes—
Eccles.[2]
Noli esse sicut leo in domo tua—Eccles.[3]
Minor est quam seruus dominus qui seruos timet—
Seneca.[4]
Oportet famulatum esse bene dispositum—
Aristoteles.[5]
Si est tibi seruus fidelis, sit tibi quasi anima tua—
Eccles.[6]
Famulum alti cordis repelle vt inimicum—Bernardus.[7]

H, f. 4a   (The drawing in ink which is reproduced opposite.)
H, f. 4b   (Blank)

H, f. 5a   Tabula

Domus regis magni	Folio 1a[b]
Domus regis Salamonis	f. 3a
Domus regis Lud	f. 5a
Domus regis Cassibellani	f. 5b
Domus regis Hardiknout	f. 6a
Domus regis Henrici primi post conquestum	f. 6b
Domus regis Edwardi tercij	f. 6b
Domus regiae magnificentiae	f. 9a
De visu et onere domus regis	f. 10a
De preceptis datis seneschallo thesaurario, etc.	f. 13b

[a] In its present state A begins only with the actual text of the Black Book,
except for a title page inserted from H. E also lacks all the preliminary
material, except the Latin index, which is, however, not so good as that of H.
The preliminary matter is therefore reproduced from H.

[b] These numbers refer to the old foliation. References to folios in Harl.
MS. 642 later than those (ff. 1a–121a (O)) containing the Black Book have been
omitted.

(Pictura ista inferius locata uti et symbola cum in hac pagina, tum in adversa exacte ab exemplaria in imis Libri Nigri limantur. vide aliam picturam fol. 71. h. postea.)

Socrates: Edere oportet ut vivas non vivere ut edas

Rex erit invictus fuerit cui copia victus

Almoniam super omnia populi plus requirunt. *Seneca*

PLATE I. DOMUS REGIE MAGNIFICENCIE

	De dieta regiae personae	f. 14b
	De oblationibus regis	f. 15b
	De expensis et dieta in curia regis	f. 16b
	De sedentibus in ea	f. 16b et f. 17a
	De regina cum venerit	f. 17a
	De principe cum venerit	f. 18b
	De ducibus in curia	f. 19b
	De marchione	f. 22a
H, f. 5b	De comite	f. 23b
	De episcopo confessore regis	f. 25a
	De cancellario Angliae	f. 26a
	De camerario Angliae	f. 26b
	De capitali justiciario regis de communi banco	f. 27a
	De vicecomite	f. 27a
	De barone	f. 29b
	De camerario regis	f. 30a
	De banerettis	f. 31b
	De militibus curialibus	f. 33b
	De secretario regis	f. 36a
	De capellanis regis	f. 37a
	De scutiferarijs pro corpore regis	f. 38a
	De depositore mensae regis	f. 38b
	De superuisore ciborum regis	f. 39b
	De custode garderobe regis	f. 40a
	De ostiarijs*a* camere regis	f. 40b
	De depositarijs ciborum camere regis	f. 42a
	De valectis corone	f. 42a
	De valectis camere regis	f. 43b
	De officio garderobe robarum regis	f. 44a
	De officio garderobe lectorum regis	f. 45b
H, f. 6a	De garcionibus camere regis	f. 47a
	De pagettis camere regis	f. 48b
	De domo jocalium regis	f. 49a
	De phisico regis	f. 50b
	De chirurgico regis	f. 51b
	De apoticario regis	f. 2bi
	De barbi-tonsore regis	f. 53a
	De equisequelis regis	f. 53b
	De magistro equisequelorum regis	f. 54a
	De armigeris hospicij	f. 55a
	De regibus armorum	f. 58a
	De seruientibus ad arma	f. 58b
	De ministrallis et trumpettoribus	f. 59b
	De vigilia noctuali	f. 60a
	De nuncijs hospicij	f. 61a
	De decano capelle regis	f. 61b
	De capellanis et clericis capelle	f. 63a

a H has here a marginal note: 'These bee the gentlemen ushers.'

	De valectis capelle	f. 64a
	De pueris capelle	f. 64b
	De clerico closette regis	f. 65a
	De instructore grammatice	f. 66a
H, f. 6b	De officio vestiarie	f. 66b
	De clerico corone	f. 68b
	De clerico operum regis	f. 70a
	De clerico marcati	f. 68b
	De wardis et maritagijs pertinentibus regi[a]	f. 70a
	Domus prouidencie	f. 70b
	De seneschallo domus regie	f. 72a
	De thesaurario hospicij	f. 73b
	De custode magne garderobe	f. 75a
	De juramento thesaurarij	f. 75b
	De contrarotulatore	f. 77b
	De eius juramento	f. 79a
	De cofferario regis	f. 81a
	De clerico panni viridis	f. 82b
	De clericis contrarotulamenti	f. 85a
	De domo (compoti vel)[b] judicij	f. 88b
	De oneribus et statutis appositis seneschallo, thesaurario, etc.	f. 92b
	De mandatis datis seruientibus ad obediendum	f. 93b
H, f. 7a	De aliis statutis et recognicionibus f. 96a,	f. 97a
	De judicio domus determinato	f. 98a
	De officio domus computi	f. 98a
	De visu[c] et punitione iuramenti in aula regia	f. 98b
	De officio pistrine[d]	f. 99a
	De officio panetrie	f. 101a
	De officio waffrie	f. 104a
	De officio pincerne Anglie	f. 104b
	De officio selario inferende	f. 107a
	De prouisoribus vinorum	f. 106b
	De officio buttillarie	f. 110a
	De captoribus ceruisie	f. 112a
	De officio picherhouse et cuphouse	f. 111a
	De officio magne spicerie	f. 113a
	De officio aquarie	f. 117b
	De officio lauendrie	f. 120a
	De officio confeccionarie	f. 115a
	De officio candellarie	f. 116a[e]

[a] Also E.

[b] H has 'This worde I added, it being alwaie called the countinghouse'; this note is written in the margin.

[c] H has here a marginal note: 'All this I added myselfe, being not found in the table of the black booke.'

[d] H has here a marginal note: 'The office of the Backhouse, I take it.'

[e] The order of items in the manuscript is as given here.

[A, p. 3] *Lectio prima*

§1 (i). DOMUS REGIS MAGNI*ᵃ* Hec est domus regis celestis dapiferi, qui se lacte virginis*ᵇ* ponit in suo paraclyto; in qua omnes celicole indefessa dei visione tanquam cibo spirituali delectantur, de qua sacratissimum viaticum diuiti et pauperi pupillo et humili*ᶜ* ministrandum committitur; per quam Israelitis pluit Deus manna ad manducandum, panem quoque celi omne delectamentum in se habentem dederat connoscendum. Volucres item celi, pisces maris, oues insuper et boues, vniuersa pecora campi, omnem quoque herbam afferentem semen et ligna fructifera, que habent sementem generis sui humanis vsibus subjiciuntur. Hic noster senescellus uberimus sua in effabili sapiencia hanc domum vniuersalem sibi edificauit, miscuit vinum et posuit mensam,[8] PONDERE., VIZ., ET NUMERO ET MENSURA.[8] Omnibus nobis prouidens nostrum panem cotidianum, aperit quoque manum suam et implet nos in rore celi et de pinguedine terre et huiusimodi*ᵈ* quibus nostre nature fruitur nutritura; vnde Evangelista, 'voluit enim Deus per orbem cibaria distribui'.[9]

Lectio secunda

§1 (ii). Et alibi, 'prestat nobis Deus omnia habunde ad fruendum'.[10] Ab eo ergo omnis paterfamilias terrenus exordium trahat et exemplum. Et quantum nostra fuerit*ᵉ* fragilitas, inuitemur vt honorabiliorem*ᶠ* viuendi statum peragamus et Deo complacentiorem, dapibus ergo vniuersis et terre*ᵍ* frugibus ad sue vite sustentamentum et defencionem moderate sumptis qualitate eorundem et quantitate proportionatis secundum suarum dignitatum distinctiones maiores pascantur et humiliores necesse est. Sic unusquisque secundum naturam stomachi sui varia alimenta suscipiat. Hii autem quibus erit super habundancia, non tantum in seipsorum replectiones vacabunt, imo verum ex hiis qui supererint secundum rationis exigenciam*ʰ* pauperibus delectando distribuant*ⁱ* et sub forma vrbane dapsilitatis ministrent, ob quod et fame immortalitatis ac hospitalitatis benedictionem premerituros ire diffinimus et apud altissimum sumopere collaudandos fore fuit. Est*ʲ* quoque fama quod hoc regnum Anglie cetera hujus seculi regna in ferclorum habundantia et varietate in tantum supereminet,*ᵏ* vt a tempore Salamonis,

---

ᵃ The words 'in qua mansiones multe sunt' have been inserted, from H, in a late eighteenth-century hand. E lacks this phrase.

ᵇ 'virginio', *H*; perhaps a corruption of 'qui selecte virginis'.

ᶜ 'humillimo', *H*.

ᵈ From H. A and E have 'huius cerino'.   *ᵉ* From H. A and E have 'fuit'.

ᶠ From H. A and E have 'honorabile'.   *ᵍ* 'terrenis', *H*.

ʰ From H. A and E have 'exigencia'.   *ⁱ* 'distribuatur', *H*.

ʲ 'hinc est', *H*.   *ᵏ* 'superemineret', *H*.

quem primum maximum quoque audiuimus in terris [A, p. 4] dapiferum huic regno simile in escarum largitate non legimus repertum; vnde quidam sic metrice: 'Angligenis multa prae multis additur esca'.[11]

Lectio tercia

§1 (iii). Vt ergo reges et magnates hospitalitatis causam suscipere suadeamus, tres causas assignauimus.[a] Prima est, vt ab ipso summo datore, in quo omnia, per quem omnia, de quo omnia, sine quo nichil, pro caritatiua distribucione bonorum temporalium indigentibus meritum consequamur,[b] vt Paulus commemorat: 'illarem enim datorem diligit Deus'.[12] Secunda est, vt tali porcione amicitias proximorum lucrentur,[c] subditorum fidelitates augmentent, amicorum corda confirment, inimicorum corda jocunda liberalitatis conuincant, et singulorum animos pro sua ingenti caritate in suam tutelam conuertat, vnde Aristoteles Alexandro: 'non opus est vallo quos dextra dapsilis ambit'.[13] Tercia est, vt tali exhibicione rem publicam a penuria per prouisiones discretas conseruent et patriam circumfusam per soluciones pro hujusmodi expensis fideliter factas ditent; vnde Cassiodorus: 'equitas regna confirmat injusticia dissoluit'.[14] Augustinus: 'regna sine iustitia publica latrocinia';[15] et alibi dicit: 'vult vetus et noua lex vt rex sua debita soluat; sin autem sua grex in murmure stat continuo'.[16]

Lectio quarta

§1 (iv). Non enim decet domum regiam in qua tanta caritas vniuersaliter ministratur, quamuis[d] parcitate corrumpi. Sed quod sit prudenter fundata et stabilita super firmam petram, sicut supra diximus in tribus, viz., PONDERE vere et secure, substancie monete, prima ordinacione assignande et stabilite, pro discreta prouidencia fiendi,[e] vt non deficiat virtus in via; NUMERO, officiariorum ex morum nobilitate electorum, per quos omnia debita conformitate in honore domicilij[f] studiose frequententur; et MENSURA, qua expense fiende proporcionabiliter in honore et proficuum regie celsitudinis moderentur et victualium copia deliciose preparentur[g] et in mensuram sufficientie porrigantur: dicitur prima secunde 'nullus potest sine delectatione ciborum viuere quoad humanum vitam'.[17] Si ergo omnis delectacio esset mala, sequeretur quod omnis vita esset mala; si bonum in quo quis delectatur, conueniat racioni est delectacione bona; si vero discordet[h] a racione, est delectacio mala. Non ergo

---

[a] From H. A and E have 'assignabimus'.
[b] 'consequatur', E.
[c] From H. A and E have 'alucrentur'.
[d] 'quavis', H.   [e] 'fienda', H.   [f] 'domialij', E.
[g] From H. A and E have 'prepararentur'.   [h] 'discordit', H.

sequamur Epicurum, quia gulosus de ventre suo facit deum, de coquina templum.[18] Tu autem [A, p. 5].

§2. DOMUS REGIS SALAMONIS, exemplar of householding and for a grounde notable in his dapsilite, for whos high wisdom, grete renomed richesse, welfare, and high largesse,[19] the noble quene Saba doth wondyrly recommend and singlerly for the sadde and studiouse direccions the orders of officers fourmed in astate and degrees, all thing executing after theyr occupacions and chargez to the high excellence of the king, to all other astatz and degrees of householde, according with so formal conueyaunce and of theyre demure wordes attemperaunce, with euery dede honorable in circumstaunce of her huge great maruelyng. Also[a] when she sawe[a] the habundance, variede,[a] and maner of disposicion of such metes as cam to king Salamonis table, hit[b] smote her from any sprite[b] to speke, thus seyng that quene, that the trouth of Salamon is worthines was more than his fame did expresse; semyng also to her that euery master officer in his sober demenyng, his honestee, his riche araye, and of all theyr[c] manerly cerimoniez don in that court, that eche of hem my3t be lykenyd to a king of her cuntree. Also for the stedfast obseruauncez of the good rulis, apoyntmentes, and ordinaunces for the householde, to kepe the ministres thereof from any breche, outrage, reproche, or nicetie, making ordynat reuerentz aftyr the distinccions of euery high or low degre, and as pepull to straungers cherefull, so many vnder obedyence in one house; this caused the wise quene to maruayle more hugely, she thou3t there that euery officer in vnitie of loue aplyed to excuse other by seruyce and attendaunce, that any man no fawte cowde aspye.[19, 20] The expenses of this householde in comyn dayes drewe to xxx chooris[21] of the [A, p. 6] moste pure floure, wich was for hymself, for his lordes, ladyes, and gentyles of his court, and lx chooris of mele for the comynaltie of his householde. A choore is called by Hugucon[22] conteyning xxx busshells; Doctor Bruto[d] [22] seyith a choore is as muche as a camell may bere. Hit may be so that the busshell of Jury is lesse than viij gallons, as hit aperith by the woman[e] Ruth that bare vij busshelles at ones.[23] And if euery busshell be viij gallons there, than hit wuld amount dayly expendid after the Englishe busshell cccxxxvij quarters and iiij busshells bred corn. Item dayly x stalfed oxen and xx grasse oxen,[f] c grete wethyrs, grete plentie of sondry venyson, grete numbyr of gece,[g] and many

---

[a] H omits 'Also', and has 'sighe' and 'varietie'.

[b] H has 'that' and 'pirt'.

[c] 'theym', E. 　　　　[d] 'Brito', H.

[e] From H. A and E have 'homan'.

[f] E has 'x stallyd oxen and xx grasse oxon'; H has 'tenn stall fedd oxen very great, and twentie gret grassed oxen'.

[g] 'geet', H.

fatte bubales,[24] almaner pultry, dayly tame fowles and wylde of lond
and water, and dayly freshe fyshes of diuerse kyndes[a] out of numbyr
for the alyens, with muche more othir stuff of vytaylys. And for the
garde of his royall (person),[b] he had logged nyghe vnto hym of horse
men xij m[l], beside the grette numbyr of othyr diuerse ordinaunces
and cariagez.[20] And for that his householde shuld neuer fayle, but[c]
that in his dayis shuld euer stand sure,[c] he ordeyned xij grete
mastyrs[d] puruyours dwelling in xij diuerse costes and contries[e] of
Jury and Jerusalem, euery to puruey apart from other by the
apoyntment of his household for one monethe in the yere all suche
seasonable thinges according and conuenyent for the astate of hym
and his honorable (A, p. 7] householde, whereof is written thus, etc.

> Testis adhuc tibi fama manet semperque manebit,
> Set fama melior. Res tibi testis erat.
> [f]Alimoniam super omnia populi plus requirunt.

> Anglia terrarum decus et flos sitiarum
> Est contenta sui fertilitate boni[g]
> Externas gentes consumptis rebus egentes
> Cum[h] fames recreat ledit et reficit
> Commoda[i] terra satis mirande fertilitatis
> Prosperitate viget cum bona pacis habet.
> Anglorum portus occasus nouit et ortus
> Anglica classis habet quod[j] multa loca jubet
> Et cibus et census magis hic communis habetur
> Nam de more viri sunt ibi magnifici
> Anglia terra ferax et fertilis angulus orbis
> Anglia plena jocis gens libera digna jocari
> Libera gens cui libera mens et libera lingua
> Set lingua melior liberiorque manus.[25]

[A, p. 8] §3. DOMUS REGIS LUD,[26] for his famous housholding is to
be remembred in Englond. He comaunded his houshold officers to haue
in dayly custume to couyr the tablez in his hall from vij in the
mornyng tyll vij in the ny3t.[k] His dayly dyet was not muche in
sotyle and delicate vyaunde, but that he kept solemply with all
suche[l] good stuff as coude be goten the iiij grete festes of the yere,

---

[a] 'many diuers kindes', H.　　　　　[b] From E and H; omitted in A.
[c] 'but as in his daies to stand sure', H.
[d] 'maister', H.　　　　　　　　　　[e] 'contrey', E.
[f] H has in the margin 'Seneca'.　　[g] 'loci', E.
[h] H has 'Cum fames ledit, recreat et reficit'.
[i] From H. A and E have 'comoda'.　[j] E omits 'quod'.
[k] 'from eight in the morning till seauen in the night', H.
[l] E omits 'suche'.

with opyn proclamacions in euery cuntrey all maner people to cume thither; he disposed his domesticall men to logge most[a] of them and ny3tly within his courte for his proper gard,[a] euery man stuffed and renned at the kinges costes of suche defence as he coude best deale with all.[b]

§4. DOMUS REGIS CASSIBELLANJ[27] standith here for a speciall nota, wiche, after his secunde triumphe vppon the emperoure, gafe out his royall comaundmentes to all the gentils of Brytaygne to come with theyre wiffis to magnifye his fest; for wich he slewe xl m[l] kyne and oxen, c m[l] shepe, xxx m[l] deere, and other wilde bestes of the woode, besides the diuerse kindes of pullayle, conyes, wylde fowle, and tame, of see and lond; with muche other purueaunce of stuffe of vytayle, with many [A, p. 9] disguisinges, playis, minstralsy, and sportes. Iste primo ordinauit[c] pro custodia corporis sui xxiiij[d] fortes doctissimos ad bella, cum gladiis accinctos et cornua gerentes propter timores nocturnos.[e]

§5. DOMUS REGIS HARDEKNOUT[28] may be called a fader noreshoure of familiaritie, wiche vsed for his own table neuer to be serued with ony like metes of one mele in another. And that chaunge and diuersitie was dayly in greate habundaunce, and that same after to be ministered to his almesdishe, he caused cunyng cooks in curiositie. Also he was the furst that began iiij meles stablyshed in oon day, opynly to be holden for worshupfull and honest peopull resorting to his courte, and no mo melis, nor brekefastes nor chambyr, but for his children in householde; for wiche iiij melys he ordeyned iiij marshalles to kepe the honor of his hall in receuyng and dyrecting straungers aswell as of his household men in theyre sitting, and for seruises and ther preceptes to be obeyed in, and for the hall, with all diligence of officers therto assigned. From his furst incepcion tyll the day of his dethe, his house stode aftyr [A, p. 10] one vnyformite.[f] Thys king reygned but ij yeres except x dayis; he deyid drinking at Lambithe.

§6. DOMUS REGIS HENRICI primi post conquestum[g] berithe the fame of an excellent mete geuer,[h] and that he ordeynyd his groundes for houshold so sure that his greete hospitalitie dayly stode wur-shuypfully without decay xxxiij yeres, his dettes and all purueaunces truly proued. The people reputed hym as a yong Salamon for his richesse, greete noblesse, wisedom, loue, and largesse. Voluit propter

---

[a] 'most part of them and nighely within his court for his proper good', H.

[b] H adds '*This noble viander reigned thus in England 32 yeares*' and gives a marginal explanation '*This last clause is not in the blacke booke, but I found it in a copie of it written in an hande of about H. 7th time'.

[c] 'Item ordinauit', H.
[d] 'triginta quatuor', H.
[e] H adds 'in vigilijs'.
[f] H omits this sentence.
[g] 'post conquestum Anglie', E.
[h] 'metez-ever', H.

otiositatem euacuandam vt omnes domestici eius se ocuparent cum omnimodis ludis honestis, cum jactu lapidum, cum hasta, arcubus, testibus, saxis, aleis, scutareis, vel cum ceterorum jocorum diuersitate, omni lite postposita, de quo scribitur:

HIC ALTER SALAMON, LEGUM PATER ORBITA PACIS.[29]

§7. DOMUS REGIS EDWARDI TERTII[30] was the house of very polycye and flowre of Inglond, the furst setter of sertayntez among his domestycall meyne, vppon a grounded rule. Notwithstanding his fader, the secunde Edwarde,[31] made many good [A, p. 11] custumes of household; thereof one to be remembered specially was to breede vpp beues and motonnes in his parkes sufficiauntes to serue his household.[a] And in no dayis afore that tyme were vsed ne feez of no maner vytayle purueyed for the expensis of his household, not to be taken by none[b] officer to his proper vse of onything that mought serue to this[c] household honestly. Also he, this iijd. Edward, apoynted diuerse duteez vnto his offices and of[d] officers by a formal and a conuenient custume more certayne than was vsed byforn his tyme, that is to say,[e] of all wages within court or without;[f] all maner of lyuerez of winter and somer; the feez of all astates and of officers and householdes and degrees, as well of yeftes of money, feez of bestes, and also feez of other stuffe perused or otherwise occupied within the[g] court and towching it;[h] the numbyr also of officers thorough all Inglond aswell of his household and thaire clothing for wynter and somer as of all other officers outward. This noble Edward had greate richesse of his lordez and grete loue of his counsell,[i] among his counsellers greate studye to make hym riche by polycy vppon straungers[j] out landez. And after his richesse was purchesed, his seyde lordez of counsayle sought many wayis and deuysed and compaced how they might [A, p. 12] assertayn the kinges house, wiche was so long and defuse of worke in theyre study to refourme the people of theyre[k] old law that this king prayd his lordes to surcesse of thyre grete[l] and almost endles labour[j] and hym self toke all on hond. And whereas in the begynnyng hym self was liberall, aftyr he did furst reforme hym self and all that would be dwellers in his

---

[a] E has 'And in no daies afore that tyme'; H has 'And anothir in his daies bifore'; A has 'in no dayis afore that tyme' written above the cancelled words 'nothir dayis nother before that'.

[b] 'any', H.   [c] 'his', E.   [d] H omits 'of'.

[e] H omits 'that is to say'.

[f] E has 'within the court or withoute'; H has 'within court and without'.

[g] From H. A has 'this', E has 'his'.

[h] E has 'hit'; H has 'that'.

[i] From H. A and E have 'comyntie'.   [j] 'strange', E.

[k] E has 'olde lawe. Then this kyng'; H has 'old lore. That this king'.

[l] E omits 'grete'; H puts 'labour' after 'gret'.

household; and so he framed all his new statutes, commaundmentes, and charges vppon euery officer, inward and outward, and so he exercised[a] his actes in honour and profit to hymself and to the favour and grete ease of all his liege people. Exemple[b] we take to bylde vpon a more perfit new house, bycause this noble king Edward the iijd. his household varyethe gretely from the householde that kinges haue kept syn that tym, and yit in thies dayes;[32] for our souerayn lordez[c] is now discharged of the priuy seale and all[d] his clerkes; of the court of marchalsy and all his clerkes and yomen, sauyng at the v festes of the yere whan with ther long typped staffis they owe to help the porters to kepe the gate and the vsshers at the hall dore and to precede the king in prees of people whythyr someuer the king go in the[e] dayis festyuall; of the warderober, also called 'clerk puruyoure,' besidez the grete warderober of houshold, wich is the countynghouse, and the houshold tresorer, called 'custos magne garderobe hospicij', also discharged of all artificers vnder hym, [A, p. 13] butt whan hym self cumyth at the grete festes or elles that he be sent for. Also in some one office were[f] ij maistyrs, the clerk of kychyn deuyded fro the pantry;[33] the butteler[34] of Englond for the most party, and diuerse many other offices[g] and officers, both conged[h] in name and dede, aswell sergeauntz of armez and messingers many, with xxiiij archers a foote before the king, shoting whan he rode by the contrie, called 'garde corpus le roy'. And therfore the king jorneyde not passing x or xij myles on a day; and as other officers in household than hauyng grete labour and toke nother wages, feez, nor clothing, expressed by the statutes, whereon was greete perell; and also the lyuerey for horses at bouge of court, of gentylmen and[i] many other requiryng a grete busynes, that now is left and putt in to siluer to encrese theyre wages. This king apoynted of offices[j] outward[35] to rewarde his household seruauntes,[k] after theyre desertes, to be parkers, some foresters waryners, kepers of manors, baylywekes, constableshippes, portershippes, receuours, corrodyes, wardes, mariages, and many other thinges of valure, in portez, and townes, citees, etc.; and for his chapelmen, chyrches, prebendes, free chapelles, and pensions,[35] etc., whan [A, p. 14] any suche fell in his gifte, or elles by his letres of contemplacions to gete suche benyfece of ony other lord for his household man. In the festyvall dayes or whan astate shuld be showed,[36] he wold be seruyd with iiij course or v, his lordes and gentyles with iii cors, and euery messe after ij

---

[a] 'executid', *H.*
[b] 'Example hereof', *H.*
[c] 'our soueraigne lordis housold', *H.*
[d] From H. A and E omit 'all'.
[e] 'thoo', *H.*
[f] From H. A has 'where' and E has 'wher'.
[g] 'diuers other many offices', *H.*
[h] E has 'chaungyd'; H has 'chaungid'.
[i] From H. A and E omit 'and'.
[j] 'officers', *E.*
[k] From E. A and H have 'services'.

G

course,[36] de quo metrice sic

MENTE SENEX ETATE VIRENS, SINE FRAUDE FIDELIS
PURUS CARNE FUIT JUSTUS[a] AMANSQUE DEUM[37]

§8. DOMUS REGIE MAGNIFICENCIE sex habet proprietates; quarum
prima est quod[b] magnificus assimilatur scienci, quia sicut ad
scientem artificem pertinet cognicio vnius ad aliud; ita eciam ad
magnificum pertinet cognoscere proporcionem expensarum ad illud
in quo sunt[c] expense. Secunda est quod magnificus expendit magna
et decencia propter bonum honestum sicut propter finem. Tercia est
quod magnificus delectabiliter expendit eaque expendit et non cum
tristicia, quia quod aliquis sit multum diligens in ratiocinio et
computacione expensarum hoc pertinet ad peruificentiam. Quarta
est quod magnificus intendit quando[d] [A, p. 15] facit opus optimum
et decentissimum quantum[e] multum possit expendere ad opus
intentum facientum. Quinta est quod magnificus expendit sicut
oportet et quando[d] oportet et hoc circa magna et decencia, quia
magnificencia est super habundans liberalitas, sicut et in domesticis
expensis. Sexta est quod magnificus facit opus admirabile et excellens
cum magnitudine expensarum; omnis[f] eciam magnificus est[g]
liberalis et non econuerso. Et sic magnificencia[h] non extendit[i] solum
circa omnes operaciones que sunt in retentione[j] pecunie, sed circa
sumptuosas expensas in quibus excellet liberalitatem vt supradixi
magnitudine. Ergo est circa magnos sumptus; ad magnum opus
requiruntur proporcionati sumptus. Rex autem magnificus largus
est sibi et suis subditis magnificus in ornatu conuiuijs possessionibus
et edificijs. Certe non possunt magna opera fieri nisi cum magnis
expensis; magnifici est dare secundum proporcionem gracie diuiti-
arum. Et ideo diligenter est intuendus quod non superhabundet ne
excedet in sumptibus magnis, quia[k] talis vocatur banna-vsus, quasi
in fornace bona sua consumens, Ethicorum iiij°, magnificus ab
equali proporcionato sumptu opus faciet magis magnificum;[l] hoc est
induratum secundum virtutem.[38]

[A, p. 16] §9. THIS IS the new house of houses[m] principall of Inglond
in tymes of pees, bylded vpon this[n] kinges foundacions, precedentes,
and vpon other mo notable[o] and husbandly householders by the
greate counsayll of lordez spirituall and temporall,[39] the Cardinal of
Canterbury, George, Duke of Clarence, Richard, Duke of Glocester,

---

[a] From H. A has 'iustans'; E has 'iustus' above a cancelled 'iustans'.
[b] From H. A and E have 'quia'.   [c] 'fuerint', H.
[d] 'quum', H.   [e] E omits 'quantum'.   [f] 'summis', H.
[g] 'et', E.   [h] From H. A and E have 'manificencia'.
[i] E and H both read 'extenditur'.   [j] 'retentionem', H.   [k] 'quoque', H.
[l] H has, after 'magnificum', 'quod est diu duraturum quia sedit virtute
recte studium quod oportet'.
[m] 'hausoldis', H.   [n] 'these', H.   [o] From E and H. A has 'notably'.

the wise and discrete jugez, and other sad, avised, and well lerned men of Inglond in all aprowmentes. And also mony of them long tym haue knowledge of the experiens^a and conduyte of kinges houses by many prudent proves and long study and^b deliberacions by theyre hole assent for thes formal direccions that ensew; whereof is diffined throughely^c this royal court to stond after thies apoynt-mentz that folowe after,^d of all the intermixtions peysed by wysedom, profyte, and by reason, answering to euery astate and degree, according to lyueres, competent wagez, clothing, feez, rewardez, and other dueties, by the wiche euery officer shall mowe sufficiently be of power in all trouth to do the kinges seruyce honorably.^e The kyng wull haue his goodes dispended but not wasted. Et sic scribitur Ecclesiastes, 'DOMUS REGIS EDIFICABITUR SAPIENTIA'.

[A, p. 17], §10

VISUS STATUS DOMUS REGIS FAMILIARIS IN HONORE THESAURARII
⎫
HOSPICIJ TEMPORE PACIS PRO XIJ MENSIBUS ET TRIBUS SEPTI-
MANIS KALENDARIJ IN ANNO;⁴⁰ VLTRA^f TERCIUM DENARIUM
⎬ SUMMA
BOUUM ET MULTONUM^g EXPENDENDORUM, PRESENTA SIUE
EXCENNA DOMINO REGI DONANDA SINE PRECIO, AC FORISFAC-
TURAS CONTINGENTES PRO HOSPICIO...... ....
⎭

xiij^{ml} li.

Inde potest dieta communis stare ad xxv li. Et si annus
⎫
bisextiles fuerit xxv li. vltra. Summa per annum....
...........ix ^{ml} cl li.

Item ad incrementum dietarum pro festo Sancti Georgij,
etc. allocatur ....cc li.

Item ad incrementum dietarum pro v festis principalibus
in anno⁴².....................................cli. ^h

Item ad incrementum dietarum pro cera, mapperia, tela,
linea, in officiis speciariae, etc., ad iiijor festa, vltra dieta
supra ....ccclxvj li. xiijs. iiijd.

Item ad incrementum dietarum pro vinis rubiis, albis, et
dulcibus, vltraⁱ quod allocatur superius in communi xj^{ml} xvj li.
dieta pro festis principalibus, adventu dominorum, am- ⎬ xiijs.⁴¹
bassiatorum, extraneorum, et aliorum^j superuenientium iiijd.
ad curiam per annum ....D li.

Ita quod prouidencia et empciones illorum vinorum fiant
per senescallum, thesaurarium domus, et contra-rotula-
torem et non per pincernam Anglie, sed inde totaliter
exoneretur pro maiori proficio et minore honore domus
hujus

Item ad incrementum dietarum pro remocionibus et cari-
agia patrie^k per annum ....ccc li.

Et sic vniuersalis dieta anni apparebit ad xxx li. ijs. q^a
plus in toto per annum, ob.q. di. quam summa dietarum
anni
⎭

[A, p. 18]

Item pro oblacionibus regis et aliis elemosinis dandis fratribus et predicantibus, ac reparacione vessellorum argenti per estimacionem ....ccc l.

Item pro libro necessariorum vadijs et expensis officium curiae, pro donis regis, pro regardis garcionum et pagettorum, estimatur per annum—Summa ....ccxxl i.[l]

Item pro feodis in moneta debita infra curiam, vltra vadiis hospicij per annum—Summa...............................cxxx li. xjs. iiijd.[m]

Item pro empcione equorum somerariorum et charretarum cum reparacione sua estimatur per annum—Summa...................cxx li.

Item pro vadiis custodis mutarum, falconum, et falconariarum regis,[n] per annum—Summa.......................................xl li.

[o]Robis xij[p] militum officij vt infra ad cvjs. viijd.....lxxxv li. vjs. viiid.

Robis xxiij magistrorum, clericorum, et seruiencium, vt infra........ ....liij li. viijs. viijd.

Robis clx armigerorum infra et extra curiam ....ccclx. li.

Robis ccxl valectorum infra et extra curiam ....ccxx li.

Robis x clericorum[q] ....x li.

Robis x clericorum seruiencium....................vj li. xiijs. iiijd.

Robis xvj valectorum et garcionum charretarum................x li.

Robis xvj valectorum stabuli ad maius............xxvij li. vjs. viijd.

Summa hujus domj........xiij[m] li.

FIGURA VNIUS DIETE COMMUNIS
REX CUM FAMILIA

		[r]		
Vinum xx sextarii, xls.		D.[r]	xxvs.	Frumentum, iij
Cera xij li.		B.	vj. li. xviijs.	quarterie iiij busselli
		G.	xxxiijs.	Inde cariagia
		C.	viij li.	cipharum allecium
		P.	xxxs.	Inde
Dieta per modum commune		S.	vis.	Inde
		S.	iijs.	Inde
		A.	xs.	Summa..xxv li. estimatur
Fenum xs.		S.	ls.	
Avena vj quarterie		V.	xls.	Indehujus litere
		E.	iiijs.	cariagia

---

[a] 'expence', H.　　　　　　　　　　[b] 'longe studied deliberations', H.

[c] From H. A and E have 'strongly'.　　[d] H omits 'after'.

[e] 'So the king . . .', H.

[f] From H. A and E have 'EST TERCIUS DERNARIUS'.

[g] 'boum et muvttonum', H.　　　[h] 'D li', H.　　　[i] H omits 'vltra'.

[j] 'alterorum', E.　　　[k] 'patet', E.　　　[l] 'DCxx li', H.

[m] 'cxxx li. xj. s. iijd.', H.　　　[n] H omits 'falconum'.

[o] H precedes this and the following six items with 'Item, pro'.

[p] '13', H.　　　　　　　　　　[q] H adds 'secundariorum'.

[r] The letters in this column stand for 'Dispensaria', 'Butelleria', 'Garderoba', 'Coquina', 'Pulletria', 'Scutilleria', 'Salseria', 'Aula et camera', 'Stabulum', 'Vadia', 'Elemosina'. H has, in the left-hand column, 'Dieta per medium communis' and, in the middle column, 'B. vj li. xvijs' and 'G. xxxiiij s'.

[A, p. 19] §11.[43] MEMORANDUM that if the kinges hyghnesse plese to kepe a lesse household than the foresayde grete summe sheweth of here, in this boke are deuysed ix other smaller houses, as one for a lower prince, another for a duke, another for a marquesse, another for an erle, for a baron, for a banrette, for a kny3t bacheler, and for a squyer, whereof the king may cheese suche as shall please hym best.[43]

§12 THE KYNG hath geuyn his grete preceptes vnto his steward, thesaurere, chamberlayne, countroller, countynghouse, and to all the officers, ministres, achatours, purueours, sergeauntz, and all other seruantes to folowe, execute, and aplye all the actes, statutes, and apoyntmentz that byn assigned in this boke,[a] DOMUS REGIS ANGLIE, vnder peyn of discharging them from any office in this housholde. Furst, for the edyfying and comfort to all officers in this householde and seruauntes therein, the kyng, wylling the good sad rulez and the encres of cunnyng seruauntez by ouersight and doctrine of the mastyrs of offices, hathe of [A, p. 20] his highe excellent grace commaunded specially iiij thinges to be seen to, be the rullers of this court. PRIMO, quod seruiens quiscunque vel minister hujus domus habeat competentem victum vnde honeste viuat et valencior fiat in obsequijs domini regis. SECUNDO EST vt officij sui curam in emolumentum domus debite et fideliter exsequatur.[b] TERCIO VT OMNINO sub correctione existat ne ea que honestatem domus regie concernunt[c] turpiter alienat aut in dedicus ejusdem sua contumacia[d] succrescat. So for this honorable houshold and lantern of Inglond hit is agreed by our souerayn lord and his councell abouen sayde, for all wey to be stablisshide for the yerely chargez in the thesaurer of houshold is ministracion, to be taken of the most surest groundz of payment in the land for[e] the conuersacion of his most high estate and contentement of his housolde royall and creditours thereof, as hit is expressid before in the astate of this seyd court, for the yere xiij^{ml} li.,[44] beside all presentz that shalbe geuen to the king for his foresayd householde euery yere, not to be preyseyd at any prise, not to be parcell of the thesaurers grete receyte, but to be taken as in ayde and relief of[f] the household; sauyng that the officers that shall receyue all suche stuff all weyes they to make thereof just and [A, p. 21] true acompt how hit shalbe dispended to the kinges vse and worshipp, with profit by ouersight and record of countrollers and clerk of kychyn, and in countinghouse. Now begynnyng furst at the seruyce of metes and drinkes for his most noble and propyr person,

[a] 'booke callid Domus Regis Anglie', H.   [b] 'exequatur', H.
[c] From H. A and E have 'concerunt'.
[d] From H. A and E have 'continuancia'.   [e] From H. A and E have 'of'.
[f] 'to', H.

shewing ensample to all other of good gouernaunce and to be after a rule according to suche astatz and tymez as shall require.

§13. [45]THE KING for his brekefast ij looues made into iiij maunchettes, and ij payne demayne, one messe of kychyn grosse, demi a gallon ale. Item, at none for his bourde sitting allone, viij loues, with the trenchers; his seruyce of kychyn cannot be expressed at certeyn, but the noble Edward the iijd. in comune dayis feryall, beyng no prees of lordez or straungers at his bourde, was serued with viij[a] diuerse disshes,[46] and his lordes in hall and chamber with v, his other gentylmen in court with iij disshes besides potage, and gromez and other with ij disshes diuerse. Than the kinges [A, p. 22] mete, ij pichers dim. wyne, ij gallons ale. Item, for his souper by hymself, viij loues, with the trenchers in all the kychyn after the day, or after the stuff that is had within forth, ij pychers wyne, ij gallons ale, besides the frutez and waferez.[b] [45] Item, bred and drinkinges for the kinges person betwixt meales cannot be ascertayned but by trewe[c] recorde of the vsshers of chamber. Item, ny3tly for the bed making, j pain, di. gallon wynne.[d] [47] Item, for the king and his chambyr also, when the day shortnyth and no prees of grete straungers, iij torches, j tortayis, and iij prikettes for the table and cupbourde, if hit be not fasting day; vj perchers, x candyls wax for syzes of chambre, ij morters wax euery ny3t; and at the festes or cumyng of lordes or other straungers worshipfull, hit must be more large by the discression and recorde of the vssher, by ouersight of the chambyrlayn and others. Item, for his own person, in the chymney brannyng day and ny3t, xviij shides,[e] viij fagottes for wynter season; and if there be mo nedefull chymneys to brenne for the kinges honour in the grete chambre,[48] then as the chamberlayn and vssher[49] thinken[f] reasonable; and dayly all thinges to be recorded by the vssher into the countynghous. Item, for the beddes and paylettes in the kinges chambre, all litter and russhes of the sergeaunt of hall by ouyrsight, for all thing that [A, p. 23] growith of thesaurere of household his charge must be ouerseen the expences thereof by the styward and countroller.

§14. [g]The King also taketh[g] for his offring by the propyr handez of the thesaurer of housholde, what greete[h] astatz som euer[h] be then

  [a] 'seauven', H.

  [b] 'fruyter and wauffrer', H.

  [c] From E. H has 'true'; A has 'new'.

  [d] From E. A has 'i p. di g.'; H has 'one pitcher half gallon measure'.

  [e] 'Item, for the persoone, one chiminey, brynning day and night, sixteene shydis', H.

  [f] 'thinking', H.

  [g] From H. A and E have 'THE KYNGES CHAMBER takith also'.

  [h] H has 'greter'; H has 'he be'.

in presence, that is to say on[a] Christmas-day, Estyr-day, Whitsonday and All Halowen-day, at eche of thees festes out of the countyng-hous vjs. viijd.,[50] called a noble of golde.[b] Also for his dayly offringes alowed to the deane of the kinges chapell of household rennyng in greete priseez of a greete plate of golde[b] to the valure of vijd. by day that the king offerith; except tho dayes in wiche the king offerith the noble. Than the countynghouse called le graunt garderobe[51] paith v dayes and in the iuelhouse xij dayis, that is to say, in All Halowen-day, Michaelmas day,[c] Concepcion of Our Lady, Cristmasse-day, Newyeresday, Epiphany, Purificacion and Annunciacion of Oure Lady, Good Friday, Estyrday, Ascencion-day, Whitsonday, Trinitee [A, p. 24] Sonday, Corporis X-day, Assumpcion-day, and Natiuitee of Our Blessid Lady.[52] So thies vijd. dayly[d] wulde draw to by the yere after iij[c] lxvj [sic][e] dayes, thereof xvij dayis abated, x li. iijs. viijd. Item, to the kinges offringes to the crosse on Good Friday, oute from the countynhouse for medycinable ringes[f] in gold and syluer delyuered to the iuel-house, xxvs. Item the king offerithe or sendithe to the shryne of Seint Thomas of Caunterbury, in the name of chyuyage, iiij[g] florynes of golde fro his priuy cofers yerely.

§15. THE KYNGES CHAMBER. Mete and souper to be sett with lordez as if thaire astate be some deale lyke;[53] often tymez a baron may be set there at the messe of an erle,[53, 54] alweyis too such to one messe.[h 54] And for a custum there sitting the confessoure, and[i] chamberlayn, the secretary, a messe;[55] of knyȝtes to serue the king of his basen and towell called 'for the body',[56] a messe; chapleyns, a messe; squiers for the body, the phisician, the kinges surgeon, a messe; of jentylmen [A, p. 25] vsshers wiche shall recorde that day the expences of the king and his chamber into the countynghous; also to be in the chamber in feryall dayes, iiij messez of yomen, as the yeman of robis, yeman of beddes, yeman[j] of the crown and of the chambre; and all other to the hall, except a messe of gromez wayters etyng in a pryuat place, as with the grome porter of chambre or within a withdrawȝt or warderobez, herknyng vpon the vsshers of chambre yf the[k] call. And if there be com such straungers that for

[a] From H. A and E have 'in'.

[b] H omits 'Also for his dayly offringes . . . plate of golde'.

[c] From H. A and E omit 'Michelmas day'.

[d] ' by the daye', E.

[e] E has 'iij[c] lxvj'; H has 'three hundrid three score and five' and 'tenn poundes three shillings seaven pence'.

[f] From H. A and E have 'thinges'.

[g] 'three', H.

[h] 'oftentymes a barron may sitt there at the messe of an earle, allwaies to such on messe', H.

[i] 'the confessor, the chamberlaine', H.

[j] E has 'yemen'; H omits the word.   [k] 'they', H.

certen causes must sett in the chambre, than[57] as the vssher thinkith best according so to be sette and serued by the assewer of the chambre.[57] Item, at the greete festes of the yere the officers of chambre. and yemen shall sitte and kepe theire meelis in the kinges chambre during the festes, sauf gromez nor pages sitte not there at no tyme, but thees gromes eten with yomen of householde in the hall. The drinkinges in the kinges chambre betwixt meles for lordes or other straungers can not be acertayned but taken by dayly recorde of the vssher of chambre as the causes shall require.

[A, p. 26] §16. A QUENE, ita quod sit regina regnans and endowed with liuelode sufficient, than if hit please the king and hur highness,[58] hit hath byn vsed by quenez to pay a certen dayly for theyre dietes, whan she cumith to this court,[58] and after the numbyr of personagez of lordez, ladiez, gentyllwomen, knyghtes and[a] squiers, and other officers such of her seruauntes as shall apoynted be, etyng within this court or yit taking any lyueres at the kinges charge within his household. We fynde of old recordes and new both, that for the quene is seruyse, wich must be nygh like vnto the king, and for her ladyes and other worshipfull men and jentylwomen, theire seruices and lyuerez after as hit[b] accordith to high and lowe degree aftyr the maner as hit is to the kinges household maynie. Thus, acountyng the charges that shall rise by her, as by resorting to hir highnes, bothe lordes and jentyls, and other comyn sutors, also to pondyr the dayis of grete festes with the dayis of abstinence; consideryng also the reparacions of napery, vesselles, and other stuffe, this must cause her comyn diette to be the more for the highe astate of her propyr person, and the higher persons to be [A, p. 27] bettyr seruyd than the lower. For the numbyr of her own seruantes and for the resorte of comers, as hit is before sayde, yf her[c] noble presence be in this court, than the dogettes in the countynghouse bere witnesse both of her VENIT ET RECESSIT AD CURIAM VEL A CURIA POST PRANDIUM SIUE ANTE, TOCIENS QUOCIENS. For her self one day with another at xls.; and euery person of her propyr seruantes, xijd.; and all the names that shall take suche lyuerey and seruyce, that the lower personnes may help the hygher. The quene is counsell,[59] or suche as be of her countynghouse to send in writing the namez of euery suche person, as oft as hit pleaseith, as to the kinges countynghouse to call aftyr, and that this apoyntment alwey be obserued. Also that the money herefore be truly delyuered to the handes of the tresorere of housold with the kyng quarterly; and elles hit wull breke and surcharge the greate apoyntment made for the honour of our souerayn lordes court, as keping ij housholdes so honorable with the groundez of one, so that one mought [A, p. 28] hurt and minisshe the othyr his greate

---

[a] H omits 'and'.   [b] H omits 'hit'.   [c] 'theire', H.

fame. Be[a] hit remembred that the thesaurere of the kinges household
be charged with such receyte as he takithe of the quene. Item, hit
hath byn that the officers for the quene hyghe and lowe taken in
seruise and lyuerey som what lesse in euery thing than dothe such
an officer beyng of the kynges propyr house holde to whom he is
lykened by office[b].

> Pro dieta proprie persone regine ⎫
> per diem xls. Summa per annum ⎭ DCCxxx li.
>
> Pro C[60] seruientibus suis infra curiam ⎫
> regis prandentibus ad xijd. per diem ⎭ M¹ viij[c] xxv li.
>
>   Summa per annum
>   MMDLV. li.[c] [sic][61]

[A, p. 29] §17. A PRINCE, the kinges eldest son, brother, vncle, or
any[d] other, beyng heyre aparent to his principalities and abydyng to
suageourne[e] in this court, he hathe byn acustomed to pay for his
diettes after the numbyr of personagez that he[f] shall have attendaunt
and taking seruice and lyuerey of the king his householde, of all
wich people the names must be acerteyned in to the kinges countynghouse and the money[g] for them monethly to cume to the handez of
the thesaurere of the saide householde. We fynde of sume princes
that haue payde in thies householde dayly a cs., and some iiij li.
after theyre persones, and as it[h] pleasith the king. The prince[i] takith
dayly[j] for his brekefast and mete and souper lesse then the quene,
and so of all other seruyses within this court. In case the prince be
but cumyng and goyng among to this houshold and nat to soiourne,
but for to see the welfare of the kinges highnes and of the quenes, or
ellez that he be sent fore, yet then[k] he to haue like seruyce, if he be
nat [A, p. 30] sitting at the king or quene is table but in his chambre
out of the highe presence, there to be couered with assaye and assewer at his towell with double seruyce.[62] Also a messe at his table
if he[l] require and the seruyce at his table and of his couppborde to be
dayly recorded in to the kinges countynghouse. Also etyng in the
kynges hall, x of his seruauntes. Also lyuerey for his chambre at
none and[m] ny3t, xij loues, vj messes of greete mete and rost, j sexter
wyne, [n]viij gallons ale. And for wynter lyuerey,[n] ij torches, a tortayis,[o] iiij perchers at souper and viij candelles wax,[o] a morter wax,

---

[a] 'But it remembred', H.   [b] 'office vnto', A and E.
[c] From H. A and E have 'M¹ viij[c]. xxv. li'.   [d] H omits 'any'.
[e] E has 'soieane'; H has 'at soiourne'.   [f] From H. A and E omit 'he'·
[g] Also E, but H has 'moneth'.   [h] From H. A and E omit 'it'.
[i] 'kyng', E.   [j] From H. A has 'day'; E has 'daye'.
[k] From H. A has 'thou3e' and E has 'tho3e' (for 'though').
[l] Both E and H have 'it'.   [m] 'at none at ny3t', E.   [n] E lacks this section.
[o] 'fower perchers soper and at eight candle wex', H.

viij candelles peric, xij tall (woods),[a] iiij faggots; and for somer lyuerey, iiij shydez, ij faggots, litter, and russhes at all tymes of the sergeaunt vssher of the hall and chambre. The prince hath within this court[b] of suche tymez of goyng and commyng,[b] not abyding in household, xx[tl] persones wayters and the remnaunt of his officers and seruauntes to be at bed and bourde at the princes household,[63] at his logynge and lyuerey in the cuntrey or in the town where as they [A, p. 31] shalbe assigned by the kinges herbergers for the tyme, wich householde is a gard vnto the king. Lette alwey be remembred to make in the kinges dogettes both *venit* and *recessit* as often as hit plesith the king the prince to come or go, and if the prince be so abyding in houshold at a sertayn, as hit is by[c] nethe estemed, then the thesaurere of household to be charged therof in his accompt.

Pro dieta proprie persone principis
per diem xxxs. Summa per annum } Dxlvij li. xs.[d]

[64]Pro 1 personis suis infra curiam regis
prouidentibus ad xijd. per diem
Summa per annum } ix[c] xij li. xs.[d]

[A, p. 32] §18. A DUKE IN THIS[e] courte sitting in the kinges chaumbre shall haue etyng in the hall i kny3t, a chapleyn, iij esquyers, iiij yomen; and for his chaumbre and brekefast, at noone, souper tyme, and lyuerey at ny3t, x loues, iiij messes of grete mete and rost for all day, iiij[f] pychers wyne, vj gallons ale, a torche, ij tortayis, j morter; [g]and in wynter season[g] iij perchers wex, vj candylls wex, viij candelles perich, x talles,[h] iiij fagottes,[i] for winter liuerie; and for sommer, when he needeth, fower tallwood, two faggottes; litter[i] and russhes for his chambre of the sergeaunt vssher of the hall; and whan he dynethe or soupyth in his own chaumbre[65] oute from the hygh presence, than to be couered in all seruyses, none assay nor his shewer no towell[66] but he be a kynge is[j] son. And if he be muche continuyng and attending vpon the kinges person, than he to haue a yoman keping his chaumbre styll in thys courte, as ofte as the duke departith tyll he com agayn, taking dayly for his lyuerey ij loues, ij messes of grete mete, ij gallons ale, and the festiuall dayis dimi a pycher wyne. Also this lord beyng present hymself hath into this court wayters on hym xij persones,[67] the remnaunt of his maynie with his houshold at his lyuerey within vij mylez to this court, and

[a] A and E have 'tall', but H has 'tallowe'.
[b] H reads 'at such tymes of comeinge and goeing'. [c] 'be', E.
[d] H includes an addition of these sums: 'Miiij[c] lx li.'
[e] 'A DUKE sitting in this court in the kinges chambre', H.
[f] 'three', H. [g] E has 'and wynter season'; H has 'one winter season'.
[h] 'tallewod', H. [i] From H. A and E lack this passage.
[j] E has 'kny3tes'; H has 'kinges'.

he payith for all his own cariagez [A, p. 33][a] harneys and other.
Item, that no purueoure of king, quene, nor prince take no maner[b]
stuffe within his lyuerey so delyuered by the kinges herbigers, but
oonly at the will of the owners, of lesse than hit be to sell as to mar-
kettes. His howsolde in the cuntrey is called a 'garde corps du roy'.
The steward and thesaurere of such a duke is houshold representith
within hit the astate of a baronne, if they be out of the kinges courte
within theyre lordez propyr housholde.

Domus propria talis ducis per se in Anglia fundata, per annum super. .

iiijM$\frac{l}{i}$. li.[68]

xx

Vnde pro dieta comunj vltra vadijs ad vj li.[c] . . . . .ijM ciiij. x. li.
Pro duobus garderobiz et elemosinis et oblacionibuz suis per annum[c]. .

ccc li.

Pro necessarijs hospicij et aliis expensis forinsecis estimatur per annum
—Summa . . . . .cccc li.
Pro donis et regardis domini et aliis contingentibus estimatur per annum
—Summa . . . . .cc li.
Pro feodis senescalli—xl marcs; thesaurarij—xl marcz; contrarotula-
toris, xx li.; et iiij (militum)[d]—xl marcz.
Summa de vendicione cepium, pellium,[e] boum, multonum, vitulorum
expensorum, etc.,

Propter medium [f]AULE, CAMERE, ET CAPELLE[f]

Pro vadijs xl generosorum et armigerorum ad vijd. ob. per diem, cum
venerint computamus[g] cum vacacionibus eorum extra per finem ad
plenam recepcionem monete; potest estimari quod quilibet contentetur
cum x marciz, et sic sufficientur in[h] summa; satisfaciet omnibus eis et

xx

vltra per mensem, xx li.,—major cum majore[i].. cciiij. vj. li.xiijs. iiijd.

xx

Pro vadijs iiij valectorum in camera, capella,[j] et hospicio, cuilibet per
diem ad iijd.—Summa cuiuslibet partis in toto, iiij li. xjs. iijd.

[A, p. 34]
Vnde cum quilibet acceperit pro tempore attendencie sue, vacationibus
deductis, per medium inter eos omnes non deuenient, et homini cuilibet
alter ad iiij li., quare licet xx plene habeant omnes alij, plene non

[a] A here has an inserted leaf which transcribes in a late eighteenth-century
hand the text from 'Domus propria talis Ducis' to 'vltra supervenientibus et
cum vacant ibus'.
[b] 'noe manner of stuffe', H.   [c] 'Summa', H (bis).
[d] 'militum' is inserted in a late eighteenth-century hand; H has the word but
E does not.
[e] 'pellium, cori, bouum', H.
[f] H omits this phrase but inserts it in the next line after 'armigerorum'.
[g] 'computatum', H.   [h] 'ista summa', H.   [i] 'xx marcz cum mid.', H.
[j] H has 'in camera eorum et hospicio', and omits 'cuilibet'.

habebunt—et ideo posuimus certum pro incerto pro vadijs, iiij li.—
Summa . . . . .CCC xx li.
Pro vadijs xxx garcionum domus,ᵃ cuilibet liijs. iiijd. per annum—
Summa. . . . . .iiij li.
Pro vadijs siue regardibuz xxiiij pagettorum laboranciumᵇ cuilibet ad
xxvjs. viijd. per annum—Summa . . . . .xl marcaz

<table>
<tr><td rowspan="6">Pro robis
estiualibus
et yemalibus</td><td>vj militum hospicij . . . . . .xij li.</td><td rowspan="6">Ciiij xvj li. xiijs. iiijd.</td></tr>
</table>

Pro robis estiualibus et yemalibus

⎧ vj militum hospicij . . . . . .xij li. ⎫
| lx armigerorum et aliorum infra |
| et extra . . . . .lx li. |
| c valectorum infra et extra ad |
⎨   xx   xx ⎬ Ciiij xvj li. xiijs. iiijd.
| xviijs. . . . . .iiijx li. |
| xl garcionum infra et extra . . . |
| xl marcas |
| xxiiij pagettorum laborancium |
⎩   viij li. ⎭

Summa domus talisᶜ . . . . . .iiijmˡ li.

ESTIMACIO PER ANNUM[69]

De frumento per septimanam estimatur ad x quarteria
De vino per annum xxiiij dolia ad Cs. per medium
De ceruisia estimatur per septimanam iij dolia ad
De bobusᵈ cxl
De multonibus . . . . .MᴵC, recentes et salsatiᵉ
De porcis. . . . . .iiijC
De vitulis . . . . .D
De damis. . . . . .iijCᶠ
De cuniculis . . . . .iijMᴵ
De pullina et aliis volatibus
De piscibus stagni et marinis

Pro ccxl domesticis[70] vltra superuenientibus et cum vacantibus

[A, p. 35] §19. A MARQUES sitting in the kinges chaumbre with duke,
erle, bisshopp, or chaunceller shall, by the chamberlayn or vssher's
discression, for few sit allone in this courte, but king, quene, or prince,
and they may be coupled with any worship. This lorde shall haue
etyng in the kingis hall ɪ knyght, a chapleyn, iij esquiers, ij yomen,
besydes hym that kepith still his chambre. The lyuerey for his
chambre, brekefast, none, souper tyme, and for all nyȝt, vij loues,
iiij messes of grete mete and rost, ij pichers dim. of wyne, v gallons
ale, j torche, a tortayis, iij perchers, v candylles wex, vj candelles
peric, viij tallwood, ᵍiij fagots in wynter season; and he wull,ᵍ in

ᵃ 'domo', H.
ᵇ From H. A and E have 'labore'; H has 'pagettarum laborancium'.
ᶜ 'Summa domus talis ducis', H.   ᵈ 'bouibus', H.
ᵉ H has 'recentis et salsati' and a marginal note, 'i.e. 11,000'.
ᶠ From E. A has 'iiijC'; H has 'iiijC' with the first stroke crossed out.
ᵍ 'fower fagottes in winter season; and if he wille', H.

somer iij talles,[a] j fagott. He is not vsed to be couered in his chaumbre
within this court butt his cuppe. And if he be often attendaunt
vppon the king to this court, than he hathe a yoman be fore sayd to
kepe his chaumbre and harneys in housholde and to make redy his
lyuerey in the cuntrey or town, dayly taking in his master's absence j
cast of brede, ij messes of greete mete, ij gallons ale, and in festiual
dayes dim. a picher wyne. The sum of all his meynie abyding with
hym in this courte, x persones wayters. The remnaunt [A, p. 36] of
his officers and seruauntes to be with his houshold at his lyuerey in
the cuntrey, logged and assigned by the kinges herbigers within vij
mylez to the kyng for a gard corps du roy. No purueour to execute
his power within the marquez logging or lyuerey as ferre as hit
strechith, but by the assent of the owners. Also he payith for his
own cariage of harneys in this courte.

Domus propria talis marchionis siue ducis per se in Anglia fundatur per
    annum super[b] ....iijM^l
Pro dieta per medium estimatur ad iij li.
             Summa anni ....M^{l}ixC viij li.
Pro alocacionibus et expensis ij garderobarum, cum oblacionibus et
    elemosinis, estimatur—Summa ....cc li.
Pro necessarijs hospicij et expensis forensibus, per annum estimatur—
Summa ....cclxvj li. xiijs. iiijd.
Pro donis et regardis domini[c] fiendis, per annum estimatur—Summa..
                    cxxxiij li. vjs. viijd.

^{d}xxx armigerorum et capellarum ad cs. per annum..Cl li.
xx
^{d}iiij^e valectorum infra et extra cum capella, ad v marcas
    per annum ....C li.
xx
^{d}xl cum capella garcionum ad xls. per annum ......iiij li
^{d}xx pagettorum laborancium ad xxs. per annum, xx li

Summa
CCCl li.

Pro feodis senescalli, xx li., thesaurarij xx li., contrarotulatoris, xx marcz,
et iiij militum, ^{f}cuilibet, x marcz per annum
Summa de vendicionibus cepium, coriorum, bouum, multonum, et vitulorum
    iiij militum per annum.................................viij li.
    lx generosorum infra et extra, ad xvjs. viijd. per annum .....l li.
    C valectorum infra et extra, ad xiijs. iiijd. per annum ....c marcz

    ^{a} E has 'ta^l'; H has 'tallow'.
    ^{b} H has 'Summa' as well.
    ^{c} H has the marginal note: 'i.e. domi vel domini'.
    ^{d} These four items are the same in A and E, but H brackets them with the
introduction 'Pro vadijs hospicij'.
    ^{e} From H, which has the marginal note: 'i.e. 8o valectorum'; A and E have
'iiij'. The arithmetic seems curious in either case.
    ^{f} 'cuiuslibet', H.

^alx garcionum et pagettorum laborancium, ad vjs. viijd. per
annum..xx li.^b

Summa huius domus iij M^l li.

[A, p. 37]

Pro cc domesticis vltra superuenientibus cum vacantibus aliquando,
^cdomino computato per se, et domina^c

These lordes rewarde theire kny3ts, capeleyns, esquiers, yomen, and
other of theyre seruauntes, after theyre desertes. Some of his chapleyns with officyashippes, deanriez, prebendez, fre chapels, person-
ages, pensions, or suche other; and for the secular men, steward-
shippes, receuours, counstables, portershippes, baylywikes, warden-
shippes, foresters, raungers, verders, vergers, shreues, eschetours,
corouners, custumers, countrollers, serchers, surueours, beryngis of
yeres giftes,[71] wardes, mariages, corrodiez, perkers, and wareners.

^dThis causeth lordes to rule at nede.

§20. A COUNTE of this courte, sittinge in the kinges chambre, with
a like pere,[72] or elles assisting hym a baron. And he to haue in the
kinges hall etyng, a chapleyn, or a kny3t, esquiers, ij yomen,[73] taking
for his brekefast and lyuerey to his chaumbre, at noone, souper-
tyme, and for all ny3t, vj loues and dim., iiij messes of grete mete
and rost, ij pychers wyne, v gallons ale; and for wynter lyuerey,
from All Halowen-tide tyl Estyr, a torche for hymself, j tortays
[A, p. 38] to sett by his lyuerey at ny3t, iij perchers wex, iiij candelles
wax, vj candelles peric., vj tallwood, iij fagots, liter and rushes all
the yere of the sergeaunt vssher of the hall and chambre; and after
wynter ij tallwood,^e ij fagottes, if hym nede. In euery place within
this court serued uncoured, and when he is absent to haue a yoman
keping his chaumbre in courte, taking ij loues, ij messes grete and
roste, j gallon^f ale dayly. In his^g houshold, whan hymself is present,
dayly^h to haue ix persones wayters: the remnaunt with his houshold
at his lyuerey in the cuntrey, assigned by the kinges herbeger within
vij mylez compace to the king for a garde corps du roy. No purueyour
to take any stuf within the precinct of his herbigage or lyuerey but
for the count is proper howsholde, but only at the will of the owner.
This lorde payeth for hys own cariage of herneys in the courte. The
steward and tresorer of an erle orⁱ of a bisshoppes houshold worship-

^a This and the preceding three items are the same in E, but H brackets them
with the introduction 'Pro robis estiualibus et yemalibus'.

^b H brackets these four items and gives the total in the right-hand margin:
'Summa Cxliiij li. xiij s. iiijd'.

^c From H. A and E omit 'domino'.

^d H has 'And this causeth lordis to rule at neede'.　　^e 'tallowe', H.

^f 'one gallon dimid. ale', H.　　　　^g 'this', H.　　　^h H omits 'dayly'.

ⁱ E omits 'or'.

fully possessed represent the romez of knyȝtes within theyre proper howsholde.[a]

Domus comitis in Anglia fundatur per annum super . . . . ijM^l li.[74]

^{b}Pro dieta communi ad xls. Summa . . . . M^l iiij xv li.^{xx}

Pro custubus duarum garderobarum cum oblacionibus et elemosinis, estimatur—Summa . . . . Ciiij^{xx} iiij li.^{c}

[A, p. 39]

Pro necessarijs hospicij et expensarum forensium, estimatur . . . . .
ccxlj li. xiijs. iiijd.

Pro donis domini et regardis fiendis per annum, estimatur—Summa
C li.

Pro vadijs et equis {
xvj armigerorum, cuilibet ad vj marcz ^{d}et trium equorum^d in liberacione domini cum vacauerit l valectorum, cuilibet ad ls., habentium singulorum^e equos in liberacione domi
xl garcionum ad xxxs. habentium^e equos per domum^f
} vnius anni Summa ccxlix Li.

^{g}Pro robis^g {
xxx generosorum, cuilibet ad xs.–xv li.
lx valectorum, cuilibet ad viijs.
xl garcionum, cuilibet ad vjs. viijd.
} Summa lxxviij li

Pro feodis senescalli xx li., thesaurarij xx li., contrarotulatoris xx marcz—Summa . . . . liij li. vjs. viijd.^{h}

This lorde may geue deaneryez, prebendez, free chapelles, corrodiez, or ellez he is ^{i}founder of a chanon house,^{i} monkes, or frierres syngers; thus he may reyse a chapell^{75} by help of yomen and howsholde chyldren, wiche after, if they may not serue in chapell, shall serue in housholde or ellez be preferrede by the lorde.

Summa huius domus. . . . . . ijM^l li.

^{j}Estimacio per annum^j

[A, p. 40]

De frumento per diem ad vj busselloz
Pro domesticis vacuis, Cxl personis
De vino per diem, ad iij sextarias

---

^{a} H adds 'or rule'. ^{b} 'Vnde', H. ^{c} 'Ciij iij. li', H.^{xx}
^{d} From H. A and E have 'et iij'.
^{e} From H. A and E have 'singulos' and 'habentes'.
^{f} Also E, but H has 'per domi, sicut domus baronis'.
^{g} From H. A and E omit 'Pro robis'.
^{h} In H this is followed by 'Memorandum pro pellibus bouum et muvttonum expendendis'.
^{i} H has 'founder of some chanons'.
^{j} From H. A and E lack this heading.

De ceruisia per septimanam ad quatuor pipas
De bobus*ᵃ* .... Cviij .... ad xvs.
De multonibus .... Mˡ .... ad xviijd.
De porcis.............. C
De vitulis C
De damis.............. Cxx
De piscinis,*ᵇ* stancis,*ᶜ* et marina, etc.
De prouidencia pulletrie, etc.*ᵈ*
De prouidencia seucerie, etc.*ᵉ*
De prouidencia aule et camere
De prouidencia stabuli
              *ᶠ*Pro Cxl domesticis vacantibus*ᶠ* ⁷⁶

§21. A BISSHOPP CONFESSOURE sitting in the kinges courte chambre*ᵍ* shall haue etyng in the hall a chapleyn, j esquier, j yoman;⁷⁷ and for his brekefast and chambre, none, souper-tyme, and lyuerey at ny3t, iiij loues, ij messes of greete mete and roste, *ʰ*j picher wyne, ij gallons dim. ale*ʰ*. And wynter lyuere from All Halowen-tide tyll Estyr, a torche wayting vppon him, a tortays to sett his lyuerey in the wynter nyghtes, ij perchers wax [A, p. 41] iij candelles wax, iiij candelles peris, iiij shides, *ⁱ*two faggottes; and for summer liuerie two shides,*ⁱ* fagott; russhes,*ʲ* litter all the yere of the sergeaunt vssher. By the statute of noble Edwarde,⁷⁸ then*ᵏ* the king founde all thinges necessary for suche a confessoure is body to be taken of his warde-rober priuate or thesaurere of Inglond;⁷⁹ he kepith in this courte v persones wayters now, but than he had horse mete for his horses, clothing, and chawcers for his iij gromez in suggeoure.*ˡ* ⁸⁰ The remanent of his seruauntes to be at his lyuerey in the cuntrey, delyuered by the kinges herbigers, paying now for all his vytayles after the prisez, as the clerke of markett⁸¹ cryethe for the king. He payith for his owne carriage of harneys in court. And if he be lette bloode or seeke, than he takith half seruice of the kychyn to his chambre; and if he be any preest of lower astate than a bisshopp, than he takith dayly his lyuerey sitting in the kinges chambre. And taking for his chambre yet of the greete spycery, at Cristmass and*ᵐ* Whitson-day, in all ij bourde clothes, conteynyng both vj ellez, and ij shorte towellez of*ⁿ* ij ellez.

[A, p. 42] §22. CHAUNCELER OF INGLOND takith for his yerely fee⁸²

ᵃ 'bouibus', *H.*   *ᵇ* 'pistr', *H.*   *ᶜ* 'Staur', *H.*
ᵈ A and E have 'pulle'; H has 'pullina et alijs volatilibus'.
ᵉ H has 'Scut' '.   *ᶠ* From H. A and E omit this line.
ᵍ 'in the kinges chambre', *H.*
ʰ 'one pitcher dimid. of wyne, three gallons and a halfe ale', *H.*
ⁱ From H. A and E omit these words.   *ʲ* 'rushes and litter', *H.*
ᵏ From H. A and E have 'that'.   *ˡ* 'soiourne', *H.*
ᵐ From H. A and E have 'at'.   *ⁿ* H omits 'of'.

out of the kinges selars, or at the port by the buttler's assignement, best for the king to the chaunceller his own housholde vse, by cause of his office, for euerey of the kalender of the yere, a dolium of wine, bothe for to shewe of wynez the more largesse to the maysters of chauncery*a* as to sewtors, straungers, and resorters to his housholde, bering the kinges greete key of worship and profit as well as for*b* to yeue his fauoure and tendur loue to the honour, sad and stedfast guyding of the kinges householde, and of all the seruantes thereof; wherefore all the lordez aforetyme wich haue byn chauncelers allwey graunted and continued this priuylege to euery astate and degree high and lowe of the felyship of the kinges housholde charged and named in the greete roll of housholde. Than he to haue alle suche writtes as he shall nede full*c* shewe for hymself by the*d* propyr name expressed in that writte of the commyn lawe of the chauncery seale free. This vsage and noble custume hath not be denyed and therefore twyes in euery yere the clerk [A, p. 43] of the hanapre*e* shold call a newe housholde roll out of the kinges countynghous by cause of newe charging and discharging of serueauntes, officers, and other, etc. This housholde rolle contaynyth many names mo than the rolle chekke.[83] Whan and as often as the chaunceler or any other lordes of greate astate resorte to this honorable courte, they must be seruyd after their astate and remembred in the kinges countynghouse, bothe of there *venerunt* and *recesserunt*.

§23. GRETE CHAUMBYRLAYNE OF INGLOND comithe to this courte at the v principall festes of the yere, take suche lyuerey and seruyse after the astate he is of. And for his wynter and somer robes, for the festes of Cristmas and Whitsontide, to be taken of the countynghouse, by euyn porcions, x li. xiijs. iiijd.[84] And for his fee of the kinges housholde at the ij termes of Estyr and Mighelmas, by euyn porcions, xx marcz in the countynghouse.

[A, p. 44] §24. CHIEF IUGE OF COMYN PLACE is callid a grete membre of the kinges house, for whos fauour, counsayle, and assistance in the lawe to be shewed to the howsold maters and seruauntes, he takethe a yerely fee by the handes of the butteler of Inglond at ij termes of the yere, by equal porcion, ij tons*f* wyne, wiche is alowed in *g*the counte of housholde.*g* [84]

§25. A VISCOUNT sitting in the kinges chambre shall haue in the hall eting, one chaplin, one esquire, one yoman,[85] and for his breakefast and chambre, at none, souper tyme, and lyuerey at ny3t, iiij loues,

---

a H has 'ministres of chambre'; as so often, the eighteenth-century editors of the *Liber Niger* have imposed H on A, scoring through 'maysters' and 'chauncery' and inserting instead 'ministres 'and 'chambre'.

b E omits 'as for'. *c* 'needfully', *H.* *d* 'his', *H.*
e 'hamperd', *H.* *f* 'dolij', *H.*
g E has 'the countynghouse'; H has 'thaccompt of housold'.

H

iij messes of greete mete and roste, j picher wyne, iij gallons dim. ale.
And for wynter lyuerey, j torche, ij perchers, and iij candelles wex,
iiij candelles peric., iiij talwood,ᵃ ij fagotts; and for somer season ij
talwood, j fagott; also hauyng in to this courte of wayters vpon hym
of his own seruauntes, vj persons, the remnaunt with his howsolde at
his lyuerey in the cuntrey within vij myles to the courte for a garde
to the king, paying for his propre cariage in this courte. And for his
yoman keping his chambre in absence of this lorde, he takethe
[A, p. 45] dayly j payn, j messe gros chare, j gallon ale.ᵇ No purueyour
to take within his lyuerey, but by assent of party,ᶜ and allᵈ his
proper purueyaunces there after the kinges prisez, as the clerk of the
merkat ys byll declareth in to the countyng house.

Domus vicecomitis in Anglia fundatur per annum super . . . .   Mˡ li.ᵉ
Pro dieta per medium ad xxviijs.—Summa anni . . . . .Dxj li.
Pro renouacionibuz in garderobis cum oblacionibus et elemosinis esti-
                    xx
  matur Summa. . . . . .iiij li.
Pro necessarijs hospicij et expensis forensibus, estimatur—Summa. .cc li.
Pro donis et regardis domini faciendis per annum, estimatur—Summa
                    c marcz

Pro vadiis x generosorum, cuilibet ad v marcas . . . . ⎫
         xxxiij li. vjs. viijd. ⎪
xxx valectorum, cuilibet ad xls. . . . . .lx li. ⎬Cix li. vjs. viijd.
xij garcionum, cuilibet ad xxvjs. viijd.   ⎪
habentes equos gyldinges ad custusᶠ domini . .xvj li.⎭

Pro robis xx generosorum, cuilibet ad xs.   ⎫
xl valectorum, cuilibet ad viijs.   ⎬Summa,
xxiiij garcionum, cuilibet ad vjs.   ⎭xxxiij li. vjs. viijd.

Pro feodis senescalj, x li., et thesaurari, viij li., consiliariorum dominiᵍ
  cum clerico, ...xls.
Summa de denarijs prouenientibus de vendicione coriorum, boum,
  cepium, pellium, multonum, et vitulorum per annum et vltra
Hic eciam potest leuari capella cantancium trina vice in septimana, viz.,
  adiutorio eorundem seruiencium huius domus electorum vt supra cum
  paruisʰ vadijs vt supraⁱ ad missas et vesperas.
      Summa huius domus Mᵗ li.

[A, p. 46]
 xx
Pro iiij domesticis, vltra superuenientibus, domino et domina computatis
 per se.

 ᵃ H has 'tallowe', although eight words later it has 'tallwood'; A and E have
'tal' in each case.
 ᵇ 'ceruoise', H.   ᶜ 'by the assent of the partye', E. ᵈ 'at', H.
 ᵉ H follows this line with 'Vnde'.
 ᶠ E has 'Custos'; H has 'custod domi'; all three manuscripts have 'habentes'.
 ᵍ E has 'de'; H has 'domi'.   ʰ E has 'p̄uis'; H has 'penitentijs'.
 ⁱ H lacks 'supra'.

De bona prouidentia

Per diem in panem, estimacione communi .... iijs.

Per diem in lx gallonis estimatur............vs.

Per diem vnius sextarij*a* vini, estimatur ....ijs.

Per mensem vj bouum estimatur .....lxvjs. viijd.

xx

Per mensem iiij multonum*b*

Per annum tempore suo, lxx porcorum

Per annum c vitulorum...................x li.

xx

Per annum iiij damorum*c*

Per annum piscinarum, stancorum,*d* viz., mororum, melewell, codde, etc.

Summa estimatur per medium domino vel domine, aliquando extra prandium vel cenam ex rogacionibus,*e* aliquando per abstinenciam, vota,*f* vel deuociones.[86]

§26. A BARONNE sittyng in the kinges chaumbre or in the hall with a person of like seruyse.[87] He shall haue etyng in the hall a gentilman and a yoman. And for his brekefast and in his own chaumbre, at none, souper-tyme, and lyuerey at nyght, iij loues, ij messes of grete mete and some roste, dim. a pycher wyne, ij gallons ale. And for wynter lyuerey, j tortayis, j percher, ij candelles wax, iij candelles peris, iij tallwood, ij fagots; and for somer lyuerey, ij fagots; and whan hym self is oute of courte, than he shall haue a yoman keping his chaumbre, dayly to ete with the chaumberlayn in the hall till his lorde com agayn. Item, a baronne to haue within this courte iiij persounez wayters, the remenaunt of his meynie to be with his houshold [A, p. 47] at his lyuerey in the cuntry within viij*g* mylez by the kinges herbiger delyuered, taking his prisez for his proper expenses, there so awayting vpon the king after the clerk of merkates cryez. There shall no purueyour of the kinges take or make any puruyaunce within his logging but by assent of the party owner. Though the king geue clothing embrawdid, yet these lordez nor kny3tes haue none but a speciall sute or warraunt vnder priuy seale, directed to the kinges warderober of chaumber.[88]

Domus baronis in Anglia fundatur per annum super ....Dli.

xx

*h*Pro communi dieta per medium ad .. xvjs. Summa anni.. CC iiij xij li.

Pro reparacionibus garderobarum et oblacionum et elemosinarum estimatur—Summa ....l li.

Pro necessarijs hospicij et expensis forensibus, estimatur per annum— Summa..lvj li.

a E has 'sex' '; H has 'sextarius'.   *b* '90 muvttonum', *H.*

c E has 'dam'; H has 'damas'.

d E has 'pisc' and 'stanc'; H has 'in piscibus stagni'.

e 'recognicionibus', *H.*   *f* From H. A and E have 'voto'.   *g* 'seauen', *H.*

h H here has 'Vnde'.

Pro donis regardis domini,^a empcionibus equorum cum husbandria, estimatur—Summa ....l li.

Pro vadijs iiij^{or} generosorum, cuilibet ad xls.

        xvj valectorum, cuilibet ad xls.   Summa—xlij li.

        et vj garcionum, cuilibet ad xxs.

habentes equos gyldynges ad custus domini,^b et cum laborauerint, ^cquilibet equus percipit bartagium, jd. q^a et pro tota nocte^c quilibet equus ijd. ob., et quociens peruenerint sic laborandum ad aliquod hospicium vel manerium domini, regardantur iij equi generosorum ad j bussellum auenarum.^d Et equus vnius valecti ad proporcionem^e

Et cum non [A. p. 48] laborauerint, quilibet equus percipit per diem j peck auenarum, vel j jactum pani equini; simili modo duces et alij domini superiores et inferiores reguntur exceptionibus.^f

Pro liberacione pannorum xxx hominum per annum, in vestura. Summa x li.

Pro feodis senescalli—x li., et receptoris et vnius clerici scribentis,^g iiij li. per annum

Summa de vendicione corrij, pellium, et cepi senellionis,^h multonum, et vitulorum, etc., per annum

        Summa hujus domus.......D li.

Pro xl domesticis vltra superuenientibus, domino et domina computatis per se

§27. A CHAMBYRLAYN FOR THE KING in housholde, the grete officer sittingⁱ in the kinges chaumbre. And whan hit requireth for maters to be comynd of the kinges counsayle, than his metes and soupers in his own chaumber, or elles with the astatz of the houshold, as hit shall seme hym best. He takith his brekefast if he wull in opyn dayes; he presentith, chargith, and dischargith all such persounez as be of the kinges chaumbre, except all suche officers of houshold as ministren for any vytayle for the kinges mouth or for his chaumbre, for all thees take her charge at the grene cloth in the countynghouse. This is the cheef hed of rulers in the kinges chaumbre.[89] Item, as often as he chargith or dischargith any [A, p. 49] new person in chaumbre, to present tho^j persones and names in to the countynghouse. Item, he hath punicion of all them that are longing to the

---

^a 'domi', H.

^b E has 'ad custos d̄ni'; H has 'ad custod'domi'. All three manuscripts have 'habentes'.

^c H has 'quilibet equum percipit pro battagio'-jd. quoque tota nocte'.

^d E has 'ad j bz. au.'; H has 'ad i bz. m.'

^e E has 'Et equus vnus valens ad precium'.

^f 'exceptis', H.   ^g 'servientis', H.

^h A and E have 'sen', for which 'senellionis'= 'measure of fur' seems the most likely expansion; H has 'De vendicione pellium et cepium, bouum, muvttonum, vitulorum, et aliorum, per annum'.

ⁱ E omits 'sitting'.   ^j 'the', H.

chaumber for ony offence or outrage; sauyng the right of the
countynghouse in chekking them for theire vacacions, or for lak of
recordz, or for mysse recording, or for losses of torches, naprye,
pottes, cuppes, woode, or suche other stuff commyng fro the
thesaurer's charge and by them so miscaried. The chaumberlayn
takith his othe and staf of the king or of his counsayle.[90] He shall at
no tyme within this courte be couered in his seruise; he may haue
etyng in the hall ij esquiers, ij yomen.[91] And for the yoman and
other keping his chaumbre, and for his proper lyuerey at ny3t, in
opyn dayes, vj loues, iiij messe of grete mete and rost, j picher wyne,
iiij gallons ale, j torche, j percher, iiij candelles wax, vj candelles
peric. For wynter lyuerey vj talwood, iiij fagots, the larger by cause
he shuld take no thing of[a] suche stuf from the kinges chamber, nor
suffer none to be taken awey, but for worshipp to the king; he takith
also for somer lyuerey iij talwood, j fagot; russhez and litter all the
yere of the sergeaunt vssher of the hall and chaumber and of
[A, p. 50] all other vytayle and stuf as he shall haue nede to within
this houshold, geuyng ensaumple of his content and moderate
costagez in court, both to the kinges honour and profit. Item, for
his robis at Cristmas and Whitsontide of the countynghouse by euyn
porcions,[b] eight marcz; and for his fees at Michaelmas and Easter by
euen portions, x marcz.[92] This growith to hym from the houshold,
and not of the jewell house, nor of the kinges warderobe, for the
fauour and help that he shulde owe in asisting the stewarde,
thesaurrer, and other offices of householde in speking to the kinges
highnes, or to his noble counsayle, for the ayde and goode continuance
of the honorable conductes of his housholde. Item, whan hym self is
absent from courte, he leuith a yoman to kepe his chaumber, and
puruey for his lyuerey of stuf in the cuntry, taking in courte at mele
tymes j payn, j messe gros de kusyn, j gallon[c] seruoice. And whan
hymself is present in this courte, to haue in all vj[d] persons wayters
within the gate; the remnaunt of his seruauntes abiden[e] with his[f]
housholde at his lyuerey in the cuntrey, a garde.[g] His lyuerey and
euery other without the kinges gates is delyuered all wayes by the
assent of the kinges herbiger, and that by his byll; and within the
kinges gates no man herborow[h] or assigne but this chambyrlayn or
vssher, or such other [A, p. 51] vnder hym of the kinges chambre
hauyng theyr power. This chamberlayn besyly to serche and ouersee
the kinges chaumbres and the astate made therin to be according,
first, for all the aray longing to his propyr royall person, for his propyr

[a] 'for', H.   [b] From H. A and E omit this passage.

[c] 'j grose seruoice', E.   [d] 'seauen', H.

[e] From E and H. A has 'abydyng'.   [f] 'the', E.

[g] 'a guard du corps le roy', H.   [h] 'shall borrowe', H.

beddes,^{a} for his propyr^b boarde at mele tymez for the diligent doyng
in seruyng thereof, to his honour, and pleasure;^{c} to assigne keruers,^{d}
cupberers, assewers, fesicyans, almoners, kny3ts, or other wurship-
full^d astate for the towell, and for the basyn squiers for^e the body to be
attendaunt.^{90} The vssher of chambre euer^f to se and quikly to remedy
euery thing lacking, or defautz as well in the kinges inner chaumbre
as in the vtter chamber,^{93} specially in sight towardes straungers of
worship if^g the king kepe astate in his chaumbre. And dayly this
vssher makith his towell or surnape as dothe a marchall when the
king is in hall.^{94}

[A, p. 52] §28. BANERETTIS^{95} IIIJ, or bacheler kny3tes, to be
keruers^{96} and cupberers in this courte of lyke degree for the kinges
person, sitting in the hall at one of the metes with a person of lyke
seruyce; or whan any of them keruith, and the cuppeberer also done
seruyse, than to sett in the hall at the furst or later mete; and the
greate awmoner with hym, if he will attende, or ellez^h with another,
but not of the hall,^{h} in like seruyse. They are called knyghtes of
chaumbre;^{97} euerych of them shall haue a gentilman and yoman
etyng in the hall, and for his own brekefaste and chambre, day or
nyght, ij loues, j messe of gros mete, dim. pycher wyne, ij gallons
ale; and for wynter season, from All Halowen-tyde till Estyr, j tortays,
j percher wex,^{i} ij candelles wex, iij candelles peric, ij talwood, ij
fagotts; rushes and^j litter all the yere of the sergeaunt vssher of the
hall. And whan they are out of court, than they haue ij yomen
abyding still to kepe theyre iiij beddes,^{98} sitting with the chamberlaynes dayly in the hall till their mastyrs come ageyn; and if there
be ij mastyrs so oute of^k courte, than to haue o^l person so keping
there ij beddes^{98} and etyng in the hall and leuyng no mo in the
courte behynde^m them; and if they do, that man to haue no mete
[A, p. 53] in this courte whyles his master absentith; nother they to
kepe no houndes in courte but at theyre lyuerey. Euery of thies
keruers takith for his attendaunce of the countyng house for his
robis, wynter and somer, at Cristmasse and Whitsontide egally, viij
marcez. And for euery of theire fees at Ester and Mighelmas egally,
x marcez.^{99} And for euerych of them comyng in to this courte, iiij
personez wayters,^{100} the remnaunt to their lyuerey with theyre

---

^{a} 'bed', E. ^{b} H omits 'propyr'. ^{c} 'place', H.
^{d} H has 'carvers and cupbearers' and 'worshipfull other astate'.
^{e} From E and H. A has 'of'.
^{f} From H. A and E has 'every'.
^{g} From H. A and E have 'of'.
^{h} 'with anothir of like seruice but not of the hall', H.
^{i} From E and H. A omits 'wex'.
^{j} From E and H. A has 'rushes, litter'.
^{k} 'out of the court', H. ^{l} 'one', H. ^{m} 'to guide them', H.

horses and housholde in the cuntrey nygh to geder. [a]A keruer at the borde, after the king is passid hit, may cheese for hym self o dyshe or ij after that plentie is among. The king will assigne a dishe to som lorde or straunger in chaumbre or hall, ellez amonges the awmoner woll[b] see to straungers in suche rewardes, and if hit seme hym worshipfull, elles all at the kinges boarde goithe to almesse.

IN THE NOBLE Edwardes dayes[101] worshipfull squiers did this seruyse, but now thus for the more worthy. Thies keruers and cupberers pay for the cariagez of theyre harneys and other in courte. Them nedith to be well sped in taking of degree in the scole of vrbanytie.[102]

[A, p. 54]

Domus talis ductoris[c] banneretti in Anglia fundatur per annum super.. CC li.[d]

Pro cotidiana dieta, vt in panibus, potulentis, victualiis coquine,[e] expensis stabuli, et aliis, ad vjs. viijd. Summa anni..Cxxj li. xiijs. iiijd.

Pro renovacione garderobe cum oblacionibus et elemosinis, estimatur— Summa... xxv. li.

Pro necessariis, reparacionibus hospicij, et aliis expensis forensibus,[f] estimatur ....xvj li.

Pro donis, regardis, et ad escambia equorum, estimatur—Summa..x li.

Pro vadiis vnius senescalli et receptoris, liijs. iiijd

Pro iiij mulieribus in vadijs per annum ....vjs. viijd.

Vnius clerici scribentis generosi pro mensa[g] domini ....xls.⎫

Duorum valectorum[h] iiij li. et vnius,[i] xxvjs. viijd. ⎪

vj garcionum laborancium[j] per annum ....vj li. xiijs. iiijd ⎬xxij li.

habentes equos geldinges ad custus magistrorum cum equitauerint ⎭

Pro liberata pannorum pro senescallo ac receptore bis ⎫

per annum, viz., estiuali et yemali ....xiijs. iiijd ⎪

Pro liberata clericis et iiij valectis yemali et estiuali,.. ⎬vj li. vjs. viijd.

xxiijs. iiijd.[k] ⎪

Et pro xvj aliis seruientibus inter eos diuidendi, iiij li. ⎭

Summa

Memorandum de denarijs prouenientibus de corrijs, pellibus, et cepium[l] boum et multonum et vitulorum per annum ad suplenda omnia alia deficiencia in fine anni.

---

[a] 'And', H.   [b] 'would', H.   [c] E has 'duc'; H lacks this word.

[d] H here has 'Vnde'.

[e] 'Pro cotidiana dieta vt in panibus potu victu conquine', H.

[f] E has 'fore'; H has 'forum'.   [g] 'pro mensa domi', H.

[h] E has 'aloc'; H has 'valector'.   [i] 'vnius valecti', H.

[j] E has 'labore'; H has 'labor'.   [k] 'xxxiijs. iiijd', H.

[l] 'cepe', E.

Summa hujus domus . . . . CC li.

Pro xxiiij personis*a* domesticis, magistro et magistra computatis per se cum filiis, etc,

[A, p. 55] § 29. KNY3TES OF HOUSEHOLD,[103] XIJ, bachelers sufficiantz and most valent men of that ordre of euery cuntrey, and more in numbyr yf hit please the kyng. Whereof*b* iiij to be continually abydyng and attending vppon the kinges person in courte,[104] beside the keruers *c*abouesayd, for to serue the king of his bason, or suche other seruyse as they may do*d* the king in absens of the keruers, sitting in the kinges chaumbre and hall, with personez of lyke seruyce. Euery of them haue etyng in the hall one yoman,*e* [105] and taking for his chambre at none and ny3t, j loue, j quart wyne, j gallon ale, j percher, j candell wax, ij candelles peric, j talwood dim., for wynter lyuerey from All Halowen-tyde tyll Estyr, russhes and litter all the yeı ? of the sergeaunt vssher. And for keping of theyr stuff and chambre, and to peruey for theyre stuffe, also at theyre lyuerey in the contrey, amonges them all, iiij men; after tyme viij of thees kny3tes be departed from court, and the iiij*f* yomen to ete dayly in the hall with the chamberlaynes, tyll theyre sayd maistyrs com agayn, so that the numbyr of kny3tes seruauntes be not oncresed whan theyre maystrs be present. Euery kny3t shall haue in to this court resorting iij personez wayters, the remnaunt [A, p. 56] of theyre seruauntes to be at theyre lyuerey in the cuntrey within vij myles to the king, by the herbygers sufficiauntly loged, and, if it may be, ij kny3tes togeder. Also they pay in this courte for the caryage of theyre own stuf; and if a kny3t take clothing, hit is by warraunt, made to the kinges warderober,[106] and nat of the thesaurere of household. (Sometymes kny3tes tooke*g* a fee here yerely of x marcs and clothyng, but by cause ray clothinge is not according for the kinges kny3tes, therefore hit was left.) Item, if he be seeke, or specially let blode, or clystered, then he taketh lyuerey iiij loues, ij messe of greate mete and roste, dim. picher wyne, ij galons ale. This lettyng blode, or clystryng, is to auoyde pestylence; and therefore the peple take lyuerey oute of courte, and nat for euery syknesse in man contynuyng in this court.

Domus talis militis in Anglis fundatur per annum super . . . . C li.
*h*Pro quolibet die estimatur j bussellus frumenti ad vjd.
Summa anni, xlv quarterii, v busselli. Summa denariorum. . ix li. ijs. vjd.

---

  a From H. A and E have 'persones'.   *b* From H. A and E have 'wher'.
  c From E and H. A has 'as abouesayd'.   *d* 'do to', *H*.
  e From H. A and E omit 'one yoman'.   *f* 'iiij', *H*.
  g From H. A and E have 'take', and omit the brackets.
  h H here has 'Vnde'.

Pro quolibet die estimatur circa xij galonas seruicie ad obolum quartam.
Summa anni circa xl pipas, summa denariorum....xvj li. xiijs. iiijd.
Pro vna pipa vini per annum estimatur ad—Summa......xlvjs. viijd.
Pro vj pipis cisere faciendis, quolibet anno crescente in ortis*a* domini; summa sine*b* precio [A, p. 57]

Pro cera, sucro, melle, et aliis speciebus, et candelis periciis,
per annum—Summa...........................l s.
Pro xiiij bobus ad x s. per xxviij septimanas*c* carnium in
anno—Summa................................vij li.
Pro lx multonibus per idem tempus,*d*.........iiij li. xij s.
Pro xvj baconis, xx s.; pro xx porcis de stauro, pro xiij vitulis
de stauro domini,*e* pro lx porcellis de stauro   } xij li. xijs.
Pro xx agnellis de stauro, pro xij damis in anno, pro capcione
canium domini plus constant quam conferunt venaciones
Pro anceribus, signis, caponibus,*f* gallinis, pulcinis,*g* heronis,
perdicibus, pocokis, cranis, et minoribus volatilibus de
stauro domini, et per falcones cum cuniculis—C. Summa..

Pro recentibus carnibus emendis, estimatur pro C iiij xx viij diebuz anni
ad xij d. per diem—Summa ....ix li. xviijs.

Pro xvj moruis, in anno x s.; pro l dry hake, iijs iiijd.; pro
xxvj stokfishe, vjs. vjd; pro allecibus rubijs*h* ixs.; pro
allecibus albis, xijs.; pro viij salmonibus precij viijs.;
pro j cade spratte, xviijd.;*i* pro casijs sine precio, pro
cepo,*j* herbis, ouis, buttyro, lacte, et ostrijs, per annum } x li. ixs. vjd.
estimatur xx s. Et pro piscibus recentibus pro clxvij
diebus abstinencie*k* in anno, ad xd. per diem,—Summa
vj li. xix s. ijd. Summa,*l* cum adiutorio riuorum et stag-
norum domini,*m* cum fructibus ortorum*l*

Pro renouatione fienda in diuersis officiis per annum estimatur,
xl s.; pro sale grosso et albo*n* xs.; pro cenapio, vinacro, per
annum, vjs. viijd; pro vergeous sine precio, pro carbone fiendo } Ciiijs.
de boscis domini,*m* xiiijs.; pro C carrectatis bosci de bosco
domini, etc., xxxiijs. iiijd.; cirpis, etc., sine precio

Pro imposicione feni, xl s.; xx quarteriarum*o* auenarum
xxxvjs. viijd.; empcione equorum et excambia,   } vij li. iijs. iiijd.
[A, p. 58] cum reparacionibus hernesiorum stabuli,
estimatur per annum, lxvjs. viijd. Summa

---

a H has the marginal note: 'Haec vocabulum do*l* significat domi vel domini in omnibus.'
b 'Summa suum precium', H.   *c* 'pro xxvj septimanis', H.
d From H. A and E have 'pro idem tempus'. The error in A and E is due to the use of the wrong abbreviation mark.   *e* H omits 'domini'.
f 'capen', E.   *g* Also E; H has 'pultrinis'.   *h* 'rubris', H.
i E has 'pro cade spratte'; H has 'cad' sprator' '.
j 'cepibus', H.   *k* 'abstinencium', H.
l A and H include this sentence in this paragraph; E has it in the next.
m 'domi', H.   *n* 'pro sale gre et all' ', E.
o 'quarters', H.

Pro vadiis senescali scribentis ad custodiam curie domini et⎫
recipientis omnia onera hospicij liijs. iiijd.; et vnius juuenis ⎮
generosi attendentis ad mensam*a* domini, xxvjs. viijd.; vnius ⎮
officiarij pistrine, panetrie, et buttillerie, per annum, xls.; ⎮
vnius coci,*b* boucheri, lardenarij *c*squylourij, per annum, ⎬x li. xvs.
xls. Et cum vno puero in auxilium senescalli, capienti per ⎮
annum, viijs. iiijd. Et pro vno custode equorum domini,*d* ⎮
xxvjs. viijd. Et pro custode canium et falconum et capi- ⎮
entium damos,*e* aues, etc., per annum xxs. Summa ......⎭

Pro aliis necessariis et expensis forensibus cum donis domini per annum
iiij li. xijs. iiijd.

Pro robis magistri et reparacionibuz camere sue, per⎫
annum ....iiij li. ⎮
⎬iiij li. xiijs. iiijd
Pro suis oblacionibuz et elemosinis, estimatur per⎮
annum ....xiijs. iiijd.⎭

Pro liberata pannorum xvj personarum. Summa, iiij li.

Summa hujus domus C li.

Pro xvj personis domesticis vacuis, magistro et magistra computatis per
se absque paruulis.

Memorandum, de denariis prouenientibus de corrijs*f* et pellibus boum*g*
et multonum et vitulorum, per annum expenditorum in hospicio

[A, p. 59] §30. A SECRETARY[107] sitting in the kinges chambre or
hall with a person of like seruyse. And he shall haue eting in the hall
j gentilman.[108] Item, for his chambre for all day, iij loues, ij messe
of grete mete, dim. a picher wyne, ij galons ale, j torche, j percher,
ij candelles wex, iij candelles peris in wynter season, and iij tallwood; ruyshes and litter all the yere of the sergeaunt vssher of the
hall and chambyr. Parchemyne and pauper sufficiaunt of the office
of the grete spycery, by ouersyght of countroller or his clerkes, and
that to be alowed in the countynghouse, and also red wex. And whan
he hathe nede of muche writing, than he to haue comaundment from
the seyd countynghouse for perchers of talowe or smaller candelles
peris. To this office ar belonging iiij clerkes,[109] sufficiaunt writers of
the kinges signet vnder the seid secretary, eting dayly in the kinges
hall. And for theyre lyuerey at nyȝt a gallon ale, and in wynter
season j candell peris; whan theyre business requireth, then by the
secretaryez propyr recorde thies clerkes to haue dyners and soupers to
theyre scriptory, taking so for one mele j peyne, j messe gros de cusyn,
dim. a gallon seruoice. The secretary and his clerkes pay [A, p. 60]

---

a Also E; H has 'messam'.   *b* From H. A has 'quoci'; E has 'quioci'.
c All three manuscripts here insert an 'and', in English.
d H has 'domi', with the marginal note 'Hoc est domi vel domini in
omnibus'.
e 'damas', *H.*   *f* 'corre', H.   *g* H has 'bouum' and 'muvttonum'.

for theire cariage of harneys in courte, oute-take[a] a litell cofer in[b]
wich the kinges warrauntz and billez assigned and other lettres and
remembraunces be kept vpon a falace.[110] This cofyr is caried at the[c]
kinges cost, where as the countroller wull assigne. The secretary he[c]
hath into this courte iij personez,[111] wayters on hym for all that
office, the remnaunt of all other seruauntes to be founden at his
lyuerey in the cuntrey, deliuerede by the herbiger sufficiauntly for
hym and all the clerkes; and when hym self is oute of courte, he hath
a yoman to kepe his chaumbre, etyng at the chaumberlayn's bourde
in the hall. Both he and his clerkes take clothyng of the kinges
warderobe.[d] [112]

[A, p. 61] § 31. CHAPLAYNS IIIJ or mo,[113] as hit pleasith the king
whereof ij alwey in the chambre be sitting at the meales, [e]for he
sayth that day matyns, masse, or before the king for graces,[e] that
other ij in the hall with personez of like seruyse. Item, eche of them
hath eting in the hall a yoman at the chaumberlaynes bourde. Item,
eueryche of thies maistyrs takith lyuerey for his chaumbre at nyȝt
dim. a payn, a quart wyne, j gallon seruoice;[f] and for wynter season
j percher, j candell wex, ij candelles peris, j talwood dim.; russhes
and litter all the yere of the sergeaunt vssher. And if ony of them be
benyfysyd to xl li., he taketh no wages in this courte; but abiding for
his attendaunce to[g] he be preferred by the kinges yift whan as hit
fallith. Item, they take clothing of the kinges warderobe but if ony
of them stand in the chekker roll.[114] Item, they pay for the cariage
of their own harneys in this court. And euery of them may haue of
wayters on them in this courte ij persones honest, the remnaunt to
be at theyre lyuerey with theyre horses in town or contree. Item,
if ony of thees chapleyns be lett blode or be syke, than to take syke
lyuerey as the knyȝtes don. Eueryche of them hath on person honest
at the chamberlaynis bourde in the hall.[h]

[A, p. 62] §32. ESQUIERS FOR THE BODY, IIIJ,[115] noble of condicions; of them[i] alwey ij be attendaunt vppon the kinges person to
aray and unray[j] hym, to wache day and nyȝt, [k]to dresse hym in his
clothes. And[k] they be callers to the chaumbrelayn if ony thing lak
for his person or plesaunce; theyre[l] business[116] is many secretes, som

<hr />

[a] 'except', H.   [b] 'the which', E.   [c] H omits 'the' and 'he'.
[d] 'wardrober', H.
[e] 'such as say the daie matinnes, masse, bifore the kinge for graces', H.
[f] 'ale', E.   [g] H has 'to', altered to 'til'.
[h] H has a further sentence—'These chapleines giuen attendantes for
matteines, messes, and other deuotions, to be readie at such season and place
as the king wilbe disposed.'
[i] 'wherof', H.   [j] 'vnarray', H.
[k] 'and to dresse him in his cloathes. And if', H.
[l] 'his', H.

sitting in the kinges chaumbre, som in the hall,[117] with persones of like seruyse, wich is called kny3tes service.[a] Taking euery of them for his lyuerey at ny3t dim. a cheteloffe, j quarte wyne, a gallon ale; and for wynter lyuerey, from All Halowen-tide tyll Estyr, j percher wex, j candell wex, ij candelles peris, j tallwood et dim. And wages in the countynghouse yf he be present in courte, dayly vijd.ob.,[118] and clothinge with the housholde wynter and somer, or xls. besides his other fee of jewelhouse, or of thesaurere of Inglonde; and besides his wachyng clothing of chaymbre, of the kinges warderobe, he hath abyding in this courte but ij seruauntes,[119] lyuerey sufficiaunt for his horsez in the cuntrey by the kinges[b] herbiger. And if ony squier of the body be lett blode or elles forwached, he shall haue syke lyuerey with kny3tes; litter and russhes all the yere of the sergeaunt vssher of the hall and chaumbre. Oftyn tymes thees stond in [A, p. 63] stede of keruers and cupberers.

§33. A SEWAR[120] FOR THE KYNG, wich owith to be full cunyng, diligent, and attendaunt. He receueth the metes by sayez and saufly so conueyeth hit to the kinges bourde with saucez[c] according[121] therto,[c] and all that commith to that bourde he settith and dyrectith, except the office of pantrie and buttre. [d]He showith at one mele and dynyth and soupith at an other meele,[d] and to sitt in the hall with a person of like seruyse. And dayly hym owith to be with the souerayns or rulers of housold present at ordnaunce, there to hyre[e] what shalbe purposid for the kinges noble person and the proporcion of as for his bourde oonly; and than there to say if ony thing be specially that the king desirith hymself. Item, if the kinges surueyour lak, than this assewer with the clerk of countrolment and the clerk of kychyn and the master cooke for the mowthe shall go see the kinges seruyse and deyntez of flesshe and fishe, that it be alwey chosen of the best [A, p. 64] endrayzt. Item, among to comyn with the master cooke of the kinges diet and appetites, so that he may deuyse his mete and dight them to his plosure. And this assewer shall not abrigge nor withdraw no dishe of seruyse that is delyuered or deuysed by other officers at the dressour, but trewely to sew tham vppon the kinges table, vppon such payn as styward, thesaurer, or countroller list to awarde, after the reason that towchith the kinges honour; this is agreed by the statutes of noble Edward. This assewer takith for his chaumbre at ny3t dim. a payn, j quarte wyne, j gallon ale, j torche of the grome porter of chaumbre, to be borne before hym to the dressoure, and whiles he seruyth the king and no longer,

---

[a] From H. A and E omit 'service'.   [b] H simply has 'the herberger'.
[c] 'accordingly', H.
[d] In H this sentence comes earlier, after 'and attendaunt'.
[e] E has 'here'; H has 'heare'.

butt to be deliuered to the grome agayn. He takith for his chambre
in wynter seson j percher wax, j candell wex, ij candelles peric, j
talwood*a* dim., russhes and litter all the yere of the sergeaunt vssher.
And whyles he is present in courte he takith dayly in the chekker
roll vijd. ob. and clothyng for wynter and somer, or elles alowed
xjs. And at eueryche of the iiij festes of the yere, of the clerk of
greete spycery, ij elles of lynen clothe for aprons, price the elle,
xijd. [A, p. 65] Item, he takith partes of the generall giftes,[122] as
they be geuyn to the householde, if he be present in court at tyme of
geuyng, ellez not. He may haue in this court ij seruauntez, the
remnaunt to abide at his lyuerey in the town or countrey. He payethe
for carriage for his harneys in court. His seruyse from kychyn is
after the sewte of squyers for the body;[123] and if he be seeke, he
takith lyuerey like to them. Also but hit be bake*b* all maner fruytes
and wafers shall come to the bourde alwey without brede,[124] the
bourde auoyded whan wafyrs come with ypocras or with other swete
wynes.[125] The king takith neuer at bourde of comfisez*c* and other
spices but stonding.[126] Memorandum how king Edmund, brothyr to
Athylston, for the trouthe and dilygence that he founde in his
assewer in his seruyse doyng, that the king loued hym so agayn,
that he put hym self in his enmyes hondes to dye to saue and defende
this*d* derely beloued assewer in suche a tyme as he stoode in perell.[127]

[A, p. 66] §34. A SURUEYOUR FOR THE KING,[128] to ouerse, with the
master cooke for the mowth, all maner of stuf of vytale, wich is best
and most holsom, and*e* the conueaunce and saufgarde of hit, with
all the honest maner of clenly handling and dylygence of keping
and couering. And dayly to be at the ordinaunce, to hyre*f* the
proporcions that he made there for the kinges person, so that hit
may be called hoole out at*g* the dressoure; and that no thing be
purlonged*h* that is so apoynted by the clerk of kychyn and maister
cooke, but that the kinges*i* estate be serued therwith, if hit may be
goten by the purueours, vppon such payne as the sofferaynes of
houshold wull awarde in the countynghouse. Item, in absence of the
kinges assewer, a squyer for the body or ellez this surueyour berith
the towell[129] to shew to*j* the king. He eteth in the hall at*k* one mele
or at the later with a person of lyke seruyse.[130] He takith with-in
this courte all such wagez, clothing, and lyuerey and othyr duetiez
as doth the kinges assewer. His charge is not vpon the maner of
sewing*l* of disshes at the dresser but to see that the ordinaunce be

---

a 'tallowe', *H.*   *b* 'but that he bake', *H.*   *c* 'comfittes', *H.*
d 'her', *H.*   *e* From H. A and E have 'at'.
f E has 'here'; H has 'hire'.   *g* 'of the dressour', *E.*
h 'purloyned', *H.*   *i* From E and H. A has 'knyȝtes'.
j 'to sewe the king', *H.*   *k* 'at that one meale', *H.*   *l* 'sorting', *H.*

sett forth and sew them, and than lette the assewer allone in the [A, p. 67] maner of setting them.

§35. WARDROBER,[a] [131] called by the noble king Edward the iijd. statutez 'clerk purueour du le garderobe de roy',[132] that tyme beyng of the body of household, aftyrward remoued by kyng Richarde ijde., assigned to kepe his office continually in London among merchauntz and artificers, hym selfe to com when the king or chaumbrelayn callith hym specially at the iiij festes of the yere as an officer of chaumbre outward. His lyuerey is like that tym to a squyer's of[b] the body; nor wages nor clothing of houshold. He takith all his receytes of the thesaurere of Inglond by hym self and yeldith his acompt in the chekker by warrauntes of the kinges chaumbrelayn.[c] [133]

§36. GENTYLMEN VSSHERS OF CHAUMBRE,[134] IIIJ, whereof on or ij countynually sittith at mete and sopers in the kinges chambre to see euerything done in dew order and to kepe silence; that other to[d] be etyng in the hall with a [A, p. 68] person of like seruyse, so that one be walking at the recorde of the kinges chaumbre[135]—all[e] the seruyse of brede, messez of kychyn, wyne, ale, wex, wood, that is dispended, bothe for the kinges bourde and for the hole messe and other of the chaumbre, and aswell the seruyse for the king of all ny3t[f] as the greete auoydez of festes and[g] the dayly drinkinges betwixt meles in the kinges chaumbre for straungers, and thereof to make trew recorde,[136] and to bring hit dayly to the countynbourde before none, there to be prouyd where[h] hit be resonable or not. Also he to sett all the astates, gentyls and straungers, at the bourdes in the kinges chaumbre in a dew order,[137] ij persones to[i] a messe, if the astates be sume deale lyke, weyyng honour with profitt; he must geue grete attendaunce vppon[j] the king and straungers. And if ony defaute be founden in the vssher of mysse recording, [k]other for other outrage[k] or losses for the kinges goode, growing from the thesaurer of houshold charge, than he to awnswer and to take suche punicion by wages and clothyng as the jugez of the countynghouse wuld think resonable to award, or ellez ferthermore vpon hym by the auyse of the chaumberlayn. He shall at no tyme make commaundmentes of brede [A, p. 69] wyne, ale, or ony[l] other out of the kinges chamber, but if the king drink in his outward disportes, but by assent or comaundement of the countynghouse of such as haue the rule. Euery[m] vssher

---

[a] From H. A and E have 'WARDEROBEZ'.
[b] 'squires for the bodie', H.   [c] 'kinges and chamberlaine', H.
[d] E has 'ij'; H has 'two'.   [e] 'at', H.   [f] 'the whole night', H.
[g] 'or', H.   [h] 'perused whether', H.   [i] 'till', H.
[j] E omits 'upon'.
[k] E has 'other for outrage'; H has 'or for other outrage'.
[l] H omits 'ony'.
[m] 'eueryche', H.

takith for his lyuerey at ny3t dim. a chet lofe, j quarte wyne, j
gallon ale; and for wynter, j percher wex, j candell wex, ij candelles
peris, j talwood dim.,[a] the larger for that none of the squyers of the
body nor vsshers[138] shold nat withdrawe ony such stuf from the
kinges chaumbre. Also hym owith to be cunyng, curteys, and glad
to receue, towche, and direct euery man in serues doyng, and to
know all the custumes and cerimoniez vsed aboute the king and
other astates according, whan they com. He hath his comaund-
mentez for euery office as for bred, wyne, ale, wex, wood, or coole,
straw and russhes to be had for the kinges chaumbre or other
straungers, as his discression ordinable[139] well.[b] He assigneth the
yomen[c] of crown and chambre, gromez and pagez, to attendauncez
and other busynes inwarde and outewarde[140] for the king. Also he
hath for hym self russhes and litter all the yere of the sergeaunt
vssher of the hall for his chambyr where vsshers lye to geder; and
euerich for theyr wages [A, p. 70] in the chekker rolle present in
court, viid. ob.,[141] and clothing, wynter and somer, with the houshold, or ellez xls. a pece. And if ony of them be lett bloode or syke,
they take syke lyuerey, ij loues, ij messes of kychyn for all day, j
quarte wyne, ij gallons ale. They pay for the caryage of theyre own
harneys[d] in courte. If the king kepe astate in his chambyr, these
vsshers make the astate in the surnape,[142] like as the marchall doth[e]
in the hall. And eche of these vsshers to haue into this courte ij
honest seruauntes,[143] and lyuerey for theyre horses to gyder if they
may,[f] in the town and cuntrey, assigned by the kinges herbigers, and
to leue by hynde them no chaumbre dekens[144] in courte but suche
as are apoynted by the countynghouse. Item, nother marshalls
nother vsshers of hall nor chaumbre of very right nor worship owe
nat to lityll or withdrawe ony hole stuf of fleshe or fishe geuyn to
the king by wey of present, mustred[g] in the hall or chambyr. One
of these vsshers, by the statutes of noble Edward, was purueour for[h]
wood and litter and russhes, wich busynes now is inned[i] to the
sergeaunt of the halle. This name vssher is now[j] a worde of Frenshe.
[A, p. 71] Item, he assigneth euery office and loggyng with in the
kinges place. The worshupfull clerk and [k]counsellor speketh thus to[k]
this officer vssher and to the marchals and porters; Terencius—'vt
homo est, ita morem[l] geras'.[145]

---

[a] 'ij candelles peris. Item, d' the larger', *E.*
[b] 'ordinarily would', *H.*   [c] 'yoman', *H.*
[d] 'their owne cariage of harneis', *H.*   [e] 'marshalls done', *H.*
[f] 'if they may be', *E.*
[g] E omits 'mustered'; H has 'by way of gret present, mustered in the hall or
chambre'.
[h] 'of', *H.*   [i] 'ioyned', *H.*   [j] H omits 'now'.
[k] From H. A and E have 'chaunceler speketh to'.   [l] 'morum', *E.*

§37. YOMEN OF CROWNE, XXIIIJ,[146] most semely persones, clenely and strongest archers, honest of condicions and of behauoure, bold men, chosen and tryed out of euery lordes house in Ynglond for theyre cunyng and vertew. Thereof one to be yoman of the robes, another to be yoman of the wardrobe of beddis in houshold;[147] thes ij in sartaynte ete in the kinges chaumbre dayly, other ij be yomen vsshers of chaumbre etyng there also; another to be yoman of the stole,[a] if hit plese the king; [b]anothyr to be yoman of the armory; another to be yoman of the bowes for the king; another yoman to kepe the kinges bookes; another to kepe his dogges for the bowe[b]; [c]or another to kepe his best[c] [148] and except the furst iiij persones the remnaunt may to the hall as the vssher, etc.;[149] and thus they may be put to busines. Also[d] hit accordith that they be chosen men of manhoode, shotyng, and [A, p. 72] specially of vertuose condicions.[150] In the kinges chaumbre be dayly sitting iiij messez of yomen, and all the remnaunt etyng in the hall, sitting togeder aboue, ioynyng to the yomen of houshold, except at the v grete festes[e] of the yere;[151] than as many yomen of crowne and chambre as may sitt in the kinges chaumbre shalbe serued there duryng the fest. And eueryche of them present in courte hath dayly alowed in the countynghouse iijd.,[152] and clothing for wynter and somer, and chauncez yerely, or ellez xviijs.[153] besides theire watching clothing of the kinges warderobe. And if ony of them be sent out of court by the kinges chambrelayne, than he takith his wages of the iewel-house and *vacat* in the chekyr roll till he be sene in court agayn. Also logging[f] in the towne or contre, sufficiauntz for theyre horsez, as nygh to gadr as the herbiger of houshold may dispose; and alwey ij yomen of crowne to haue an honest seruaunt in to[g] court. In the noble Edwardes statutes these[h] were called the 'xxiiij archers a pe currauntz enchierment deuaunt le roy pur payis pur gard corps du roy'; thes[i] were called the kinges wachement. At thys[j] dayis a yoman toke but xs. for his gowne and iiijs. viijd. for his hosen and shoone.[154] They haue nothing ellez with the houshold sauf [A, p. 73] cariage of theyre beddes, ij men togeder, by deliueraunce or assignment for that cariage of the controller,[k] and litter for theyre beddes of the

[a] 'stoole', H.

[b] This passage is the same in E, except that E omits 'another to be yeoman of the bows' and places 'for the king' after 'armory'; in H the passage is as follows: 'another to be yoman of the armorie, another to be yoman of the bowes for the king, another to keepe his dogg for bowe, or another to keepe his best'.

[c] In A and E this phrase comes later, between 'vssher, etc.', and 'and thus'.

[d] H omits 'Also'.   [e] 'five gret soleme festes in the yeare', H.

[f] 'in the countrie townes', H.   [g] 'the', E.   [h] A and E have 'and these'.

[i] 'and these', H.   [j] E has 'thies'; H has 'those'.

[k] From H. A and E have 'countrollers'.

sergeaunt vssher of hall and chambyr. And if ony of them be syke or lette bloode, he takith for all day a caste of brede, j messe of grete mete, j gallon ale; and if hit be of greet sekenesse he must remoue out of courte, or ony othyr. Also whan they make wache nyghtly, they shuld be gurde with theyr swerdes or with other wepyns redy and harneys about them.[a]

§38. YOMEN OF CHAMBRE, IIIJ,[155] to make beddes, to bere or hold torches, to sett bourdes, to apparayle all chambres, and suche othyr seruyce as the chaumbrelayn or vsshers of chambre comaund or assigne; to attende the chambre; to wache the king by course; to go messagez.[156] Taking for theyre wages as yomen of crowne do in the chekker roll,[157] and clothing alike, beside theire waching of the kinges warderobe; the statutez of noble Edward[158] wull geff but one of thes for his expenses out of courte but iiijd. And hit hath be seen often that on of thes yomen hath ben also yoman surgeon[159] for twey causez. [A, p. 74] Also ij of these dyne and soupe in the chaumbre; also theyre expenses oute of courte sent by the chambrelayn or vsshers than to be payd in the iewlhouse. And alwey ij of thes yomen haue an honest seruaunt into court, the remnaunt at theyre lyuerey assigned by the kinges herbiger, togyder, or with the yomen of crown,[160] sufficiauntly logged. And if ony of them be lett bloode or syke, they[b] to haue as the yomen of crown, and cariage by the countroller,[c] ij men to a bed.

§39. OFFICE OF WARDEROBE OF ROBIS[161] hathe one yoman eting in the kinges chambre, taking lyuerey for his office at nyȝt in wynter season from All Halowentyde till Estyr, j candell wex, vj candylles peric, j talwood dim., j gallon ale. And if hit require more wood for the kinges necessarijs, in moyste weder, or in othyr nedefull tymez, hit to be vnderstond in the countynghouse, and by theyre discression to commaund more larger for that tym; russhes and litter for this office all the yere of the vsher of hall and chambre. This yoman hath byn most acustumed to be one of the [A, p. 75] yomen of crown alwey,[d] [162] lyke euyn to whom he takethe wages, clothing, and all other thinges in courte.

GROMES in this office, ij, eting with in the same office, wich take in etyng dayis ij loues, ij messe of grete mete, j gallon ale. And eche of them takith a reward in the countynghouse at euery quarter's end, xld., and clothing with the household yerely, or eythyr of them, vjs. viijd., besidez there waching clothing of the warderobe. And if any grome be syke or lette blood for the grete sykenesse in

---

[a] H has 'harneis aboutis thair shouldris'.
[b] From E. A has 'there'; H has 'then'.
[c] 'controller competent', H.
[d] 'to be one allwaye of the yomen of the crowne', H.

I

court, he takethe lyuerey a loue, a messe of grete mete, dim.*a gallon
ale, for all day. These ij gromes haue into court*b one honest childe;
no part of yeftes made *c to the houshold to this office.*c

A PAGE also to be attendaunt herein,*d takith for his lyuerey for*e
all day, etying in this office j loffe, a messe of grete mete, dim.
gallon ale; and at euery quarter end rewarded in the countynghouse,
xxd., and clothing with the houshold alowed *in precio vesture*. In
noble Edwardes housholde pages were none officers, nor yet long
sene,*f 163 beryng no charge nor [A, p. 76] sworn in the countynghouse: but now they be permytted for an ayde *g of euery office chosen
oftyn tymez. Thes officers of both wardrobes put to theire hondz to
amend many defautz with the nedle worke, but specially they clense
and puryfy all that longeth to chambre workes, by the maysters
of offices as for labours.*g So by*h theyre vertuous disposicion may
grow and by succession to*i be preferred to hygher seruyse; and
therefore the charge is that no man shall draw in any office in this
court any chylde or seruaunt but he be com of clene byrthe, clene
lymed, personable, and vertuously disposed. And whyle they be pagez,
the maysters of office, as sergeauntez or yomen in theyre absence, vse
resonable correcions vppon theyre defautez. They haue not bene
vsed in old dayes, these nor other mennys seruauntes, to be homely
in the pyles at none of the ij offices but by ouersight. To this office
longeth a carre with vj horses, whereof all such thinges as are*j
purueyde or taken out of the charge of thesaurere of houshold, as
for the apparayle and reparacions, except that this thesaurere
purueyith for horse mete and shoying and the wages and clothing of
[A, p. 77] yoman and the grome of this carre, as hit is expressed
after in the office of the stable.164 In this carre, among other thinges,
are caryed suche bokes as pleseth the king to studye in. Thies officers
hath theyre compotent beddyng caryed in this office by ouersight
of the countroller and as he wull assigne. Also they haue theyre
lyuerey in contrey or towne for theyre horsez sufficient, by the
herbiger of houshold. Thes ij wardrobes haue all theyre fumigacions,
that the kinges robes, dublettes, shetes, and shertes be fumyd by
all the yere of the yoman potycary, and that to be truly recorded to
the chambyrlayn.*k

a 'a gallon ale', *E.*
b A and E have 'for one honest childe'.
c A and E have 'to the household to this houshold to this office'.
d 'Also a page attendaunt herein', *H.*
e E omits 'for'.   *f* 'since', *H.*
g E also has this passage; but H reads 'to euery office chosen by the maister
of officers as for labourers'.
h 'be', *E.*   *i* H omits 'to'.   *j* From H. A and E have 'is'.
k 'chamberlaine office', *H.*

§40. ^aOFFICE OF WARDEROBE OF BEDDES^a hathe one yoman[165] etyng in the kinges chambre, takyng lyuerey for this office at ny3t j gallon ale in wynter season, from All Halowen-tyde tyll Estyr, j candyll wax, vj candyls peris, the tortays or torche to bring in the kinges stuf for [A, p. 78] all ny3t of the grome porter of chaumbre without waste, j tallwood dim., russhes and^b litter for theyre paylettes all the yere of the sergeaunt of the hall. And this yoman, or this grome, berith vp nyghtly stuf for the kinges bed and bideth thereby till hit be made; and in the mornynge^c they fett hit down^c to their office ageyn saufly and clenly, that no stranger shall touche hit. In wynter or somer, and^d hit nede, the berer vpp of this stufe shall haue a torche before hym of the grome porter, borne by the grome or page of warderobe or^e chambre; and if this office require more largesse of wood or coole, then to haue comaundement there fore by the countynghouse or^f such a nedy tyme. This yoman hathe be^g acustumed to be one of the numbyr of yomen of crowne;[166] he takith wages, clothing, and other lyke with the yomen beforesayde, and the fees of his office acustomed; this office takith no part of gyftes yeuen to the houshold. The officers of this office serue the king for all thing that longeth to his body day and ny3t in tym of pees; they bringyth hit vpp and fett^h hit down, and brusshe hit, and clense hit, and saufly keepe hit; and the stoole is hereⁱ kept. Nothyr^j this office nor none longing to the kinges chaumbre owe to take no maner feez but by ouersyght of [A, p. 79] the chaumbrelayn. Also in this office GROMES, ij,[167] etyng in the office, taking lyuerey ij loues, ij messe of grete mete in^k etyng dayes, j gallon ale. Eueryche of thes gromes takyn rewarde, clothing in all wises, like to the gromez of warderobe of robes beforeseyde. Thes ij gromez haue into court on honest childe. Also in this office, A PAGE,[168] keping and atending in this office, to sett in all maner lyuerez, to kepe, trusse, and bere the harneys and stuf, to wayte vpon the caryagez. They^l should be sumewhat vnderstanding with nedyll worke; etyng in this office or with his next fellow, taking dayly for his lyuerey j loffe, a messe of grete mete, dim. a gallon ale, and reward[169] and clothing as the page of robis beforesayd dothe. To this office belongith a charyette, horsez, corps,[170] with all the aparayle, horsmete, with all reparacion founden in the charge of thesaurer^m of houshold for the kinges stuf only by ouersight of the countroller. Thes officers haue theyre competent beddyng caryed in this office by ouersight of the

<hr>

^a 'WARDROBE OF BEDDIS', H.   ^b 'rushes fower litter', H.
^c 'they sitt downe', H.   ^d 'if', H.   ^e 'and', H.
^f 'for', H.   ^g 'bene moch', H.   ^h 'sett', H.
ⁱ 'there', H.   ^j 'nor', H.   ^k From H. A and E have 'j'.
^l From H. A and E have 'the'.
^m From H. A and E have 'thesaurers'.

countroller, and lyuerey for theyre horsez in the cuntrey with this
yoman, delyuered by the herbyger. Also [A, p. 80] for this office
sompter horses for the kinges stuf, resonable as the chambrelayn
wull assigne, xij or mo or lesse; but nat in the thesaurer's charge,
but for wages and horse mete; and for one male man at iiijd. a day
by the stable roll and etyng in the hall. Thes gromez and pagez of
thes both wardrobes shold gadyr for the kinges gownes and shetes
and othyr clothes the swete flowres, herbis, rotez, *a*to make amonges
them othyr swete fumes, thinges*b* to make them brethe most hole-
somly and delectable; and all thinges to be*c* preciously and dylygently for mothes and all other vnclennesse attended,*d* and from
towching of straungers' hondes the verry spores that the king shall
were.

§41. GROMES OF CHAMBYR, X.[171] Thereof one is grome porter that
berith wood, straw, russhes for the kinges chambre, making the
kinges litters of his bed and to fylle the paylettes. And he fettith
nyghtly, after the seasons of the yere, torchys, tortays, candylles of
wax, morters; and he settith vp the sises in the kinges chaumbre
with out ony wast or giftes or taking of [A, p. 81] fees, but that the
jentylman vssher assigne hit in*e* the kinges honour with profit, and
dayly recordith that he settith*f* truly in the countynghouse by
tayle, [172] so that his good dealing may be knowe. And if he lese eny
thing hereof, than to awnswere therefore*g* and to make hit good as
the juges of the countynghouse woll award. He takith a dayly peny
alowed in the byll of the hall, and for his reward and clothing with
the houshold lyke to the gromez of chaumbyr and wardrobes afore-
sayd, besydes his waching, clothing and othyr; but he takith no
part, nor none of thes gromez nor pages of chambre, of ony gyft
that shall be made to the houshold. And he etith dayly out of the
kinges chambre, to be nyghe the vssher's comaundmentes or callinges,
taking in opyn dayes ij loues, ij messes of grete mete, j gallon ale for
all day; he is permitted to haue into this court a seruaunt to help
hym bere such necessarijs. And dayly iiij other of thes gromes, called
wayters, to make fyres, to set vp trestyls and bourdes, with yomen
of chambre, and to help dresse the beddes of sylke and arras vppon
the vssher's apoyntment, and to [A, p. 82] geue the yoman water
after dyner and souper, and to help hang the chambre*h* and to kepe
hem clene from dogges and other vnclennes. Thes gromes also ete
with out the grete chambre[173] pryuatly, as theyre course goith about
dayly in opyn dayes, taking iiij loues, iiij messe of kychyn of grete

---

a 'and to make', *H.*
b ' other sweete fuminges to make them breathe', *H.*
c 'soe preciously', *H.*   *d* 'accordid', *H.*   *e* 'to', *H.*
f 'he setteth it truly', *H.*   *g* 'herefore', *E.*   *h* 'hange the cloathis', *H.*

mete, ij gallons ale; the remnaunt of all thes gromez dyne and soupe
in the hall with yomen of houshold. Another of thes gromes is called
'of the armory[174] for the kinges person'; another callid 'grome
surgeon';[175] another 'grome pulter';[a] and another as the chambrelayne
woll apoynt. Euery grome quarterly as the countynghouse reward-
ithe, xld.,[176] and clothing with the houshold or ellez vjs. viijd.,
besidez there waching clothing of the warderober; and besidez the
grete reward yeuen yerely from the kinges priuy cofers to the gromes
and pages of his chambre. Also ij gromes of chambre be suffred to
haue in to this court j honest seruaunt, and they haue lyuerey for
theyre horses assigned in the contrey by the herbiger; also the kinges
chambrelayn to assigne for the ij garderobes and the kinges chambre,
for the male and stoole and other stuf nedefull, to the some of xij
or xvj sompters,[b] whereof the thesaurere of houshold [A, p. 83]
berith no charge but for horsmete, shoyng, kepers' wages, and other[c]
clothing. Thes gromez of chaumbre, one of them fettyth[d] ny3tly
bred, j lofe, a gallon ale, for the kinges bedmaking, with a torter of
the grome porter of chambre.

§42. PAGES OF CHAMBRE, IIIJ,[177] besidez the bothe wardrobes, to
wayte vppon and to kepe clene the kinges chambre, and most honest
fro fautes of houndez as for other, and to help trusse and bere
harneys, cloth, sackes, and other thinges necessary as they be
comaunded by such as are abouen them. And at no tyme a page to
ete in the kinges chambre opynly but in priuat other places, as
warderobes or with grome porter of chambre; eche of thes take
lyuerey dayly, on loffe, j messe of grete mete, dim. gallon ale hole or
syke, and rewarded and clothing as the pagez of wardrobes before-
said[e] in the countynghouse; but no page of chambre shall haue part
of no gift geuyn to the houshold. They take competent beddyng,
caryed and assigned by the ouersight of the countroller; and [A,
p. 84] amonges thes iiij pages to haue one honest child resorting
into thys court. By the statutes of noble Edward the iijd. both
gromez and pages of ij warderobez and chambre toke all theyre[f]
necessarijs and findinges of shone, hosen, shertes, dublettes, gownez,
etc., of the kinges warderober, but now hit is turned into money
and other wise.

§43. THE OFFICE OF JEWELHOUS hath an architectour called clerk[178]

[a] 'pelter', H.
[b] H has 'summer'; none of the three manuscripts has 'sompter horses', as
does the 1790 printed version.
[c] H omits 'other'.
[d] 'settith', H.
[e] From H. A and E have 'besidez'; all three manuscripts have 'rewarded'
unlike the 1790 printed version, which has 'rewarde'.
[f] 'the', H.

of the kinges, or keper of the kinges jewelles, or thesaurer^a of chambyr;¹⁷⁹ ^b(this officer taketh *per indenturam*^c betwext hem and the king all that he findith in this office of gold, syluer, and preciouse stones, and the merkes of euery thing; also he receueth yerely yeftes by recorde of the chambrelayn. Also^d he receueth by indentur of the thesaurer of housholde, and by ouersyght of the chamberlayn);^b sitting in the kinges chambre or in the hall with a person of like seruyse. And for his chambre at nyȝt dim. a chete lof, j quart wyn, j gallon ale; and for wynter lyuerey, j percher wex, j candell wax, ij candelles peris, j dim. talwood. And present in court, vijd. ob. in the chekker roll, and clothing with the housholde for wynter and somer, or of the countynghouse, xls.; his lyuerey is a^e knyȝtes, and if he be syke, he takithe in etyng dayis lyke the esquiers for the body whan they be lette bloode or syke. Also in this office is a clerk vnder [A, p. 85] hym,¹⁸⁰ etyng in the hall,^f taking for his lyuerey at nyȝt dim. a gallon ale, j candell peris, dim. talwood,^g and clothing by the countynghouse or yerely xxs.; and if he be syke, he takith for all day a loffe of brede, j messe of grete mete, dim. gallon ale. And for this office a yoman, etyng in the hall with yomen of chambre, taking for his wages in the countynghouse^h if he be present, alowed by the chekrolle iijd.,¹⁸¹ and clothing with the housholde wynter and somer, and chauncez and all other party or xviijs.,¹⁸² besydez his reward of the jewelhouse, for trewe and diligent kepinges of the foresayd jewelles, etc.;ⁱ and if he be syke, he taketh such lyuerey as doth the clerk. A GROME, etyng dayly in the office,^j taking for his lyuerey j lofe, j messe of grete mete, dim. gallon ale; and he fettith^k in the lyuerez for this office in season, j candell wex, ij candelles peris, j talwood dim., [A, p. 86] and rushes and litter for this office all the yere of the sergeaunt vssher of the hall and chaumbre. Also this grome fettith^k nyghtly for this office a gallon ale, for^l he helpith to trusse and to bere to this charyott, and waytith

---

^a From H. A and E have 'tresory'.

^b This passage, given here between brackets, comes later in A and E, between the phrases 'taking for his wages in the countynghouse' and 'if he be present, alowed by the chekrolle iijd'. H has the passage in the position to which it has been moved, which seems to make better sense. See footnote h on the next page.

^c 'bin indenture', H.   ^d 'Item', H.

^e 'as knightes', H.

^f 'in the hall eatinge', H.   ^g 'dimid, tallwood shide', H.

^h A and E give here a passage which will be found on the previous page, enclosed in brackets, in the position where H has it. See footnote b on the previous page.

ⁱ 'keeping of the kinges joalxe yerely, etc.', H.

^j 'Also in this office a groome eating dayly', H.

^k 'setteth', 'setting', H.   ^l H omits 'for'.

there vppon the saufgard; and the yoman also to attend vppon this
caryage. And this office hath also logging in the cuntrey^a or town
for all theyre horsez and seruauntes sufficiauntly, by the herbiger.
And the chief of this office to haue into this court ij wayters and the
clerke an honest seruaunt; the remnaunt to go to theyre logging in
the cuntrey, and the yoman and grome to haue a seruaunt. And for
this office is assigned a charyet with vij horsez, and all theyre
apparayle, horsmete, shoyng, and the yoman and gromez wages
therefore, founden of the charge of thesaurere of houshold to cary
the stuf of the kinges in this office, and none other mannes, by the
ouersight of the countroller. Betwext the thesaurer of houshold and
this office be^b many interchaunges of syluer vesselles, hole and broke,
receued or delyuered by officers by indenture, as hit woll apere in
the acompt of houshold. And [A, p. 87] as for other thinges towching
this office, behold in the title 'de oblacionibuz regis' capituled
before.¹⁸³ All thinges of this office, inward or outward, comyth and
goyth by the knowledge of the kyng and his chambrelayn recorde¹⁸⁴.
Also if ony kny3t or squyer presume to were the kinges lyuerey but
he com ^ctherby by^c auctorytie or ellez by recorde in this office.

§44. ^dDOCTOURE OF PHYSYQUE¹⁸⁵ stondith muche in the presence
of the kinges meles, by the councelying or awnswering to the kinges
grace^d wich dyet is best according, and to the nature and operacion
of all the metes.¹⁸⁶ And comynly he shuld talke^e with the steward,
chambrelayn, assewer, and the master cooke^f to deuyse by coun-
sayle^f what metes or drinkes is best according^g with the kinges dyet;
and whan he woll^g at mete and souper^h in the kinges chambre or
hall or in his own chambre,ⁱ deuysyng the kinges medecens. And
dayly hauyng in the hall j yoman¹⁸⁷ sitting with the chambre [A,
p. 88] laynes, taking dayly for hym self to brekefast, mete,^j and
souper in etyng dayes, and lyuerey for all ny3t, v loues, seruoyce^k
from kychyn as squiers for the body,¹⁸⁷ j picher wyne, iij gallons ale
for all day, if he kepe his chambre;^l and for wynter lyuerey, from
All Halowen-tyde tyll Estyr, j tortayes, j percher wex, ij candylls
wex, iij candylles peris, iij talwood;^m russhes, litter, all the yere of the

^a 'countrie towne', H.   ^b From H. A and E have 'by'.
^c From E. A has 'by by'; H has 'thereby'.
^d 'DOCTER OF PHISIQUE standeth moch in the kinges presence at his mealis,
councelling or answering to the kinge', H.
^e From H. A and E have 'take'.
^f 'to' is from H. A has 'by deuyse by counsayle'. E has 'by there deuyse and
by counsayle'.
^g 'with the king, when he woolle', H.
^h 'at mete tyme, dyner and super', E.
ⁱ 'or in his owne chambre at tymys be commaundement', E.
^j 'diner', E.   ^k 'seruice', H.
^l 'if he kepte his chambre by commaundment', E.   ^m 'and rushes', E.

sergeaunt vssher. And wages and clothing present in the court as squyers of houshold,[188] and caryage for one cloth sack; keping in this court ij honest seruauntes in all, taking lyuerey for his horsez in the cuntrey or town by the herbyger. This physycyan, of right and of old custume, shold haue no part of the generall yiftes geuyn to the houshold, thouȝe he were present. Also him owith[a] to aspie[a] if ony of this court be infected with leper or pestylence, and[b] to warne the soueraynes of hym, till he be purged clene, to kepe hym out of courte. There owith no perileous[c] syk man to loge in the court, but[d] auoyd within iij dayes. And than, by fauour as the souerayn think according, to contynewe his lyuerey if he logge nyȝe to the court, as within a mile, long or short tyme by fauoure; [A, p. 89] and no man to take syke lyuerey at no time, but he were an officer. The costes for all medycens long to the chambrelayne is audyzt[e] in the jewelhouse.

§45. MASTYR SURGEOUNE[189] sitting in the kinges chaumbre, but most party in the kinges hall, with a person of like seruyce, as knyȝtes lyuerey,[190] taking at nyȝt j lofe, j quarte wyne, j gallon ale; and for wynter season j percher wex, ij candelles wex, iij candelles peric, j. dim. talwood; russhes and litter all the yere of the[f] sergeaunt vssher of the hall and chambyr. And dayly, if he be present in court, by the cheker roll, xijd., and clothing as squyers for the body or[g] xls. of houshold; and yerely to hym by petycion alowed in the end of the yere before steward, thesaurer, countroller, coferer, at the countynghouse, for medycynes geuen to the[h] syke and hurt officers bouȝt by this[i] seyde master surgeoune, xls.[191] And if hym be syke or bleed, than he takith syke lyuerey with squyers for the body. He hath into[j] this court lycensed ij honest persons, wayters on hym, and [A, p. 90] caryage for his own[k] cloth sak by the ouersight of the countroller. Also in this office one[l] yoman surgeon, etyng in the kinges chambre or hall if he be one of the numbyr of yomen of chambre;[192] and for his dayly wages, if he be present in court, presented in the chekker roll, iijd., and clothing with the houshold, and chauncez or xviijs.[193] He and the grome of this office haue j honest child, a seruaunt,[m] into this court and lyuerey for theyre horsez in town and cuntrey to gyder by[n] the herbiger. To this office is deliuered a part of the old broken meteclothes and towelles perusyd in the[o] ewry, delyuered and remembered by the countroller or

---

[a] From H.	[b] E omits 'and'.	[c] 'no personnys sykman', E.
[d] 'to auoyde', H.	[e] 'this paid in jewelhouse', H.	[f] H omits 'the'.
[g] H omits 'or'.		[h] From H. A and E have 'this'.

[i] From H. A and E have 'the'.

[j] E has 'in this courte'; H has 'into the court'.

[k] 'one', H.   [l] From E and H. A has 'o'.

[m] 'or seruant', H.   [n] 'with the herbiger', H.   [o] E omits 'in the'.

countynghouse, that may recorde where they be spent, to make
playstyrs for the syke officers of this court and other longing therto.
Also this yoman, if he be let blood or othyr wise syke, he takith ij
loues, j messe of grete mete, j gallon ale for all; and he hathe[a] his
competent beddyng caryed by ouersight of countroller for the grome
and hym togedr. O grome in this office, if he be nat amitted grome
of chambre, then he sittythe in the halle with gromez of houshold
at the towell. He takith reward and clothing of the countynghouse
as othyr lyke of chambre done; also syke lyuerey. And he fettith
for this office[b] j gallon ale; and in wynter dim. talwood, ij peric
candelles; [A, p. 91] russhes and litter for this office and caryage
for his bed by the countrolloure. And in this office a small cofer,
with playsters and medycens for the king and his houshold, assigned
by the countroller. All thes persons haue byn acustomed to haue
part after theyre degrees of suche giftes as be geuyn generally to
the houshold, if ony of them be present at the tym of yeuing; also
if[c] they stand not affermed as yoman and grome of the chambre.

§46. POTYCARY,[194] etyng in the hall or chambre among, if he be of
the numbyr of [d]yomen of chambre,[d] and when and as often as the
vssher of chambre woll assigne, taking wages and clothyng of the
countynghouse lyke to other yomen aforesayde; caryage with one
cofyr of the kinges stuffe resonable by ouersight of the countroller,
and half[e] bed for hym self and a gowne;[f] all the payment[g] of his
medycyns [h]and ingredients[h] payde of the jewelhouse, by ouersight
of fysycean[i] and by audyzt of chambrelayn of the king.[195] And if
he be syke or lett bloode, than he takith syke lyuerey as the yoman
surgeon; and parte of [A, p. 92] the general yiftes yeuen to the houshold, if ony be, except alwey that suche as be perfitely of the
numbyr of the kinges chambre, they take theyre part with the
chambre and nat with both. He hath nother grome nor page, but if
ony able grome be in the ewry.

§47. A BARBOURE[196] for the kinges most high and drad person, to
be taken in this court aftyr that he stondith in degree, gentylman,
yoman, or grome. Hit hath byn muche acustumed to one or ij well
known officers of the ewry in houshold, [j]suche as byn of the mowth
gladly sergeaunt[197] or other;[j] also, we find how this hath be vsed
among by a welbetrusted yoman of chaumbre, for lak of cunnyng
of this other men. Hit is acustumed that a kny3t of chambre, or

---

[a] A and E have 'he hathe in his competent beddyng'; H omits 'in'.
[b] 'fetteth for this office liuerey', H.   [c] 'if also', H.
[d] From H. A and E lack 'yomen of'.   [e] 'halfe a bedd', H.
[f] From H. A and E have 'grome'.   [g] 'remanent', H.
[h] From H. A and E lack 'and ingredientes'.
[i] ' by ouersight of officers', H.
[j] 'daily of such as bene for the mouthe sergeant or othir', H.

ellez squier for the body, or both, be present euery tym whan the king wull be shaue. This barbour shall haue euery Satyrday at ny3t, if hit please the kinge to clensse his hed, legges, or feete, and for*a* his shauing, ij loues, j picher wyne; and the vssher of chambre owith to testyfye, if*b* this is necessaryly dispended or nou3t.[198] Also this barbour takith his shauyng clothes, basons, and all his other [A, p. 93] toolys,*c* and thinges necessary*c* by the chambrelayn is assignement of the jewelhouse. No feez of plate nor syluer but hit be in this instrumental tooles perused by ocupacion, and that by alowaunce of the kinges chambrelayn.

§48. HENXMEN, VJ ENFAUNTEZ,[199] or mo as hit shall please the king. All thees etyng in the hall and sitting at one bourde togydr, and to be serued ij or iij to a messe as the souerayns apoynt, taking dayly for thyre brekfastes, amonges them all, ij loues, j mess of grete mete, j gallon ale; also for thayre souper in fastyng dayis acording to*d* thayre age; and lyuerey ny3tly*d* for them all to thayre chambre, j lofe, j gallon ale. And for wynter lyuerey, ij candylles wex, iiij candilles perich, iij talwood for them all; russhes and litter all the yere of the sergeaunt vssher of the hall and chambre.*e* And if thes gentylmen, or ony of them, be wardez, then after theyre byrthes and degrees the steward and thesaurere with the chambrelayn may apoynt theyre seruyce more larger in fauoure by theire discressions whan as often as them nedith till the king*f* hath youen or sold ther [A, p. 94] landez and wardez. And all theyre competent harneys to be caryed, and beddinges,*g* ij logged togeder at the kinges caryage by ouersight of the countroller. And eueryche*h* of them an honest seruaunt to kepe theyre chambre and harneys, and to aray him in this court whyles theyre masters be present in court, or ellez to alowe*i* here no chambre dekyns, etc. And all*j* other finding for theyre bodyes*k* they take of the kinges warderober, by sewte of the master of henxmen made to the kinges chambrelayn for warrauntez.

§49. MASTYR OF HENXMEN to show the scoolez of vrbanitie and nourture of Inglond, to lern them to ride clenly and surely, to drawe them also to justes, to lerne hem were theyre harneys; to haue all curtesy in wordez, dedes, and*l* degrees, dilygently to kepe them in rules of goynges and sittinges, after they be of honour. Moreouer, to teche them sondry langages and othyr lernynges vertuous, to

---

a H omits 'for'.
b From H (which has 'if this be necessary dispended or not').
c From H. A and E have 'towellis' and 'necessaries'.
d 'till there age; lyuerey nightly', H.
e 'sergeaunt vsher of the chambre', H.
f 'kinge's grace', E.   *g* 'bedding', H.   *h* 'euery', E.
i 'to haue here', H.
j 'And other fyndyng', E.   *k* 'beddis', H.   *l* 'and in degrees', H.

herping, to pype, sing, daunce, and[a] with other honest and temperate
behauing[b] and pacience; and to kepe dayly and wykely[c] with thees
[A, p. 95] children dew conuenitz, with correcions in theyre chambres
according to suche gentylmen; and eche of them to be vsed to that
thinges[d] of vertue that he shalbe most apt to lerne, with remembraunce dayly of Goddes seruyce accustumed. This maistyr sittith[e]
in the hall next vnto benethe[f] theez henxmen, at the same bourde,
to haue his respectes vnto theyre demenynges, how manerly they
ete and drinke, and to theyre comunicacion and other fourmez
curiall, after the booke of vrbanitie. He takith dayly, if he be present
in court, wagez, clothing,[200] and other lyuerez as other squiers of
houshold, saue he is not charged with seruyng of the hall. Caryage
also for harneys in court, competent by the countroller, to be with
the henxmen is harneys in court.[g] And to haue into this court[h] j
seruaunt, whyles he is present, and sufficyaunt lyuerey for his horsez
in the town or cuntrey by the herbiger. And if he be syke in court,
or lett bloode, he takith ij loues, ij messes of grete mete, j gallon
seruoice; and[i] for the feez that he claymyth amongis the henxmen
of all theyre aparayle, the chambrelayn is juge.

[A, p. 96] §50. SQUYERS OF HOUSOLD, XL,[201] or mo if it please the
king, by the auyse of his counsayll to be chosen men of theyre
possession,[j] worship, and wisdom; also to be of sondry sheres, by
whome hit may be knowe the disposicion of the cuntries.[202] And of
thees to be continually in this court xx squiers attendaunt vppon
the kinges person,[203] in ryding and going at all tymes; and to help
serue his table from the surueying bourde, and from other places
as the assewer woll assigne; also by theyre comon assent to assigne
amonges them self to serue the kinges chambre, at one day, wooke[k]
or tym; som to serue the hall at another tym, of euery messe that
cumyth from the dressing bourde to thayre handez for suche
seruyce, so that thereof be no thing withdrawe by the squiers, vppon
suche payne as steward, thesaurer, or countroller, or in thayre
absence othyr jugez[204] at the countyngbourde, woll awarde after
demeritez. [l]They ete in the hall, sitting togyder at ony of the bothe
meles, as they serue, som the furst mele,[m] some the latter, by assent;

---

[a] E has 'and daunce, with'; H has 'daunce, with'.
[b] 'behauiour', H.   [c] E has 'wekelye'; H has 'weekely'.
[d] From H. A and E have 'thinges'.   [e] 'sitting', H.
[f] This word is cancelled in A, but all three manuscripts have it.
[g] H omits 'in court'.   [h] 'but one seruant', H.   [i] 'as for the fees', H.
[j] 'pocessions', E.   [k] E has 'weke'; H has 'wole'.
[l] In H this sentence comes after the following sentence and ends with the
words 'and ease to them selfe'. None of the three manuscripts has an 'and'
between 'honour' and 'profit'.
[m] 'meate', H.

this hath be alwey the maner amonges them for honour, profite to
the king. Hit may be that the kinge [A, p. 97] takith into houshold
in all lx squiers, and yit amonges them all xx take not the hoole
wages of the yeare*[205] wherefor the numbyr of persons may be
receued and suffred the bettyr in the chekker rolle for a wurshipp, and
the kinges profit saued, and ease vnto them selfes.*[b] Euyryche of
them takith for his lyuerey at ny3t dim. gallon ale; and for wynter
season eche of them takith ij candelles peric, j*[c] faggot or dim. talwood; and whan any of them is present in court, he*[d] is alowed for
dayly wages in the chekker roll, vijd. ob., and clothing wynter and
somer or ellez xls.[206] Hit hath euer byn in speciall charge to squiers
in this court to were the kinges lyuerey custumably,[207] for the more
glory and in worshipp*[e] this honorable houshold. And euery of them
to haue into this court an honest seruaunt, and sufficient lyuerey
in the townes or cuntrey for theyre othyr seruauntes*[f] by the herbiger,
ij gentilmen logged togyder and*[g] they be copled bedfelowes by the
gentylmen vsshers. And if ony of them be let blood or syke in courte
or nyghe*[h] court, he takith lyuerey in etyng dayes, ij loues, ij messes
of grete mete, j gallon ale for all day, and litter all the yere of the
[A, p. 98] sergeaunt vssher of hall for theyre beddes in court. And
if ony of the squiers be sent out of court by steward, thesaurer,
countroller, or othyr of the countynghouse, for mater towching the
houshold, than he hath dayly alowed hym xijd. by peticion. Also
they pay for theyre caryage of harneys in court; they take no part
of the generall yiftes, nothyr with chambre or hall, but if the geuer
geue them specially a part by expresse name or wordez. None of
these shuld depart from courte, but by lycens of steward, thesaurer,
or by*[i] soueraynes of the countynghouse, that know how the king is
acompanyed best; and to take a day whan they shold com ageyn,
vpon payn of loss of wages at his next cumyng, that no sergeaunt
of office nor squyer nor yoman nor grome, but as be apoynted in
this boke, to dyne or*[j] sope out of hall or*[k] kinges chambre, nor do*[l]
withdraw ony seruice, or ellez to hurt or lytell the almesse of hall or
chambre, vppon such payn as the soueraynes of household woll
awarde. By the statutes of noble Edward the iij, in none office etc.,
hit hath byn often in dayis before comaunded by the countynghouse,
that in feriall dayes after that the king and queen and theire chambres

---

*[a] From H. A has 'of there'; E has 'therof'.
*[b] In H this sentence comes before the previous one and does not, as in A
and E, end with the words 'and ease vnto themselves'. E has 'worshipfull'.
*[c] 'j dim. faggot', E.
*[d] From E. A and H have 'hym' and 'him'.   *[e] 'worshipping', H.
*[f] 'for theire horses, and other seruantes', H.   *[g] 'as they be coupled', H.
*[h] E has 'ny3e the courte'; H has 'nighe therto'.   *[i] H omits 'by'.
*[j] From H. A and E have 'to'.   *[k] 'and', H.   *[l] 'to withdrawe', H.

and the soueraynez of houshold in the hall be served that then suche honest yomen of houshold be called or assigned [A, p. 99] to serue from the dressour to the halle the remnaunt, specially such as bere wages, that if seruyse*ᵃ* be withdrawen by them that then they to be corrected therefore. Thes esquiers of houshold of old be acustumed, wynter and somer, in after nonys and in euenynges, to drawe to lordez chambrez within courte, there to kepe honest company aftyr theyre cunyng, in talkyng of cronycles of kinges and of other polycyez, or in pypyng, or harpyng, synging,*ᵇ* other actez marciablez, to help ocupy the court and acompany straungers, tyll the tym require of departing.*ᶜ*

*ᵈ*Domus nona et ultima que hic fundatur*ᵈ* sub tali tali forma;⎫
   viz., vnius armigeri de possessione clare in Anglia, per ⎪ 1 li.
   annum super .... ⎬
Prouideat senescallus siue gubernator cujuscunque domus ⎪
   capiat primam septimaniam per policiam²⁰⁸ in adjutorium ⎪ Si potest
   tocius anni sequentis. ⎭
Et quod habeat de remanenciis, stauri, etc.

Quando incipit*ᵉ*

⎧xviij loues bake in housholde; .... iijd.
 viij gallons mene ale in housholde; .... iiijd.
 sydre to helpe the dayis,*ᶠ* sine precio; in beef dayly and
  moton freysh; .... vd.
 or ellez [A, p. 100] moton dayly bouȝt all powdred is more
*ʰ*Pro dieta   auayle; .... iijd.*ᵍ*
media ad ⎨ Bacon, porkes, velis, venison, pigges, lambes,⎫ Totalium
xxd. Inde   capons, hennes, chekyns, cony, pejons,⎪ dietarum
   egges, milke, chese of iiij kyndes to the⎪ summa
   payle or greete,²⁰⁹ ewen herbage,*ⁱ* on-⎬ anni—
   yonys, garlik, etc., by husbandry and help⎪ xxiiij li.
   of on day with another de stauro.*ʲ* Item,⎪ vjs. viijd.
   for wood, coole, candelles, sawce dayly,⎪
⎩salt, and ote mele .... iijd.⎭

    ᵃ 'if any seruice', *H*.
    ᵇ Also E; H has 'or other actes marcealls'.
    ᶜ In E the next section, of estimated expenditure for a squire's household, is lacking.
    ᵈ From H. A has 'Domus nona qui [*sic*] hic fundatur et vltima'.
    ᵉ In H 'quando incipit' is placed at the end of the previous sentence.
    ᶠ 'sidre to helpe the dayes or mede', *H*.
    ᵍ 'in beefe daily or mutton, fresh or eles all poudred is more availe, vd. Motton dayly bought . . . ijd', *H*
    ʰ 'Pro dietar', ad xxd.—inde', *H*.
    ⁱ 'of fower kyne to the paile, herbage', *H*.
    ʲ H has 'de stauro—vjd.', and does not include the next sentence in this bracket.

In like wise these xxd. in fisshe dayes must be deuyded by husbandry
and help of ryuers and pondez. ᵃItem, to make vergeouse there selfes.ᵃ
Pro camera et. reparacionibus vesture et cum oblacionibus et elemosinis, per annum..iiij li.
Pro necessarijs domus emendis, reparandis, cum expensis forinsecis,ᵇ
etc.—Summa ....c s.
Pro empcione et excambijs equorum, cariagiorum, feni, et aliorum, per
annum estimatur ....iiij li.
Pro vadijs vnius clerici, xls., ij valettorum, iiij li., ᶜduorum garcionum ad
xls.,ᶜ et ij puerorum, xxs., per annum—Summa................ix li.
Pro robis x personarum per annum in liberata—Summa...........ls.
Pro canibus et nisis plus constant quam conferunt—Summa..iijs. iiijd.
Pro feno et auenis de pratisᵈ domini, per annum, et proᵉ falcacione et
imposicione feni et litterij—Summa ....xxs.

Summa hujus domus............l li.

Pro vj honestis personis vacuis et seruientibus absque paruulis et omnibus laborariis infra, j bussellus brassijᶠ boni potest satis respondere ad
xij gallonas communis seruisij, ad valorem fere cuiuslibet gallone...j s.ᵍ

[A, p. 101] §51. KINGES OF ARMEZ, HEROLDEZ, AND PURSEUNTES,
comyng to this royall courte to the wurshupp of thes v festes in the
yere,[210] sitting at metes and soupers in the hall; and to begynne
thatʰ one end of the table togyder vppon dayes of astate, by the
martyalles assignacion,[211] at on mele. And if the king kepe astateⁱ
in the hall, than thez walke before the steward, thesaurer, and
countroller, comyng with the kinges seruyce from the surueying
bourde at euery course; and aftyr the laste course they crye the kinges
largesse, shaking theyre grete cuppe.[212] They take theyre largesse of
the jewelhouse, and during thes festiual days they wayte vppon the
kinges person, cumyng and goyng to and fro the churche, hall, and
chambre before his highnes in theyre cotez of armes. They take
nother wages, clothinges, nor feez by the countynghouse, but
lyuerey for theyre chambre, day and nyȝt, amonges them ij loues,
j picher wyne, ij gallons ale; and for wynter season, if there be present
a king of armes, for them all a tortayis atʲ chaundry ij candelles wex,
iij candelles peris, iij tallwood. Thes kinges of armes ar serued in
the hall as knyȝtes, seruyce and lyuerey, for theyre [A, p. 102]
horsez nyghe the courte by the herbiger; alwey remembred that the

---

ᵃ H omits this sentence.   ᵇ 'forum', H.   ᶜ From H.
ᵈ 'de pratis et campis', H.   ᵉ H omits 'pro'.   ᶠ 'brasilij', H.
ᵍ In A is inserted between pp. 100 and 101 a leaf with a transcript in late
eighteenth-century italic hand of pp. 99 to 100, from 'Domus nona . . .' to
'. . . cuiuslibet gallone, js'.
ʰ All three manuscripts have 'that', unlike the 1790 edition, which has 'at'.
ⁱ A and E here repeat 'by the marcyalles assignacion'; H does not.
ʲ 'and chandrye', E.

cup wiche the king doth create any king of[a] armez or harold withall,
hit stondith in the charge of the jewelhouse, and not vppon the
thesaurer of houshold. The feez that they shall take at the making of Kny3tes of the Bath, hit apperith after the capitle of
squiers.[213]

§52. SERGEAUNTES OF ARMES, IIIJ,[b] [214] chosen prouyd men of
conducion and of honour,[b] for the king and his honorable houshold
whereof ij alwey to be attending vppon the kinges person and
chambre and to auoyde the prees of peple before, where as the king
shall com; in like wise at the conueyaunce of his mete at euery
course fro the surueying bourde. Also obseruing for[c] the kinges
comaundmentes, and so after steward, chambrelayn, thesaurer, and
countroller for the king or for his houshold.[d] They ete[d] in the hall
togeder or with squiers of houshold, taking theyre wages[e] xijd. by
day[215] or iiijd. as hit please [A, p. 103] the king after theyre abyltees,
by lettyrs patentz; and clothing also to be taken of the issue and
profitts growing to the king in diuerse countez of Inglond, by the
handes of the receyuours of them; no more hauyng in houshold but
euerych[f] of them, whan he is present in court, at ny3t j gallon
ale;[216] and for wynter lyuerey, j candell wex, ij candylles peris, j
tallwood; russhes, litter for thaire chambyr of the sergeaunt vssher
all the yere. They pay for caryage of theyre propyr harneys and
bedding, and eche[f] of them to haue into this courte j honest
seruaunt.[216] By the statutes of noble Edward were xxxti sergeauntes
of armez[217] sufficiauntly armed and horsed, rydyng before his
highnes whan he iourneyde by the cuntrey, for a gard corps du roy.
And if ony of thes be lett blood or be sike, he taketh dayly ij loues,
ij messes of mete, j gallon ale, and thus[g] to be breued in the pantry
roll; also sufficiaunt logging assigned thes sergeauntz togyder nat
far from court, for hasty erandez whan[h] they fall.

[A, p. 104] §53. MYNSTRELLES, XIIJ,[218] whereof one is veriger that
directeth them all in festiuall dayes to theyre stacions, to blowinges
and pipinges, to suche offices as must be warned to prepare for the
king and his houshold at metes and soupers, to be the more redy
in all seruyces, and all thies sitting in the hall togyder, whereof sume
vse trumpettes, sume shalmuse and small pipes. And sume are

---

[a] 'or armes', E.

[b] 'chosen proued men, and of hauiour and condition', H; 'chosen prouyd
men of conducion and of honour and conduction', A and E.

[c] 'of the kinges commaundmentes', E.

[d] 'the eating', H.   [e] 'of twelve-pence by day', H.

[f] E has 'euerye' in both cases.

[g] All three manuscripts have 'thus', unlike the 1790 edition, which has
'this'.

[h] H omits 'when'.

strengmen,[a] coming to this courte at v festes of the yere, and than
to make theyre wages of houshold after iiijd. ob. a day[219] if they be
present in court; and than they to auoyde the next day after the
festes be don. Besidez, eche of them anothyr reward, yerely taking
of the king in the resceyte of the chekker, and clothing with the
houshold wynter and somer or xxs. a piece;[220] and lyuerey in court,
at[b] euyn among them all, iiij gallons ale; and for wynter season iij
candelles wex, vj candelles peric, iiij talwood;[c] and sufficiaunt logging
by the herbiger for them and theyre horsez nygh the court. Also
hauyng into court ij seruauntes honest to bare theyre trumpettes,
pipes, and other instrumentes, and a torche for wynter ny3ts, whyles
they blow to soupers and other reuills,[d] delyuered at chaundry. And
allwey ij of thes [A, p. 105] persons to continue in court in wages
beyng present to warn at the kinges ridinges whan he goith to
horsbak, as oft as hit shall require, and by theyre blowinges the
houshold many[e] may folow in to[f] the contrez. And if ony of thes ij
minstrelles be sicke in court, he takith ij loues, j messe of grete mete,
j gallon ale. They haue no[g] part of ony rewardes geuyn to the houshold. And if hit please the king to haue ij streng[h] minstrelles, to
contynue in[i] like wise. The king woll[j] not, for his worshipp, that his
minstrelles be too presumptuouse nor to familier to aske any rewardes
of the lordes of his lond; remembring de Henrico secundo impera-
tore,[221] qui omnes juculatores suos et minstreles[k] monuit vt nullus
eorum in eius nomine vel dummodo steterunt in seruicio suo, nichil ab
aliquo in regno suo deberent petere donandum; set quod ipsi domini
vel donatores pro regis amore sitius [l]pauperibus erogarent.[l]

[A, p. 106] §54. A WAYTE,[222] that ny3tly, from Mighelmasse til
Shere Thursday, pipeth the wache within this court iiij tymes, and in
the somer ny3ghtes [sic] iij tymes; and he to make bon gayte, and
euery chambre dore and office, as well for fyre as for other pikers or
perelliz. He etith in the hall with the minstrelles and takith lyuerey
at ny3t, dim. payn, dim. gallon ale; and for somer ny3tes, ij candylles
peris, dim. bushell coolez. [l]And for winter nightes halfe a loafe,
dimid. gallon ale, fower candles peris, dimid. busshel coles.[m] And
dayly, if he be present in court, by the chekker roll, iiijd. ob. or iijd.,
by the discression of steward and thesaurer and aftyr the coning

---

   [a] All three manuscripts read thus, unlike the 1790 edition, which has 'and
sume as strengemen'.
   [b] 'and euen', H.   [c] 'tallowe', H.
   [d] From H. A and E omit 'reuills'.   [e] E has 'meny'; H has 'men'.
   [f] H omits 'to'.   [g] E omits 'no'.   [h] 'strange', E.
   [i] E omits 'in'.   [j] 'would', H.
   [k] E has 'a'nnes'; H has arnnos'.
   [l] From H. A and E omit these two words.
   [m] This sentence is taken from H. A and E omit it.

that he can and good deseruyng; also clothing with the houshold yomen or minstrelles,[a] according to the wages that he takith. And if he be syke or lette blood, he takith ij loues, j messe of greete mete, j gallon ale; also he partith with the generall giftes of houshold, and hath his bedding caryed, and his gromes togeder, by the countroller's assignement. And vnder this yoman a GROME[b] wayte; if he can excuse the yoman in his office and absence, than he takith reward,[c] clothing, mete[d] rewardes, and other thinges like to the other gromez of houshold. Also this yoman waytith at the makinges of Knyghtes of the Bath,[223] waching by ny3tes tym vpon them in the chapell; wherefore he hath of fee all the [A, p. 107] waching clothinge that the knyghtes shulde[e] were vppon.

§55. MESSAGERS, IIIJ,[224] attending to this courte for the king, obeying the comaundmentes of the chambrelayn for the messagez concernyng[f] the king, or secretary,[f] or vssher of chambre; also the steward and thesaurer for the honour and profit of houshold, if hit require. Thes sitt togeder in the hall at theyre meles; and whyles they be present in court, eueryche[g] of them takith by the chekker roll iijd., and[h] euery man for his clothing, wynter and somer, yerely j marc, and eche[i] for his chauncez iiijs. viijd. And as oftyn as ony of thes be sente in message by the chambreleyn or secretary, than he takith his wages of the jewelhouse; [j]and if he be sent by the heedes of the countynghouse,[j] than he takith out of court, wagez and all, vd. be day, as other yomen of houshold. And if ony of them be sike in court, he takith j loffe, j mess of greete mete, dim. gallon ale; and ij of thes haue in the court one clene[k] childe and logging for there horsez nyghe to [A, p. 108] the courte. They haue part of the yeftes geuyn to the houshold, if they or ony of them be present when hit is geuen, but none aprons.[225] None of thes to depart from court but be leue of steward, chambyrlayn, thesaurer. In the noble Edwardes houshold there[l] were xij messagers,[224] wich were minnisshed[m] by the avoydance[n] of priue seale from houshold.

§56. DEANE OF CHAPELL.[226] Hit is but an office geuen withous presentacion or confyrmacion of ony bisshop, [o]called the kinges chyef chapleyn aftyr the confessoure,[o] sitting in the hall and serued like to a baron seruise, and begynnyng the chappell bourde; hauing in the court a chapleyn vnder hym wyche he may assign to be by hys power confessour of the houshold, also j gentylman, bothe etyng

[a] 'as minstrell', H.   [b] A repeats 'grome'.
[c] All three manuscripts have 'reward'.   [d] 'meere rewardes', H.
[e] 'do', H.   [f] 'secretaries', H.   [g] 'euerey', E.
[h] 'to euery', H.   [i] 'eueryche', H.   [j] E omits this passage.
[k] 'cleanely', H.   [l] From H. A and E have 'thus'.
[m] 'munished', H.   [n] From H. A and E have 'habundaunce'.
[o] In H this clause comes immediately after 'Deane of Chapell'.

K

in the hall. He takith also lyuerey to his chambre, for all day and ny3t, iij loues, ij messe of grete mete, dim. picher wyne, ij gallons ale; and for wynter season, j torche, j percher, ij candelles wex, iij candilles peric, iij talwood; litter and russhes all the yere of the sergeaunt vssher of the hall and [A, p. 109] chambre, and the dewtes of the kinges oblacions as hit is expressed before in title of the kinges offeringes.[227] Item, he hath all the offeringes of wex that is made in the kinges chapell on Candylmasse-day, with the moderate feez of the beame in the festes of the yere whan the tapers be consumed into a shaftmount, by ouersight of the countroller. Also the deane assigneth all the sermonz and the personz. He takith yerely clothing with houshold for wynter and somer, or[a] money at the countyng-house viij marcs,[228] and cariage for his compotent beddyng and harnes in the office[b] of vestyary, by the vewe of the countroller; hauyng also in this court iiij honeste persons; and whan hymself is out of court his yoman[c] [229] shall ete in the hall at the chambrelaynez bourde. Also he to haue assigned logging sufficiaunt for his horsez and the remnaunt of his seruauntes bourde at his lyuerey, and other chapleyn's men oute of court togeder if they woll. This deane hath of fee all the white swordes[230] that the Knyztes of the Bath offer vpp[d] to God in the kinges chapell. Also this deane is curate and confessoure of all this houshold. 'Ex consuetudine hujus curie regalis singuli ministri ac eciam inhabitantes quatuor anni festis [A, p. 110] solennibus ad certas oblaciones e jure tenentur; ipsarum tamen quantitas ac species apud singulos voluntarie consistunt, eciam mortuaria quam tociens apud decanum sunt reperta. Omnes enim laici de suis patrimonialibus in eisdem diocessibus quibus sua possident dominia decimarum tenentur; verum tamen in domo ista regia nullus episcopus quicquam habet juris, nisi sibi committatur; rex enim patronus est et regimen sue capelle eciam hospitalis et spiritualis cure cujuscunque presbitero ydoneo immediate potest committere.' [230]

This deane was determyned by kyng Herry the V for euer to be a bachelor of diuinitie or a doctour, because of the apposile that was made vppon zyma vetus, etc. He hath all corrections of chapellmen *in moribus et sciencia*, reserued some causes to the steward and countynghouse.[231] Nothyr this deane nor other of this chapell at no tym part not with the houshold of any generall gyftes, except the office of vestyary. The dean makithe the sad rules of the personez, clerkes, and all theyre ceremoniez in this chapell; he assignethe the subdean and the chaunters to guyde, kepe, and to rule all the quere in stedfast seruice and honorable demeanyng, to ouersee theyre

---

[a] 'in money', H.

[b] 'offices', H.

[c] H omits 'yoman'.

[d] H omits 'vpp'.

seruice [A, p. 111] and songes. He assignethe also the order howe euery preest and clerke shall take his rome after othir; hym owith euery Friday to kepe a conuenite with them all, and there to reherse the fautez, and to appoynt the remediez; and suche as be defectif or disobedient, the deane or his deputie to send to the*a* countynghouse to putt hym out of wages as ofte as hym thinkith nedefull.*b*

§57. CHAPLEYNS AND CLERKES OF CHAPELL, XXVJ,[232] by the kinges choyce or by the dean is eleccion or denominacion, of men of worship endowed with vertuouse, morall and speculatiff, as of theyre musike, shewing in descant[233] clene voysed, well relysed and pronouncyng, eloquent in reding, sufficiaunt in organez playyng, and modestiall in other maner of behauing. All thies sitting togyder in the hall at the deanes bourde, and loggyng togyder within the court in one chambre, or nyghe therto, because of lyuerez:[234] and whyles [A, p. 112] they be in court, euerych hathe dayly alowed in the chekker roll, vijd. ob., if the dean or vnder-dean complayn not in lacking of his seruyce withdrawen in this*c* chapell. And euerych of them for wynter and somer clothing of the grette warderobe of houshold, xls.;[235] and lyuerey to theyr chambre at ny3t, amonges them all ij loues, j picher wyne, vj gallons ale; and for wynter lyuerey, from All Halowen-tyde tyll Estyr, amonges them all ij candelles wex, xij candelles peris, viij tallwood.*d* The houshold partith not of no yiftes that is yeuen to the chapell; they pay for theyr own cariage of bedding and other harneys; they haue all the yere litter and russhes for theyre chambres of the sergeaunt vssher of the hall and*e* chambre. And euery chapleyn hath unto this court whyles he is present j honest seruaunt;[236] and for euery gentylmen clerkes into this court j honest seruaunt, and lyuerey sufficiaunt for theyre horsez and for theyre othyr seruauntes in the towne or nye. The kinges grace auauncith thes preestes and clerkes by prebendes, churches of his patrymony, or by his lettres recomendatory, free chapelles, hospitalles, or pensions.[237] Also Oure Lady massepreest and the gospeler are assigned by the deane; and if the king be present whan he redithe the passion on Palme Sonday, hit [A, p. 113] hath be acustomed the gospeler to be serued with a lamprey. *f*Also, *g*if ony of these people be seke or lett blood, that

---

a 'their', *H*.

b H has in addition: 'And then the styward is warnyd wher the king liketh to keepe his Christenmasse', with the marginal note: 'These words had a line drawne through them, as if they had bin to be rased out.'

c 'the', *H*.   *d* 'tallow', *H*.

e From H. A has 'or chambre'. E ends the sentence with 'hall' and has 'rushes and lytter' instead of 'litter and russhes'.

f This section has been moved to the place it occupies in H; in A and E it comes at the end of the section on 'Chaplains and clerks'.

g 'and', *H*.

than he withdraw in to the town, taking dayly ij loues, j messe of
grete mete, j messe of roste, j gallon ale. And whan the chapell syng
matyns ouer nyght, called blanke matyns, or ellez solempne dyrygez
for the kinges fader or moder, than is there alowed to them comfettes
and wyne. The statutes of noble Edward the iijd. apoynted the
numbyr of vj. cunnyng preestes, tyll they were auaunced, to take
vijd. ob., and all other gentylmen clerkes singers iiijd. ob. by day.[f] [238]

MEMORANDUM that the king hath[a] a song before hym in his hall
or chambre vppon All Halowen-day at the later graces, by some of
thes clerkes and children of chapell, in remembraunce of Cristmasse,
and so of men and children in Cristmasse thorowoute; but after the
song on All Halowen-day is don, the steward and thesaurer of houshold shall be warned where hit likith the king to kepe his Cristmasse.

[A, p. 114] §58. YOMEN OF CHAPELL, IJ, called pistelers, growing
from the children of chapell by succession of age, and after that
theire voicez chaunge; and yit that by the deane is denominacion
and for thaire connyng and vertu. Thes ij yomen etyn in the hall at
the chapell bourd,[239] taking dayly in court of wages and clothing,
lyke in court by the chekkyr roll, iijd. And clothing as the household
doth, playne and no party, or ellez eche of them be way of reward,
alowed by petycion, yerely[b] liijs. iiijd., by the discrecion[c] of steward
and thesaurer and deane; and cariage for thaire competent bedding
with the caryage of chapell.

§59. CHILDREN OF CHAPELL, VIIJ,[240] founden by the kinges jewelhouse for all thinges that belongith to thayre apparayle, by the
hondez or ouersight of the deane, or by the mastyr of song[241] assigned
to teche them. Wich maister is apoynted by the seyd dean and
chosen one of the numbyr of the seyd felyshipp of chapell; and he to
draw thees chyldren all as well in the scoole of facet as in song,
organes, or [A, p. 115] suche other vertuouse thinges.[d] Thees children
etyn in the hall dayly at the chapell bourde next the yomen of
vestyary; takynge[e] amonges them in lyuerey for all day, brekefastes
and nyȝt, ij loues, j messe of grete mete, ij gallons ale; and for
wynter season, iiij candelles peric, iij talwood; and litter for theyre
beddes of the sergeaunt vssher. And cariage at the kinges cost for
theyre compotent bedding be ouersight of the countroller; and
amonges them all to haue one seruaunt into this court to trusse and
bere theyre harneys and to fett theire liuereys[f] in court.[242] And
suche dayis as the kinges chapell remouith, euery of thes children
than present receuith iiijd. at the grene feald[g] of the countyng house,

---

[a] 'haue', H.
[b] From H. A and E have 'yere'.
[c] 'direccion', E.
[d] H omits 'thinges'.
[e] From H. A and E have 'takinges'.
[f] From H. A and E have 'harneys'.
[g] E has 'seale'; H has 'feld'.

for horse hyre dayly as long as they be iournaying. And whan ony of thos children be sike, they take lyuerey as with the syke yomen of houshold. Also when they be growen to the age of xviij yeres, and than theyre voyces be chaunged, ne can nat be preferred in this chapell nor within this court, the numbyr beyng full, then, if they wull assent, the king assigneth euery suche child to a college of Oxenford or Cambridge, of the kinges fundacion, there to be in [A, p. 116] finding and study sufficiauntly tyll the king otherwise list to avaunce hym.[a]

§60. CLERK OF CLOSETTE[243] kepith the stuf of the closet. He preparith all things for the stuf of the aultrez to be redy, and taking[b] vpp the trauers, [c]leyyng the cuysshyns[c] [d]and carpettes; and he settith[e] all other thinges[d] necessary for the king and the[f] chapleyns. [g]There he helpith the chapleyns[g] to sey masse; and if this clerk lose torche, taper, morter of wex, or such other, growing of the thesaurer of houshold is charge in ony part, than he to awnswer therefore as the steward, thesaurer, countroller, or the jugez vnder them at the grene cloth wull[h] award by reason. Also this clerk etith in the hall with the sergeaunt of the vestyary by the chapell gentylmen, and takith for his lyuerey at ny3t dim. gallon ale; and for wynter lyuerey ij candelles peris, dim. talwood; russhes for the closett and litter for his bed of sergeaunt vssher; and dayly for his wages in court by the chekker roll iiijd. ob., and clothing for wynter and somer [A, p. 117] with the houshold or ellez xxs. And at eueryche[i] of the iiij festes in the yere shall take of the greete spycery a towell of work conteynyng iiij ellez for the kinges houssellyng,[j] and that towell so onys ocupyed is fee to this clerk; but he partith not with the yeftes of houshold. And if he be sike in court, he takith ij loues, j messe of grete mete, j gallon ale, and lyuerey by the herbiger for his horse. He hathe one honest servaunt into this court to help hym, etc. and for his caryage of this closett ys[k] assigned a sompter horse, j sompter man, founden by the thesaurer his charge of houshold by ouersight of the countroller. The chambrelayne is this clerkes auditor and opposer; and[l] this clerk warnyth suche chapleyns as likith the king or the chambrelayne to attend to do seruice any day or wyke to the king.

[A, p. 118] §61. MASTYR OF GRAMER;[244] 'quem necessarium est in

---

[a] 'theym', E.   [b] 'takith', H.   [c] 'beyng kushoyns', H.
[d] The 1790 edition omits this passage.
[e] E has 'fettithe'; H has 'settith'.
[f] 'his', H.
[g] Both E and H omit this passage.   [h] 'would', H.   [i] 'everye', E.
[j] From H. A and E have 'of the kinges household'.
[k] From H. A and E have 'j'.
[l] H omits 'and'.

poetica*a* atque in regulis positionis gramatice expeditum fore quibus
audientium animos cum diligentia instruet ac informet'; scilicet, the
kinges henxmen, the children of chapell, after they can theyre
descant, the clerks of the awmery, and othyr men, and*b* children of
court disposed to lern in this science, if they be of ordinate*c* maistyrs
within this court. Wiche maistyr of gramer among, if he be a preest,
must syng Our Lady messe in the kinges chapell, or elles amonge
to rede the gospell at the hygh masse, and to be at the greete processions. And this to be by the dean is assignacion, taking his mete
in the hall, sitting with the sergeaunt of vestyary and clerk of closett,
and lyuerey at ny3t dim. gallon ale; and for wynter lyuerey j candell
peric, dim. tallwood, or ellez j fagott; and for his dayly wages in
court, by the chekker roll whyles he is present iiijd. ob., or ellez
reward of*d* v marcz by discression. And clothing with the houshold
wynter and somer, or xxs., caryage for his competent bed and bokes
with the children of chapell by countroller; nor parting with no giftes
of houshold, but abyding the kinges auauncement after his
demerites; and lyuerey assigned [A, p. 119] for his horse by the kinges
herbiger; and to haue into this court with him one honest seruiture.*e*

§62. OFFICE OF VESTYARY hathe in hym a sergeaunt,[245] preest or
layman as the king, by the dean is auise, seemethe best according, for
to ward saufely and ouersee all suche sacred stuf of Holy Churche,
and other richesse longing to the chappell and vestyary. The stuf
of this office is taken by indenture of euery parcell, and twey tymez
in the yere vewed and dewly examynyd by the kinges chambrelayn
and dean for the tym being; and making the chaungez of the awlter
clothes and vestymentes in sewtes and colours as the sayntes and
festes require, with all other ornamentes accordauntes, whereof the
purueaunce lyeth in charge to the kinges warderobe and to his jewelhouse. And the auditte and viewes of all this stuff longith to [A, p.
120] the chambrelayne and dean, as hit is abouesayd, except for
synging—bred, wyne, holy-bred euery Sonday a chiet lofe, waysshing
of surplyse of all the chapell, incense, torches, taperis, morters, and
small candelles of wex, and the lynnen cloth for the sepulcre and
font; wich lynen cloth of the sepulcre is aftyrward fee to this
sergeaunt, and this apperteynith to the charge of thesaurer of houshold. Also this*f* sergeaunt wages out of court in shewing for his office
of vestyary, by record of countroller, hath ben vsed to be alowed
in the countynghouse after viijd. a day, as them think reasonable;*g*
hit semeth more according to haue his wages out of jewelhouse,

---

a 'postria', E.   *b* From H. A and E omit 'and'.
c 'ordinately maist', H.   *d* 'or', E.
e E has 'seruaunt'; H has 'seruitour'.   *f* 'the', E.
g From E. A and H have 'reason'.

because he shewith by the*a* chambrelaynes warraunt. The*b* sergeaunt of this office etith in the hall and takith lyuerey for his chaumbre at ny3t dim. gallon ale; and for wynter lyuerey j candell wex, j candell peric, dim. talwood, and lyuerey for all this office nyghtly in wynter season, j candell wex, ij candelles peric, j talwood*c* dim. And for his dayly wages by the chekker roll whyles he is present in court, iiijd. ob., and clothing with the chapell wynter and somer, or xxs.²⁴⁶ of the [A, p. 121] countynghouse. Russhes and litter for chapell and vestyary all the yere of the sergeaunt vssher; and at euery of the iiij festes in the yere, naprons of the grete spycery, ij ellez of lynen cloth, price ijs. And hauing into this court j honest seruaunt, and lyuerey for his horses; and for the officers of this office sufficiauntly*d* by the herbiger, and cariage for his competent bed by the ouersight of the countroller. ONE YOMAN, OR IJ,²⁴⁷ as the steward and thesaurer think nedeful, eting with the sergeaunt in the hall at chapell bourde, proued trewe men and diligent to kepe this office and grete richesse with the sergeaunt, excusing all that longith to the aparayle of this office as the dean and sergeaunt woll assigne them for the king. Taking for theyre dayly wages by the chekker roll euery yoman iijd.²⁴⁸ in court; and for thayre wages dayly*e* out of courte in the seruise of this office, vd. by recorde of the countynghouse. And clothing with the houshold wynter and somer and chauncez, or ellez xviijs.²⁴⁸ a piece, and the lynen cloth about the font, being fee to this [A, p. 122] yoman; they take naprons also at euerych of the iiij festes, j yoman j elle clothe, price viijd., and cariage for*f* theyre competent bedyng by the countroller. And allwey ij*g* yomen of houshold to haue one honest child whiles they be present in court. O GROME²⁴⁹ to kepe and to attend vppon this office dylygently, helping to dresse the chapell, kersse sure and trusse*h* the stuff, wayting on the caryage, fetting*i* in the lyuereys, trew prouyde and obedyent to the sergeaunt and yoman, as for the king. And this officer sitting in the hall beneth the yoman of this office at the chappell bourde, or by the children of chapell, taking his rewardes like the gromes of houshold. And if ony grome be sent out by the power of the countynghouse, than he takith for expenses dayly iijd. after the old custume; and hit be by the jewelhouse, hit is allowed more largely. Also caryage of harnes competent for all the gromez, by the king by countrollement.

[A, p. 123] §63. CLERKE OF CROUNE,²⁵⁰ of the kinges chauncery, receuith the old commissions, made for the purueyaunces of the kinges houshold,²⁵¹ the date being expyred at euery half yere; and

---

a 'that', *H.*   *b* 'One', *H.*   *c* 'tallow', *H.*   *d* 'suffisaunt nye', *H.*
e H places 'dayly' after 'office'.   *f* 'of', *H.*   *g* 'they yomen', *H.*
h 'keepe, sewe, and trusse', *H.*   *i* 'setting', *H.*

so to make newe as the thesaurer of houshold dothe endose the sayd comissions, or ellez by other newe billes of warrauntes vnder this seale, as often as hit shall require by the seyd thesaurer so to be examined. Wherefor this seyd clerk takith a yerely reward in the countynghouse of xls.,[251] remembred alwey that he take nothing ellez for his writinges, ne for the kinges seale of the seid purueours.

§64. CLERKE OF MARKETTE[252] is ordeyned to attend vppon this honourable houshold, callid the kinges presence.[a] [253] He makith examinacion in citeez, boroughez, townez, and fraunchisez, within and withoute, of the assisez of bred, wyne, ale, and the assisez of all maner mesurez, elles, yerdes, and weyghtes [A, p. 124] and the prisez of all maner of greynys; and also of other excessiff wynnynges by vytayle or other stuf of marchaundise that be vsed 'infra virgam curie seu regie presencie proprie'. This clerk shall punissh all suche trespassours and disobedientes that thus[b] mysseuse of sisez, ageynst the old statutez or new of Inglond and agaynst the kinges proclamacions.[254] Rex Johannes fecit acclamari vt legalis assisa panis inuiolabiliter sub pena colistriagiali obserueretur per superuisionem hujus clerici. Et eciam in omnibus franchesijs; et tunc probatur ita[c] quod pistor poterit sic vendere vt sequitur et lucrari tres denarios, exceptis brennio et duobus panibus ad furnarium, et iiij seruientibus suis iiij obulos, et duobuz garcionibus vnum quadrantem, et pro sale obulum, et candelis quadrantem, et pro bosco tres denarios, et in buletello[d] obulum; quando quarterium frumenti venditur pro vj solidis, tunc panis albus de quadrante bene coctus xvj solidos de viginti lora. Et panis de tot blado debet esse bonus et bene coctus, ita quod nihil subtrahatur et ponderabit viginti quatuor solidos; et sic descende per omnes quarterios vsque ad quarterium frumenti benedicti,[e] precij xviijd., [A, p. 125] vt patet in cronica regis Johannis, fratris regis Ricardi.[255] Also the clerk ridith in the contries before the kinges commyng to warn the peple to bake, to brewe, and to make redy[f] othyr vytayle and stuff in to theire logginges. Also in euery goode market town, as hit shall seme hit most expedyent, he may charge xij the saddest men of dwellers to preyse the greynys and to sesse the prises of bred, wyne, ale, mannes mete, and horsmete, and othyr stuf, by theyre othis, for the king and his houshold. And than this clerk sendith this presentment vnder the seale of his office into the countynghouse, and that[g] seale to be broken vpp by suche as for that tym haue more rule at the grene cloth; there to[h] also the peple of the court may resort for to knowe

---

[a] 'presentes', E.   [b] 'this', H.   [c] From H. A and E have 'ista'.
[d] 'bubatello', H.   [e] H omits 'benedicti'.
[f] From H. A and E omit 'redy'.
[g] E omits 'that'.   [h] 'wherto', H.

the prisez aftyr wich the kinge and his housholde dothe alowe and pay to the countrey. This clerk serchith also of the good rulez and of riottes that ben vsed[a] in the cuntrey by the soiournauntes of all the housholde and hit reportith to the steward [A, p. 126] and thesaurere of houshold. By the statutes of noble Edward the iijd. this officer had more businesse in the marshalcye and also in this houshold, but now he is acomptaunt in the kinges escheker of all his issuez.[256] Hit may accord well that this chief clerke of market be a squyer of this houshold[257] as hit pleasith the soueraynes; and than to take lyuerey in euery[b] as an housholde squier; elles he takith no thing in this court as of lyuerey but by warraunt, but after the guyse of marchalcye, whan they com at festes. The steward of houshold most specially owith to haue herknyng vpon this clerkes demeanyng in the contriez for oppressions or othyr extorcions, iniury, or wronges don to the kinges peple.

[A, p. 127] §65. CLERKIS OF WORKES, called by the noble Edward 'clerk dez eouers[c] du roy, pregnaunt sa gagez, feez, et l'autre choisez appurtenauntez a son office par l'assignement du thesaurer d'Angleterre de hors le charge de l'oistiel du roy'.[258] This clerk hath no duetie longing to hym in this houshold by vertue of this office outward; but if he be apoynted by the soueraynes of houshold to take wages and clothing with the houshold, hit mought cause hym to be the more attendaunt for necessary byldinges in offices in this house;[259] and so he may take lyuerey as a squier of houshold.

§66. AT THE WARDES MARYAGEZ that growyn to the kinge by right or by fauour. Suche take wagez or rewardez of the kinges pryue cofyrs or jewelhouse, and all theyre other necessaryes for theyre bodyes of the kinges warderobe after theyre astate or degrez; but allwey lyuerez of mete and drinke and other by the thesaurer of houshold tyll they be accepted to theyre londez or ellez sold by the king.[260]

[A, p. 128] Blank, except for a late eighteenth-century transcript of the contents of p. 129.

[A, p. 129] §67. [d]DOMUS PROUIDENCIE in qua quecumque multa requiruntur ad vnum necesse est vnum eorum principale, ad quod omnia alia ordinantur. Vnde et in quolibet toto necesse est vnam partem formalem et predominantem, a qua totum vnitatem habet; et secundum hoc prouidentia est principalior inter omnes partes prudencie; quia omnia alia que requiruntur ad prouidenciam ad necessaria sunt, vt aliquid recte ordinetur in finem. Et ideo nomen ipsius prudencie sumitur a prouidencia sicut a principaliori sua parte non speculatorie sed et in practicis. Dicitur itaque prouidencia, id

---

[a] 'made', E.   [b] 'every thinge', H.
[c] E has 'ouerers'; H has 'covers'.   [d] E omits this paragraph.

est, procul videns, et est ipsa diuina racio in summo omni principe constituta que cuncta disponit. Ac eciam prouidencia est cura et solicitudo circa licita cum policia presentis vite admixta et specialiter ad justum, que sunt necessaria esse procuranda in futurum, propter imminentem famem vel scitim*a* vel frigus. Non ergo improbat deus si quis humano more ista temporalia procuret sibi et alijs, sed si quis propter ista non deo militet: vnde Philosophus, 'Prouidencia ad finem caritatis ordinata est commendanda, nisi sit superflua; tunc non est ibi virtus quia secundum virtutem omnia fiunt recte, id est, secundum quod oportet'.²⁶¹

[A, p. 130] Blank.*b*

[A, p. 131] §68. STEWARD OF HOUSOLDE receyuith his charge of the kinges highnes and propyr person, and the staff of housold, by thes wordes folowing: 'Senesshall tenez la baton du nostre hostiel', by the wich he is also forthwith steward*c* of the hoole court of *d*marchalcye,²⁶² that is, the court of*d* housould, in wich he is juge of lyf and lym; and except thoez causez, the thesaurer, countroller, cofyrrer, ij clerkes of the greene cloth, and the chief clerk of countrolment, for ony maters ellez don with in the housould or apertaynyng thereto; they sitt with hym at the bourd of dome within the housould, that is, at the grene cloth in the countyng house as recorders and witnessers to the trouth. The secundary astate and rule vnder the king of all the excellent housould is holy comitted to be ruled and guyded by his reson, and his comaundmentes principally to be obeyed and obserued for the king.²⁶³ Also with in this housould, except in the kinges chambre, all wey in his seruises to be serued couered²⁶⁴ out of the kinges presence only, what grete astate ellez that be present; as for his cupe, cupbourde, and disshes with doubell seruise,²⁶⁵ but none assaye. *e*Item, he hath the office to call the names of [A, p. 132] knyȝtes, cytezens, and burgesses at the parliament door the furst day of comencement, and to amerce*f* suche

---

a 'sitim', *H.*

b H here has a pen-and-ink sketch of the 'Domus Prouidentie', which is reproduced in the plate facing this page. The figures of Ratio, Circumspectio, Discretio, Intellectus, Prouidentia, Deliberatio, Concordantia, are seated round a table with a roll of parchment, pen and ink, and coins on it. Surrounding this group are scrolls bearing the words: 'Seneschallus dicitur rector sub rege, imperans servientibus, dux excercitus, praepositus domus regiae, gubernator officiariorum, custos formae et bonae regulae complens officia domestica': and the steward stands in a doorway on the right-hand side, bearing his staff of office. In the top left-hand corner are the words: 'Ista pictura reperitur in dicto Libro Nigro, cum omnibus scriptiunculis, ita vti heic exprimuntur circumfusis.'

c 'by which forthwith hee is allsoe styward, *H.*   *d* E omits these words.

e This passage is in H given in the margin with the explanation 'All this is to bee added, and was part of the booke'.   *f* 'ouerse', *E.*

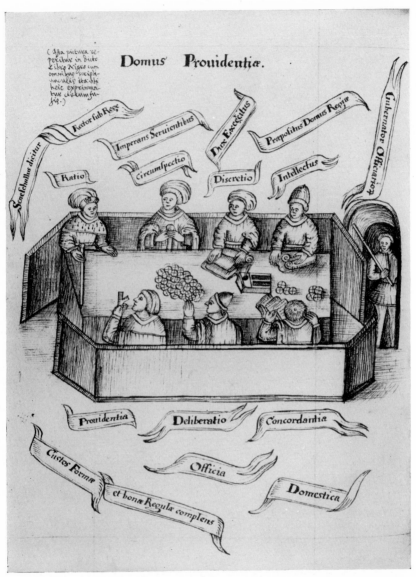

PLATE II. DOMUS PROVIDENCIE

as fayle by the certificate.[266] Also, he may licence suche as wold
depart as hym thinkith pleasing to the king. Item, he with the
thesaurer and countroller shall, vpon All Halowen-day, whedder the
king kepe [a]hall or chambre,[a] shewe the king iij names of the able
places,[b] where[c] of the king shall name one to purpose to abyde at
his Cristmas, hereof the officers to haue knowledge.[d] Also, whiles he
is present in court, there owith no newe comaundmentes nor chargez
of officer or ony other person be made with out the comaundment
furst of his mouthe. Also, in all the houshold rulez and jugementes
he representith the kinges astate; his staff is taken as for[e] comission.[267] Also, he may in this courte[f] adnulle ony custome nat medled
with wurshipp and profit, but chaunge hit and edyfye anewe suche
as shal seme his wisdom by the auyce and counsayle takyn at the
countyngbourde for the better, and to the king and his houshold
of more honour and profit. And for that he is hed officer, he geuithe
ensaumple to all other to be of good gouernaunce [A, p. 133] with
an ordinat rule to be contented with moderat costagez within this
court,[268] in lyuerez, seruices, taking diuerse metes and soupers,[g] in
the hall most specially, or in his chambre, or in ony other office, as
often as hit pleasith hym to serche and see the good sad rules, and
the dirreccions of officers in them. He hath dayly in the hall etyng
j chapleyn, ij esquiers, iiij yomen;[269] and to his chambre dayly for
his brekefast and his chambrelayn is mete and souper and lyuerey
for all ny3t, viij loues, iiij messe of greete mete, ij rewardes of roste,
ij pichers wyne, and [h]vj gallons ale in potts of siluer for the liuerye.[h]
And from All Halowen-tide till Estyr, j torche to attend vppon hym
self, j tortays to fett[i] his lyuerey by[j]—basyn, ewer, and towell,[270]
iij perchers wex, vj candelles wax, viij peris, viij talwood,[k] iiij
fagottes; litter and russhes all the yere of the sergeaunt vssher of
the hall; and after wynter season iiij shidez, ij fagottes. And whan
hym likith to haue more largely in ony thing, than his keper of
his chambre doth fett[i] hit and make thereof a record by tayle or
bill in the countynghouse for his fee at Estyr and Mighelmas, xx
marcez;[271] and for his robes for wynter and somer, at the festes of
Cristmasse and Whitsontide, [A, p. 134] xvj marcez;[271] and for his
napery at the iiij principall festes of the yere, by euen porcions, in

---

[a] H omits these words.   [b] 'hoomes', H.
[c] From H. A has 'whethyr of'; E has 'wherof'.
[d] This passage is in H given in the margin with the explanation 'All this is
to bee added, and was part of the booke'.   [e] E omits 'for'.
[f] 'courte of household', H.   [g] 'diuers mealijs and suppers', H.
[h] From H. A and E have 'pottes of siluer for his lyuerey, vj gallons ale'.
[i] 'sett', H.
[j] From H. A and E have 'to fett his lyuerey—basyn, ewer, and towell—by'.
[k] 'tallow', H.

prisez of lynyn clothe in the greet spycery, or in mony therefore by
a bill in the countynghous, Summa xiij li. xvjd. Item, he hathe a
yoman of his chambre stylle abydyng in court to kepe his chambre
and stuff; and he purueyith *for his lyuerey of hey and otes in the
cuntrey* ageynst his master or lordes comyng. *His yoman takyth to
his chambre dayly in court j cast of brede, ij messe of greete mete
for none and nyght, j gallon ale whyles his master is absent. The
steward, and thesaurer in hys absens, within this court* represent
vnto the astate of an erle; he hathe in to thys court x personez.[272]
'Ecclesiasticus—Qualis est rector domus, talis in ea habitantes.[273]
Idem Ecclesiasticus—Noli esse sicut leo in domo tua.'[274] And if this*
steward be but a squier[275] he wereth his robis of the same* shappe,
but hit is another furre of coloure. This steward, thesaurer, or countroller, of verry duetee, one of them or all, oweth to be at the
dayly accomptes to here the complayntes of* offences of court and
to correct them or pease them as hit accordith by dew examination.
Hy* owith to haue the propyrties* of all these names that be
ascryued vnto hym, in rewardyng of officers [A, p. 135] for there
well doing and as* in punicion for theyre offences; and that streytly,*
for more or lesse, by his dyscression, that pees may be kept in court,
and with manasing or thretynges outward,* specyally amonxt
officers.[276]

§69. THESAURERE OF HOUSHOLDE, wyche takith his charges
before the kynges hyghnes or hys counsayle of lordes, as hys othe,
hereafter writon, doth declare. He is the secund astate next the
steward in this honorable court, and in this* steward is absence, bothe
in the hall, in his own chambre, as in othyr offices, the kinges
chambre excepted, he hathe be vsed to be couerd, cupbourde, cuppe,
and other with double seruisez, thouȝe the old seying be that non of
them both shuld be couered out of the kinges hall, for there they
represent the greete astate opynly; vnto whom also all officers of
court shalbe obedyent and seruizable as for the kinges part and the
honour of this his* royall court. He doth bothe correcions in this
court and gyfe pardons with the [A, p. 136] steward. Also the grete
charge of polycy and husbandry of all this houshold growyth and
stondyth most party by hys sad and dylygent purueyaunce and

---

a Also E and H; unlike the 1790 edition, which omits this passage.
b 'This', *H.*   *c* 'housold', *H.*   *d* 'the', *H.*
e E omits 'same'.
f From H. A and E have 'accomptes day'.   *g* 'and', *H.*
h E has 'Hy owght'; H has 'Hym ought'.   *i* 'proprieties', *H.*
j Also E and H; unlike the 1790 edition, which omits 'as'.
k 'strictly', *H.*
l E has 'of thretnynges owteward'; H has 'or threatening a styward'.
m 'the', *H.*   *n* H omits 'his'.

conduytez. Also he ys a geuer of exaumple to all other to be of good
gouernaunce vnder a rule, contented with moderat costagez in this
courte, of his lyuerey and seruise, takyng dayly metes and soupers
in the kinges hall, or in ony office ellez whan hit pleasith hym to see
the rules and demeanynges of profit or no profit in offices so named
or supposed not worshipfull. Also he hath dayly whyles he is present
in court j chaplen, ij esquiers, ij yomen etyng in the hall;[277] and
for his chambre-brekefast, none, souper, and lyuerey for all ny3t—
vij loues, iiij messe of greete mete, ij rewardes of rost, ij pychers
wyne, v[a] gallons ale. And from All Halowentide tyll Estyr, a torche
wayting for hymself, a tortays[b] to fette by hys lyuerey, ij perchers
wex, iiij candylles wax, vj candylles perich, vj tallow, iiij fagots,[c]
litter and russhes all the yere of the sergeaunt vssher of the hall;
and after wynter lyuereyz, iij talwood,[d] ij faggots; and whan hym
pleasith to haue more large in ony thing, than his chambrelayn to
record all this[e] he hathe by [A, p. 137] a tayle[d] or bylle in the
countynghouse duly[f] whan hit requiryth. This thesaurer taketh
no fee in houshold, but for his robys wynter and somer, at the festes
of Crystmasse and Whytsontide xvj marcez,[278] and as for hys napery
at the iiij festes of the yere, by euyn porcions in lynyn clothe out of
the spycery, or ellez by a bill from thens into thys[g] countynghouse,
by euen porcions, xiij li. xvjd.; and for euery day that he ys out of
court for the kinges maters towching thys[g] houshold, xxs. He hathe
all weyes continuyng in court j yoman to kepe hys chambre and to
puruey for his lyuerey, for his horses in the cuntrey, taking lyuerey
daily,[h] ij loues, ij messes of greete mete, j gallon ale. Hit belongith
to the thesaurer with the steward and controller to remembre the
kinges highnes of his disposicion and purposes ,of[i] his remembringes
and most abydinges[279] shalbe most[j] for his propyr person and for hys
houshold from terme to terme,[k] by the wyche [l]he may[l] logge redyly
the kynges wynes, and [m]to make prouision[m] for wood, coole, hey, otes,
for that season,[n] and, if pollycy wull hit in that coostes,[n] bothe for
whete, ale, beef, moton, and suche other as the cuntry may bere.

---

[a] 'vj', *H.*

[b] 'one torches', *H.*

[c] 'fower f*' and the marginal note '*Id videtur fagots', *H.*

[d] E has 'towe talwood'; H has 'three candles'.

[e] 'all that he hath', *H.*　　　　　[f] 'talley' and 'daily', *H.*　　　　[g] 'the' *H.*

[h] From H. A and E have 'day'.

[i] All three manuscripts have this reading, unlike the 1790 edition, which has
'howe his remembringes'.

[j] 'shalbe both for his person', *H.*

[k] 'from time to tyme', *H.*　　　　　　　[l] From H. A and E omit 'he may'.

[m] From H. A and E have 'to take prouisiones'.

[n] 'and, and if pollicie would it in that coastes', *H.*

To declare what [A, p. 138] the thesaurer owith to do, euery office and officer in this courte shewith to him his part.[a] Thes greete officers haue sume tym vsed to kepe chariottes at theyre own costes, founden at theyre lyuerey with thayre othyr horsez in the cuntrey. After the noble Edward the iijd. he is called 'custos magne garderobe hospicij domini regis'.[280] This thesaurer in absence of the steward, is serued with dowbyll seruyce;[281] he hathe into this court viij personez. Also this[b] thesaurer, countroller, cofferer, and, in theyre absence, clerkes of grene cloth and the chiefe clerk of countrolment shall punyshe offencers[c] vnto the stokkes by theyre dyscression for theyre offences after as the[d] fynde the mater worthy suche correccions or lesse.

§70. *JURAMENTUM THESAURARIJ,*[e] 'Ye woll swere by that booke to be after your power and cunyng a good, wurshipfull, true officer to the kinge your[f] souerayn lord, whose hyghe astate[g] is here present,[g] and dylygent seruis to do[h] hym as thesaurer of his[i] noble houshold,[282] [A, p. 139] and not to be knowing nor consenting to ony thing that mought be ageynst him in his body naturell or of his goodes temporall; but that ye let hit after your power, or elles to geue hasty knowlegge thereof to hymself or to suche aboute hym that wold do hym to witt or to let hit and amend hit. And all suche good as ye shall receue of the kinges by the thesaurer of Inglond or other officers for the astate and conseruacion of hys royall houshold and for the expensys of hit, ye shall truly charge your self therewith and thereof due accompte yeld into the kinges exchequer, full[j] and hoole, by euery ij yeres end at the furthest,[283] and no councelement make. Also to behaue you truly and honestly in making of all your paymentes with fayre demeanynges, cherysshing loue betwext the king and his peple; and that suche paymentes by vsed and made continually at the[k] grene clothe in the countynghouse of houshold. Also that ye[l] take oftyn tymez vyews and suche oversightes of maner of[m] vytayle and stuff comprised with in your charge and parcelles in euery office, so that the vtteraunce of hit be guyded to the kinges most worship and profitt. And that in all your sessions and jugementes in [A, p. 140] the countynghouse vppon ony matter, cause, or thing,[n] to sey and geue your doomes truly, after good conscyence,

---

[a] 'shall show to him his part', H.   [b] 'the', H.
[c] E has 'officers'; H has 'offences'.
[d] E has 'after the ffynde'; H has 'after as they finde'.
[e] From H. A and E have 'Thesaurarie'.
[f] 'our', H.   [g] has 'yow here present', H.   [h] E omits 'do'.
[i] 'this', H.   [j] E omits 'full'.
[k] H omits 'the'.
[l] H has 'he', although it later reads 'within your charge'.
[m] From E and H. A omits 'of'.   [n] From E and H. A has 'thinges'.

ryght reason, and all^a the rulez of this courte wyll require betwixt the king and party, or^b ony other party and parties, cheryssying the good officer and punisshing the euyll doer, not by affeccion nor loue only, nor in magry nor euyll wyll, but retourn trouth to euery party as nyghe as ye can. ITEM, ye shall ^cnother aske nother consent^c to none alowauncez but^d as shall be rightfull and dew to be done and and that ye demeane yow in charginge or discharginge of the expencez of household alweys to the kinges worship and profit; and in your own person to be ensampler to other of the court. Also, suche parcelles or purueyauncez as shalbe brought into the countynghouse of your tyme be^e trewly purueyed and parcelled by indentures betwext suche officers and yow by good examinacions or serches in the cuntreys, as truly as ye can charge all the purueyours; and that hit be duly apposed in the countynghouse monethly for the king. And also that ye serche the good, old, sad, worshupfull, and profit-ables rulez of the court vsed before [A, p. 141] tym, and them to kepe, vphold, or bettyr if ye can, as God helpe yow and^f by that booke'.

THIS thesaurer forthwith takith his staf of the king; and in the next mornyng erly after, in euery office of houshold, the remanentes must be taken,²⁸⁴ and in all the contreys there^g the kinge hathe ony stuff loggyng to be hastyly syowed^h for the old thesaurer's discharge and to the new thesaurer ys charge. And if he be a bacheler kny3t, he werythe his robys and hoodez at iiij festes of the yere in the kinges presence, lyke of fourme as dothe a greate baron of Inglond and the kinges keruers; and if he be a sqyer,²⁸⁵ he hathe his robys of another furre after the same shappe.

Tempore Henrici iiijti. regis quidamⁱ magister Bokyngham, thesaurarius hospicij, (sed postea electus est episcopus Lincolniensis), hic primo abstraxit de modis et formis et abbreuiacione dietarum hospicij regis sub breuiori composicione et superficiali dieta et com-potacione de omnibus expensis alicuius hospicij majoris^j status. Et [A, p. 142] postea dedit opus suum Domino Henrico, Episcopo ac Cardinali Wyntoniensi, qui tunc conformauit familiam et domum suam secundum idem opus. Non tam perfectum facit compotum neque^k omnez finalez conclusionez^l sicut modus et forma hospicij domus regis.²⁸⁶

§71. COUNTROLLER OF THIS HOUSHOLDE royall takithe his charge in the kinges presence, as hit aperyth in his othe. He is iijd. in^m astate

^a 'as the rules of the court', H.   ^b 'and', H.
^c 'never aske nor graunt', H.
^d 'but such as shalbe righteful', H.
^e 'by trewly purveyde', E.   ^f From H. E omits 'and'.
^g All three manuscripts have 'there'.   ^h E has 'syewid'; H has 'viewed'.
ⁱ From H. A and E have 'quondam'.   ^j 'nostrorum', H.
^k 'nos', H.   ^l 'conclusionem', E.   ^m E omits 'in'.

of thys house aftyr the steward, but at no tyme nor place within thys
court couered in seruyse and but singylle saruyd,[a] [287] by whos
superuision and witnes the thesaurere of houshold is dyscharged fro
many partycular accomptes of thynges dyspended in houshold, wych
by hys record is comprysed and alowed within the thesaurer is
accompt in groose that ellez shuld be expressed in euery small
partycularytie, [A, p. 143] as of euerie[b] pewter dysshe, cup of tree,
pottes of lethyr or erthe, as of othyr many small and[c] infinite spyces
and other thinges; and so passith by hys countrollment as well as
of vytaylle or ony other gold or syluer; in whom next after the steward
and thesaurer the power of houshold restyth; to whom also the
officers and ministres of thys court owe obedyence for the king. He
geuyth ensaumple to all other of lower astate and degrees to be
content with moderate costagez of lyuerey and seruyses in thys
houshold, sytting dayly at metes and soupers in the hall[288] after the
syght that he takyth, furst of the seruyce of alle[d] hoole court, or
ellez then he syttythe in other place or office with in the court to
see the good gouernaunces thereof and the dylygence of offycers and
theyre conueyaunce in worship and profitt to the king. And whyles
he is present in court, he hathe etyng in the hall j gentylman, j
yoman[e] [289] and for hys chambre for brekefastes and lyuerey [f]for
none and souper tyme and for all ny3t,[f] v loues, ij messes of grete
mete and rewarde of rost, j pycher wyne, iiij gallons ale; and from
All Halowentide [A, p. 144] tyll Estyr, j torche for hym selfe,
j tortays to fett[g] his liuerey by, j percher wex, iiij[h] candylles wex,
iiij candylles peric, v talwood, ij fagots, litter and russhes all the
yere of the sergeaunt[i] of hall; and for somer lyuerey, ij talwood, ij
fagots;[j] and whan he woll haue more larger in ony thing to hys
chambre, than hys chambyrlayn to record hit by bylle or tayle in to
the countynghous; and whyles hymself is present in court, he takyth
dayly by chekker roll xvd., by the statutes of noble Edward iiij seyne,
tyll he be preferred by the kyng to asmuch lyuelode in other placys
terme of hys lyfe.[290] Also for hys robys, wynter and somer, for the
festes of Crystmasse and Whystontyde, by the wardrobe of houshold,

---

[a] E omits 'and but singylle saruyd'. A has 'but singylle saruyd' crossed out
and the words 'but duble saruyd' are inserted above.

[b] From H. A and E omit 'everie'.

[c] 'smale and smale infinite spices', E.

[d] E has 'alle and hole corte'; H has 'the whole court'.

[e] 'j gentleman, iij yomen', E.

[f] E omits this phrase; H has 'for noone, sooper, and for all night'.

[g] All three manuscripts agree here, unlike the 1790 printed version, which
has 'sette'.

[h] 'three candles wex'. H.   [i] 'sergeant vssher', E.

[j] H has 'two *f' and the marginal note ' *Id videtur fagots'.

wiche is the countynghous, viij marcez;[291] and for hys napery at the
iiij festes yerely by egall porcions in lynyn cloth of the grete spycery,
^aor elles^a by byll dyrected to the countynghous as for so much stuf
bou3t of hym, xiij li. xvjd; and for hys wages out of court dayly,
whan he is in busynesse for the houshold maters, to be payd in the
countynghous, xiij s. iiijd.[292] And also he hath on yoman to kepe hys
chambre and to make purueyaunce for [A, p. 145] hys horses at hys
lyuerey in the cuntrey; ^bthys yoman takyth dayly in court j messe
of greete, j gallon ale.^b

§72. JURAMENTUM CONTRAROTULATORIS. 'Ye woll swere by that
booke to do vnto the king our souerayne lord good,^c true, and
dylygent seruyse after your power and connyng, as countroller of
hys honorable houshold; and not to knowe nor consent to ony thyng
that may be hurting to hys hygh astate or to hys body or goodes,
butt that ye shall lette hit after your power, or ellez warne them in
hasty tyme that may lete hit. Also to countroll^d the receytes and all
the yssuez of the thesaurers office of houshold; and^e that to record
in playn acompt into the kinges escheker after the old fourme of
the countynghouse. Also truly and justly to help make the prisez of
almaner stuffes, of vytayle and other, purueyde for [A, p. 146] thys
household; and that ye see and knowe that hit be good and holsom
vytayle in euery thing for the king and hys houshold and for the
kinges houshold and worshypp.^f Also that hit be lyke wurth to the
syluer that the king must pay therefore or bettyr, by your wysedom
and discression; and ellez such vytayle of mete and drink be dampned
and adnulled so that hit be not dispendyd within thys houshold.
And to shew and comyn such maters at the grene clothe byfore
steward and tresaurer, that hit may be vnderstond not done for malyce,
and there to counsayle vpon hom to cast the losces of suche mysse-
purueyauncez. Also ye to be conscyensly assentyng in and to all
dew alowauncez to be made or geuyn in the countyn house betwyxt
the king and hys people, and to apply your besynesse vppon the good
guyding and ouersyghtes of all such maner charges and expences,
within thys court and without, also longing to thys houshold. Also
in your party to make good serche and dew to enquere of^g and vppon
condycions of purueyoures, and of theyre [A, p. 147] prouisyons
inward and outward,[293] and of all the demeanynges of the officers of
thys court, that there is^h no sclaunder by theyre dedes vnto thys

^a From H. A and E have 'iiij ellez'.
^b 'this yoman taketh dayly in the court two loves and messe of gret mete,
one gallon ale', H.
^c H omits 'good'. ^d 'to compte', E. ^e 'all', H.
^f 'for the kinges worship', H.
^g 'Also in your partie to make due search and to enquire of', H.
^h 'there arise noe sclander', H.

L

famous court. And that ye see that the officers vnder you, for the
kinge, putte them in theyre dylygens to take oftyn the vyewes of
offices, that the alowancez of expenses[a] passe not theyre charges of
reysceyte. Ye also to make acompte of all the thesaurer of houshold
ys charge and discharge for all the resceytes, purueyauncez, and
the expenses, and no councelement make thereof, but truly to
engroos hit and to put hit in to the kinges eschequer. And in your
offyce to attend and preferre the kinges wurshyppe and profyt
as nygh as ye can deuyse, and ye to serche, kepe, and vphold the
good, sad, wurshypfull, and profytable rulez and the statutes vsed
before tyme in thys court and them to encrece and that your
demeanyng be exampler to all othyr vnder you in thys court of good
gouernance. And also that ye or your vndyr-clerk or bothe be at
the coupage of flesshe and at the departing of fysshe at the seruyce
of the kinges chambre and hall, and to knowe the verry dewtiez of
lyuereys[294] [A, p. 148] dayly in houshold, and to see with the awmoner
that the messez thereof be smytyn in a suffycyaunt and acording
maner after the old custumez, and so to serue hit to the kinges hall
and to other offycers[b] dew. Also ye or your vndyrclerkes truly, as
oft as hit requiryth, shall take the remanentes and vyewez in officez[295]
and surely make the booke of wyne; and all thys present into the
countynghouse as often as ye be desyred by the steward, coferer,
and the clerkes of grene clothe, wyche must nedes engroose the grete
acompt of houshold by your record. To all wyche thinges ye woll
confourme you after your[c] power and vnderstondyng; so God help
you and by thys[d] booke'. Forthwith he receyuyth hys staf of the
king or of hys greate counsayle.

§73. COFFERER of the kinges houshold, wych takyth in charge all
the receytes for the thesaurer of houshold, as of money specyally by
indentures made betwext them tweyn; and he delyueryth to all
other offycers purueyoures theyre prestes vppon reknyng; and he
also payith to the cuntriez in the countynghouse for all dew prouisyons [A, p. 149] towchyng the expenses of houshold, with the
presence and recorde of the clerkes there, after the noble Edwardes
statutes;[296] and he to dyscharge the thesaurere of and for all suche
sumes as thys cofferer receyuyth by the sayd indentures. Also he
takyth acompt of the receytes and paymentes made by the clerkes
of grene clothe; also of euery other acomptaunt and theyre partyculer
acomptes in houshold, bothe inward and outward, for the seyde
thesaureres party dayly, monthely, and yerely;[297] also he payeth
feez, wagez, and rewardez, and for all other necessaries bought for

---

[a] 'allowances of expensis ther', *H*.

[b] 'office', *H*.

[c] H omits 'after your'.   [d] 'that', *H*.

the housholde and alowed in the countynghouse. All*a* the wyche purueyauncez, expenses, and paymentes, he with the clerkes of grene-clothe and secundary of countrolment engroose in the grete acompt of the hole houshold. Thys ys a greate offycer and key-berer of thys noble court; and he also to ete in the hall, countynghouse, or in ony other offyce, aftyr hys busynesse doth require, geuyng good exaumple. He hathe also etyng in the hall j vnder-clerk[298] contynually*b* to wryte hys resceytes, paymentes, to pure*c* the jornall, to joyne doggettes, to make the mensall,[299] and mony othyr wrytinges for the thesaurere is acompt and things nedefull towchyng to the countynghous; takying rewarde and clothing by dyscressyon and alowaunce yerely by petycion of the soueraynes at the grene clothe, more or lasse aftyr hys connyng, trouth, and [A, p. 150] dylygence. Thys clerk takyth none othe at the countyngbourde as an offycer *d*but as conduyte. For the coferer's chambre,*d* or for brekefast whan he woll, and lyuerey for all day and ny3t, to geue ensaumple to othyr men to be vnder a rule, he takythe iiij loues, ij messes of grete mete, dim. pycher wyne, iij gallons ale; he loggyth in the countynghouse with suffraunce*e* of woode, coolez, litter, russhes nedefull; and for hys ny3t lyuerie in wynter season, j torche, j percher, ij candles wex, iij candylles peric; and hys other resonable comaundmentes in court after the steward, thesaurer, and countroller. And for hys dayly wages present in court by the chekker roll, vijd.ob.; and for hys robys wynter and somer with the houshold, in clothe or money, viij marcez;[300] and for hys napery at the iiij festes yerely, in*f* lynyn clothe of the spycery or ellez by byll in money, xij li. xvjd.; and hys seruyce in hall lyke a grete baroun, stonding saler[301] and hys spone.*g* And if he be oute of court in busynesse for the housholde, than for hys wages outward, in the countyng house, dayly vjs. viijd. Also a rewarde; and he also partyth with such yeftes that shalbe yeuyn to the householde, beyng present in the time of yeftes or ellez than [A, p. 151] being of recorde in labouryng for houshold Also he hathe in to thys courte ij seruauntes;[302] the iijd. kepyth styll hys chaumbre and harneys in court and makyth*h* hys lyuerey for hys horsez in the town or contrey, wyche seruaunt, in absence of the coferer, etyth in the hall at the chambrelaynes bourde.[303] The coferer hath caryage of hys harneys with stuffe of countynghouse in the charyot, longing to that office, specially ordeyned for the caryage of mony and bokes, etc. The cofferer hathe suffycyaunt logging of

---

a 'And the which', *H.*   *b* 'continueing', *H.*
c H has 'procure'; the 1790 edition has 'prove'.
d 'but as a conduct. Also for the coffrer his chambre', *H.*
e 'suffisaunce', *H.*   *f* 'of', *E.*
g 'standing sale and his spoones', *H.*   *h* 'maketh ready', *H.*

the herbyger in the town or nyghe court in the contrey. The honour of thys court ys to make trew, opyn, and hoole paymentes for the king in the countynghouse.

§74. CLERKYS OF GRENE CLOTHE, tweyne, wyche, after the statutes of noble Edward, were callid ᵃ'clerkes du table de la counte, suffisauntez pur feere toutz chosez touchantez le graunte garde-robe et la counte de ceel'.³⁰⁴ In all jugementez [A, p. 152] or sessyons to be don or made by ony estate within thys housholde at the grene clothe thyes clerkes and the chyef clerke countroller owe to sitte thereat with the juges as audytoures and councelloures,ᵇ to helpe kepe in course the statutes and the formall order of housholde according to lyke actes edyfyed before tyme. Also vnder the stewarde, tresorer, countroller, and the cofererᶜ theis ij clerkes haue power comytted vnto them consernyng for all the rulez and guydyng of thys housholde, as at the ordynaunce taking, to knowe and to modyr thereᵈ howe the king and hys housholde shall fare, and the proporcions of all by a clere vndyrstonding; also at the accomptes in many apposylys, and also vppon many correccions; and they to be proue with the countrolment of all alowauncez,³⁰⁵ how they be asked and geuyn, remyttyng the verre grete and defuse maters vnto the comyng of the hygher sufferaignes as they think accordyng. And for that the offycers shall not oftyn tymes trouble for euery mocion the sayde soueraygnes abouen in small, acoustomede, and cotydyan thynges and questyons, hit ys geuyn to these clerkes at the countyngbourde to make awnswere and to determyne vppon mony causez and correccions; they haue also comaundmentes [A, p. 153] vppon officers for mony maters necessary andᵉ to be done in housholde by theyre ouersyght, wysedom, and counsaylez. The bookes of the house be vnder theyre power for euery partyculer mater and groose.³⁰⁶ Them owithᶠ among to help see the king and soueraynes seruede, and so to be priuy and knowing of the sad demeanyng of all. They etyn in the hall with a person of lyke seruyce, or ellez with some straunger of wurship, to sitte with them; and yf theyre busynesse require,ᵍ to haue theyre brekefast, metez, or soupers resonable into the countynghouse. Also for theyre chambre day and ny3t, eueryche of them, iij loues, ij messes of grete mete, dim. pycher wyne, ij gallons ale; and eueryche of them for wynter lyuerey from Al

---

ᵃ A has here the phrase 'clerkes du table de la count de ceel, in all jugementes or sessions to be don'; this has been dropped on the evidence of H. E has 'tweyne, which were callyd after the statutes of noble Edward, clerkes du table de la cunt de ceele, in all jugements or sessions to be done, clerkes du table de la counte, suffisauntz', etc.

ᵇ 'comptroller', E.   ᶜ 'next after the coffrer', H.   ᵈ 'them', H.
ᵉ H omits 'and'.
ᶠ E has 'The owght'; H has 'Them out'.   ᵍ 'required', E.

Halowentyde tyll Estyr, j tortays, ij candylles wex, iij candylles peris, j talwood dim.; russhes and litter*a* all the yere of the sergeaunt vssher of hall. And caryage of theyre harneys with the countyng-house; and dayly present in court euery by the chekker roll, vijd. ob.;[307] and clothing with the housholde, wynter and somer, or xlvjs. viijd.,[308] and at*b* the iiij festes of the yere pryncypall eche of them takethe of the grete spycery j napron of lynyn cloth of ij ellez, price of j elle*c* xviijd. And eche of them for theyre wages out of court in busynesse or*d* sutez for the housholde, dayly*e* iijd. iiijd., [309] and a rewarde; also, they part [A, p. 154] with the generall gyftes with the housholde, beyng present when hit is yeuen or ellez*f* by recorde send out in erandes of the houshold. Also they haue ouersyght for*g* the thesaurer's party in euery office, both of the self stuff and the ministracion, how hit passith, as often as them seme nedeful to be seen and apposed of euerything; and to take the remanentes with the clerk countroller often, to know the astate of housholde by suche vyewes, whethyr the alowauncez passethe the chargez or not. Also they to*h* help appose[310] truly and monethly all the parcelles of prouisyons, to helpe to examen and proue the jornall,[311] to helpe total the memorande,[312] helpe tytle and engroos the vnder,[313] help ioyne the dyettes,[314] helpe make the mensale, and the booke of hoole remanentes yerely of euery offyce[315] surely and truly, and thys*i* to help redy to the thesaurer's acompte, and with the coffyrer to help appose all the partyculer accomptes of offycers of thys houshold, and to call vppon and for the credytoures at*j* the yeres ende; also to yelde theyre own*k* accomptes or vyewes of theyre receytes and paymentes clerely to*l* the seyde cofyrrer. Also hit hathe byn accos-tomede [A, p. 155] muche for the lesse charge, that*m* one of the*n* clerkes delyuer the clothing of household; and at euery Mighelmas term to ryde with other offycers to all the kinges homez and soiournez, to take all such remanentes growing to any charge by purueyaunces or other to the thesaurer of houshold or officer*o* of thys court.[316] Eueryche of thees clerkes haue permitted ij honest seruantes into thys court;[317] the remanent with theyre horsez at theyre logging suffycyaunt nyghe to the courte, as suche offycers seruysablez and attenders must alwey be redy to help dyrect the hole court and to help answer the people of the cuntrey. Theyre seruyse in thys court and the chyef clerk countroller is taken as pety barouns.[317] The

---

a 'rushez and litter for thair Chambre all the year', H.
b From H. A and E omit 'at'. H has 'sixteene shillinges eight-pence'.
c 'price the elle', E.   *d* 'of', E.   *e* E omits 'dayly'.
f A here repeats 'being present'.   *g* From H. A and E have 'of'.
h From H. A and E have 'to'.   *i* 'thus', H.
j From H. A and E have 'of'.   *k* E omits 'own'.   *l* 'of', E.
m 'then', E.   *n* 'theise', H.   *o* 'offis', H.

clerkes of grene cloth be not exempt from ony ouersyght[a] of countrolment in none office of housholde, for theyre doing is the thesaurer's
doyng pryncypall.

[A, p. 156] §75. CLERKE OF COUNTROLMENT. After the statutes of
noble Edward, the clerkes of grene clothe and he 'girount ensemble
en[b] le garderobe'.[318] Hys charge ys to see to all maner of purueyaunces
grete and smale longyng to the thesaurere of houshold hys charge;
as for weyghte of brede, wex, weeke, all maner spyces; syluer vessell,
pewter, tyn, coppyr, brasse, lede, iron; and of delyuerauncez of
mesure of napry and all othyr lynyn cloth of the full content;
mesurez of tonnez, fates,[c] buttes, pipes, hogges, rundelettes, barelles,
to the lowest mesure of pottes of ale, wynez, and all other maner of
vessels and drinkes or botels vergis, etc.; busshelles, half busshelles,
peckes, and suche othyr necessary[d] for thys houshold lyke as a clerk
countroller owith to execute and apposer to thys[e] clerk of market
in thys court. Also of all othyr maner of[f] stuff purueyed for the
householde, as hit is wurthe, hym owyth to recorde and testyfye
at the countynghouse before the steward and thesaurer. Thys clerk
also owith to be at the coupage of fleyshe specyally with the clerk
of kychyn in the grete larder, as hit requiryth nyghtly to knowe the
proporcion of beof and moton [A, p. 157] for the expenses of the next
day and to see the feez thereof to be iustly smytten by the yoman
cooke; also at the breking vp of the panyers of fyssh and the departing thereof for the kinges chambre and hall and housholdez[g] dew
and necessary lyuerez outward.[319] And thereof to kepe suche remembraunce that no thing ellez after be asked by the accomptauntes but
as was truly necessary and wurshupfully dyspended for the king;
the same ouersight that the countroller himself owith to haue of
all maner achatez, prisez, alowauncez, dysalowauncez, and the
conueyauncez; the same in[h] lyke owith thys chyef clerk to haue in
euery offyce in houshold, and to do thys[i] greate busy dylygence, to
aspy and to lett the wasters, raueners, and miscaryers to[j] the kinges
goods, agaynst the ordynaunce of thys court, and such persons to
opyn and declare and to help punyshe in the countynghouse. Also
he countrollythe the thesaurer's resceytes and paymentes, and that
to entyr into a iournall of countrolment; also the dayly dyettes of
houshold, so that no doggettes aftyrwarde be broken but by the
assent of bothe partyes. Also he makyth the booke of remanentes
[A, p. 158] and the booke of wyne, [320] truly and duly to be entendyd
vpon of euery *venit quo die a quo loco in quem locum*: and thes[k] to

---

[a] 'from anny sight', *E*.   [b] From H. A and E have 'in'.   [c] 'vates', *H*.
[d] 'necessarijs', *E*.   [e] 'the', *E*.   [f] H omits 'of'.
[g] 'howsold', *H*.   [h] 'and', *H*.   [i] 'his', *H*.   [j] 'of', *H*.
[k] 'theise bookes', *H*.

be redy whan so euer they be called aftyr in the countynghouse. Hys othe ys muche after the controller's charge. Hit besemethe thys clerk offycer that shall testyfye all prisez and alowaunces with the clerkes of grene clothe to be prouable, resonable in hys dyscressyon, of good concyens, and in all maters betwext the kinges court and other partyez to be vpryght and indyfferent. Also he doth ouersee with the clerk of kychyn in the ministracions of the messes and other seruyses into^a the kinges hall and chambres, to help see with the awmoner^b that hit be according of^c largenesse, and ellez to be strykyn more or lesse after the astates and degrees and^d for the kinges worshyp done require, and so to help amend hit. Thys clerkys is in euery duete and seruyce of thys court lyke to the clerkes of grene clothe, except that he makyth no paymentes. All suche herneys of mennys as shalbe caryed at the kinges cost ^{e}that hit passe not hys competent clothys,^{e} and yett that to be after the astate that they be of and [A, p. 159] acording to such other degrees; and allwey to be ouerseen by these countrollers; and yf ony passe suche apoyntment than he to be modyfyed by this countroller.^{321} Thys clerk owyth to haue a booke of remembraunces of all maner purueyauncez of beofes and motons, by whom hit ys brought yn, and fro whens, that the pasture and fugacions take trew alowaunce;^{322} and for the delyuer-auncez of napry; of all^f other vessel of^g wyne or ale dampned or yeuen to any almesse, and of muche other small thinges, that when the petycions comyn at the yeres end, hit may clerely by vnderstond and recorded by thys offyce. Also one vndyrclerk,^{323} or yf hit be thouȝt nedefull by the auyse of styward, thesaurer, countroller, and othyr to make one mo, they to wryte and make redy all the bookes towching^h the office of countrolment and the acompt of the same; and to entyr dayly the prouysyons of beofs, motons, and other achates, so that the sergeauntes accountauntes^{324} shall not haue alowauncez of none hygher prisez than they bring in by the furst record; also to enter dayly with the clerkes of kychyn all maner vytayle and stuf that cumyth in to be dyspended, and [A, p. 160] to be at the petycions thereof, and to^i testyfye hit at the accomptes, and that^j remaynythe in the lardre so that there be no double alowaunce asked; thys to do in the absence of the chyef clerk or by hys assignment. Thys vnder clerkes ete in the hall, not serued with trenchers but as squyers,^{325} taking for one lyuerey at nyȝt euery dim. gallon ale,^{k} j candyll peric, dim. tallwood, lytter, russhes^l for

^{a} 'in', E. ^{b} 'awmeners', E. ^{c} 'with', E. ^{d} H omits 'and'.
^{e} 'that is passe not his awne competent clothis', H.
^{f} 'also', H. ^{g} 'or', H. ^{h} 'touchand', H.
^{i} 'so to testifie', H. ^{j} 'what', H.
^{k} E omits 'every'; H has 'everyche dimid. gallon ale'
^{l} E has 'rushes and lytter'; H omits 'rushes'.

hys paylete of the sergeaunt vssher. And for the rewarde of suche
one, by the dyscressyon of steward, thesaurer, countroller, at the
yerys end by petycon after hys desert, x marcez or vnder; and clothing with the household, wynter and somer, as the houshold hath
playn at the termez of Crystmasse and Whytsontyde, or elles for all
xxs. and caryage for hys bed togyder; and at*a* eueryche of the iiij
festes princypalles, of the offyce of spycery, ij ellez of lynyn clothe,
price the elle xijd., and part of the yeftes generall, if he be present.
Thys vnder-clerk ys accompted for a yoman and a grome in hys
degre in thys court; and he is permytted to haue one honest chyld
into thys court but no lyuerey of kychyn, but yf the king deuyde
often tymez hys houshold into iiij partes; [A, p. 161] elles here nedyth
but one vnder-clerk.[326] Also one of thes clerkes dayly to be at the
weyghtes of wex in the chaundry to se the *infra* and *extra* and the
expenduntur,[327] and thys also to record at the accomptes. Also as
oftyn as the king or hys houshold remouyth from ony place, to se
and wryte if there leue ony remanentes in offyces, as of whete, brede,
wyne, ale, wood, coolez, or other thinges of ony charge; and that to
entyr in there memoranda truly, in whoos kepinge hit ys left or how
othyr wise disposed hit ys. The chyef or the secundary clerk owith
to be at the receyte of ony stuf or other goodes purposed,*b* purueyde
and brou3t in for houshold into ony offyce, and to see the entrie
thereof, and the ministracion dayly or as often as he may.

[A, p. 162] §76. DOMUS COMPOTI*c* CONSILII ET JUDICII, called also
by the noble Edward thyrde 'le graunt garderobe du loistyel du
roy'[328] in*d* which the worship and welfare of the hoole houshold is
purposed, in wyche the correccions and jugementes be geuyn; in
whom ys taken the audyte of all thinges of thys court, beyng of the
thesaureres charge as princypall*e* of all other offices, in whom euery
offycer of houshold takyth hys charge on hys kne, promyccyng
charge*f* and obedyence to the king and to the rules of thys offyce;
for at the grene cloth ys alwey represented the kinges power in
towching maters of thys houshold. Thys offyce beryth armes for a
chyef grounde and defence vnto all other offycers, a felde of grene,
a key, and a rode of syluer, saultre;*g* sygnyfying that thys offyce
may close, opyn, and punyshe other offycers, beryng markez from
hens. Also hit ys shewyd by bookes of kinges housez that the grete
courtes of Inglond toke theyre orygynalles in thys offyce, be chyef
the steward, thesaurer, countroller, and aftyrward the coferer; and so
in theyre absence the [A, p. 163] ij clerkes of grene clothe and the

---

a 'to', E.   *b* H omits 'purposed'.
c 'compotis', H.   *d* From H. A and E omit 'in'.
e Also E; H has 'principall heede'.   *f* 'promitting trouthe', H.
g A here has in the margin a pen-and-ink drawing, thus

THE ARMS OF THE COUNTINGHOUSE

chyef clerke of countrolment to appose and determyn all charges
and dyscharges of prouysyons and expensys ministered in thys
houshold; and also by the same they haue power vpon many correccions in absence of the aboue sayd soueraynes. Thys offyce^a takyth
all tymez at hys commaundementes breede, wyne, ale, mete, wood,
coolez, candylles, lytter, russhes as hit shall nede, more or lesse, by
and for suche^b as kepe the sessyons for the tyme at the grene cloth;
and in thys offyce is the receyte of all the golde and syluer, as well
of coigned syluer as of plate, for euery offyce in thys houshold his
charge except the Iwelhouse. And the delyueraunce of all suche plate
longyth to thys offyce, ^cbetwext the thesaurer and euery other
partyculer offycer, by indentures to be left in thys office;^c and yerely
so to call the plate hyder, to proue the wast and to know if ony lak
thereof, than to sett along thereof in the thesaurer's acompt in to
the escheker. Thys countynghouse is neuer voyde of one ouerseer,
wyche shall charge and dyscharge all other acomptauntes of the
court by record.

[A, p. 164] §77. THYS OFFYCE OF COUNTYNGHOUS hath in hym a
sergeaunt vssher³²⁹ to kepe the dore, to kepe the tresour, to kepe the
bookes, ^dand attend dylygently vpon thys offyce and all the stuff
within furth as he shall awnswere to for suche thinges as shalbe leyde
in hys keping and charge, so that hit be not lost in hys defaute.
Also a part of hys wothe ys to kepe the counsaylle of thys howse.
Also that he make herbygage by the assignment of the chyef herbyger
for all the officers and clerkes of the countynghouse and to be
attendaunt vnto theyre comaundmentes for the king and the
execucions of thys offyce. And after the statutes of Edward the
iijd.³³⁰ he shuld fett theyre al thyr lyuerey nyghtly and for the
offyce also; and he shold logge within thys offyce next to the dore.
All the sergeauntes of thys court owe specyally to were theyre ray
hoodez furred with whyte lambe and a coyf of silk, whyte, at the
iiij festes of the yere. By the ordynaunce of Henry the furst³³¹ thys
sergeaunt shold not be lettred for many causez; he shall ete in the
hall with other sergeauntes; and for hys lyuerey at nyʒt a gallon
ale; and for wynter lyuerey from All Halowentyde tyll Estyr j
candyll wex, j candyll peric., j tallwood. And for wages in the
chekker roll, whyles he [A, p. 165] is present in court, dayly iiijd. ob.,
or ellez by the dyscression of souerayns and after his demerytes,
vijd. ob., and for his clothing, wynter and somer with other sergeauntes, or ellez in mony xls.;³³² and at euery of the^e iiij festes
princypall of the yere ij ellez of lynyn cloth of the grete spycery

for naprons, price the elle xijd.; and part also of the generall gyftes
yeuen to thys houshold, and caryage for hys competent bede with
the countynghouse; and yf he be lett bloode or othyrwyse syke for
a season, to haue dayly a cast of bred, j messe of greete mete, a messe
of rost,[332] j gallon ale, besydys hys lyuerey; and yf he be sent out of
court for maters of thys offyce or of houshold, he takyth dayly xijd.
by peticion. He hath into thys court one honest seruaunt; hys dwetie
ys also to call aftyr the recordez of the kinges chaumbre, queenys,
princes, and all other the recordes,[a] any thinges at the acomptes,
and saufly to kepe them, and so warne suche othyr offycers as be
here vnder hym [b]for the king. O yoman also in thys offyce, called
ye messager of the countynghous,[b] etyng in the hall; he shold be
redy horsed and loged nyghe, to serue suche erandez as the countynghous woll send hym in; taking [A, p. 166] for hys wages dayly, being
present in court, in the chekker roll iijd., and[c] bouche oute of court,
in message, ijd. more dayly; and for hys clothing wynter and somer,
j marce; and for hys chaunces iiijs. viijd., and at euery of the iiij
festes princypall of the yere j elle of lynyn cloth for naprons,[333] price
the elle viijd., and part of the generall gyftes[334] of houshold; he
helpythe and assystethe the sergeaunt, and to be ready at the
comaundementes of them that kepe the sessions at the grene clothe
for the king and execucion of thys office; and betwext hym and the
grome here they haue into thys court one honest seruaunt. O grome
also in thys office, dylygent in attendaunce[d] vppon thys offyce vnder
the sergeaunt and to the comaundmentes of the clerkes at[e] countyngbourde, keping the secretys of thys house and[f] office and the dore;
and to shewe and help make the bookes of thys office, and truly and
clenly to kepe them and also the tresoure of gold and syluer in thys
office, and all other stuf longing thereto; and to se and[g] suche harneys
be saufly trussed [A, p. 167] and attended vppon, and to remembre
what seruyce and lyuereys come in to thys countynghous, yf he be
called[h] to record dayly; hys part is to kepe clene the countyngbourde
and the offyce. He takythe hys mete and souper into thys offyce
for all day ij loues, ij messe of grete mete, j gallon ale; and for hys
reward of household quarterly in the countynghous, xld., and
clothing yerly or ellez vjs. viijd., and his part of the grete reward
that the king geuythe yerely among all[i] the gromes and pagez of
houshold; and at the iiij festes princypall[j] of the grete spycery euery

[a] 'record', H.
[b] 'for the kinges yoman. Also in this office called message of the countinghouse', H.   [c] 'and for bouche', H.   [d] 'atendyng', E.
[e] E has '& countyngborde'; H has 'at the countynbourd'.
[f] H omits 'house and'.   [g] 'all such harneys', H.   [h] H omits 'called'.
[i] From H. A and E have 'the gromes and pagez all of houshold'.
[j] 'iiij festes of the yere principall', E.

tym j elle for naprons of lynyn cloth, price vjd., and caryage of hys
competent bedding with the countynghouse. O page in thys offyce;
in the noble Edwardes dayes pagez were none officers, as hyt ys
before seyd;³³⁵ but syn that tym sergeauntes haue be suffred to
draw furth to connyng and permitted to chese and suffer suche yong
apt personez to lerne to serue, and to help the yomen and gromez to
fett lyueryes among, and to bere wood, coole, and trusse harneys,
and to wayte vppon the caryagez of offyces; andᵃ by cause [A, p. 168]
they meddyll among with the kinges stuf, euery sergeaunt in hys
offyce by lycence of the countynghouse geuyth them theyre charge.
A page etythe in hys offyce or withᵇ hys next felow, not in the hall
at no plase, taking dayly a lof, j messe of grete mete, dim. gallon
ale, one reward quarterly in the countynghouse, xxd., clothing whan
the household hathe *inᶜ precio vesture* at euery of the iiij festes, j
napron of j elle, price vjd.; and part of the kinges grete rewardes
yerely youen amonges them in houshold gromez and pagez of the
kinges priuy cofyrs. In euery partycion in thys court ijᵈ pagez make
awnswer to a grome, ij gromes to j yoman, ij yomen to a gentylman,
of vijd. ob. wages in court. Thys countynghouse hathe assigned hym
a charyot complete and a somter horse³³⁶ for the grene cofyrs, all
thoroughly to be founden by the king in the charge of houshold.
The porters of the gate haue by custume in thys charyot a payre of
small stockes caryed for trespassours.

[A, p. 169] §78 (i). ITEM, THE KYNG confermythe to thys office of
countynghouse all the actes of Kyng Herryᵉ the furst after the
conquest,³³⁷ and the actesᶠ of housholde of noble Edward the iijd.;
and by thys newe auctoryte, and of his hygh propyr power, chargythe
thys offyce and officers to kepe and execute thys ordynauncez for
thastate of thys housholde royall as the soueraynesᵍ do and shall
appoynt by the kinges counsayle and as hit ys after wryten.

§78 (ii). FYRST,³³⁸ the steward and thesaurere, or one of them, ys
bounden by vertu of offyce to be in the countynghouse at the audite
of the dayly accomptes and dietes of housholde. And by the statutes
of noble Edward the iijd.,³³⁹ in case the accomptes passe for lak of
apparence of one of them iij dayes iijʰ vnacompted, that then
steward and thesaurer shall acquyte the costages of the kinges houshold for one day of theyre propyr pursez; and in semblable wise,
if the [A, p. 170] sargeaunt and mastyr clerkesⁱ accomptantez be
nat redy dayly to shewe theyre expensez, they shall bere the chargez,

ᵃ 'and for because', E.   ᵇ From H. A and E have 'within'.
ᶜ From H. A and E have 'j'.   ᵈ 'ij gromes pagez', A.
ᵉ 'Henry', E. H has 'Harry'.   ᶠ E has 'chartez', H.
ᵍ 'soueranz of hit do', H.   ʰ All three manuscripts have this version.
ⁱ From H. A and E have 'clerks'.

and if the king or hys houshold trauayle by the cuntrey, than at the ferthest aftyr iij dayes past yit thes soueraynes to take accompt of all at theyre restyng places by the wey, vppon payn to them to pay for half the expensez of the kinges journey. The king nowe hathe enlarged thys; for hit shuld not fayle by a playne power comitted to the countroller, cofferer, ij clerkes of grene clothe, and clerk countroller or by ony of them as the steward and thesaurer's excusers and atturneys, that ony of them may take hit in absence of the gretter and elder; and in lyke wyse to kepe the dayly ordinaunces for peryle of leuyng hit vndone, wych mought grow to the offycers a breche of theyre due fourme and a settyng asyde sure dyrreccion and order of the kinges house.

[A, p. 171] §78 (iii). ITEM,*a* that the sergeauntez and clerkes offycers, with all other accomptauntes of housholde, present in court, dayly appere[340] before steward, thesaurer, countroller, cofferer, and theyre lyeutenayntes at the grene cloth to awnswere to suche apposyles as shalbe leyde vnto them there for the king.

§78 (iv). ITEM, that the clerkes offycers bryng in theyre parcelles of purueyaunces indented into the countynghouse at euery moneth is end, vppon the paynes of houshold; at euery wiche delyerauncez the sergeauntes shuld swere that all suche parcelles[341] as they so*b* present be good and true, vppon a booke at the grene clothe.

§78 (v). ITEM, that all the minstrez foreynes[342] make theyre accomptes*c* quarterly without ony excusacion.

§78 (vi). ITEM, that euery sergeaunt and maister of offyce kepe good and sad rule within*d* theyre offyces, and no ryot, nor to suffer theyre own seruauntes much conversaunt within whyles the king specyally shalbe asseruing, nothyr to kepe ony houndez in officez, nothyr dayly straungers, nothyr to kepe furettes[343] within thys houshold to geue ony seruaunt occasion to furet or hunt ony mannys wareynes, chasez, nor parkes without leue of the owner or of hys depute suffycyaunt.

§78 (vii). ITEM, the [A, p. 172] statutes of Edward the noble wold that if ony sergeaunt or othyr accountaunt dwelle in arerages, he to be sent into the ward of marchalcye.[344]

§78 (viii). ITEM, that none astate, hygh nor lowe degree, kepe within thys court mo personez than be *e*to hym appoynted,*e* vppon the payne of houshold.

§78 (ix). ITEM, that none officer nor knyȝt nor esquier charged depart from thys court any tym without hys dewe lycence,[345] in

---

a E has the same arrangement of paragraphs in the following section as A (to A p. 180); H has a fresh paragraph for each 'ITEM'.

b 'doe present', H.   *c* 'viewz of accomptz', H.

d 'with', H.   *e* 'heryn to him appointid', H.

houshold or in chambre, as by the steward, thesaurer, chambrelayn, or countroller, or of other that rule in the countynghouse in theyre absence; and that*a* the chambre decons voyde with theyre maistyrs sauf suche as are assigned her to abide.*b*

§78 (x). ITEM, that the rascals and hangars vppon thys court be sought out and auoyded from euery offyces monethly.

§78 (xi). ITEM, that no maner person bere out at the gate mete nor drink, torche wood, coole, or other vytayle but suche as are commaunded lyuerez for hole men or syke, except the awmoners; but that hit be vnderstoud in the countynghouse for the kinges worship or that the vsshers of chambre vppon theyre own charge send or lend out [A, p. 173] ony suche stuf for worshipfull straungers in tyme of nede.

§78 (xii). ITEM, that no lyuerey be made oute from none office, wynter nor somer, after vij in the euenyng.[346]

§78 (xiii). ITEM, that no sargeaunt of household make purueyaunce but by commission, nor to be a marchaunt of ony suche stuf as apperteynyth to his*c* offyce.[347]

§78 (xiv). ITEM, that euery clerk of officez make truly debentoures of euery duetee as hit shal be alowed to the contrey without delayes or ony fee taking there fore, that the people grucche not agaynst the king.

§78 (xv). ITEM, that none other person make suche debentoures or byllez but the clerkes of the self offyce, so that theyre wryting and hond may be certaynly known to them that pay in the countynghouse, and that no clerk countyrfete othyr's hond.

§78 (xvi). ITEM, that there be dewe examinacions made wykely by the countynghous for all suche maters, and of the wasting*d* offycers, and of suche as woll not execute worship, connyng, and profyte for the king in thys court; and to enquire what seruice and profyte the kinges houndez do,[348] [A, p. 174] specially such as take lyuerey for bred in the pantrey rolle dayly, and so of all other maters expedyent with the seasons of the yere.

§78 (xvii). ITEM, that the justice soueraynes of thys court royall kepe ferme the pece in hit and aboutez hit, that no fyghting nor occasion thereof be suffred by the wych any blood shading might fall, or ony other perturbaunce ellez so nyghe to the hyghe presence and hys*e* famous houshold, nother for fere nother for loue of no party but dewe punicions be had. SENECA—MINOR EST QUAM SERUUS

---

a A and E have 'in the'.   *b* From H. A and E have 'voyde'.
c From E and H. A has 'thys'.
d Also E and H; but in H 'waysting' is crossed out and the word 'wayting' is inserted above.
e H has 'this'.

DOMINUS QUI SERUOS TIMET; and also BERNARDUS—FAMULUM ALTI CORDIS REPELLE VT INIMICUM.[349] Yf hit be vppon life and lym, the steward hathe his souerayntie soole within thys house;[350] and ellez for other affrayes the thesaurer, countroller, cofferer, eche in absence of other, may punysshe after the quantyte of offencez, and also dyspence there with in nede and absence of theyre aboue.

§78 (xviii). ITEM, if ony wronges be don to the kinges officer or seruaunt of houshold by ony dede malycyous, [A, p. 175] for executing of his comission, offyce or seruyce, or yet for malyce toward hym self by ony other forener, hit shall please the soueraynes to send for bothe parties, thou3 that other party be of the queenes house, prince's house, or chaunceler's *hous, or of the chyef justyce house, or seruauntes of the kinges benche* or common place, or ony other lordes seruaunt in Inglond, to appere in thys countynghous and here to appease[b] suche debates after the discressyon of thees soueraynes of thys most hygh court temporall.

§78 (xix). ITEM, that euery purueyour bring into thys countynghous at euery half yere is end his lettres of comission with the seale, there to be seene and new assigned with a newe superscription by the thesaurer of houshold vnder hys seall enclosed and directed to the clerk of crown to be renoued.[c]

§78 (xx). ITEM, if ony offycer or minister longing to this court be noysed or by suspeccion be a thoef or outrageous royatour in much haunting sclaunderous places, companyes, and other, then he to be rehersed hereof [A, p. 176] afore the soueraynes and to be sent by the stewardes power to the marchalcye prison, there to abyde as tyll he be declared and as the law woll award.

§78 (xxi). ITEM, if ony officer of this noble houshold be known for a comyn dayly drunkyn man, *that then hit be claryfyed and charged by the sitters* at the countyngbourd, that he bere no keyes nor minister no stuf of the kinges tyll hys conduccions be refourmed. EBRIETAS TOLLIT INTELLECTUM ET OCULOS DEUORAT.[e] [351]

§78 (xxii). ITEM, hit is here enacted by the king that euery man of this court wyche shall draw furth ony seruaunt in hit, that suche yong seruauntes be comyn of clene blood, good of condycions, vertuouse, and of person lykely, that if hit fortune them to growe to the kinges seruice, the worship of the courte to continue by suche chosen people.

§78 (xxiii). ITEM, that no man of this household support in none

---

a 'of or of the chiefe justicez seruauntes of the kinges benche', *H.*

b From H. A and E have 'appere'.

c Also E and H; unlike the 1790 edition, which has 'removed'.

d Also E; except that it has 'than' instead of 'that'; H has 'that then it be chargid by the sitters'.

e H has 'vorat'.

office ony maner^a [A, p. 177] man or chyld vnder colours of wrong
don ^bto ony maner man,^b as keping prenticez, renners about, pykers,
malefactours of outward people or inward, but suche as may be the
kinges vnchanged officers, vppon the payne of houshold.

§78 (xxiv). ITEM, in this countynghous may be taken the bond of
reconysaunce of ony party; and if hit be broken aftyrward, the
soueraynez here may send hit with the testibuz vnder theyre seales
into the chauncerie^c and therby the party greued may haue the
processe of law as thouze the very dede had be made in the chauncery;
thys custom hath byn of olde and newe.³⁵²

§78 (xxv). ITEM, that no maner^d man of hygh or low degree longing
to this houshold presume by ony coloure to hawke, hunte, or to
fysshe in ony mannes chase, parke, wareyn, or ony^e other seuerall
grounde in his pondez and watyrs^f by lycence of the owners thereof
or theyre deputez, but by comission for the kinges disshe onez or
twyez in the yere at the most, by^g prerogatyf; but and the parties so
greued and wronged complayn to the soueraynes for such abusion,
the offensers by theyre discressions to make amendes, for euery
shylling fourty pens.

[A, p. 178] §78 (xxvi). ITEM, the king woll and chargithe that the
statutes of olde and newe rules, actes, customez, and comaundmentes, nowe made and edyfyed aftyr^h this court, to stond stable
and to be kept and obserued vpon thes peynes asⁱ here be rehersed.
First, vpon warning in fayre maner at the countyngbourd^j opynly;
the second, vpon lesing of his wages for one moneth; the thyrd, in
peyn of prisonment for a moneth; the iiijth., to be put out of court
and to forswere the comyng into hit, or to com nyghe thys court
wetyngly purposed for euer by vij myles,^k his name of reproche
alwey lyke^k to be in the memorande of thys countynghouse yerely
tyll thys mynde of hym be past out. The old charge was that he
shuld ^lswere never^l to com within vij mylez to this court, but alwey
to voyde the kinges comyng or his houshold.³⁵³

[A, p. 179] §78 (xxvii). ITEM, that no sergeaunt, yoman, nor grome,
officer, purueyoure, nor other, furst as officers of bakehous shall not
kepe comyn bakehous for sale bred, nor none of the seler to kepe
comyn tauernes to sale wyne, nor butlers of ale to be comyn bruers,
nor none of catery to be comyn merchauntes to sale^m beoffes, motons,

---

^a 'any maide, man, or child', H.   ^b 'to othir men', H.
^c From H. A and E have 'cuntrey'.   ^d E omits 'maner'.
^e H omits 'ony'.   ^f 'but by lycence', H.
^g 'by his prerogatyf', H.   ^h From H. A and E have 'aftyr'.
ⁱ 'that', E.   ^j 'countynghouse', E.
^k H omits 'by vij myles' and 'lyke'.
^l From H. A and E have 'never swere to com'.
^m 'to sale for boefs', H.

nor graciers, but for the king; nor none officer of houshold to be ony comyn merchaunt of suche stuf as he handylyth of the kinges within this court, but by lycence of the countynghouse, vpon the peyn of statute of this houshold.

§78 (xxviii). ITEM, the kinges vertuous disposicion remembrith a text—VIR MULTUM IURANS REPLEBITUR INIQUITATE, etc.[354] He chargyth in hys hous his marchals of the hall that of what astate euer he be vnder the astate of a baroune vsyng to swere customably by Goddes body, or by ony of his other parties vnreuerently, and they can record hit, that they charge the butler to giue hem no wyne at the[a] melez; and if the butler do, to lese his wages in the countynghous by record of the marchals, etc. There was a lyke mocion to be made for the customable word of hourson.

[A, p. 180] §79. OFFICE OF BAKEHOUSE hathe a sergeaunt, wich apoyntyth the kinges garners in diuerse contriez [b]where as the apurueyaunces[b] of whete shalbe made, by the auyse of the purueours vpon[c] theyre comissions, nyghe to the kinges homez and soiournez to spare caryagez; and there to receue iustly and indifferently by a busshell sealed. And he to delyuer the king be lyke mesure, vppon the payn of houshold, remembring alwey that the king is intytled by old custome in Inglond to be awnswered[d] of euery xx quarte whete so purueyd for thys houshold, to haue one quarter of encres of the mesure vppon the sergeauntes accompt, wych he may well awnswere, and more by help of euery quarter; and that no seller nor constable[e] be compelled to lede or carye hys whete toward the kinges garner[f] or storehous at his proper cost and charge ouerpassing x myle, but that the party be payd for the ouerplus of the mylez. Also the king geuith no tolle at ony myll but geuyth money for euery quarter grynding, and caryage after the distance of a myle to the bakehous, in all iijd.; hit were better the myller to toll then[g] make caryage, etc. Another custom to make [A, p. 181] of a busshell flowre xxx[h] loues by a comyn bulter one brede[i] thorowe all the hous, euery loof weying, and no black brede but[j] for trenchours or houndez, and thereof euery quarter than shall awnswere ij busshells branne. To make a proporcion for the expenses of this houshold for an hoole yere, hit may be esteemed aftyr v quarters,[355] one day with another at largest, amounting by the yere to m¹ viijc xxv quarters, euery busshell to yeld one yere with another, beyng in some yeres or in

---

[a] 'that', H.
[b] 'as puruaiance', H.
[c] From H. A and E have 'that'.
[d] 'to answare', H.
[e] 'noe seller and constable', H.
[f] 'his wheate soe purveyed for this houshould towards the kings garner', H.
[g] From E. A and H have 'and'; H omits 'make'.
[h] '20 loaves', H.   [i] E omits 'one brede'.   [j] E omits 'but'.

M

sundry cuntreys thynne wheete or thyck husked or *a*bettyr or*a*
heuyer of*a* yelde, sume tyme whitter flowre *b*or browner, or in*c* some
place kutte or hit be rype; thys hathe be proued by many old yeres
husbandes, *d*and yett my3t there be made alweyis for a busshell*d*
xxix loues after the olde weyghtes. But for the more party than hit
ys to brown and therefore *e*now of long tyme continued hit hath be
put into a more certayntie, *e*and not to bult hit to*f* sore vppon the
gurgeonez of branne;³⁵⁶ determined and assented to the sergeaunt
of thys offyce to make continually of euery busshell half chiet half
rounde,³⁵⁷ besydez the flowre for the kinges mouthe, xxvij loues,
euery*g* weying, after one day olde, xxiij vncez of troy weyght; [A,
p. 182] wyche brede shall thus *h*be honest ynough to serue*h* this
honorable houshold. Memorandum, that the other twene loues be
called*i* vnder the name of hogman, wich mought be made acording
to seruice ne were the auenture of distaynyng³⁵⁸ of all that other
part. Thys twey loues growen into branne, that*j* woll be of euery
busshell ij loues, into branne of euery quarter xvj loues, and so vp
to euery hundred quarters whete thus dispended in housholde;
*k*sergeaunt is charged to awnswere the king therefore viij quarters*l*
bran, and that to be delyueryd for the kinges horsez be taylez
betwyxt the auener*m* and hym; and euery quarter of this bran so
delyueryd to be breued and alowed in the auener's*m* bookes at*n* the
myddell pryses of whete *o*of that yere, for the baker's discharge,
both the whete*o* and of the mony to awnswere to his parcell of charge
purueyde by hys prouysyon and not dispended in his office. And if
the auener*p* receue nat suche bran, hit shalbe hurt to the king, for
the baker must haue hoole alowaunce; and for to sell hit, he can
not haply passe for a busshell ijd. or jd. ob. or jd. wich might better
help stoppe lyuereys of otes or other*q* prouender [A, p. 183] in the
auerey; and if the sergeaunt baker sell ony thereof, he shalbe sworn
on a booke vpon his acompt *r*howe he sellith hit.*r* Also some iiij
busshells of good whete, euyn strykyn by the bourde,³⁵⁹ woll
awnswere well to vj busshells mele. This sergeaunt etith in the hall;
his lyuerey for all ny3t is j gallon ale; wynter lyuerey, j candyll wax,

---

a H has 'and' in all three cases.
  b H omits 'flowre'.   *c* E omits 'in'.
  d E has 'and my3t therbe alweis maide of a busshell'; H has 'it might there
be made allwayes of a busshell'.
  e 'of longe tyme it hath bine continued and bine put into a more certaine', H.
  f 'soe', H.   *g* 'euerye one weighinge', H.
  h 'shall thus honestlye enoughe serve', H.   *i* H omits 'called'.
  j H omits 'that'.   *k* 'the serieant', H.
  l '8 bushells branne', H.   *m* 'owners' and 'owner's', H.
  n 'of', H.   *o* H omits this passage.   *p* 'owner', H.
  q H omits 'other'.   *r* 'what he selleth it for', H.

ij candylles peris, j talwood, litter and russhes^a of the sergeaunt
vssher, wages in court vijd. ob.,^a clothing wynter and somer or
xlvjs. viijd. yerely;³⁶⁰ he makethe his petycions ones in the yere for
losses of whete, wasting of floure, some etyn by byrdes, some wasshen
by waters, ^bin houses or in caryages, some brede^b all to broken and
etyn with rattes or suche other causes resonable,^c and ^dfor bying of
berm, salt, and candylles^d all the yere; this must be recorded by
countrolment. o CLERK vnder the sergeaunt in this office to be at the
receyte of the whete, of bought brede, and of all other thinges
purueyd; and at the delyueraunce outward to the pantre othyr^e for
a recorde in thys office; and he to recorde^f the foylez of prouision
wykely and truly to make thereof entre, ^gand truly to awnswere
and to make euydence thereof to the people owners,^g so that [A, p.
184] they be not defrauded; and justly to make the tayles of delyueraunce betwyxt this office and the pantry, and wafry, the saucery,
and the auery;³⁶¹ and saufly^h to kepe the bookes of this office, and
to be dylygent to awnswere to that office of clerk or kychyn wyche
accomptyth for this office, and monethly to bring vp his parcelles,
vppon the payne of housholde. This clerk etyth in the hall with yormen
and hath a reward yerely by the sergeauntes petycion, afty his,
desert, by dyscression of the soueraynez; and clothing with yomen
of housholde for wynter and somer, playn, or ellez xiijs. iiijd.,³⁶² and
he partyth with the generall gyftes of houshold, if he be present.
The chyef clerk of kychyn engrosith ones in the yere the acompt of
this office hole, and by the clerk of kychyn is bookes ⁱall the alowauncez for this office be asked.ⁱ o YOMAN in this office for the kinges
mouth,^j receuyng the mayne floure of the sergeaunt by tayle, and
woode^k to bake with, the mayne chete, and payne de mayne, and
alwey ij loues of these to wey a chete lof; he hath also sakkes, lethyr
bagges, canvas, candylles, bulters, [A, p. 185] berm,^l and all other
necessarijs of the sergeaunt by countrolment. This yoman etyth in
the hall and takith wages, clothing, and all other dueties as the
yoman of the countynghouse dothe. Othyr iij honest yomen
purueyours,³⁶³ sad, discrete, and of good auice conscience^m to bere
the comissions of the worship and profit of this court, to puruey
suche stuf as belongyth to this office, whereof alwey one to be
attendaunt in court; and none of them to puruey for malyce of ony
maner person, nothyr to spare there as hit is to sale, orⁿ may be

^a 'russhes and litter', and '2d. ob.', H.   ^b H omits this passage.
^c E omits 'resonable'.   ^d 'for bringinge of salt, berme, and candles', H.
^e 'otherwyse', H.   ^f 'receaue', H.
^g 'and true answare and evidence thereofe to the owner', H.
^h 'fully', H.   ⁱ 'and the allowance of thease offices be asked', H.
^j 'month', H.   ^k 'weyghed', H.   ^l H omits 'barm'.
^m H omits 'conscience'.   ⁿ 'and', H.

ryght well forborn for ony loue. [a]And so he to haue them by reason
for the king,[a] that the owner be nat hurt nor this famous court
disclaundryd by ony outrage of crauing or crakyng[b] or ony other
raueyn in theyre purueyauncez; [c]and they to bring into this vnder-
clerk, called 'clerk for the sergeaunt',[c] of the foylez of theyre purueyauncez by viij dayes next after that hit is made in the cuntrey, and of
all bought brede bryng the taylez to the clerk forth wyth. [d]They
eting in [A, p. 186] the hall[d] [e]and taking wages, clothing, rewardez,
and other deuties in this court[e] as dothe the yoman baker de payne
de mayne, except that[f] the purueyours stond alowed dayly in and
out of court in the chekyr roll iijd. and no more, and yit that if the
sergeaunt or clerk record theyre occupacion.[364] O YOMAN furnour also
in this office, making the weyght of brede and to kepe the balaunce,
seasonyng the ouyn, and at the making of the leuayne at euery
bache; he shall truly delyuer into the brede house, to be saufly kept,
the hole numbyr of his bacche; he shall nother wast nor geue this
brede, but se[g] that hit be woll seasoned and saufe to the kings behoue,
vpon payne of houshold. He etith with the yomen in the hall, taking
clothing and[h] wages, but if hit be recorded; and all other dewtez in
court as his felowes[i] do, except that when that he is out of court,
than he to be chekked out of wages, but if hit be recorded that he is
out of bouge[j] in busynesse for his office. O GROME in this office,
[k]with the yoman for the mouth, cunyng[k] in this science and trewe;
eting in the hall with gromes at the towell; taking ellez[l] for his
rewardes, clothing, and other duetiez in court as the grome[m] of
countynghous. O GROME garnetour[n] to receue, to kepe, and to delyuyr
the wheete comyng from the [E, p. 103] [o]cuntres and sendyng hit
to the mylls, and so into the pistrin; and in absences of other he
kepithe the keyse of the bredehouse as the sergeaunt woll assigne.
He etith in the hall at the towell, taking yerelye for his atendaunce
by peticion xls., and clothing and other dutes with the gromys of

[a] 'And soe to behave them with reasonne for the thinge', H.

[b] E and H have 'crakyng' and 'crakeinge'.

[c] 'and to bringe in this vnder clarke for the serieant', H.

[d] 'they eate in the hall', H.

[e] Also H, except that it has 'take' instead of 'taking'; E has 'and taking
wages, rewardes, as other dothe in this courte'.   [f] E omits 'that'.

[g] H has 'soe'.   [h] From H. A and E omit 'and'.

[i] 'dutyes in courte as followes', H.

[j] E has 'charges'; H has 'that he is out of busines'.

[k] 'with the yeoman beinge cunninge', H.

[l] H omits 'ellez'.   [m] 'groomes', H.   [n] 'garourtour', H.

[o] Pages 187 to 230 inclusive of A are missing; they were presumably still
with the manuscript in 1888 when W. H. St. J. Hope noted, on 29 May, that
pp. 239 to 274 of the manuscript were wanting; otherwise so careful an
antiquary would surely have noted this earlier gap as well.

houshold, and no other wages by the countynghouse. OTHER VIJ gromys, callyd laborers,[365] chosyn and chargyd by the sergeant to bolte, bake, bere water, hewe wood, and other thinges necessary to this*a* workes, and *b*to wayte on the carryage*b* as the sergeant woll assigne for the housholde. Euery of thies takith dayly allowid by the pantrye role ijd. and ffyndyng them self, not etyng in the kynges hall; and whan clothing shalbe yeuin, thes laborers takyth hit *in precio vesture.*[366] Carryage to this [E, p. 104] office for their compitent beddyng, and for the kinges stuf be controlment. No dogges to be kept in this office. ITEM, euery sergeant of office must answer to the sad*c* rule, and also to the ryotes*c* in his office, or elles hit ys thought to hym a grete rebuke.

§80. OFFYCE OF PANETRY hathe a sergeaunt, which is callyd 'chief pantrer*d* of the Kinges mouthe and maister of this office', vnder the kinges power of the countynghouse, as*e* all other officers and sergeauntez of this corte be.*f* He receyuythe the brede of the sergeant of the bakehouse by tayle,*g* and by the viewe of clerk of kichyn as chief clerke of thoffice accomptaunt, which clerk is nowe, and hathe be syne the reigne of the noble Edward the iijde, chief clerk of kychyn.[367] This pantrer, or the yoman breuer, or grome, dayly to breue*h* and answer this clerk of pantry or to his vnderclerkes, breuers*h* for the tyme in the hall and after to present hit in to the countynghouse, how resonably hit ys dispendyd, and there to be vnderstond whither*i* the ministracion of hit be the kinges worship and profit, or not; so that if anny waste or riotous expenses be fonde, then hit to be knowne by whom. This sergeaunt etithe in the hall, taking*j* for wages vijd. ob., daylye in corte, clothing for wynter and somer, or ellis in money xlvjs. viijd.,[367]*k* and ny3t lyuereye, napors,*k* and parte of the generall giftes, with wages oute of corte, lyke as the sergeant of the contynghouse. *l*He makithe his peticion at the yeris end for the waste of*m* brokin and lost brede*m* in his office, etc. He and his office haue compitent carryage of harneys be controlment, and he to haue in to this corte one honest seruaunt.*n* This sergeant endentythe with the thesaurer of housholde for such plate of syluer, gilt, or gold of salers,[368] sponys, and chaundelers*o* that he takythe of

a 'theise', *H.* *b* 'to weight one carriage', *H.*

c 'sayd' and 'remanent', *H.* *d* 'panter', *H.* *e* 'and', *H.*

f H omits 'be'. *g* From H. E has 'entaile'.

h 'brewe', 'brewers', *H.* *i* Also H.

j 'and takethe', *H.* *k* 'aprons', *H.*

l The 1790 edition omits all the material on this page and the next, from 'He makithe his peticion' to 'as doth the grome of countynghouse' inclusive, resuming only with 'O PAGE for the mouthe'.

m 'his broken breade', *H.* *n* 'man', *H.*

o 'silver spoones or chandeleres', *H.*

the countynghouse for this office. Also he takythe by^a recorde of controlment of the grete spicerye, towellis of rynys^b and other of worke fynne, and pleyne nek towelles^{369} and hangers for the dore, and porters for brede. He takythe the keruing knyuis of the jewel-house, trencher knyuis, paring knyuis, gardeuiandes, and other necessarijs allowed by the countynghouse; and whan such thing is renewid and the olde stuf perusyd, than the sergeant by the assent of controlment and ouersight shall haue such olde woren stuf to his fee. And he hath lyuerey for his horses and for all this office in the towne or contrey^c by the sergeant herbiger; and if he be let blod or other wise sicke^d for a season, he or such lyke sergeauntes by cortesy of [E, p. 105] corte take daylye oute of courte ij louis, ij messes of grete mete, one gallon ale, besydes his lyuereye. O YEMAN for the mouthe,^{e} to ^{f}serue the king in absentes of the sergeaunte, which makythe^f seruythe the kynges chamber and ^{g}recordythe to the yoman breuer the trouthe of his expencijs and howe, declaring to hym alwey the personis that he hathe so seruyd;^{g} and he makythe the kinges saler.^{370} He etith in the hall at the oon of the mettes with yomen, taking for his wynter clothing chaunces,^{h} napors, parte of the giftes generall, and caryage for his harneyse resonable, lyke as the yoman of the countynghouse; and he to haue his parte of feez of^i chippinges of brede;^{371} alweyse ij yomen in this corte to haue one honest seruaunt. O GROME in this office for the mouthe, wich cuttythe trenchers, parithe the brede for the kinges chamber, and makythe the saltes for chamber;^{372} and in absentes of sergeante or yoman he seruythe the kyng. The statute of^j Edward the iijde. woll that no grome aproche to the kinges table.^{373} This grome etithe in the hall with other gromes officers at the towell,^{k} takyng of all other thinges of dutie in this corte as dothe the grome of countynghouse. O PAGE for the mouthe to helpe kepe the office and stuf for the king, to pare brede, and for the chamber, to helpe bere with^l porters when he is commandyd, to make and kepe clenne knyuis, and clene the^m office, to trus and bere ^{n}brede or harnes,^{n} and to attend vpon the carryage for the kynges goods to be sauid. No page shall ete in the hall, but in his office or with his next fellowe in office,^{o} takyng for aldaye one lof of brede, one mes of grete mete, dim. gallon ale, and all other rewardes and duites as the page of countynghouse, alwey

---

^{a} From H. E has 'the'. ^{b} 'raynes', H. ^{c} H has 'courte'.
^{d} From H. E omits 'sicke'. ^{e} 'month', H. ^{f} H omits this passage.
^{g} H has 'recordeth to the yeoman brewer his expences, trulye declaringe vnto him allwaies the personnes he hath serued', H.
^{h} From H (which has 'aprons'). E has 'chaunges'. ^{i} 'and', H.
^{j} 'noble Edward', H. ^{k} 'at the towell, with other groomes officers', H.
^{l} From H. E has 'the'. ^{m} From H. E omits 'the'.
^{n} 'hedd and harneys', H. ^{o} 'or in his next fellowes office', H.

to be obedyent to such as be aboue hym in thoffice. O YEMAN breuer
that dayly makythe breuementes with the clerk of kychin, or with
his vnder clerkes, of all thexpences of brede dispended in this housholde the day biforn; this brefmentes be made in the mornyng, at
viij of the clok in the hall, by custom of all such lyuereys and
seruyces, and that day he to cum to the apposile and accomptes in
the countynghouse, there to answer to. Hym^a owghte to make his
lyuereys a lytelle before that metes and suppers go, to auoydyng
such prese and combraunce,^b that the hall and chambers may be
quykly seruyd, withoute lyttyng afterward, when hit is callyd for.
The statutes of noble Edward the iijde. wolde that this yoman
shulde serue the halle at one mele, and dyne at the other mele;^c 374
but now hit ys assentyd, for more worshipp and sure answering^d to
the kynges profit, daylye to haue ^ehis lyuereye in to this office^e
allowid [E, p. 106] vpon an eting day ij louis, ij messes of grete mete,
one gallon ale, wages in countynghouse iijd. daylye, for clothing
xiijs. iiijd., ^fand for chaunces iiijs. viijd.,^f 375 of napors at euerye of
the iiij festes princypall of the grete spicery one elle lynyn clothe,
price viijd., parte also of the generall gyftes of housholde and his
parte of the fees of chepynges^g and that the comptroller^h oftin tymys
see that theieⁱ be not parde to ny the crome. 376 No yoman of this
office, grome, nor page, ought to bere or to take^j oute of this anny
brede, but ^kbe knowing of the breuer or his deputie by which he may
declare his discharge.^k OTHER III YEMEN^l in this office, 377 panters
attendyng vpon the hall, other astates in there chambers 378 by commandmentes of the soueraynis and^m rulers in the countinghouse or
vsshersⁿ of the kinges chamber, to make trewe and worshipfull
seruyce in the hall by the marshallis preceptes, in other places by
recordes,^o 379 and all his expences, and howe to declare to the yomen
breuer^p or to his deputie that nothing be mysusyd^q by them to the
damage of the king or sergeant. Thes yomen by assent serue the hall
at^r one mele, and dyne and sup at that other mele;^s they set the
saltes in the hall and take theym vp last; they take^t in all other

---

^a 'there to answere. Hee ought', H.

^b 'to avoydinge such place of presse and combraunce', H.

^c 'and dine at annother', H. ^d 'and for answaringe', H.

^e 'his liuereyes into his offices', H.

^f H omits this phrase and has 'for aprons'.

^g 'his parts of chippinges and fees', H. ^h From H. E has 'controllers'.

ⁱ From H. E omits 'that theie'. ^j 'make', H.

^k 'by knowledge of the brewere of his deputyes by which he maye dis-
charge', H.

^l H omits 'yeomen'. ^m 'or', H. ⁿ 'vsher', H.

^o 'record', H. ^p 'brewer', H. ^q 'misused', H.

^r From H. E has 'an'. ^s 'at another', H.

^t H omits 'they take'.

duites in this corte lyke to the yoman breuer;[a] and this sergeant assignythe of these yomen or of the gromys as hym thinkythe beste to make lyuereys and to breue and answer in absentes of the yoman breuer,[a] or ell is he assignythe one of the gromys, such a persone as the sergeant of countinghouse thinkythe most apt and redye therto. None astate of Ynglond ought to be seruyd within this corte but be one of the kynges officers of euerye office, etc. OTHER II GROMYS[380] in this office to help serue the hall or other lordes in absentes of the yomen, and to kut trenchers, to make saltes, to helpe bere the porters after yomen in the hall or chamber as they be commandyd be such as ar[b] aboue theym in office; etyng in the hall with gromys[c] officers at the towell, taking of all other rewardes, clothing and duites as the grome of countinghouse and the grome of the mouthe in this office aboue writtin do within this corte. OTHER II PAGES[380] in this office, taking lyuereys, clothing, and rewardes, in this housholde as page of the countynghouse dothe. Yf hit nede, the[d] bere the porters after the gromys in the hall; theym[e] ought to kepe clenlye the bynnys of brede and the office, to fet the brede dayly from the cart in to this office, to chip brede but not to nye the cromme, to wayte vpon carryage at the remouinges; and other necessary thinges [E, p. 107] to do as[f] they shalbe commandyd by theym that ar aboue theym[g] in this office, [h]or else to take the correccion of the office, lyke as euerye office within this corte haue nedefull correccions within theym self vpon reasons, tyll the countynghouse call before theym.[h] O sompter hors longithe to this office for the kinges gardeviaundes, founden in alle charges by the purueyauns of the thesaurer of housholde. No dogge to be kept in this office. This office hathe [for][i] wynter lyuereye, one candyll wex, ij candeylles peric, one talwood dim., yf he haue a chymmyney,[381] and[j] elles one busshell of coolys; and all other ny3tes throghe[k] all the yere, one gallon ale; also lytter for the beddes or palettes, as hit shall nede; besydes the sergeauntes lyuereye, if he serue the king at ny3t, a torch.

§81. OFFYCE OF WAFERS hathe one yoman makyng wafers, and safflye and clenlye to kepe theym couered and vnder lok, and by assaye [l]to delyuer for the kinges mouth[l] to the shewer; and for other men to the assewers of chamber for the astates[m] as the countynghouse

---

[a] 'brewer', *H.*   [b] 'be', *H.*   [c] 'other', *H.*   [d] 'hee', *H.*

[e] 'theye', *H.*   [f] H omits 'to do as'.   [g] H omits 'aboue theym'.

[h] 'or else to take the corrections of this office within. That courte hath needeful corrections within themselves vppon reasonne, till the comptinghouse call it before them', *H.*

[i] E has 'no', which does not appear to make sense; H omits 'this office hathe no'.

[j] 'or', *H.*   [k] 'throughout', *H.*

[l] 'to be delivered to the kings monethe', *H.*   [m] 'after theire estates', *H.*

apointythe; and so afterwarde to the assewers of the hall for dayly
seruice. And at the festes principall of the yere than hit is assentyd
to be seruyd to other lower officers more generall; the cotidyan
seruyce is to the king, to dukes, to erllys,[a] to the steward of housholde, thesaurer, comptroller, cofferer, and to such straungeours as
they assigne for that seruyce as hit shall requier. He takythe for the stuf
of this office after the [b]prees of astates beyng present in corte;[b] furst,
for his[c] flower of the sergeant of bakehouse dayly or wekelye as he
hathe nede by a taile betwixt theym bothe; and sugar of the grete
spicery; towelles of reynnys, towelles of work and of playne, cloth
fyne,[d] cofyrs, smale gardeviaundes, and bakyng yrons of the office,
if hit nede, egges. This yoman etith in the hall, taking wages, clothing, [e]naprons, rewardes, and fees of his proper office, perused after
the forme as yemen[e] of the pantrye,[382] by ouersyght of countroller
or countynghouse. The lyuerey of this office in wynter season, for
comyn dayes, a candyll wex to bake for the kinges mouthe, ij
candylles peric, iij tallwoodes, and lytter all the yere for[f] his owne
bed of the sergeant vsher; and for all other thinges necessarye by
commandmentes of the soueraigns [E, p. 108] of the countynghouse.
The statutes of noble Edward iijde, for[g] sertayne reasonnys vsyd in
those[g] dayse, gaf this[h] office grete wages, clothing, and higher
lyuereye then he takythe nowe because his busynes was much
more.[383] And if this yoman be let blod, syk, or otherwise clistred[i]
for a season, he takythe a cast of bred, a mes of grete mete, j gallon
ale; and carryage for his office, and there harneys and beddyng
compitent by ouersight of[j] controlment; and his charge is daylye to
answer into the countynghouse for the resaite and of the ministracion, and for all the yssues and expences of this[k] office. O GROME in
this office[384] that can make wafers, as be vsyd in this corte, to helpe
kepe theym clenlye and saflye for the kynges mouthe, and afterward
for the worship of this corte and sauegarde of theym that shalbe
seruyd with theym, and to helpe serue the hall and chambers in
absentes of the yoman, the yoman at that[l] mele, the grome at that
other; and he to kepe the kinges goodes in this[m] office and stuf that
is receuyuyd therfore, withoute losces reasonable and withoute
riottes, gyftes inordynate. This grome etithe in the hall at the towell,
takyng in rewardes[n] and clothing of the countynghouse, and other
generallyties as the grome of pantrye. O PAGE in this office, yf hit

---

[a] 'or earles', H.   [b] 'prices of estate beinge in present in courte', H.
[c] 'the', H.   [d] H omits 'fyne'.
[e] H omits this passage, from 'naprons' to 'yemen'.
[f] From H. E has 'of'.   [g] From H. E omits 'for' and 'those'.
[h] 'his', H.   [i] 'glistered', H.   [j] 'and', H.
[k] 'that', H.   [l] 'the', H.   [m] 'that', H.
[n] 'The groome eateth at the towell in the hall, takeinge rewardes', H.

nede,*a* by discreccions of the countynghouse, to geue atendaunce in
kepyng of this office and the kynges mete and stuf longyng therto, to
lerne the cunnyng seruice and duites*b* of this office, to fet the
lyuereys longyng nedefully*c* therto, and to waite vpon the saf
conduyte therof in reknynges; which daylye takythe rewardes,
clothing and other generall giftes of this corte as do pages of pantrye.

§82. OFFYCE OF BUTLER OF YNGLOND capitall, vnto whome steward
and thesaurer of housholde make yerelye warraunt vnder their seals*d*
or vnder the seale of countynghouse, at Michelmas, by the kinges
assent, assigning the saide butler howe much conuenable wynnys of
all kyndes he shall pourueye for the yere next following expressyd
in that warraunt; and the namys of the places of the kinges or elles
where hit shall please the kyng to pourpose his moste abydyng, that
there the saide wynnys shuld be loged in, for his expenses and of*e*
his housholde. This chief butler and his [E, p. 109] vnder butler
deputie sufficiant takythe his receipte of moneye and assignmentes
of the thesaurer or by his apointment in the countynghouse or in
thexchekker for all the empciones of this office;*f* and wages, rewardes,
feez, and other necessarijs, for all his pourueyaunces of housholde,
wynnys, and almes wynnys to houses of relygyon,385 and for*g* wynnys
of gift, by pryue seale. And he endentith with the thesaurer of
housholde for such receites as can be founden in the kynges peele
takyn oute by his houndes.*h* 386 And herefor*i* he is bounden by olde
custum to make his viewis in to the countynghouse of all his receiptes,
charges, and discharges,*j* and remanentes bref yerelye at ij termys,
the furst viewe in the morne*k* next after Sent Hillarij, this*k* other
viewe at the fest of Sent John Baptist, and the trewe smale accompte
of euery thing particular*k* expressed by his propir othe, a nother to be
made at the contyngborde before the soueraynys, etc., at the fest
of Sent Martyn. Thies butler's purueyours be charged by statutes of
the land and of*l* this royalle cort, that all achates and pourueyaunces
maide with the merchauntes be withoute anny disturbance or
damage escewing the sclaunder of this courte or of the dishonour of
hit; and if anny such be, then to make large amendes to the party
so wrongyd. Also steward, thesaurer, countroller, or thother maister
clerkes of the countynghouse, to viewe the kinges cellars*m* and of the
wynys thereof, to knowe the profet and the verrey diligences*n* that
thees butlers make vppon the saf kepyng thereof, by the whiche

---

a 'One page if neede be in this office', *H*.   *b* H omits 'and duites'.
c H omits 'needfully'.   *d* 'seale', *H*.   *e* 'for', *H*.
f 'emprises of his office', *H*.   *g* H omits 'for'.
h 'hands', *H*.   *i* 'therefore', *H*.   *j* 'charged and discharged', *H*.
k 'morrowe', 'the', and 'particulerlye', *H*.
l From H. E has 'if'.   *m* From H. E has 'sealers'.
n 'to knowe the verrye perfecte dilligences', *H*.

viewes the butler's trouthe in his office doyng may be knowe,[a] and
therby to take his[b] rewardes yerelye after the[c] desertes, more or les;
remembring alweye that the paylyng of euery pype or ton ought to
be takin according to[d] the inche of the square[d] that the carpenter
vsythe. This sergeant capitall butler's fees be delyueryd and takyn
be ouersight and recorde of the comptroller[e] whan thinges beene of
wynne and vessaulx feeble[e] perusyd; he takyth wages of housholde,
vij. ob., and clothing, xlvjs. viijd., with the sergeauntes lykewise;[f]
and[f] by the statutes of noble Edward the iijde, he shulde take in
corte for all his fee and wages xx marces yerelye,[387] payed[f] by his
owne [E, p. 110] handes till he were auaunced by the kyng or by[f]
his meanys to the summe of xl li. yerelye duryng his lyf;[f] at tho[g]
dayes he had but xxvjs. viijd.[387] allowid yerelye for his clothis;[g]
clothing syn that tyme he hathe be vsyd to take in seruices and
lyuereys of corte, [h]if hym self be present after such astate and degre;
sittyng in the hall or in the kynges chamber with a persone of lyke
seruyce. And alle his pourueyaunces of wynnys for this housholde
wikely to be knowin, serchid or tasted, as can be thought nedefull;
if eny be corrupid wynnys,[h] reboylyd, or vnholesum for mannys
bodye, then be the comptrollers[i] hit to be shewid at the counting-
borde, so that by assent alle such pips or veseulx defectyue be
damnyd and cast vppon the losses[j] of the saide chief butler; and
forthewith the wynne to be auoydyd oute of the kinges selers opinly
into the corte to auoide all suspeccion.[388] The namys and the properties of the officers of this office,[k] as for[k] vnder butlers, cunter clerkes[k]
of selers, men of counsaile, atterneys, yomen, pourueyours, and
gromys nedefull longyng to this office of chief butler, they be expressyd in his fynall accompt.[l] The kyng hathe hit entitled by his
prerogatif to haue of euery ship, [m]from xxj dolia tight before the mast
and behynd to haue ij dolia of wynne;[m] and so of euerye ship till he

---

[a] 'by the which viewes of buttlers theire truth in office doeinge mey be
knowne', H.

[b] 'theire', H.   [c] 'theire', H.

[d] From H. E has 'with' and 'squier'.

[e] From H. E has 'controllers' and 'fyeable'.

[f] H omits 'lykewise', 'and', 'payed', 'by' and 'duryng his lyf'.

[g] H has 'those' and omits 'clothis'.

[h] H has 'if himselfe be present after such of like service and all his purveyances of wynes. Soe this househould weekelye to bee knowne, searched or
tasted as shalbe needefull; yf any wines be corrupted'.

[i] H omits 'for man's body', has 'comptrouller', and omits 'hit'.

[j] From H. E has 'a losces'.

[k] H omits 'of this office' and 'for', and reads 'counter clarkes'.

[l] 'this small accompt', H.

[m] H has 'from 16 dolia before the mast and 2 dolia wyne'; the printed version
of 1790 has 'xx dol' instead of 'xxj'.

cum to the ti3t of iijC dolia, ^athan the kyng hathe of euery such ship before and be hynde iiij dolia wyne; and anny bere more, the king getithe more.^a Hit hathe lykyd the king now, be thaduyce of his full sad and noble counsaile, to discharge this grete butler of all the pourueyaunces of wynnys for the kyng and his housholde and to exempt hym fro this corte, lyke as ys nowe thoffice of priue seale, the office of marchalse, office of warderober, tailor, armorer, pauilloner, the clerkes of croune, of market, and workes,³⁸⁹ and other mo that sum tyme wer here incorporate; and now be lyke polecy be remem-bred^b which lyghtenythe to no blemyshe but to grete profet shall proue and worship before the kyng.^{b 390} And the saide butler to execute his office as hit hath be acustomyd beforetyme for this almes wyns to housses of religion and for other wynnys of gift that the kyng giuith, [E, p. 111] to sume men terme of lyff and to sume menn but o season by his lettres of priuey seale,³⁹¹ and to medill and take of the kinges prices and other in the portes as he dyd befforetyme. But he is put here aparte to pouruey for thexpences of housholde; wherfor the kyng hath now assignyd pourueyors of wynne and tasters for hym self and householde, abydyng vpon the asignementes and comaundmentes^c of the stewarde, thesaurer, comptroller, and countynghouse within housholde as hit^d ys here after writin. Re-membred alwey that the chief butler of Ynglond and his deputes sauely and surely kepe^d the furst venus of wyns in vessels or shipps in anny portes or other places from anny sale^e till the kynges housholde pourueyours^f haue take for the kyng and his expences^g of his corte and asmuch as theym nedithe, with trewe paymentes accordyng to the kynges olde inheritable prices^h by verry discreccion; and the butlerⁱ of Ynglonde to enter for his office after and thereof^j to yelde his viewz and accomptes vp to the kinges escheker yerely.³⁹² And the sergeant of ^kthe cellare^k to be chargyd with all particuler wynnys of all manner ^kof kindes^k pourueyde and expendid in ostries and the kinges loggeyng whan he remeiuithe, be ouersi3t of counting-house and comptrolment, and this to be chargid in the memorandum.

§83. OFFYCE OF POURUEYOURS OF WYNNE, attendyng for the more parte in this housholde to herekyn vpon the preceptes of steward and

---

^a 'then the king has behind and before and euerye such shippe 4 dolia wyne; and if any beare more than hee to haue more', H.

^b 'which littleethe this courte to noe small blemyshe but the great post shall prooue and be worshippe for the kinge', H.

^c H omits 'and commandments'.

^d H omits 'hit' and 'kepe'.   ^e From H. E has 'seale'.

^f 'purveyor', H.   ^g 'kings expences', H.

^h 'kings charitable prices', H.   ⁱ 'and then the buttler', H.

^j 'other', H.

^k From H. E has 'seler' and 'kind'.

countynghouse, to know the kynges remouinges, or elles *to be sent
owte* to make pourueyaunces of wynnys for this*b* corte; and to ryde
and ouerse the places there as the kinges wynnys be loggyd, that hit
be safly kept from perell of lekyng or*b* brekyng of vesselles of*b* lak
of hopyng or other copage;*b* and all other craft for the rackyng,
coyning, rebatyng, and other saluacion of wyns, etc.[393] IIIJ YOMEN,
leuable and discrete,[394] prouyde in that facultie of chesyng, bying,
and keping of all cuntreye wynns, that*c* euery of theym pouruey
by the kinges commyssion, to be had by the thesaurer of housholdes
recorde and seale directed*d* to the clerk of crowne to make such
commyssion for such pourueyours accordyng to the statutes, and
at euery half yere to be brought into countynghouse, that hit may
be there subscribed [E, p. 112] vnto the clerk of croune, and so to
haue oute*e* a newe commyssion. Also*f* at anny grose pourueyauncez
or grete paymentes for wyne the thesaurer, cofferer, or one of the
clerkes of grenne clothe, with one of the controlment, owght*g* to be
there*g* to knowe and enter alle maner of charges and the trewe
conueyauns thereof forthe to*h* the kynges homys, and there to be
delyuered by one indenture therpartet,*i* that one to remayne with
thies butlers pourueyours till alle the hole yere be accomptyd, that
other partye with the clerk of butelary and seler otherwise callyd
clerk of the kychin in this housholde, the thirde party to remayne in
the countynghouse.[395] Thiese yoman take*j* dayly by the chekker role
in and oute of corte in the kinges seruyce iijd., etyng in the hall
with yomen, and *k*clothing and*k* other parte as the yomen of the
pantrye; and when anny of theym pourueyith wynnes, that at the
discrecion of steward, thesaurer, comptroller and countynghouse,
after his desert, for bouge*l* of corte and for his hors, dayly ijd., that
he be nother extorcioner, oppresor, nor shamfull in his demeanyng.

§84. OFFYCE OF CELLAR*m* within the kynges housholde hathe a
sergeant[396] that shall receiue alle the wynnys in euery place that the
kyng or his housholde shall cume to, aswell bought wyne at the
kinges prices as other wynnys of present. And he to answer roundly
*n*therto for euery galon,*n* potell, and pint by mesure, and so as
treuly to delyuer the remanentes[397] as oftin as the kyng and his

---

a From H. E has 'to present'.
b 'the' and 'and' and 'for' and 'compage', *H*.
c 'thus', *H*.
d 'tresaurer of househould, recorded, sealed, and directed', *H*.
e Also H, unlike the printed version of 1790, which omits 'oute'.
f H omits 'Also'.   *g* H omits 'ought' and has 'present'.
h From H. E has 'with'.   *i* 'tripartite', *H*.
j 'This yeoman taketh', *H*.   *k* H omits 'clothing and'.
l 'beinge', *H*.   *m* From H. E has 'SEALER'.
n 'there to every gallon', *H*.

housholde shall departe and^a remeue, by ouersight of the countroller,
or clerkes of grene cloth and clerkes of kychin, or by sume of there
vnder clerkes,³⁹⁸ that a^b trewe booke of wynne may be made at the
yers end. And in lykewise to take euery inuencion^c as oft as the king
cummythe to ony place of his owne or of anny other mannys, for
a declaracion of trouthe with the butlers and kepers of the kinges
selers, receyue^d the remanentes of wyne of prise, and delyuer them
agayne at euery inuencion as oft as the kyng cummyth, by indenture.
And the countynghouse wull assent for euery polle and inch for ^ethe
butler of seler in housholde is discharge,^e and then to answer of
almaner expences of wynnys. This saide sergeant, or the yoman
tryour, or yet^f the grome tryour, by the sergeauntes assignement
[E, p. 113] dayly to be redye in the hall as the yoman pantrer and
butler of ale shalbe, at viij of the clok in the mornyng or bifore,
there to abyde^g one of the clerkes of kychin the breuementes of
thexpences of all there offices in the daye next before, therby to
knowe howe honorably and husbandly the officers handill and
minister the kinges goodes. This sergeant seruythe the kynges
persone of wyne and ale; he hath also in kepyng and charge of^h all
maner of plate, syluer, golde, ^h and gilt delyueryd from the countynghouse or jewell house by indentures, ewers, lauers, and coberd-
clothis, cup-clothis, hangers, barelles, fferys,ⁱ and portatiffes. He
takith in euerye dutye in^j this corte, of wages clothing, gyftes, lyke
the sergeaunt of pantrye, for hym self, in season of the yere, one
candell wex in tymys of nede,^j one torch to serue the king for wyne
and ale, ij candelles peric, ^kdim. talwood or dim bushell of collys;^k
and ny3tly one gallon ale, and lytter rushis^l for his bedd, and lyuerey
for his office ny3tly of wex candell and peric candell, and ^motherwhilles
after that they brou^m in derk selers, coolis as shalbe thought nedefull
by the discrecion of the countynghouse. This office hathe a somter
man and hors and also a botelhors ³⁹⁹ foundon by the thesaurers
charge. The brede andⁿ wynne that hit be onestlye kept by the wayse
vndispendyd ^ountill it be brought in againe^o by the botell man; and
all other carryages for this office and for there compitent beddyng^p
be ouersight of controller, etc. O YEMAN for the kinges mouthe^q ⁴⁰⁰

---

^a 'or', H.   ^b From H. E has 'be'.   ^c 'an inventorye', H.
^d 'receauinge', H.   ^e 'the buttler or cellars in houshoulde's discharge', H.
^f H omits 'yet'.   ^g 't'abide that', H.   ^h H omits 'of' and 'gold'.
ⁱ H has 'fferrers' and omits 'barelles'.
^j H has 'of' and omits 'in tymys of nede'.
^k 'dimid. bushell coles', H.   ^l 'lytter and rishes', H.
^m H and the 1790 edition omit these five words.
ⁿ From H. E omits 'and'.
^o From H. E has 'oute to be brought and in agayne'.
^p 'abydinge', H.
                                              ^q 'monethe', H.

that with the sergeaunt chesythe the wynnys most pleasunt to the kinges drinkyng and most holesum; *a*and he safly with all his diligences to kepe hit*a* that no persone but for the mouthe medill*b* therwith. He seruythe*c* the kyng at the cupborde and barre*c* [401] in the absentes of the sergeaunt, both with the cupbordecloth, pottes and cuppis, for wyne and ale; *d*the saide sergeant, this yoman, or the grome here for the mouthe in their absentes,*d* shall treulye enforme the yoman treyour or the grome trayour*e* in his absentes of as much wyne and ale as they haue mynystered there by the vsher's recorde, so *f*tha(t) the entre thereof*f* may be made at the brefmentes. This yoman takythe in housholde for wages and clothing and parte of the giftes generall [E, p. 114] lyke to the yoman of pantrye etyng in the hall. O GROME of seler[402] for the kinges mouthe, to giue attendaunce vpon*g* thoffice, to drawe wynne, or*g* to fet the ale for the king and his chambre, and other gardevyaundes and cofers, and to kepe his parte clenely and onestly, and all the vessellis, both pottes and cups and clothis and to bere theym inward and outeward at euery carryage. He etithe in the halle*h* dynner and supper, as the gromys of pantrys for the mouthe; and rewardes, clothing, and other, etc. O YEMAN trayour of the seler*i* which draweth and delyuerythe at the barre alle the wynns for the hall, chambre, all lyuereys and other duites of alle this corte. He daylye shall breue as the yoman pantrer dothe in hall with clerk of the kychyn, at the our assigned, lyke as he woll answer to all recordes of vshers, marshallys, and other dew lyuereys, or to any other commaundmentes. Hym ought to delyuer his wynnys be just mesure and to take so*j* his allouauncez by sextaries, pichers, dim. pichers, and quartes in the countynghouse at the accomptes contynually. He with the clerk controller and clerk of kichin receyuythe the contynualle inuencions*k* of wyns as oftin as the kyng and his housholde cummythe to ony place; and euery remeuing he or the sergeant *l*or the grome treyour*l* shall delyuer the remanentes of alle such wyns receued by hym. And hym ought by the statutes to haue noe fees of cleane wyne*m* as long as hit may renne, but droppinges and spillynges, but the kokyrs and the lyes, and that*n* be ouersight and recorde of comptroller*n* or

a 'and safelye to keepe it with all his dilligence', *H.*

b 'monthe' and 'intermeddle', *H.*

c H omits 'He seruythe' and 'and barre'.

d 'the serjeant, yeoman, and groome for the monthe in theire abscence', *H.*

e H omits this word.　　*f* 'that the same', *H.*　　*g* 'in' and 'and', *H.*

h E has 'at one mele'; H omits this.

i 'and other for the yeoman trier of the sellor', *H.*　　*j* 'for', *H.*

k 'receaveth continuallye inventions', *H.*

l E has 'or the groom or the grome treyour'; H omits 'or the grome'.

m From H. E has 'And hym ought by no statute, to have anny fee clene wyns'.　　*n* From H. E has 'the' and 'countrollers and clerkes'.

clarke[n] of kychyn. Nothir this sergeant, nother yoman grome, nor othir officers, owte [a]to kepe anny continuaunce of personnys dynyng nor suppyng much in this office but[b] byd va.,[403] sauf onlye such as be longing to the office in dewe tymys but by the soueraign's commaundmentes for the kynges worship, nothir to kepe there propir seruantes within this office to be ouerconuersauntes, vppon the payne of housholde.[b] This yoman, because of[c] his grete busynes, and the grome trayour,[d] shall haue in to this office in etyng dayes ij payns, ij mes de gros de cusin, and one mes rost, j gallon seruoice, [e]all thinges of[e] wages, clothing, or giftes generall lyke to the yomen of pantrye; and to be obedient vnto the preceptes of the soueraigns of housholde in alle such appointementes [E, p. 115] as they[f] shall make in the countynghouse for the kyng and his corte. This yoman helpithe the sergeant yerely to make his peticion for his discharge of wynnys by lekage, and of wynnys lost at breuementes, or disalowid in the countynghouse for lack of commandementes or other auctoriteez, and for damnyd wynnes[g] [404] not allowid, or othir causes resonable, by record of countroller.[h] He hathe one seruaunt honest in thys corte, but nat abydyng in[i] this office; also that[j] this yeman bere not the kayse of this office anny tyme oute of corte, not[j] to be ferre absent, nor continually abidyng in the seler but at mele tymys, but[j] as hit shall requier for the kyng and straungers. Hit fyttyth that thees officers be of jentill condicion in answering to all people and temperat in all there guydyng, for the honour of this corte. OTHER IJ GROMYS vnder the trayour, to helpe hym to drawe and bring the vesselx with wynnys to the barre or to other places within the corte as the soueraigns of corte will command them for the king in tyme of nede and commyng of strangers; and for the kinges chambre and hall to kepe safly the wynne, vesselx, stuf, and oneste of thoffice, that there[k] be nothir ryot ne waste, but to be atendaunt, secret, and diligent for worship and profet of this corte. Thies gromys take alle othir duetes, rewardes and clothing, etc., as do the gromys of the pantrye; alwey ij gromys betwixt theim to haue one onest man or childe seruaunt in to this corte, but not vsed[l] in the seler.[405] O PAGE in this office, to help washe barellys, portatiffes, tubbus, pottes[m] or

---

[a] E has 'nat' which H omits.

[b] H has 'by the souerainges commaundement for the King's worshipp and honnor, nor keepe there onye proper servantes within this office to be over-conversant'.

[c] From H. E omits 'of'.   [d] 'triors', H.   [e] H omits 'all thinges of'.

[f] From H. E has 'he'.   [g] 'for dampned wynes or for singinge wynes', H.

[h] 'comptrollers', H.   [i] From H. E has 'on'.

[j] H omits 'that', has 'nor', and omits 'but'.

[k] H has 'there', which E omits.   [l] 'vseinge', H.

[m] From H. E has 'bottes'.

cupis, and[a] to helpe kepe clenlye the office, to helpe to trus the stuf,[a] and bere to and fro the carryage at alle remeuinges, and to waite therupon, safly to gyde and kepe hit. Pages haue oftin tymys be choson and abled by the maisters of office;[b] [406] and than presentyd in to the countinghouse, ther to be entrid and vnderstond of his [c]vertuus, condicions, and properte[c] of persons, and therfore[d] the maisters or the sayd[e] yomen haue the coreccions of pages within theym self, vpon reason, [f]but hit be in anny grete case[f] that the countynghouse lyst to call before theym. This page takyth clothing and rewardes of the countynghouse, and daylye one mes of grete mete, one payne, dim gallon ale in to this office, lyke pages of the pantrye. Hit hathe bene oftymys in yeris to gither that the kyng [g]hath had the advantage of the feeble and dull wynes[g] to make thereof vinegar and to delyuer hit to the [E, p. 116] sergeaunt of saucery. O chariot for the gardevyaundes of the pantrye, cofers of waffrye, gardeviaundes with syluer vesselles of bothe selers, and barrelles of wynne, gardeviaundes of picherhouse, gardeviaundes of the ewrye, some gardevyaundes of skolery and saucery, the kynges almesdishe, alle other stuf be ouersight of countrolment as hym thinkyth conuenyent to saue the caryage and accordyng [h]to euery mannys degree.[h] The king ought of right to be furst merchaunt to euery mannys fee within this housholde, and so hee[i] ys entitled be noble Edward the iijde.[407] to bye of his yoman trayour as many cokers[408] of his fee within the [j]selers as[j] the pourueyors of the butel-arye and pourueyours of squylery shall nede at anny tyme or place, highe or lowe, for viijd. apece the best. The soueraynnys of housholde owe to haue a priuate enquiere of anny officer of[k] butry or seler take anny rewardes of the brewars of ale, or of the butler pourueyor of wyne take onny giftes of the parties oweners, for to vtter their euill ale or wynne or other stuf by ony colour within the housholde; and he that so receyuythe such stuf to be cast vpon hym and the owner therof.

§85. OFFICE OF BUTELARY OF ALE vnder the sergeant of selers charge, one chif[l] sobir yoman versour,[409], to receyue alle the ale or bere that shalbe pourueide be entaile, to viewe hit in the cummyng in, to receue tailles foylls,[m] to call the countrollers or clarkes of buttrye, that

---

[a] 'to helpe cleanlye the office, to helpe and trusse', H.
[b] 'masters of offices', H.
[c] 'vertuous disposition, condition, and propertyes', H.
[d] H omits 'therefore'. [e] From H. E has 'sad'.
[f] 'but if it be vppon anye greate cause', H.
[g] From H. E has 'be avauntage the feble or dull wynnys'.
[h] H omits these four words.
[i] From H. E omits 'hee'. [j] 'cellare if', H. [k] From H. E omits 'of'.
[l] H omits 'chif'. [m] 'to receaue the tayles', H.

N

is the clerk of kychyn, to gawge the pipse, to mesure or proue anny othir vesselx, to assay, tast, or set the prise of alle such drink vpon the foylles be ij or iij dayse next after cummyng in therof to this office. *The olde custome of this corte is to pay* after as the clerk of market dothe*b* present for euery gallon ale, and that is for kinges housholde after as malt goythe in the market, for euery shiling of the quarter malt that*b* brewers by, the king to paye so many quadrans for the gallon ale in to this housholde if the ale be so worthe; than the countrollers of buttrye and kychin to make such entre in to there bookes and such allowaunces therfore in the counting-house, and euer that they be praysed*c* trulye and indiferently as hit is worthe without*d* loue or hatred, so that no sclaunder [E, p. 117] arise agaynst this courte. This yeman hathe speciall charge vnder the saide*e* sergeant of the keping of this ale, bere, or such other*e* stuf, and ministracion therof at the barre for alle the housholde. Hym*e* ought to be of temperat conducion and to preferre worship to straungeours with profit with such as hathe duites to lyuereys,[410] with honest and manerly demeanyng; not to kepe dyners nor suppers customably within this office but for hym self *for the page as dothe the yoman pantrer breuer.* Hit fittithe the grete officers of countynghouse, oftin tyms*g* and sodenlye, to visite the officers and offices, to se and know *hif any riotous*h* rulis be vsyd within forthe the kynges hurt, and to amend hit. Also of deute, because he takyth hoole allouaunce be euery gallon or dim. gallon, hym*i* ought to make delyueraunce to halle, chambre, and lyuereys by euin, playne mesure.[411] Also to geue atendaunce dayly to the breuementes with the clerkes of botrye in the hall and to giue answer therto at accomptes; also that he or the gromys of this office be attendaunt with the keye, if they be callyd for the kyng, soueraigns, or straungers, not to*j* long abidyng in thoffice of*j* melles, with opyn window*j* or dorys[412] but as the kinges worship with profit do requier. This yoman by the sergeauntes aduyce makythe at euery Mychelmas a peticion in to this countynghouse for abatementes and disalowaunces of his ale; and for ale giuin to *k*almose; how much and wherfore ale lackyng*k* in the vesselx and spylt by drawinges. Also he askyth allowaunce for tubbis,*l* treyse, and faucetes occupyed all the yere before by

---

a 'Of ould custome this courte is paye', *H.*   *b* 'will' and 'the', *H.*
c 'that theye be priced', *H.*   *d* From H. E has 'for'.
e H omits 'saide' and 'other' and has 'he'.
f H, and the 1790 edition, omit these ten words.
g 'sometymes', *H.*   *h* From H. E has 'of ony riotes'.
i 'he', *H.*   *j* H omits 'to' and has 'at' and 'windowes'.
k H has 'almes; howe much and wheare, and for ale lackinge'. The 1790 edition has 'almesse; how muche and wherefore; and for ale leakinge'.
l 'Allsoe for tubbs', *H.*

recorde of controllers and clerkes of the buttrye. In lyuerey season
he hathe for his office asmuch coole and candilles as shalbe thought
nedefull by the commaundementes of countynghouse. OTHER IJ
GROMYS versours[413] in this office, to helpe lodge there ale, to help
drawe hit, and to helpe kepe thoffice clenne; and in absentes of the
saide yoman to make ministracions at the barre for the kynges
chambre and halle and for lyuereys, and so to receyue hit as the
yoman dothe when he is present. Thees officers shulde be markyd
and ordeynyd after there manerly condicion and behauour[a] in all
there ministracions, and elles to be at the doctryne be conueniteez
[E, p. 118] to the countynghouse[a]. They ete in the halle at the towelle
and have[b] all othir duites of clothinges and rewardes in this corte
lyke to the gromys of pantrye. O PAGE[414] in this office, to helpe the
yoman[c] and gromys to kepe clenne the office, to helpe lodge in the
vesselx, and to fet in lyuereys. There owght no page in no office to
kepe the barre; he hath his lyuerey into this[d] office daylye lyke to
other pages. Of old vsage ij pages wolde dynne togither with one of
there messes, so that they may spare that other mes for ther soper.[e]
This page takith lyuereys, rewardes, and clothinges of the countinghouse as the[e] pages of pantrye.

§86. OFFYCE OF PICHERHOUSE AND CUPHOUSE. IIIJ ONEST YEMEN[415]
and diligent, wherof ij serue the furste mete of wyne[f] and ale, and
that other ij serue the secund mele. Hit fittythe this office to be
right quyk and seruyzable, to obey the marshallys preseptes, and
vshers in there absentes. They intaile with bothe butlers of wyne and
ale for how many pottes the receiue[g] by mesure, and that taile the
bring in to the countynghouse. Theye owe to fet the potes with drink
in to the halle at the highe dease,[h] that marshallys, vsshers, and
awmoners may se the full mesurys or elles they to make hit vp as
the countrollers and clerkes of botry and kichin[i] haue markyd the
pottes. The chef yoman of this office hathe in charge vnder the
sergeant of seller the kepyng of all the [j]pootes and cuppis of syluer,
pottes of lether, tankardes of yerthe, asshin cuppis,[j] cofers, gardeviaundes, hangers, and all that other stuff of this office, and he to
answere therto. This office hathe in lyuerey season iiij peric candilles
or more, and colles as the countynghouse thynkythe reasonable.[k]
And alle these etyn in the halle and in[k] there wages, clothing, and

---

[a] 'in all the mynistracion, or elles to be at the doctryne convenient in the
countinghouse', H.

[b] From H. E has 'in'.   [c] 'page', H.   [d] 'his', H.

[e] 'till supper' and 'as do', H.   [f] 'the first meale with wyne', H.

[g] 'theye have receaved', H.   [h] 'on the heighe dayes', H.

[i] 'clarkes of kitchine and butterye', H.

[j] H has 'pottes and cupps of silver, tankards of earthe, ashen cupps'; E has
'tankards and yerthe'.   [k] 'reasonne' and 'have', H.

^ageneralle thinges of corte they take lyke to the yomen of pantry.
OTHER IJ GROMYS⁴¹⁶ in this office, to assist the saide yoman as they
shalbe commaundyd, to help fett wyne, ale,^b to help washe clenly^c
the barelles, potatiffes, pottes, cuppis, of^d this office, or^d as the sergeant wolle assigne theym, and to bere the saide vesselx with^e wyne
and ale from the seler and buttry in to the halle or chambre by
trewe record; and trulye to kepe the remanentes [E, p. 119] to the
kinges vse in to thoffice agayne, if the hole mesurys^f be left after
the seruice of the hall and other straungers,'^{f 417} and bring in hole
alle the pottes and cuppis agayne ^gin lakkyng of thes ij yomen, and
to help fet^g euerye mornyng the pottes and cuppis that be oute for
lyuereye; and to trus the kinges good, and bere hit to the caryage
safelye, and so to helpe to receyue hit that nothing be lost in there
default. Theye ete in the halle ^hat towell; in alle the rewardes,^h
clothing and other duites lyke the gromys of pantri. O PAGE in this
office, by the assent of countynghouse, yf hit be tho3t nedefull, to
helpe kepe and atend, to bere and washe, and holsomlye to kepe
barelles, portatyus, pottes, gardeviandes, and cuppis, ⁱand oftin to
kepe theym clenelye and wipe theymⁱ and saue the kinges stuf; ^jto
help trus and bere to the carriage,^j and to help fet other lyuereyse
in season, as wood or coole, as the yoman woll assigne hym. And he
with the yoman euery morenyng tellyth the pottes and pellys and to
fet theym home euerye mornyng, so that the halle and the kinges
chambre be not vnseruyd, vpon blame of alle thes officers. This page
takythe lyke lyuereye, rewarde, and clothing as doth the pages of
panetrye. The butler for the mouthe delyuerythe ny3tly at the buttry
barre, for the king for alle ny3t, with the ale in newe asshen cuppis,
and ij other for the watche, which of right shulde be delyueryd agayne
at the coborde in the mornyng, with the pottes to serue men of
worship in the halle; and whan other men of worship bring to this
office their olde soylyd cuppes of ashe, then^k to haue newe.

[E, p. 120] §87. OFFYCE OF ALE^l TAKERS hathe one yoman⁴¹⁸
discrete and much temperat to make trew and good pourueyaunce
for ale and bere for the kyng and his housholde, and be as lytelle

^a 'other generall things of the courte', *H.*
^b 'to helpe to fetche wyne and ale', *H.*
^c 'to helpe to wipe and washe cleanelye', *H.*
^d 'for' and omits 'or', *H.*   ^e 'of', *H.*
^f From H which has 'messe' instead of 'mesurys'. E has 'leve the serue the
hall and other straungers'.
^g 'and thease 2 yeomen to helpe to fetche', *H.*
^h 'at the towell, and have theire rewardes', *H.*
ⁱ 'after to wipe them cleanelye', *H.*
^j 'to trusse and beare in the carriage', *H.*
^k H omits 'then'.   ^l 'ALL', *H.*

troble as may be with the people. And that he and the grome vnder hym make and mark truly the tailles betwixt them and euerye partye, how much they take; and tho taillis to be delyuered to the sayde parties for there euidens *forthe withall*, and the foyllys *to the butrye* with the ale, there to be receyued of recorde and the good prysyd[419] and the foylles markyd as hit ys worthe, and so to be delyuered to the clerk of the buttrye to make oute the billis and the prises to the ale parties and to dampne the taillis, that the playnely fet there moneye at the countynghouse, or els forthewith to be paide be acreditour[b] and the taillis togither.[420] And that this yoman grome, or page in his absens, see and knowe alle such playne mesure and stuf for the king and his corte to be good and holsom, well brewen in to clene vesselles, and soote[c] vpon their charge and specially to the charge of the owner; and elles after the daye of prof[d] and resting in the buttrye, if hit be foundon vnholsom, then[e] to be ouer-seen be countroller and[e] clerkes of kychin and buttery, and that alle such defectyue drink be had oute of thoffice opinly in to the corte dampnyd, and therof to smyte oute the heddes of the vesselx at large,[f] and forthewith to cancell the foyllis[421] and drawe them oute of alle entre. The statutes of noble Edward the iijde gaf this wages[g] but ijd. by daye;[422] nowe be cause his busynes is much out of corte and to be trewe and diligent in all his pourueyaunces, he is apointyd dayly by the cheker role iijd. in and oute,[h] sitting in the halle with other yomen of housholde, and lyke clothing and other duites of this corte. He presentithe the hoppis and other coperage,[i] done for the kyng in his office, [j]vnto the comptrollers and clerkes of buttryes bookes.[423] And by there recorde[j] he hathe the commyssion vnder the kynges grete seale, by the thesaurer of housholdes bille and seale,[424] for hym and for his grome and page[k] to take ale, beere, carryages, horses, and men to serue the king as oftin as hym nedithe, and at the kynges prises and olde custumes. O GROME[425] [E, p. 121] in this office, to help the yoman and to be much attendaunt and diligent to ouersee the vesselx brought togither to be clenne wasshen and well fauoryd, and elles to refuse theym; and safly to helpe guyde[l] the ale, bothe inward and owtewarde, to the kinges vse. He takythe dayly, for bouche oute of corte in the kynges seruyce by

---

^a H omits 'forthe withall' and has 'of the butteryes'.
^b 'by a creditour', *H.*
^c Also H, unlike the 1790 edition, which has 'putte'.
^d 'or elles after the daye of prowes', *H.*   ^e 'that' and 'or', *H.*
^f H omits 'at large' and has 'heade of the vessell'.
^g H omits 'wages'.   ^h '3d. and out 3d.', *H.*
ⁱ 'hoopes and other cooperage', *H.*
^j 'vnto the comptroller and clarke of buttrye; and by record', *H.*
^k From H. E has 'bage'.   ^l 'and safelye to guyde', *H.*

record of his yoman, jd. ob., allowid in the buttrye role, and he to help to mete the vesselx,[a] that the kyng be not diffraudyd in mesuris. He etith in the halle at the towelle; and in alle other rewardes, clothing, lyuereys, and giftes he takythe lyke to the gromys of the panetrye. O PAGE in this office, to helpe conduyte saflye alle such drinkes, and to helpe charge and discharge the caryages therof as he may goodlye atend, and to go therwith; and in some tyme of nede to help pourueye and to bring in the tailles trulye to be entryd with the ale, and trulye [b]to help messure the vesselx. Which page[b] in case the grome be attendaunt in corte and he in pourueyaunce, than takythe he for his bouch oute of corte the saide jd. ob. tille the grome come; then this page hathe in corte his lof, one mes of grete mete, dim. gallon ale in the buttry and picherhouse, and lyke in[c] alle other duites to the pages of pantry.

§88. OFFYCE OF GRETE SPYCERY hath in hym a chief master clerk,[426] which hathe the charge of pourueyaunce of alle maner stuf[d] longyng to this office and to thoffice of confeccionary, to the office of chaundry and thoffice of naperye, as for wex, weke, almaner spicery be weightes, napry and alle other lynyn clothe by the elle, also parchmyne, pauper, fygges, apples, and other fruites accordyng, stuf belonging to anny of the saide offices, with all the prices be recorde, and to bring be parcelles monythlye to the countynghouse of alle his prouycions; and of the delyueraunce of ony such stuf,[427] [e]the saide chef clerk shall dayly accompt for euery particularite therof to the countynghouse.[e] There owe to be at delyueraunce of any maner of thing of charge in this office [E, p. 122] thesaurer, countroller, or one of the sufficient clerkes vnder theym, for a testimony to the officer[f] and for a charge to theym that shall receyue hit; and so the saide countrolers[f] to put hit in there[f] bookes of remembraunce[f], and to recorde hit in the countynghouse whan hit shalbe demaundyd of theym. This chif clerk etith in the hall with a persone of lyke seruyce, wich is lyke[g] after the clerkes of grenne clothe,[428] bothe in seruyce in the halle[g] and in corte lyuereis, wages, and clothing. Hit[h] hathe not be accustomyd of olde that he shulde take for wages[h] oute of corte dayly xld., but by a grete consideracion of the soueraigns; in

[a] 'and he to helpe the vesselles', H.
[b] 'to measure the vesselles which the page', H.
[c] From H. E has 'to'.
[d] H has 'belonginge to this office of confectionarye, to the office of chaun-drye, and of naperye, as for wex, wykes, and all manner spicerye, figgs, apples, and all other fruits, and stuffe belonginge to any of thease sayd offices'.
[e] The 1790 edition makes this a separate sentence.
[f] H has 'this office', 'comptroller', 'his' and 'remembrances'.
[g] H omits 'lyke' and has 'and in the hall'.
[h] H omits 'hit' and 'for wages'.

makyng of pourueyaunces to the kynges grete auaile*a* but xijd. a
daye, and yet the countynghouse to vnderstond hit or he go therfore
oute of courte or elles by his othe vpon a booke as oftyn as hit dothe
requyre by peticion; and alle such moneye or assignmentes*b* as he
receyuythe of the thesaurer, that he truly content the merchaunt
withall.*b* By statutes of noble Edward iijde this was callyd *c*'vssher de
la graunde robe que prendra pur sa gages iiij [d.] ob le iour et seruera
lez carriages que coufrez et aultre chosys comme sez litz dez clerkes
de garderobe'.*c* [429] He sittythe nat at the grenne clothe at no tyme
of accomptes but ther is takin alwey as*d* a peticion for hym self and
for alle thoffice vnder hym at euerye iij termys of the yere. This
chif clerk owght to make viewse in the countinghouse of alle his
pourueyaunces, delyueraunces, and remenauntes, and at the iiijth.
term a playne, opyn,*e* particular accompte. [430] Sometyme the*e* office
dyd shape, sowe, and make redy vnto the writing alle the bookes of
countynghouse. He takyth other*e* lyuereye and herbygage for hym
and for his office of the herbiger and compitent caryage of his
harneyse with the kinges stuf in this office by the countroller.
o SECUNDARY clerk in this office of grete spicery, sufficient to receiue
and trulye to kepe the kynges stuf of this office, and to write the
daylye bookes of the delyueraunces therof, and of alle that other
iij offices, as hit shall requyre; and he to aunswer to euery parcelle of
theym into the countynghouse, as for sugar to the wafry [E, p. 123]
or *f*seler, to the kychyn*f* with alle other maner spices nedefull, *g*to
the confectionarye and sawcerye*g* as to alle other commaundmentes
of such as hathe auctorite, as well as to*h* thoffice of chaunderye of
wex, weke, candyll peric. Hym*h* owe dayly to proue and to be at
the weight of wex, and also to make a booke of all maner napery and
lynyn clothes delyueryd to office or persone at any time. He helpithe
engrosse*i* the parcelles [431] monthlye with the chief clerk, and shal
bring them to the countynghouse vpon an othe and hit to be apposyd*j*
by the clerkes of countynghouse. He takythe in seruyce in the halle
lyke gentimen, and he deseruyd*k* yerelye a reward by peticion of
x marces; clothing or xxs. lyuerey nyʒtlye, and carriage of compitent
beddyng, and parte of the generall giftes lyke to the secundary

---

a H omits 'grete availe'.

b H omits 'as he receyuythe . . . the merchaunt withal'.

c 'vssher de la garderobe auxibien des coffres et oultre choses come ses litz
de garderobe', H.

d H omits 'as'.   *e* 'even', 'this', and 'bothe', H.

f 'to the cellare or kytchin', H.

g From H. E has 'and to the confeccionary, sawsery'.

h H omits 'to' and has 'he' and omits 'dayly'.

i 'and helpeth to engrosse', H.

j 'oposed', H.   *k* ' and if hee deserue it', H.

clerk of countrolment; yf the king go ouersee, ^athe secundary clerke be takin at fyndyng and wagis as custellers^a. ON OTHER CLERKE in this office, to helpe write and make the bookes daylye, to helpe receuye, kepe, and delyuer the stuf for the kyng, to help attend vpon alle that other iij offices, and dayly to the brefmentes and accomptes in ^babsentes of chief or secundarye clerk;^b to help proue the *expenduntur* of wex,⁴³² and if anny lightes be lost, to shewe dayly be whome or whose defalts and^c how much, and to helpe se the lyuereys of wex and peric candelles ny3tlye delyuered accordyng to the^c duites withowton waste; and to helpe saue and trus the kynges stuf to carryages, and diligently to ouersee hit. He takith yerely rewarde at the countynghouse by the chiefe clerkes peticion, after his demerites v marces, vj marces, or Cs. at the discrecion of the soueraigns. He takithe in all other duites and lyuereyse in corte and clothing, if the soueraigns wolle assent, lyke to the secundary clerk; and yet but in^d late days such iijde clerkes wer callyd in none office but as yomen clerkes be.⁴³³ O YOMAN powder-better^d in this office and berer of the cofers, bagges, spices, wex, and other stuf in to this office, and to charge and discharge the carryages whan they^e cum and safly guyde hit ^eand to helpe kepe the journaile by the cuntrey for the king.^e He takythe daylye for his wages in corte by the spicery roll ijd., and other^f clothing, rewardes, or parte of giftes generall as don [E, p. 124] other yomen of housholde. O GROME⁴³⁴ in this office to helpe attend hit in alle busynes and to saf kepe thoffice and goodes, to waite vpon the carryages, and to obey theim that arne abouen^g hym in this office at ony^g commaundmentes, and for thoffice to fett^g in alle maner lyuerye in absentes of the yoman, and to helpe trus and bere the stuf^h in and oute when hit shall nede. He takythe in clothing, rewardes, and other lyuerys ⁱlike otherⁱ gromys of housholde. MEMORANDUM, this offyce haue lyuerey of kychin daylye.

[A, p. 231] §89. ^jOFFICE OF CONFECCIONARY hath in hym a sergeaunt⁴³⁵ to serue the king. He resceyuyth of the office of grete spycery all such stuf by indenture, all maner spyces to make confeccions, cardqwyns,^k plaates, sedes,⁴³⁶ and all other spycerez nedefull; dates, figges, raisons^l greate and smale, for the kinges mouth and for his housholld in Lente season; wardens, perys,⁴³⁷ apples, quincez,

---

^a 'takinge fyndinge and wages as custellans', *H*.
^b 'the absence of the cheife secondaryes clarke', *H*.
^c 'or' and 'theire', *H*.   ^d 'of' and 'powder-beater', *H*.
^e 'it' and 'and helpe to keepe their journeyinges for the countrye', *H*.
^f H omits 'other'.
^g 'aboute', 'all' and 'sett', *H*.   ^h H omits 'the stuf'.   ⁱ 'as'.
^j A here resumes after the missing section, pp. 187–230.
^k 'garquinces', *H*.
^l E and H have 'reasonnys', 'reasonnes'.

cheryez, and all other fruytez after the seasons longing to this office.
He resceuithe the spyce plates both of the countinghouse and
iewelhouse, according to*a* rychesse after the dayis of astate,[438] by
indenture for the kinges voyders, whan the vssher of chambre
comyth therefore; all the plates of peautyr by the purueyaunce of
sergeaunt squyloure, and indentures thereof betwext countinghouse
and hym, by countrolment of all weyghtes and numbyr; by the
delyueraynce of the seyd chief clerk and*b* his deputes, cofers,
[A, p. 232] gardevyaundez, towelles of raynes, of work, *c*and other,
and couertours*c* and hangers *c*and other necessarijs,*c* panys, basyns,
and ladylles that he maketh his confecions withall dayly. Hym*d*
owith to breue with the clerkes of grete spycery what he spendith
of*e* his office. The kinges plate is*e* estemed on a grete day of astate,
*f*j lb. dim., and other whiles but j lb., and so afterward duke, bisshop,
erle.*f* The seyd chief clerk hath claymed the perused cofyrs, gardevyaundez, and other of this office sometyme,*g* but nowe hit is
determined to this sergeaunt*g* by ouersight of the said clerk of
countrolment,*g* whan such*h* stuf here is perused. This sergeauntes all
sitt togeder in the hall; he takith wages and lyuerey ny3tly in
season like to the other sergeauntes, except for his clothing but
xls. for the office in season; and in winter for the kinge j tortoyse,*i*
j candille wex, ij candylles peric, wood and coole whan they worke*j*
by comaundment from*k* the countinghouse; and nyghtly j gallon ale,
litter and rushes all the yere; and for the sergeauntes lyuerey*l* at
ny3t j candyll peric, j gallon ale and [A, p. 233] in season dim talwood
or j fagot,*m* thes officers shold haue connyng in thes workes, o YOMAN
to be both*n* for the mouth and for the hall in tyme of nede and
chambre aftyr his power,*n* and to be well lerned in this*o* making
of confeccions, plates, and chardquinces*o* and other, sauely and
clenly to kepe and honestly to minister hit forth at tymez*p* of the
kinges worship and to make trewe awnswer thereof by weyghtes
inward and outward,[439] and so to breef hit; and to be redy to shewe
the remanentes as the clerkes woll call to vndyrstond this office.
This yoman takith his wages and clothing and other dewtiez in this

---

a From H. A and E have 'of'.   *b* 'or', *H.*
c H has 'and other counters' and omits 'and other necessarijs'.
d 'he', *H.*
e 'in' and 'thus', *H.*
f 'and soe afterwardes of dukes, earles, and bisshops', *H.*
g 'sometymes', 'the serieantes', and 'clarkes of comptrollement', *H.*
h E omits 'such'.   *i* E and H have 'torche'.   *j* 'hee worketh', *H.*
k From H. A and E have 'for'.
l 'of the serieant vssher; liuerye', *H.*
m 'or fagottes', *H.*   *n* H omits 'to be both' and 'aftyr his power'.
o 'the' and 'gardequinces', *H.*   *p* 'at all tymes', *H.*

court like the yoman of pantry but no feez; and if he be*^a* besy in working spices, than he hath his brede, mete and drinke for hym and his felyship into this office by commaundment of the counting-house. O GROME in this office,⁴⁴⁰ to help make the confeccions, to help*^b* serue the houshold in tyme of nede, both hall and chambres,*^b* to fett in the lyuereys for the office and kepe hit clenly, to help trusse harneys, to waysshe and wype and [A, p. 234] gader home the plates of syluer and peauter into the office dayly, and to wayte vpon the caryage, and to bere the*^c* fruyte and in tyme of yere to kepe hit in hourd. He etith in the hall at the towell, taking rewardez and clothing and naprons etc., like to the gromez of pantry. This*^d* office hath one somter man and hors for fruytez, spices, confeccions and spice plates*^d* in the purueyaunce of thesaurer of houshold by the countinghouse.⁴⁴¹ Thez officers make prouysyons in seasons of the yere, according for fruytez to be had of the kinges gardynez without prisez; as cheryez, perez, apples, nuttes, greete and smalle for somer season; and lenton wardons, quinces, and other, *^e*and also of presentes geuyn*^e* to the king; they be purueyours of blaundrels pepyns, and of all other fruytez; and so to present in theyre bookes.

[A, p. 235] §90. OFFICE OF CHAUNDELERY hath in hym a sergeaunt⁴⁴² seruing the kinges table, cupbourde, and his chambre of lightes vpon plate*^f* of syluer and brede.⁴⁴³ He resceyuyth of the chief clerk of spycery all wexe and weeke, peric candyll and other stuf necessary to this office, by indenture; and*^f* for the expenses he is accomptable to the seyde clerkes, if they think hit necessary,*^g* iiij tymez. He prouyth the expensis of wex of journay*^h* dayly by weyght before the clerkes and one of the countinghouse*ⁱ*; ⁴⁴⁴ *^j*if he resceyue any candylstykkes of syluer or gylt of the countinghouse*^j*, he endentythe with the thesaurer or with the jewelhouse. All other necessarijs, as balaunces, grete and smale, and weyghtes and pannys, long cofyrs, gardevyaundez,*^k* hote irons, caryagez, and other necessaryez for this office, is charged in the office of great spycery; and he makith the hoole accompt ons in the yere to the countinghouse for all this office. If ony of the porters of the kinges gate haue offended, that*^l* [A, p. 236] shalbe emprysoned or put to ward for ony trespasse within this court, he must be committed to the keping and stockes*^m*

^a From E and H. A omits 'be'.   *^b* H omits 'help' and has 'chamber'.
^c 'in', *H*.   *^d* 'His' and 'confections of spices, plates', *H*.
^e 'allsoe presentes given', *H*.   *^f* H has 'plates' and omits 'and'.
^g Also E. H has 'fyttinge and necessarye'.
^h H, and the 1790 edition, omit 'of journay'.
ⁱ 'comptrollement', *H*.   *^j* E omits this passage.
^k 'weightes, gardeviandes, longe coffers', *H*.
^l 'hee', *H*.
^m E has 'to kepyng of stokes'; H has 'to the keepeinge and to stockes'.

in this office of chaundry. This[a] sergeaunt etith in the hall with other sergeauntes, and[b] like of wages, dewtez, and clothing as the sergeaunt of confeccionary.[445] Here hath byn vsed a sompter man and hors for the king and chambre and hall to cary the long cofyrs,[c] with grete and smale lightes[d] redy at nede when there is working, of torches, smalle lightes, or of[e] peric candylles; then by commaund-ment fro the continghous they haue brede, mete, drynk, woode, and coolez as shalbe necessarij and sufficyaunt. OTHYR IIJ YOMEN in this office,[446] whereof that one is assigned more specyally in absence of the sergeaunt to serue the king and his chambre; and such loues as he fettyth of the pantry for chaundelers[f] [447] truly to present them to the vssher's recorde and to bring to the pantry[g] the remanentes vndispended,[g] vpon payn of his wages; and so to present all the expenses of lightes to the vsshers, and to be redy to[h] his preceptes for the kinges worship [i]and profit by reason and so that the yoman breuer of chaundry[i] and clerkes of spycery [A, p. 237] may vnder-stond the trouth of this yoman is ministracion ny3tly. That other yoman to make lyuereys and to see and know how all thing is delyuered, and what comithe in agayne for[j] a record. He helpith to make all lightes and geue euery man his lyuerey after the astate or[j] degre that he is, and to fette them that be greete lightes home,[448] and to call vpon that other yoman and gromez to go for them to euery mannys chambre in the mornyng. The iijd yoman attender and helper to work in this office and to ministyr hit in the hall and chambrez when he is commaunded, truly[k] to record and help bring hit fro mennys chambres in the mornyng, as for[k] morters and torches and tortays. This yoman to be[l] cunyng in wex making and true[k] to present by the marchal's record all the louez[447] of[l] chaundlers dis-pended in the hall, and the ouerplus to yeld agayne to the yoman pantrer breuer, and all othyr sisez and smale lightes not dispended in the kinges vse[m] to bring home to the yoman recorder of chaundry; and euery yoman to help excuse other for [A, p. 238] his busynesse in absence, and to declare euery partyculer lyuerey of wex and peric candylles to the clerkes of spycery whan they shalbe apposed. They ete in the hall with other yomen of houshold and lyke wages, clothing, and dewtiez. OTHER IJ[n] GROMEZ in this office[449] to help

---

[a] 'the', H.
[b] H omits 'and'.
[c] 'to cary for the kyng and chambre to long cofers', E.
[d] 'candle readdye at neede', H.
[e] 'other', H.
[f] 'fetchethe of the pantrye the chandlers', H.
[g] 'panter' and 'unspent', H.
[h] 'at', H.
[i] 'and profittes and allsoe that the yeoman brewer of chaundrye', H.
[j] 'of' and 'and', H.
[k] H omits 'truly' and 'for' and 'true'.
[l] From H. A and E omit 'to be' and 'of'.
[m] 'kinges' service', H.
[n] H omits 'ij'.

make lightes of wexe and peric candylles, to help serue the hall and chambrez and ^agader the lightes dayly from the grome porters' chambre, and other mennys chambyrs,⁴⁵⁰ that all lyuerey morters, torchys, and tortayis be brought in dayly be ix of clock before none^b or elles to tell hit the clerkes^c of spycery where and by whom hit lackith. Thez gromez help serue the court in lacking of the^d yoman; they sitte in the hall at melys at the towell, and in all other rewardez and clothing like to^e gromez of pantry. o PAGE⁴⁴⁹ to help kepe the office clenly, ^fto be a lerner and laborer and attender, to fett in wood, coole, and other thing necessarij, obedyent to them^f that be aboue hym in this^g [E, p. 127] office, and altymys to bere to and fro the carryages, and to waite vpon the safte of the kynges stuf; and lyuereye of mete, rewardes, clothing, and other casuelties lyke the pages of pantre.

[E, p. 128] §91. OFFYCE OF EWARY AND NAPRY hathe in hym^h a sergeaunt⁴⁵¹ to serue the kynges persone in coueryng of the borde with holsom and clenne vntochyd clothis of strangeors and with clene basons and moste pure waters, asseyde as oftin as his mosteⁱ royall person shalbe seruyd. He receyuith the charge of alle naprye be mesure for the kyng and his chambre and halle, andⁱ to be renouid if nede be at anny of the iiij festes principalle in the yere⁴⁵² by^j delyueraunce and recorde of comptroller^j and the chief clerk or his deputes^j by indenture, wherof this sergeant or deputies,^k yoman or grome of this office, shall shewe and geue reknyng to the countyng-house as oftin as the comptrollers command.^l He indentith with the thesaurer of housholde in the countynghouse for all the basons, yewers, cuppis, and napkins of syluer and gilt⁴⁵³ that he receyuith be weight in his charge. And if he receiue such things of jewelhouse, this sergeant shall do shewe^m all the newe and olde clothis, towelles, and napkins to be viewid by the countynghouse or comptroller's ouersight, if they be lost and be whome; or if they be perusyd clothis,

---

^a 'to', H.

^b 'at 9 of the clocke in the forenoone', H.

^c 'clarke', H.

^d 'this', H.

^e 'the', E.

^f H has 'and to be a labourer and attender, to fett in woods, coole, and other thinges necessarye, to be obedyent vnto them'.

^g MS. A breaks off here; pages 239 to 274 were already missing in 1888, as W. H. St. J. Hope noted on 29 May of that year.

^h 'it', H.

ⁱ H omits 'moste' and 'and'.

^j 'the deliverance', 'comptrollers' and 'his deputye', H.

^k 'his deputyes', H.

^l From H. E lacks 'command'.

^m 'such thinges of the jewell house, this sarieant shall shewe', H.

so that with oneste they may*a* no longer serue, then the*a* clothis of the kynges borde, clothis surnape, fote clothe,[454] and such other therto longing ys fee to*a* the sergeaunt, except at anny coronacion, by ouersight of comptroller. Alle other clothis so verely*a* perusyd to be assignyd, *b*sume to the awmery, to the squilery, to the picher-house,*b* to wipe and kepe cuppis cleane,*c* to the surgeons and other, by the comptrollers' discreccion. This sergeant hath tholde cofers and gardeviaundes and clothe saks, when they be fully perusyd, to his fee, but he shall presume to take nothing by his owne auctoryte tyll the comptrollers haue senne theym so greatly defectyue that they may no longer be amendyd nor serue for honeste and suertie of the kynges stuf; and all thinges so delyueryd to be merkyd in the comptrollers' memoranda. In kyng Henry's days the third*d* there was a grete contenccion bitwixt this sergeant and the auener*e* for loggeing of garners in the places of bissopis paleys, abbeys, and prioryes,*f* which oftin tymys*f* was furst entryd by this sergeaunt and*f* so long debatyd till by bothe assent they besought the king wich of theym before his presentes prouyd hymself the byggest*g* man, or*g* more deffensable might possede the garners in alle such place for euer, for the logging of his*g* office, and to haue fulle [E, p. 129] jugment by the king, to make delyueraunce of otes accustomyd to diuers offices, and alle other graynnys therin safly to kepe to the owners behoue.*g* This conflicte donne, the sergeant had the maistry; the juge alle wardyd*h* that he shulde alwey *i*forthe loge in that office, and the signe vpon the dore to be a sword,*i* none vssher to put hym oute.[455] He hathe herbigage in the towne or nyghe *j*in countreye for alle the horsses*j* of his office, and carriage compitent. O somter man and hors[456] for the kinges stuf foundon by the thesaurer is charge of housholde. This office hath, in tyme of yere, lyuerey, one talwood*k* or 1 busshell coolles, j candell wex, ij candelles peric j gallon ale;[457] and if hit*k* nede more wood or coole to dry naprye in

---

a H has 'will', 'these', 'is the fee of', and omits 'veely'.

b 'some to the amerye, squillarye, saucerye, confectionarye, and picherhouse', H.

c From H. E omits 'cleane'.

d 'In kinge Henrye the thirdes dayes', H.

e H (followed by the 1790 edition) has 'almoner'.

f H has 'prioryes' and 'often' and 'and soe longe debated'; E has 'pryors' and omits 'and'.

g 'highest', 'and', 'this' and 'behalfe', H.

h H has 'the judge awarded'; the 1790 edition has 'the Juges all awarded'.

i 'for the lodgeinge in that office have the signe vppon the dore to be a sword', H.

j 'or in the countrye for all his horses', H.

k H has 'tallie' and omits 'it'.

lack of wedring, ^athan to haue commaundement of the countyng-house for that that shalbe necessarij.^a Hym^b ought to gyue aten-daunce whan the vsher of chambre cummythe for the king to serue hym for alle ny3t. O YOMAN in this office for the kynges mouthe,[458] to serue hym in absentes of the sergeant, and to serue the chambre and saflye to kepe the napery and other stuf of the ewry, aswell the plate as clothis to the smallest sorte with all that longith therto, to bere the chaufirs^c with water, and, in tyme of yere, to see hit hote after the noble^c old custume, and to be diligent and obedyent to the preseptes of the vsher of chambre that occupiethe for that tyme. This yoman or sergeant in^d wynter season shall fett a torche or tortays at^d chaundrye to serue by^d the kyng and his chambre, and to bere the stuf sauelye in^d and oute of this office, taking in such season^d a lyght of the grome porter of chambre for the ewrye bourde, etc. This yeoman^e etithe in the halle at on mele, taking wages and clothing and other giftes generall lyke to the yoman of pantrye. Hit hathe be acustomed that he or the grome for the mouth most partye kepe and make answer for alle^f such plate and clothis and other stuf as the king and his chambre is seruyd withall. O GROME for the kinges mouthe,[458] attendaunt vpon his office, much diligent in saf and honest kepyng and applying to^g the kinges stuf and to^g the seruyce of his able person, and vpon his chambre in absentes of the sergeauntes and yoman abouesaide; and to help awnESwer for euerye grete parcell and smale of plate and clothe of reynis and workes and playne clothe [E, p. 130] and^h other lynyn clothe, bothe to the polles and mesure,ⁱ [459] to bere the chaufers with waters and in season to hete hit, to bere basons and ewers, to help trus and keepe^j them saf in caryage, and other to waite vpon hit. Theis yomen nor^k gromys of this office shulde nat be the furst rulers of kynges houshold to set anny basons nor other vesselx at Cristmas or Ester or ony other tyme before the people in the halle nor^k in chambre to begg money therbye to their rewarde, for hit goithe against the honour of this royall corte. This grome etithe in the halle at the towell; and in alle^l other rewardes, clothing, giftes generalle in this corte lyke to the gromys of pantrye. OTHER IJ YOMEN ewers for the halle that receyuyth of the sergeaunt alle naprye, basons, ewers,

---

^a Also H, unlike the 1790 edition, which has 'then to have by commaunde-mente of the counting-house, what shall be necessarye'; E adds 'for him'.
  ^b 'Hee', *H*.   ^c H has 'chaferers' and omits 'noble'.
  ^d H has 'in the', omits 'by' and 'in' and has 'take in seasonne'.
  ^e From H. E omits 'yeoman'.   ^f H omits 'alle'.
  ^g H omits 'to'.   ^h 'or', *H*.
  ⁱ 'measures', *H*.   ^j From H. E omits 'keepe'.
  ^k 'or' and 'to begge moneye to theire rewardes', *H*.
  ^l H omits 'alle' and 'coffirs'.

chaffers, coffirs,^{l} clothe sackes, necessarye gardeviaundes for the
halle; one of these yomen haue a speciall charge to receue alle maner
naprye vnder the sergeant, saflye to kepe and merk hit and answer
therto, and to serue offices and chambres, and to gader theym togither, and to make the chaunges. And theese attend specyallye to
the assignmentes of the marshallis; they owe saflye to kepe^a the
kynges goodes and to aunswer therto whan they be aposyd by the
countynghouse. If the vsshers of chambre call ony ewers for ony
straungeours sittyng oute of the halle in to any other place within
corte, thes yomen or the gromys must quyckly attend. Yf ony clothis
or other be lent oute by theym extraordynary, they to fet hit home
agayne or send at their perelle.^{b} They ete in the halle at one of the
melles by assent with yomen, takyng wages, clothing, in housholde
lyke^c the yomen of pantrye. OTHER IJ GROMYS in thys office for the
halle to brusshe^d the bordes clene, to kyuer^d theym, to serue theym
of water, to be attendaunt to the^d preceptes of marshallis or vsshers
for the honour of this house and obediences to theym that be aboue^d
them in thoffice for the king, ^{e}to trusse in safegarde, to keepe it
togeather clenlye, and waite on the carriage.^{e} They ete in the halle
at the towell at one of the metes^{460} by their owne assent, after that
the busynes dothe requier,^{f} takyng clothing, rewardes, and giftes
lyke to the gromys of pantrye. ON PAGE in^g this office^{461} to serue
thoffice and [E, p. 131] to fullfylle hit in nede of that other officers,
to be chosen personable yong men of good and trewe conducion,^{h} to
attend and kepe safly this office, to lerne to excuse the higher offycers,
and to fet in lyuereys, wood, and coole, lytter and rushis,^{i} to kepe
the office clenly, to trus the stuf to carriage, ^{j}and waite vpon^j and
safly to guyde hit, and to be vnder obedyens and coreccion reasonable
of theym abouin in this office for the kyng. They take clothing,
rewardes,^{k} in alle thingse as do the pages of pantrye. The table
clothis and towelles shuld be chaungyd ^{k}twyese euerye weke at lest,^{k}
more if nede require.

§92. OFFYCE OF LAUENDRYE, ij yomen,^{462} wherof one moste^l

^{a} 'they ought to keepe safelye', H.
^{b} 'they fet it hoame againe and send att theire perill', H.
^{c} H omits 'lyke', which E has.
^{d} 'burnishe', 'cover', 'theire', and 'about', H.
^{e} From H. E has 'to truse safgarde togither, to kepe hit clenlye and waite of carriage'.
^{f} 'after as their owne busines doth require', H.
^{g} From H. E has 'of'.
^{h} 'good and true of conditions', H.
^{i} H omits 'and rushis'.
^{j} 'wayte vppon hit', H.
^{k} 'and reward' and 'everye weeke twyse at the least', H.
^{l} H omits 'moste'.

specially shall fet or receyue be taile, *a*safly to kepe and tenderly to
wasshe*a* and preserue diligentlye the stuf for the kinges proper
persone of the warderobis of beddes and robez,*b* ewery, and of alle
other offices in houshold that minister such naprye or lynyn clothe
for the kynges vse, and truly to delyuer such stuf agayne to euerye
office be tale as he receyuyd*b* or by mark,*463* and that any*b* straungeors
set none handes vpon hit. That other yoman shall with a grome or
page fet and receiue of thofficers of ewry all sortes of napry, table
clothis, long towellies, short napkyns, and other soylyd lynyn cloth
be tailles and mark; and of alle other offices the kynges stuf soylyd,
as alle the surplices of syngers of chapelle and awbis*c* and amices
soylyd from the vestery*464* the neck towelles of pantry, ewary, con-
fessionary, courters, hangers, liggers, and all that is the kinges stuf,
and truly to delyuer hit agayne vpon payne of makyng good therfor
or for the leste pece therof. This yoman shall fet of*d* the grete spicery
asmuch white sope, gray, and blak, as can be thought reasonable,
by prof of the countrollers,*d* of which sope the saide clerk spycer
shall take allowaunce in his dayly dogget by the recorde of the saide
yoman lauender. Also they haue, by peticions, allowid in the roll
of the grete spicery for the*e* grete basons. for vatis*e* and asshis bought
for the vse of housholde, yf hit nede; but the custom is that they
shall haue asshis clothis of the spicerye to fet asshis in theym from
euery man's chamber and kychins*f* within the*f* corte. They haue
[E, p. 132] carryage for the*f* compitent beddes and for the kinges
stuf of countrollment in the carryage of office of ewerye. Thies yomen
etyn in the halle with yomen of housholde; but in tyme of there
grete busyness then they and there ij gromys and one page *g*take in
eting amonges theim in alle*g* vj loues, iiij messes of kychyn, iij gallons
ale, wood, coole, candill in season more or les after their discrecion
in the*h* countynghouse and so to be breuyd by the vsher of the halle;
in lyke wise other whillis for driyng of the kinges stuf. They take
clothing, wages, and other fortunys of this corte and herbigage
as other yomen of housholde. OTHER IJ GROMYS*465* in the office,
wherof that on ys more attendaunt for the kinges proper stuf in
absentes and presentes of the chief yoman*i* as hit ys aforesaide
to help him thorowlye, that other grome to help fulfyll the rome
and absens of the*i* householde yoman; notwithstandyng, alle the

---

a 'and safelye keepe, orderlye washe', *H.*
b H omits 'and robez' and has 'receaveth' and 'noe stranger'.
c 'abbayes', *H.*
d 'set at the greate spicerye' and 'comptroller', *H.*
e 'theire' and 'waters', *H.*
f 'chambers and kytchin', 'this' and 'theirs', *H.*
g 'taketh in eatinge dayes amongst them all', *H.*
h 'theire', *H.*   *i* 'the yeoman' and 'that', *H.*

yomen and gromys for the person [a]as euerye in others absens[a] and in distres ar boundon to fulfill others seruyce asmuch as they may[b] of nobles of the[b] corte. [c]Thies gromys helpe bere,[c] washe, and bring home the stuf of this corte longing[d] to the king, and trus harneys and asshis, whan hit shall nede, [e]to carryage and office. Theis gromys,[e] and the be not in busynes of there office, the set at melles in the halle at the towelle, and take rewardes and clothing and other duites generall lyke other gromys of housholde. And if ther be a quene in housholde, than there be women lauenders for the chambre, wardrobe, and the commune of her,[f] etc. This officers owe and be sworne to kepe chambre counsaile.[g]

[a] 'euerye each in others absence', H.
[b] 'as much as maye be' and 'this', H.
[c] 'this groome is to fet, beare', H.   [d] From H. E has 'logging'.
[e] 'to carriage and the office of thease groomes', H.
[f] H omits 'and the commune of her'.
[g] 'Thease officers ought be sworne to keepe the chambre counsell', H.

THE BEGINNING OF THE ORDINANCE OF 1478 FOLLOWED BY PROVISIONS OF 1471

Harleian MS. 642

[f. 177b] A COPPIE of the newe booke of the kings household of Edward the Fowerth   Anno domini 1478

§1. In the moneth of June, the yeare of our Lord one thowsand fower hundred seauentie eight, Wee, Edward, by the grace of God, King of England and of France, and Lord of Ireland, being right desireous to sett within our household a pollitique, reasonable, and vertuous guiding in euery behalfe . . . [The preamble continues as in the Queen's College, Oxford, MS. 134, below, p. 211, except for differences of spelling and four slight variations of reading, and ends, on f. 178b, '. . . as hit appeareth by the ordinances and directions heere ensueing and followeing in writing.']

For the assignement and charging therof[a]

[f. 178b] §2. FIRST, it is ordeyned that after any such assignations that the king ordaineth at any tyme for the expence and charge of his said household, bee incontinent a paire of indentures made betwixt the treasorer of England and the treasorer of the household, whereof the one partie shall remaine with the treasorer of England and the other partie to remaine in the kinges accompting house and there to be entered into a liggar.

The Treasorer and Cofferer be two persons and the money to be brought into the countinghouse

§3. ALSO it is ordeyned that the treasorer and the cofferer bee two seuerall persons and that euery of such, as soone as the said treasorer shall receiue of any of the said assignations, within fiue or [f. 179a] six daies at the furthest after the receipt, it be brought in the counting-house and deliuered vnto the kinges cofferer by ouersight of comptrolement, and soo to be entered into the said liggar.[1]

Obeysance of officers

§4. ITEM, that euery officer in the house obey all such as bee aboue them in office, that is to say, the yeoman the seriant, the groome

---

[a] This and the following cross-headings, printed in italics, appear in the manuscript in the left-hand margin.

the yeoman, the page the groome, in all such thinges as shalbe thought for the kinges honor and profitt, and that vpon paine of six daies wages as often as it is complained of.[2]

Orders and attendances for the king's chamber

§5. WE WILL that these articles following by us ordained and ordered for the guiding and directions of our chamber be duely and surely kept by all our seruantes, as theire desire is to continue in our seruice and as they will auoyd our greuious displeasure.

§6. AS THE first attendance to be giuen the last day of October, the eleauenth yeare of our raigne, and to endure the space of eight weekes then next followeinge [f. 179b] is thus vnderwritten.

Sir Thomas Mongomery
Sir John Dune
Sir Thomas Brought
Sir William Parre   }Knightes for the body[3]
Sir John Pollington
Sir Roger Ray for the bodie and
    deputie to my Lord chamberlaine

Thomas Haward
John Chany
Thomas Porte   }Squires for the body[4]
John Sapecote
John Wykes

§7. AND for the second attendance to be giuen imediately after eight weekes abouesaid be ended:

Sir John Parre
Sir Raphe Hastings
Sir Maurice Barkly   }Knightes for the bodie[5]
Sir Thomas Gray
Sir Roger Ray, deputie for my lord
    chamberlain for both attendances

Humphrey Shalford
Thomas Salinger
Thomas Bagham   }Squires for the bodie[6]
John Blonte

[f. 180a]

Sir Henry Feris }Sewers of the chamber[7]
John Strangwis

Thomas Teringham   Surueyor for the king[8]

Richard Pomery }Sewers for the chamber[9]
John Alton

Sir William Dennis ⎫
Sir Gilbert Dabeny ⎬ Keruers and cupbearers[10]
Sir William Morreis ⎪
Sir John Fynes ⎭

John Younge ⎫
John Heruie ⎬ Gentlemen vshers[11]
Brian Talbot ⎪
Robert Ratcliffe ⎭

Hughe Sherley ⎫
Bryan Middleton ⎬ Yeoman Vshers[12]
Edward Argill ⎪
Robert Burton ⎭

As for the directions aboue said to bee daylie and surely kept, WEE will that Sir Roger Ray, deputie to my lord chamberlaine, two gentlemen vshers, and two yeomen vshers at the least, be allwaie attending vpon us.

Noe roomes be supplied but by licence

§8. ITEM, that noe man take vpon him any of the said offices, that is to say, if it fortune any said persons to absent them, then the said [f. 180b] lord chamberlaine or his deputie or one of the vshers to come to vs to vnderstand our pleasure whome wee will shall occupie for the tyme.

A squire for the body to be charged with the cubbard till the king hath drunken

§9. ITEM, that one of the squiers for the bodie nightly make our cubbard,[13] and to keepe it, and not to depart therefrom vntill the tyme that wee haue drunken for all night; then hee to charge one of the yeomen of the watch therewith at his departing.

Making the bedd

§10. ITEM, that one of the knightes for our bodie and gentleman vsher nightly bee at our beddmaking.

Charging of the watch and wel keeping

§11. ITEM, that the said deputie to my lord chamberlaine and one of the squiers for our bodie with a gentleman vsher see that the watch bee surely sett nightly; and if any default bee, to certifie vs of it, and in likewise of the releise of the watch in the morning, at seauen of the clocke at the furthest.

Attendance of groomes

§12. ITEM, that all yeomen, groomes, and pages of the chamber daylie attending, according to their waiting, aswell when wee ryde as when [f. 181a] wee be abyding; and if any default bee, wee to be certified thereof by the officers abouesaid.

Attendance of all other gentlemen

§13. ITEM, that all the said keruers, cupbearers, and sewers, knightes for the bodie, squiers for our bodie, and vshers for our chamber, shall daylie and continually waite for the tyme that they bee appointed to attend, and not to depart at any tyme without lycence of vs or of our chamberlaine or his deputie in that intent hee may lett vs haue knoweledge thereof.[14]

What persons shall enter the dyneing chamber at meet tymes

§14. ALSO, that noe manner of man come within our chamber where wee bee, saueing only such lordes as shall please vs and our knightes for our bodie and our vshers and all other to vnderstand our pleasure, and that all the yeomen and groomes at the tyme of their awating be heere, and keepe daylie theire due attendance vpon vs, either on horsebacke or on foot as shall please vs.

Attendance of gentlemen both for noone and afternoone

[f. 181b] §15. ITEM, wee will that our sewer ordaine and see that wee bee daylie serued with squiers at our table, and the squire for our bodie to beare our podage both both dinner and supper; and for our sitting at meate at our supper, wee will noe more attend there but such as wee haue signed or shall assigne, after wee be sett and serued. And that dayly all our knyghtes and squiers awaite vpon vs at seauen or eight of the clocke in the morninge in the middle or upper chamber, and that afternoone at one of the clocke; and that our inner chamber doore be daylie kept with a gentleman vsher, and in the second a yeoman vsher, and the third doore with a yeoman of the chamber.[15]

Fifteene Messe appointed for the king's chamber

§16. ITEM, wee will that there be ordained daylie one messe for my lord chamberlaine when hee is heere, one messe for lordes, two messes for knyghtes for the body, two messe for squiers for our bodie, one messe for the confessor and the secretarie, one messe for the chapleines, and one messe for groome porters, and one messe for groomes wayters.[16]

Avoydance when the king is at councell

[f. 182a] §17. ITEM, wee charge all our vshers of our chamber, yeomen, groomes, and pages, that none of them depart from our attendance

without our lycence, or of our said chamberlaine or his deputie in his
absence, and that yee obey him in his office as to euery of you it
apperteyneth, vpon the paine aforesaid; and that yee suffer noe man
to come to our chamber when wee bee at our councell, saue onely
but such as bee admitted for our said councell, without yee haue
comaundement from vs to the contrarie.

*Gentlemen vshers and groome porters bring in their records to the
Accompting-house*

§18. ITEM, wee will that euery day one of the gentlemen vshers
bringe in their recordes of our chamber into the counting house by
eight of the clocke at the furthest, and semblable wyse the groome-
porters, vpon paine of six daies wages for euery of their offences
as they seuerally offend.[17]

The yeoman vsher to goe to euery office

[f. 182b] §19. ITEM, wee will that one gentleman vsher, or in his
absence a yeoman vsher, send noe meane person to the pantry, buttry,
seller, or any other office, but that hee come in his proper person, or
els to send such one as hee will abyde by on the morrowe.

THE DRAFT OF
THE ORDINANCE OF 1478

Harleian MS. 642

[f. 183a] THE ORDINANCE made for the stablishment of the kings house by the aduise of his councell which his highnes straightly chargeth and comaundeth euery his officers and other within his household to obserue and keepe as to him apperteyneth, vpon the paines in the articles followeing comprised.[1]

Chapple

§1. FIRST, that the chapple be guided according to such articles as is committed to the deane of the same.[2]

Officers keeping the hall at meale tymes
Houres to be kept for dinners and suppers in the hall

§2. ITEM, that all manner officers except such as be deputies to attend vpon the kinges chamber, and all other persons that haue a roome in the hall come to the hall and sett there, vpon paine of loosing there wages for six daies. And that there sitt none there but onely such as be appointed, of whose names the marshalls shall haue notes by writing, except strangers such as to the said marshall shalbe thought reasonable and to the kinges honor. And that euery eating day the first meate be readie anon vpon nyne of the clock at the furthest, and in [f. 183b] likewise that the first supper beginn at fower of clocke, and on fasting daies that the dinner be readie at eleauen of the clocke.[3]

Noe other liueries to be made

§3. ITEM, that there be noe liueries of meate and drinke giuen to any person, of what degree or condition he be of, at the tyme of dinner or supper, for the comaundement of any officer, but vnto the porters of the gate.[3]

Boughe of court

§4. ITEM, that such liueries as shalbe giuen to any person at night be deliuered in manner and forme followeing, that is to say, to a duke, to a bishop, etc., which appeareth yn a booke made remaineing in the countinghouse.[4]

What personages is to be suffered to sitt in the hall

§5. ITEM, that noe man, of what degree or condition hee bee of, haue any seruantes to sitt in the hall but such as is honestly cladd, and a man of person that may doe the king or his maister manseruice if the case soe shall require. And that the marshalls*a* take heed and obserue these, vpon pain of loosing of their monethes wages.[5]

Kinges breakefast

§6. ITEM, at euery eating day there be ordained a large breakfast for [f. 184a] the kinge, to the intent that such lordes, knightes, and squires, with other that shall awayte vpon his person shall nowe*b* breake their fast, and that for the queene it be ordained in likewise and to the same intent.[6]

Noe other breakefasts but by comandement of the steward, etc.

§7. ITEM, that none other breakefastes be ordained ne giuen within the household, nor hole beafe therefore cutt, but if it be by spetiall comaundment of the steward, treasurer, and comptroller of the same household.[6]

Seruing of the king for all night

§8. ITEM, that the liueries for all night for the king and the queene bee sett by day from Candlemas to Michaelmas, and in winter tyme by eight of the clocke at the furthest.[7]

Auoyding of officers after the king be serued for all night

§9. ITEM, that after the kinges and the queenes liueries deliuered as is aforesaid, none officers to abide in his office nor resort to his said office againe after his departure, without espetiall comaundement of the king or the queene, or els by a spetiall token from the steward of the household, or from the king or queenes chamberlaine.[7]

Boardwages being sicke

§10. ITEM, that euery sicke man for the tyme of his sicknes be sett at his [f. 184b] boardwages, and allowed by the clerke of the controllment and by his said allowance weekely paid in the countinghouse.[8]

Porters to keepe that nothing passe the gate

§11. ITEM, that the serieant porter, and other porters vnder him, see*c* that neither messes of meate, ne vessell, nor pottles of wyne, or pottes of ale, or other victuall passe the gate without a spetiall

---

a H has 'marshall'.

b Misreading for 'mowe'; cf. O 1478, §6.

c H has 'soe'.

comaundement of the steward, treasorer, or comptroller. And if it
happen any such vessel of siluer or peuter to be lost in the said porters
default, and soe prouided, that then newe be bought vpon their
wages.[9]

§12. ITEM, that dayly at the first dinner awaite for to see that
euery man haue his dutie of meate and drinke, and for to take vpp
broaken meate for the almes, a poore clerke, a yeoman, and a groome
of the office of almonrie; and that soe taken vpp to be surely kept to
the second dinner be done, att which dinner for the causes aboue said
shall attend an other poore clerke, a yeoman, and a groome of the
office aforesaid. And such broaken meate as shalbe had at the said
dinner shalbe put to the other broaken meate of the first [f. 185a]
dinner, and all these with such as shall come out of the kinges and
queenes chambers shall daylie bee distributed to such poore people
as shall attend at the gate for the kinges almes; at which distribution
the vnder almoner shalbe present, without it be soe that he attend
vpon the king in absence of the great almoner.[10]

§13. ITEM, that euery two persons sitting in the hall haue a loafe
of bread, fower men a gallon of ale, three men a messe of the
kitchin.[11]

Imbeselling of the almes

§14. ITEM, that if the yeomen or groomes aforesaid imbeasell any
of the said broaken meate, or otherwise dispose that without the
comaund of the great almoner, or in absence of his vnder almoner,
that euery of them soe doeing be punished by the losse of six daies
wages.[12]

For preseruing the almes

§15. ITEM, that if any person sitting or beeing in the hall or
chamber giue or deliuer to any person waiting vpon him or other,
broaken meate without licence of any of the almoners, hee shall loose
his wages for one day as oft as hee soe doth and is complained vpon
by any of the said officers.[13]

Knights and squires to weare collers

[f. 185b] §16. ITEM, that euery lord and knight within the household dayly weare a coller of the kinges liuery about his necke
as to him apperteyneth, and that euery squire, aswell squiers for the
bodie as other of the household, likewise weare collers of the kinges
liuerie daylie about their neckes as to them apperteyneth, and that
none of the said squiers faile, vpon paine of loosing a monethes
wages.[14]

Squiers for the seruing the king and the queene

§17. ITEM, that dayly there awaite 24 squiers to serue the king and the queene, of whome twelue to serue at the first dinner and to dyne at the second, and the twelue sitting at the first dinner to serue the second diner and there to awaite to serue the king and queene.[15]

Vshers to serue in their owne persons
Carrying the king's pottage

§18. ITEM, that noe vsher of the chamber send his rodd by any meane person or persons to pantrie, buttrie, seller, or any other office, but goe in his owne person, but if it [sic] bee occupied soe that he may not, and then that hee send such a person for him with his rodd as he will brefe for on the morrowe, and that vpon paine of six daies wages. And that euery day a squire for the kinges bodie beare the kinges pottage.[16]

Vshers to bring there record into the counting house

§19. ITEM, that all vshers and all other accountantes within the kinges houshold [f. 186a] daylie bring their bookes into the counting house of such thinges as haue bene spent in their offices vpon paine of loosing of a monethes wages; and that the clerkes of the greene-cloath daylie make vpon the said bookes for the whole expence of the said household, and if any default be found in them, they to runne in like paine.[17]

Serieants shall indent for their negligence

§20. ITEM, that euery serieant or other officer within the household shall receiue such stuffe as belongeth to his office by indenture, whereof the one part shalbe deliuered to such officer and that other shall remaine in the countinghouse. And if any of such stuffe soe deliuered may not serue in the said office, then that it be deliuered in the countinghouse, and nowe prouided for at the kinges charge and costes. And in case that any thereof be negligently lost, that then newe be prouided at the costes and charges of them that soe hath lost it.[18]

Three warnings for defaults

§21. ITEM, that euery officer duely and truely exercise the office which hee is in; and hee be found defectiue therein, first hee shalbe thereof [f. 186b] warned to amend, at the second tyme punished in a monethes wages, and if then hee be found faultie the third tyme in like offence, that hee bee vytterly putt out of office and of the house-hold without receiueing in againe.[19]

For the taking of oathes of officers

§22. ITEM, that euery of the said officers and other persons that shalbe admitted to exercise any office or doe seruice within the said howsehold shall come to the countinghouse, there to be sworne vpon the holy euangelist to fulfill duely and truely all such thinges as to him apperteyneth. And if any person refuse to take that oath, that hee be not admitted to any office or other seruice. And if any person after hee bee there sworne execute not his office or seruice according to his oath, that then hee haue such punishment as is afore ordeyned.[20]

The cofferer's receipts to be entered in a liggar remaining in the counting house

§23. ITEM, that there be yearely made a great ligar to lye in the countinghouse, in the which are the cofferrer's receiptes [f. 187a] and paymentes to be entered, and all other clerkes within the household that shall for the tyme handle any of the kinges money to be entered into the said ligears and to remaine in the countinghouse in the officer's absence. And that euery of the said clerkes enter their paymentes in the said ligear within fower dayes of the king and queenes comeing home, vpon paine of loosing of a monethes wages; and that all the cofferer's paymentes and other clerkes within the kinges howsehold that the comptroller take a double of the said paymentes and receipts, vpon paine of loosing of a fortnightes wages.[21]

§24. ITEM, that these debentures of the said expences to be entered into the journall vnder the paines as is abouesaid.[22]

Seruice to be done by the treasorer or comptroller

§25. ITEM, that the treasorer and comptroller soe appoint betwixt them that one of them dayly see the hall serued for the good rule and guiding of the same, and also that they in likewise [f. 187b] soe appoint betwixt them, that one of them be daylie present in the court; for if it weere the contrarie, the rule and guiding weere soon like to bee broken.[23]

Seruice to be done by the lord steward

§26. ITEM, that once in a quarter of a yeare the lord steward sitt in the countinghouse and see the state of the household, that is to say, all that is oweing that tyme, to the intent of such goodes as there is in hand in money, tayles, or assignementes, payment may be made.[24]

No seruants to be suffered within any office
Giueing out but by breuement
Obedience

§27. ITEM, euery officer and other within the kinges household keepe noe child nor man within his office noe tyme of the day, and also that man of office within his presence to giue any thinge within his office, but hee that hath the charge of the breuement of the said office, and that euery man in his office obey his serieant, and other to obey them that is aboue in the said office. And that noe man breake the aforesaid vpon paine of first warning, and soe if hee after trespasse to be punished according to the order of the kinges household.[25]

Bringing againe torch ends & morters
Making the breuement at length
Breuemente of all offices to be brought to the countinghouse by 8 of the
  clocke

[f. 188a] §28. ITEM, that euery officer shall receiue any torches or morters out of the office of the chandry that hee make deliuerance againe to the said officers on the morrowe by eight of the clocke at the furthest, to the intent that the clerkes of the comptrollment and the vnder clerke of the spicerie may see the *infra* of the said torches and morters; and imediately the said vnderclerke to bring in his breue-ment of the same into the countinghouse. And if any be found at any tyme defectiue in the foresaid, hee to be punished according to the statute aforesaid. And also that the yeoman brewer of the pantry, buttry, and celler dayly come into the kinges hall by eight of the clocke at the furthest, and thereto breue with the clerke of the kitchin, and see his deputies for the expence of the day afore. And also that all other clarkes come into the counting house and bringe theire bookes of expence of the day aforesaid, to the intent that the whole expence [f. 188b] of the kinges house of one day be cleerely vnderstanded vpon the next day following. And if any person be found defectiue in this, hee to be punished according to the fourth article next before specified.[26]

Noe fee to be taken but by assignement of the countinghouse

§29. ITEM, noe officer within the kinges howse presume to take any manner of fee in his office, but such as shalbe assigned or limited to him by a bill out of the counting howse. And if any doe the contrarie, to runn in the paine abouesaid.[27]

The ingrossing of the accompt yearely with a penaltie for default

§30. ITEM, that the clerke of the greenecloath nor clerke of the controllement haue noe part of the yearely reward of twentie poundes nor retaine it in theire owne handes vntill such tyme which they haue ingrossed vpp the whole yeares expences, to the intent that the treasorer of the household may within two monethes after the yeares end be readie to bring his accompt into the exchequour, and the king thereby euer within a quarter of a yeare next followeinge the whole expences of his household.[28]

The treasorer shall declare the order of the assignement

[f. 189a] §31. ITEM, that the treasorer of the household bring the indentures of all the receiptes of his assignementes for the household vnto the kinges highnes, or to such as his highenes will appoint the said treasorer to bring vnto, to the intent that his highnes may quarterly see that the said treasorer hath deliuered vnto the cofferrer or for other expences of his said household as much money as the said treasorer hath receiued within the said quarters for his declaration in that behalfe.[29]

Groome porter bring in dayly his record

§32. ITEM, that the groome porters of the kinges chamber and queenes bring daylie into the counting-house the recordes of all such sises, prikettes, wood, coale, or other thinges had of any office vpon paine of six daies wages, as ofte as they offend.[30]

Saue conueyance of the seruice into the hall

[f. 189b] §33. ITEM, that all such persons as shalbe limited to serue in the kinges hall giue noe messes of meate to noe bodie, but bring them to the sewer of the hall, vpon paine abouesaid.[31]

Licence for absence

§34. ITEM, that noe squire nor other officer within the kinges house depart out of the house into his countrie without licence of the steward, treasorer, or comptroller, vpon paine of six weekes wages.[32]

Steward and grand officers to keepe the hall

§35. ITEM, that the steward, treasorer dayly keepe the hall, for it is thought, if it should be broken in them, other would doe the same.[33]

Wafers

§36. ITEM, that the king be serued with wafers daylie, and with all other fruite as it apperteyneth to the yeare.[34]

Admission of officers

§37. ITEM, that noe officers be admitted into the house but by the whole aduise of the steward, treasurer, or comptroller.[35]

Noe resort to be suffered into offices

[f. 190a] §38. ITEM, that noe officer suffer noe man in his office but

such as the head officer would comaund for the kinges honor and
profitt for diuers causes, and that vpon paine as aforesaid.[36]

*In decretu [sic] domini Roberti Willoughby, tunc seneschalli hospicij
domini regis Henrici 7. Seruing the hall orderly*

§39. ITEM, that the squires of the household bee imediately serued
after the marshalls and seruantes officers in the kinges hall and soe
next after the chappell, and after the chappell yeomen of the crowne
and yeomen officers, and soe forth euery man after his degree.[37]

WARRANT UNDER THE SIGNET FOR THE ENGROSSMENT AND SEALING UNDER THE GREAT SEAL OF THE ORDINANCE OF 1478

P.R.O.—C81/File 1386, Warrants under the signet No.8

(monogram) R E By the king

Righte reuerend fader in God, righte trusty and wellbeloued, We grete you wele. And where as we by thaduis of our counsell haue made certain ordinaunces for the stablysshing of oure howshold comprised in a booke whiche by oure commaundement shal be deliuered vnto you by oure trusty and righte welbeloued clerc and counsellour, Maister Thomas Langtone, We woll that ye do put alle the said ordinaunces in writing seled vnder oure great sele, and the same so seled send vnto vs by oure said counsellor without delay. And theese oure lettres shalbe youre warrant and discharge anempst vs in that behalue. Yeuen vnder oure signet at oure monastery of Syon the ixth day of Juylle, the xviijth. yere of oure reign.

(Across the dorse is the address:)

To the right reuerend fadre in God oure righte trusty and welbeloued the Bisshop of Lincolne, our chanceller of England.

THE ROYAL HOUSEHOLD ORDINANCE OF 1478
from the Queen's College, Oxford, MS. 134

[f. 1a] Orders in his majesties household*a*

§1. IN the moneth of Juyn', the yere of oure lord MCCCClxxviij, We, Edward, by the grace of God, King of England and of Fraunce, and Lord of Ireland, beyng right desirous to sette withynne oure household a politique, raisonable, and vertuouse guyding in euery behalf, to thentent that by good and wise ordonaunces the same oure household establisshed myght' perseuer and contynue in honneur and prosperitie, to the loouyng of God, oure comfort and

---

a This line is in a later hand, as is also a marginal note by the second line of the text—'Anno. 19. Eduardi 4ti'.

good pleasir, and the wele of vs and oure people, We didde to be
called beforn' vs the chief officers of oure said household, and the
clerkes in euery of thoffices, commaunding theym after a clere vewe
seen of the state of the household vpon the assignementes somes of
money deliuered and receyued and employed vpon the costes and
expenses, with' a clere rekenyng of thempcions, solucions, and
contentacions of allemaner prouysions, that they shuld openly shewe
and declare the rules, ordres, and direccions thrughly by alle the
household, how at that tyme it was guyded and directed. And so
it was doon, whereby appered certayne enormytees and mysse-
guydinges by twoo wayes: one in thexpenses, whiche in some behalf
seemed exceeding and wastful, and in other behalfes wantyng or
diminute: the other way, in empcions, prouisions, entrees, solucions,
contentacions and rekenynges, not so ordrely and justely demeaned
as was [f. 1b] according to the honneure of vs and the good state
of the same oure household. The premysses diligently peysed, We
toke consideracion that no thing was more behouefull' for the good
and politique administracion of alle that to suche an household
might' apperteigne, than that the same shuld be established vponne
certayne ordonaunces and dirrecions grounded pryncipaly vpon the
two vertues that be mooste requisite in suche maner guyding and
rulyng. First, as it is knowen notorily that in politique administracion of outward goodes and expenses that the two extremytees be
vicious,[1] whereof that one is by excesse and superfluyte, and the
other vice is by defaute and skarsete, and the meane of both the
vices is the vertue wherby euery suche administracion' oweth' to be
modered and guyded, as so is liberalite dewe meane bitwix auarice
and prodigalite, whiche in regard to that vertue be extremytees
vicious, We, ne willing that oure said household be gyded by prodigalite,[2] whiche neyther accordeth with honneur, honeste, ne good
maner, ne on that other partie, that it be guyded by auarice whiche
is the werse extremite, and and [sic] a vice moore odiouse and
detestable, We haue taken ferme purpose to see and ordeyne
thadministracion of oure said householde, namely, in costes and
expenses to be grounded and establisshed vpon the forsaid vertue
called liberalite. And forsomuche as equyte and [f. 2a] rightwisnesse
is the grettest renommed vertue, that may best serue in euery good
policie the administracion of oure said household, as touching the
receiptes of moneyes behouefull' for expenses and costes, touching
also the dewe paymentes, accomptes, and rekenynges for the same,
We haue fermely grounded and establisshed vpon the moost noble
vertue, justice, whiche by philosophres is named of all vertues quene
and emperesse, like as may appere by the ordonaunces and direccions
here folowing in writing.

[f. 2b] (See footnote[a]).

[f. 3a] §2. First, it is ordeyned that after any suche assignacions that the king at ony time ordeyneth for the expenses and charges of householde, be incontinent a paire of indentures made bitwix the tresourer of England and the tresourer of household, wherof the one parte shal remayn with the tresourer of England and the other parte to remayne in the kinges comptinghous and also there entred into a ligger.[3] Item, it is ordeyned that the tresourer and cofferer be two seuerall' personnes[4] and that euery suche summe as the said tresourer shal receyue of eny of the said assignacions, within v or vj dayes at the furthest after the receipt therof it shalbe brought' into the comptinghous and deliuered vnto the kinges cofferer by ouersight' of the comptrollement and entred into the said ligger.

§3. Item, yf the king or the quene ride in jorneying and that they for their expenses deliuer vnto eny clerkis or other officer oute of their coffres money, that the said clerkes or other shal receyue the same money by indenture and within iij or iiij dayes at the furthest after their comyng home do entre the receipt' of the same money in the saide ligger; and the indenture shalbe deliuered [f. 3b] vnto the tresourer, and the rest of the money, if eny be, be deliuered vnto the cofferer, and the hoole debenture of the said expenses shalbe entred into the journall', and this vpon payne of losing of a monthes wages.

§4. Item, that the comptrollement take the double of the receite and payment of the cofferer and other clerkes of the household, vpon payne of losing of a fourtenyghtes wages.[5]

§5. Item, that the chapell' be guyded according to suche ordenaunces and good custumes as hertofore hath ben vsed and ben commytted to the deane of the same.

§6. Item, that euery eting day be ordeyned a large brekefast for the king to thentent that suche lordes, knyghtes, and squyers with other awaiting vpon his person shal mowe breke thair fastes with that remayneth' of the same.[6] And that for the quene be ordeyned in like wise, and to the same entent. And that none other brekefastes be ordeyned ne yeuen within the household ner hoole beof therfore kytt but yf it be to the kinges children or elles by the comaundement of the steward, [f. 4a] tresourer, or in their absence the cofferer, clerkes of the greneclothe, or chief clerc comptroller.

§7. Item that all' manere officers except suche as been deputed

---

[a] Folio 2b is blank save for the words 'Humbly complaynethe compelled of necessyte and nede youre seyde pore oratour that where I beyng a pore man having no lyving but that as I may get'. This fragment of a petition is in a rougher, more cursive hand than the text of the Ordinance and is evidently a later, unofficial intrusion.

to attende vpon the kinges chambre and the quenes and all' other
persones that haue a rome in the haulle come into the haulle and
sitte there, vpon peyne of losing of vj sayes wages; and that than
sitte non other but only suche as be apointed, except straungers
suche as to the marshalles and huisshers shalbe thought' raisonn-
able.[7]

§8. Item euery eting day the first dyner be redy anon' vpon ix of
the clok and in likewiese the first souper begynne at iiij of the clok
at the furthest, and on fasting dayes the first dyner to-begynne at xj
of the clok.[8]

§9. Item that ther be noo lyuerees of meete ne drink yeuen to any
personne, of what degre or condicion he be of, at the tyme of dyner
or souper for the comaundement of any mesne officer but vnto the
porters of the yate and suche other as to the King and the chief
officers shalbe thought in all' wiese nedefull' and expedient.[9]

[f. 4b] §10. Item that dayly at the first dyner ther awaite for to
see that euery man haue his duetie of meete and drynk, and for to
take vp broken meete for the aulmes, a pore clerc, a yoman, and a
grome of thoffice of thaumosnery; and that soo taken vp be surely
kept vnto the second dyner be done, atte whiche dyner for the causes
abouesaid shall' attende another pore clerk, a yoman, and a grome
of the office aforesaid; and suche broken meete as shalbe had at the
said dyner to be putte to the other broken meete, and all' this with'
suche as shall' come out of the kinges or the quenes chambre shall'
daily be distributed to suche people as shall' attende at the yates for
the kinges aulmes, at whiche distribucion the vnder aumosner shalbe
present, withoute he attende vpon the king in the absence of the
grete aumosner.[10]

§11. Item it is appointed and ordeyned that euery two personnes
sittyng in the haulle haue a loef of brede, iiij men a galon of ale, iij
men a messe of kechyn. And that at euery festfull' tyme and other
when by the huisshers and maresshalles it shalbe thought for the
kinges honneur, euery two messe of kechyn of gentilmen haue half
a picher of wyne. And euery iij messe of kechyn of yomen haue half
a picher of wyne. And that the sayde [f. 5a] marshalles and huisshers
see the haulle dayly to be rewarded with' brede, wyne, and ale, what
as by thaim shalbe thought nedefull' and conuenyent.[11]

§12. Item that be the ausmoner seen that the pottes with' wyne
and ale be filled, and in likewise he see the messes of mete come
from the kechyn sufficiently staked out and largely furnysshed[12] for
the kynges honneur, and that he suffre no maner man to yeue away
his meete, that shuld go to the kinges aulmes.

§13. Item yf the yomen and gromes abouesaid embesill' eny broken
meete or otherwise dispose it, withoute comaundement of the grete

aumosner, or in his absence of his vnder aumosner, that euery of theym soo doyng be punysshed atte leste in vj dayes wages.

§14. Item yf any person sittyng or beyng in the haulle or chambres, the steward, chamberlayn, and tresourer, comptroller, and other grete officers except, yeue or deliuer to eny person awaiting vpon him or other eny broken meete without licence of one of thaumosnery, he shall' lose his wages for one day, and as ofte as he is compleyned vpon by eny of the said officers.[13]

[f. 5b] §15. Item that all' knyghtes for the body, cupberers, and knyghtes keruers, squyers for the bodye, chaplayns, and gentilmen huisshiers, and squyers of household be putt to their attendaunce, and a boke therof deliuered from the kinges highenesse into the comptynghous for a quarter of a yere, that is to say, the iiij quarters to begynne at Octobre, January, Aprile and Jule.[14]

§16. Item that the chaplains make their attendaunce from halue yere to halue yere, som at oo tyme and som at another. And that for the same half yere they shalbe absent from their saide attendaunce they kepe and be reseant and abiding on their cures, onles then they *by oure holy fader the pope be* otherwise be [sic] dispensed with', vppon peyne.

§17. Item that euery day after the seconde meete ther be kept an ordenaunce, yf to the steward, treasurer and comptroller it be thoughte behouesfull', or elles at the leest thries a weke. And that of theim iij be there present ij or j at the least, to see that good rule and guiding be of the said household, and for prouysion of the same for the days folowyng.[15]

§18. Item that the stuard of the said household [f. 6a] yf he be present in the court be at the lest oones in a weke in the comptinghous, there to see the obseruyng of suche rules, prouisions, and direccions as ben ordeyned for the weale and politique rule of the same.[16]

§19. Item that oones in a quarter of the yere the steward sitte in the comptinghous and see thestate of the household, that is to say, all' that is owyng that tyme to thentent that of suche good as ther is in hand in money, tailles, or assignement, payemente may be made to the creditours in the sergeantries by thaduyse and discrecion of the steward and thofficers.[17]

§20. Item that the tresaurer and comptroller so appoynte bitwixt theym that one of theym daily see the haulle serued for the good rule and guiding of the same or elles in their absence the cofferer, or the clerkes of the grenecloth', or the clerc comptroller. And in that like wise they appointe bitwixt theym that one of theym be present in the courte at all' tymes.[18]

... This passage has been erased—presumably after the Reformation.

§21. Item that the maresshall' ne huissher of the chambre sende his rodde by eny mesne [f. 6b] personne or personnes to panetrie, buttrye, or seler, spicery, chaundrie, or eny other office, but goo in his owne personne; but yf he be occupied soo that he may not, and then he sende suche one with his rodde as he woll' aunswer fore on the morowe and also that he woll' breue fore, vpon the peyne of vj daies wages.

§22. Item, that the huisshers of the chambre come daily with' their recordes into the comptinghous withe thexpense of the kinges chambre, and that he that recordeth' sette his name in his recorde, for this entent, that yf soo they doo any excesse, that it may be sene, and sene who doth best his devoyr for the kinges auauntage. And that they sette noo thing in their recordes, but that is spente in the chambres.[19]

§23. Item, that the maresshalles come in their owne personnes daily in the comptinghouse with their recordes and that they sette noo thing in thair recordes but suche as is spended in the haulle; and that they sette their names in their recordes to thentente it may be sene, who doth' best his deuoir as before. And that they comaunde noo thing out of the halle to noo maner personne, but yf it be to straungers, yf soo eny come to courte out of meale tyme, [f. 7a] and that in thabsence of the souuerayns of the court; and that by theym soo done to be putte in thair recordes, as aboue, and that thordre of sitting in the haule be kepte after the olde rule and custume.[20]

§24. Item, that the huisshers of the haulle kepe oute of the haulle doore all' men at meale tymes, but such as shuld come in of duetye and straungers suche as they can think by their discrecions be for the kinges honneur. And yf eny be sette at meete, without a maresshall', that they take theym vp, and that they kepe the haulle that noo persone bere oute noon' almes.

§25. Item, that daily ther awaite atte lest [a]xxiiij squyers in the court to serue the king and the quene, of whom xij to dyne atte first dyner in the haulle and xij atte later dyner. And in likewiese atte first soper and last, soo that atte lest xij be euer redy to serue the king and the quene when it shall' plese them to be serued of their seruyce.[21]

§26. Item, yf soo the fulle nombre of the squyers abouesaide assigned to serue the king and the quene be not fully present in the court,[22] [f. 7b] that then of suche as ben present a maresshall' of the haulle, or an huissher in thabsence of a mareshall', atte warnyng of the king or the quenes sewer shal yeue warnyng vnto then beyng present to serue the king and the quene. And yf they or eny of theym disobbeye the seid warnyng of the maresshall' or huissher, then he

<hr>

[a] 'atte lest ther awaite' is the order in the MS.

or they lose a wekes wages by reason of their disobeisaunce. And yf it can be vnderstande that eny maresshall' or huissher that so haue warned and his warnyng disobeyed, he conceiling the same, not openyng it to the heed officers, that then like peyne be executed on theym.

§27. Item, that wekely ther be warned and appointed by the huisshers of the chambre who shall' attende and serue the king for the weke next folowing, that is to say, as keruers, sewers, cupberers, squyers for the body, and other, and in thabsence of theym, theym whom they thynk moost hable for the same. And yf eny disobbey the said warnyng or appoynted, they to be warned as afforesaide.[23]

§28. Item, that euery lorde, knyght', and squyer, aswele squyers for the body as other within the household, were daily a coler of the kinges lyuerye aboute their nekkes as to [f. 8a] theym apperteyneth, and that none of the said squyers faille herof, vpon payne of loosing a wekes wages.[24]

§29. Item, that thoffices of panetrie, butterye, and seler, and all' other offices be kepte that noo man come within theym, neyther to meete ne soper, ne at noone other tyme, but suche as be ordeyned therto. And that thofficers of the said panetrie, butterie, and seler, deliure no man brede, ale, ne wyne by the commaundment of the huisshers of the chambre and maresshall', but yf it be to straungers oute of meale tymes in thabsence of the souuerayns. And that noon' of thes said officers deliure ne breue vpon noo man moore than they delyure after the fourme and appoyntment and is truly spended for the kinges worship.

§30. Item, that the butteler abroche noon' ale vnto the tyme that it be sene by the clerc comproller and the prises made. And if it be not for the kinges honneur, to dampne it and sende it hoome ayen'.

§31. Item, that the clerc of the spicery deliure no thing that longethe vnto his office to noo man, but after the fourme of appointment [f. 8b] made by the heed officers of the house. And that he spende noo thing that longeth' vnto his purveyaunce vnto the tyme it hath' ben sene by the comptrollement and the prises therof knowen reasonable or not, and the stuff sene whether it be good or not.

§32. Item, that the clerc of the kechyn and the maister cokes take hede that ther be no wast done by theym in their offices, ne by other vnder theym, and that euery man of the said office goo to the haulle at their meales, but suche as be ordeyned the contrarye.[25]

§33. Item, that the maister cokes of both' kechyns[26] see that suche meetes as ben dressed by them, and them that be vnder theym, be wele and seasonablie dressed for mannes body; and that they dresse no manner of meetes but suche as shall' be thought' by theym for the kinges honneur, and that aswele rost as soden. And yf any suche can be founde by thaumosner after suche tyme as it is serued, and that then he present it vnto the heed officers, and that at euery defaute the said maister coke to lose a dayes wages, and he that hath' hadde the rule of it vnder him to lose asmoche.

[f. 9a] §34. Item, that the comptroller, or one of the clerkes with' the clerc of kechyn, see that noon' of the saide officers haue no fee in theyr said offices, but according to thappoyntement that is comprised in this boke folowing. And that noon' of theym take noo meete oute of the kechyn neyther for theym self nor for noon' other but by the deliuerance of suche as haue the gouernaunce therof.

§35. Item, that the clerk of the kechyn sette the nombre of the messes, both of the chambres, the haulle, and the lyuerees daily in the panetrie rolle.

§36. Item, that thuisshers of the kechyn suffre no mannes man ne other personne to come into the kechyn, but suche as ben of the office self and suche as ben sworne for the kinges mouth' and the quenes.[27]

§37. Item, that the sergeaunt of the squyllerye, saucery, and picherhous deliure noo vesselles, pottes, ne cuppes to noo man, but lyverey vesselles to suche as shall' haue of duetie and as they shall' haue warnyng oute of the comptinghous.

[f. 9b] §38. Item, that euery seke man be sette at his borde wages and allowed by the clerc comptroller and by his allowaunce wekely payed in the comptinghous.

§39. Item, that the sergeant porter and other porters vnder him see that neyther messes of meete ne vesselles nor botelles of wyne ne pottes of ale or other vitaille passe the yates withoute a speciall' comaundment of the steward, tresaurer, or comptroller. And yf it happen eny suche vesselle of siluer or pewter to be lost in the seid porters defaute, and so proued, that then newe be bought' vpon their wages; ne that they suffre no straunge man to come in atte yate, but suche as by their discrecions be for the kinges worship and also pore men to come for their payementes at all' seasons.[28]

§40. Item, that the lyuerees for all' nyght' for the king and the quene be sette by daylighte from Candelmasse to Michelmasse, and in wynter tyme by viij of the cloc at the furthest.

§41. Item, after the king and the quenes lyuerees deliured as abouesaid noo officer abide in his office nor resorte vnto his said office after his departing, withoute a speciall' comaundement [f. 10a] of the king or of the quene or elles by speciall' token from the stewarde of household or from the king or the quenes chamberlains.[29]

(Then follow in a different ink, and in another hand, a repetition of the words previously given on f. 10a, viz., 'of the king or of the quene or elles by speciall' token from the stewarde of household or from the king or the quenes chamberlains'.)

(The rest of f. 10 is cut away, and the leaf therefore measures merely 3 in. long instead of the full length of 11·4 in.)

[f. 10b] §42. Item, that euery offycer duly and truly exercise the offyce which he is in. Fore and he be found defectiue therein – – –.

(This fragmentary passage is written in a much more cursive and careless hand than the very formal, regular hand of the rest of the manuscript.)

[f. 11a] *a*Item, that euery officer duely and truly exercise thoffice whiche he is in. For and he be founde defectyue therin, first he shalbe warned to amend, and the second tyme punysshed by prison by discrecion of the heed officers; and yf he be founde the thridde tyme in like offence, that he be vtterly putt out of office and the household withoute receyuyng ayen'.[30]

§43. Item, that euery of the said officers and other personnes that shalbe admytted to exercise eny office or do seruice within the said household shall' comme into the comptinghous, there to be sworne vppon the holy Euangelist to fulfill' duely and truly all' suche thinges as to him apperteyneth'. And yf eny personne refuse to take the othe, that he ne be admitted to eny office or other seruyce. And yf eny personne after he be there sworne execute not his office or seruyce accordingly to his othe, then he haue suche punycion as is afore ordeyned.

§44. Item, that noo sergeant of the kinges house putte into his office by his own auctorite noo maner officer withoute thaduyse of the steward or one of the heed officers of the kinges house.[31]

§45. Item, that euery officer and other within' the [f. 11b] household kepe noo childe nor man within his office noo tyme of the day, ne also that no maner officer withyn his office presume to yeue eny thing but he that hath' the charge of the breuement of the saide office.[32]

§46. Item, that euery man in his office obeye the sergeant, and other to obeye theym that is aboue him in his office, and that noo man breke the forsaid vpon peyne of the first warnyng, the second to be punysshed by prison. And yf he efte trespasse, to be punysshed according to thordre of household.

§47. Item, that euery officer that shall' receyue eny torches or morters oute of thoffice of the chaundrie, that he make deliuerance ayen' to the saide officer on the morowe by viij of the cloc atte furthest, to thentent that the clerc of the comptrollement and the

---

a f. 11a has a faint marginal note in a cursive hand—'be yt knowen to alle men that . . . . . . of'.

vnder clerc of spicery may see the *infra* of the saide torches and morters; and immediatly the said vnderclerc to bring in his breue-mentes of the same into the comptinghous, and yf eny be founde defectyue, to be punysshed according to the statutes aforesaid.³³

[f. 12a] §48. Item, that the grome porter of the kinges chambre kepe the light' and the wood that he fecheth' for the kinges chambre and that he yeue awaye noon' to noo man; but yf and eny leue in his keping that it be kept and spended at the kinges vse, and the same wiese for the quene.³⁴

§49. Item, that the gromes porters of the kinges and the quenes chambres bring dayly into the comptinghous the recorde of all' suche wax, sises, prikketts, woode, coole, and other thinges hadde of eny office the day before, vpon peyne of vj dayes wages as often as he offendeth'.³⁵

§50. Item, that the yomen breuers of the panetrie, butterie, and seler comme daily into the kinges haulle by viij of the cloc at the furthest, and there to breue with' the clerc of the kechyn or his deputees for thexpense of the day afore. And also that all' other clerkes come into the comptinghous and bring their bokes of thexpenses of the day past, to thentent that the hool' expenses of the house may be clerely vnderstande the next day folowing, Sondayes and solempne festes excepte.³⁶

§51. Item, that in all' places where the king resorteth' vnto where ther be parkers, kepers of [f. 12b] beddes, gardyners, and suche other foreyn officers, they haue no lyuery of the courte ne bouche of courte but only the kepers of places. And in case be that eny suche kepers be of the kinges house, and haue bouche of courte, that they haue noo suche lyuerye.³⁷

§52. Item, that suche personnes as shalbe lymitted for seruyng of the kinges haulle or chambre, that noon' of theym yeue noo messe of meete other wiese than to bring it to the sewer of the haule or chambre, vpon peyne that for euery messe so yeuen he that soo yeueth' lose a dayes wages.³⁸

§53. Item, that noo squyer nor other officer within the kinges house depart out of the house into his countre withoute licence of the steward, tresaurer, or comptroller, vppon peyne of vj dayes wages.³⁹

§54. Item, it be ordeyned for the kinges profuyte that all' his grete horses ordeyned for to soiourne mowe from hensforth' soiourne togeder in certain places, to be lymitted after thaduyse and dis-crecion of the steward, tresaurer, and comptroller, and not in dyuers places as it hathe ben vsed, withoute by the said officers it be thought' behouefull'.⁴⁰

[f. 13a] §55. Item, that ther be noo hors logged within the kinges yates but the kinges owne, and that the soiorne be logged from the kinges courte v myle atte lest. And that therbe noo man kepe no hors atte kinges cost moo than be appointed, ne that noon' other officer haue noo hors standing emong the kinges.[41]

§56. Item, that all' the purueyours and yomen of the stable lose their wages and their horsmete when they be oute of court, but yf so be they be in the kinges seruyce, and that the auener recorde it daily in his accompte, and that noon' of theym eete in the haulle daily but suche as ben appoynted.

§57. Item, that no manere lord, knyght, squyer, ne other personne or personnes haue noo cariage of the kinges cariage ne of the contrey, but by the kinges prouision and price at their owne costes, ne that noon' of the gardrobe, vestery, ne other officer, trusse eny mennes herneys in their offices emonges the kinges cariages, but the kinges owne and their owne.[42]

[f. 13b] For payementes and prouisions[43]

§58. First, that noo payement be made in money nor in taylle or assignacion by the saide tresaurer, or coferer, or the clerkes of the grenecloth', but only in the comptinghouse, being present the steward and comptroller or the clerc comptroller atte leste.[44]

§59. Item, that all' the debentours payed by the cofferer, or by the clerkes of the grenecloth' in his absence, shal not be cancelled vnto suche tyme as the comptrollement haue a veue vppon the same and they entred into the journall', and that the comptroller or the clerke comptroller to cancele theym, and not to be canceled by the cofferer ne the clerkes of the grenecloth'; and that the debentours be cancelled ones in the weke atte lest, and that at euery monethes ende a rekenyng to be made betwixt the tresaurer and the cofferer of all' money by him receyued.[45]

§60. Item, that the saide cofferer nor clerkes of the grenecloth' in his absence make noo payement vnto the kinges creditours by weys of marchaundise, but onely of the kinges owne money as it is receyued, in payne of forfeiture of the said payment vnto the king.

[f. 14a] §61. Item, that noon' officer of the kinges house, of what estate or condicion he be, nor officer's clerc, ne sergeant, or other seruaunt, from the highest vnto the lowest, bye by hym self or eny mesne personne to his behoue eny taille, obligacion, bille, debentour or assignement of eny creditour vppon peyne to be putte out of his office and the kinges seruyce for euer.[46]

§62. Item, that all' purueyours and catours for the kinges household be made in the presence of the steward, tresaurer, and comptroller, and by their ordenaunce, and that suche as shalbe named and taken therto be sobre and peasible men, and men of good suffisaunce and power, suche as woll' see that the purueyaunce and accates by them made be for the kinges worship and profuyt, and in such wise that the grete clamour had before tymes vppon purueyaunces and accates made for the kinges household mowe ceasse; and that suche puruyours be not chaunged without grete and notable causes, and that in the presence aforesaid.

§63. Item, that euery purueyour of eny office and accatour before his admytting to suche office make his othe in maner and forme [f. 14b] folowing. That he shall' truly, iustely, and egaly, withoute oppression of the pore or favour of the riche, obserue and vse his commission and occupie his saide office to the mooste profuyt and behoue of the king, and in eschewing of the hurte of his pore people, and in especial obseruyng thies poyntes folowyng: that is to say, he shall' no thing take vppon him to doo by eny deputie in eny place there as he shall' make eny accate or purueyaunce by force of his commission or office, but that he shall' before then he eny suche accate or purueyaunce make, or eny good take of eny personne in presence and sight of the constable, bailly, or other officer, hauyng the rule and auctorite in places wher he shall' purueye or take, bifore the people there openly shewe and make to be reed his commission; and that neyther for affeccion nor fauoure of eny persons, ne for receyuyng of eny rewardes or goodes, ne for hope to receyue eny goodes, he ne shall' forbere to take in due maner and mesure for the king there as he shall' mowe take; ne for euyl will' or hate of eny personne, nor to thentente to hurt or to compelle eny personne to doo eny thing to the assithing and fulfilling of his owne or eny other personnes pleasir, nor to auenge his owne nor eny other personnes displeasir, take stuff or vitaille belongyng to his accate or puruey-aunce of eny of the kinges subgiets, nor vnder coloure of his office eny thyng [f. 15a] take to the behoue of him self or eny personne, saufe only for the king and his household; and that the prouysion, suche as he shall' make or take in eny maner of thing, he shall', withoute eny sale therof or chaungyng or applying therof to his owne or eny other personnes profuyte, truly, withoute fraude or malengin or lessing therof, bring it or do it to be broughte to the vse of the king and his household, and make a true and feithefull' certi-ficacion therof to the kinges comptinghous by discryuyng clerely all' the parcells of his accates and purueaunces and the prises, and the personnes names that the said parcelles be taken of.⁴⁷

§64. Item, that all' prouysions that shalbe made for the household be made in due tyme, and a fourtenyght atte leste before it shalbe spended, to thentente that yf it so be not for the kinges honour, or that the prises be not reasonable, other may be prouyded, or it shall' nede to be spente.⁴⁸

§65. Item, that the clerkes of the greneclothe ne chief clerc of the comptrollement take ne receyue eny part of their yerely reward vnto the tyme they quarterly haue made vp the bokes of allowaunce for the quarter paste. [f. 15b] And soo from quarter to quarter to the yeres ende, to thentente the king may haue a veue quartrely of thexpenses of his household. And the tresaurer haue no cause to delaye the bringyng in of his accompte into theschequier, but that it be redy within vj monethes after the yeres ende at the furthest, and that then the said clerkes of grenecloth' and chief clerc of comptrollement, jmmediatly after the saide bokes soo by theym engrosed, to be payed by the handes of the kinges coferer in the comptynghouse.[49]

§66. Item, that within a monethe after euery yeres ende the names of all' the creditours belongyng vnto the household, with their summes due and the causes expressed, be by euery clerc in his office pured and brought' into the comptinghous, where they shall' stille remayne, to thentente that the tresaurer of household may haue a double of theym and vnderstande what is due in his office and entre them in his accompte. And in like wise the comptroller a comptrollement of the same, whiche done, that the steward, tresaurer, and comptroller make a due certificacion to the king of the saide creditours, to thentent that he may yerely knowe the state of his household and by thaduyse of his counsaile ordeyne for contentacion of the same.[50]

[f. 16a] §67. Item, that all' pardons to be graunted to eny of the sergeauntes of the kinges household of eny thing wherof they shall' stande chargeable in their offices be examyned by the by the [sic] steward and the heed officers of the household, before eny sute be made therof vnto the king, to thintent that the king may be clerely enformed of the causes that shuld meoue his grace to pardone theym. And yf eny thing be done into the contrary herof, that it be of none effecte, but stand for nought' and voide and of noon' auaille.[51]

[f. 16b] (Blank except for scribbling).

[f. 17a] §68 (i).

| My lord of Yorke[53] | { xx tall(wood) shides, viij[52] fagots, iiij bundles coles. |

(ii)

| Duke and duchesse | { j chapleyne, ij gentilmen, and iij yomen sitting in the haulle, and for his lyuerey at nyght' j cast of bred, j picher wyne, and a gallon ale | iij shides tallewood, ij fagots j priket, ij sises of wex, iij c(andeles) of whitelight |

(iii)

Erle and
countesse
{ j chaplayne, ij gentilmen, and ij yomen sitting in the halle, and for his lyuerey at nyght' a loof of brede, demi p(icher) wyne, j potelle of ale } iij shides tal- wood, j fagot, ij sisis of wex, iiij c(andeles) of whitelight'

(iv)

Bisshoppe
{ j chapleyn, ij gentilmen, and ij yomen sitting in the haulle, for his liuerey at nyght' as an erle } iij shides tall- wood, j fagot, ij sises of wex, iij candeles of whitelight'

(v)

Baron and
baronesse
{ j chapleyn and ij yomen sitting in the haulle, and for his liuerey, j loff, demi picher wyne, j potelle ale } ij shides tall- wood, j sise of wex, iij candeles whitelight'

(vi)

Lord
chambreleyn
{ j chapleyne, ij gentilmen, and ij yomen sitting in the haulle, and for his liuerey at nyght', j loff of brede, demi picher of wyne, and j gallon of ale } iij shides tall- wood, j fagot, ij sises of wex, iij candeles of whitelight'

[f. 17b] (vii)

Lord steward
of
household
{ j chapleyn, ij gentilmen, j yoman, and a grome sitting in the halle, for his lyuerey as the chambreleyne in euery thing

(viii)

Tresaurer
{ j chapleyn and ij yomen sittyng in the haulle, and for his liuerey at nyght', j loffe of brede, demi picher of wyne, and j galon ale } ij shides tall- wood, j fagot, j sise, iiij candeles whitelight'

(ix)

Comptroller
{ j gentilman, ij yomen, and a grome sitting in the haulle, and for his liuerey at nyght', j lofe, demi picher wyne, j potelle ale } ij shides tall- wood, j fagot, j sise, iiij candeles whitelight'

(x)

Secretary,
the deane,
ij aumosners,
and coferer
{ Euery of theym ij yomenne sitting in the haulle, and for their lyuerey at nyght' j lof, j galon ale, and the coferer to haue a clerc atte kinges wages sitting in the haulle } ij shides tall- wood, iiij candeles of whitelight'

(xi)

Chapleynes and phisiciens — Chapleyns and phisicience, eueryche of thaim j man sitting in the haulle, and for thair liuery at nyght', j loof brede and a potelle of ale — j shide demi tallwood, ij candeles of whitelight'

[f. 18a] (xii)

Clerkes of the grenecloth', clerc comptroller, clerkes of spicery and kechyn — ij clerkes of the greneclothe, clerc comptroller, clerc of the kechyn, clerc of the spicerye, and the auener, euery of them a man sitting in the haulle, and for their liuerey at nyght', a loff of brede and a potelle of ale — j shide demi tallwood, iiij candeles of whitelight'

(xiii)

Sergeauntes of household — Euery sergeaunt in the house a man sitting in the haulle, and for his liuerey at nyght', half a loof and a potelle of ale — j shide tallwood, ij candeles of whitelight'

(xiv)

Knyghtes for the body keruers, and cupberers — Knyghtes for the body, euery of thaim ij yomen sitting in the haulle, and for thair lyuerey at nyght, j loff, demi gallon of ale — j tall shide demi, iiij candeles of whitelight'

(xv)

Knyghtes[54] wayters, and squyers for the body — Euery ij men sitting in the haulle, and for theyr liuery at nyghte, j loof and a potelle of ale — j shide demi tallwood, ij candeles of whitelight'

(xvi)

ij Sewers for the king and for the quene — Euery of them a man sitting in the halle, and for their lyuerey as a gentilman huyssher

[f. 18b] (xvii)

Gentilmen huisshers and maresshalles — Euery of thaim, a man sitting in the haulle, and for thair lyuerey at nyght', demi lof and a potelle of ale — j shide tallwood, ij candeles of whitelighte

(xviii)

Gentilwomen waiting on the quene — Euery of thaim, a man sitting in the haulle, and for thair lyuerey at nyght', demi lofe, j potelle ale — j shide tallwood, ij candeles whitelighte

(xix)

Vnder aumosner and clerkes of the closetts. — Vnder aumosner, ij clerkes of the closettes, euery of thaim in wages at iiijd. ob. withoute eny other lyuereye.

(xx)

Herbyiours, maister cokes, and squyers	j gentilman herbyiour, iij maister cokes, xxiiij squyers wayting, euery of thaim a man sitting in the haulle, and for his lyuerey at nyght', demi lof of brede, j potelle of ale	j shide tallwood, ij candeles whitelightes

(xxi)

Wages of household	Euery squyer at wages by the day, vijd. ob.; euery yoman, aswelle yomen of the corone, yomen of the chambre, and yomen of household, at iijd. euery day; euery grome at xls. by the yere; euery page at xxvjs. viijd. by the yere.

[f. 19a] (xxii)

Comptynghouse	Coferer .... ij clerkes of the greneclothe ...... j clerc comptroller .... j vnder clerc of the comptrollement j clerc for the coferer .... j yoman .... j grome.........................	For thoffice, ij tallwood shides, vj candeles of whitelighte

(xxiii)

Bakehouse	j sergeaunt...................... j clerc.......................... iiij yomen .... j grome......................... v conductes	viij candeles of whitelight'

(xxiv)

Panetrie	j sergeaunt...................... j gentilman for the quene .... vj yomen .... iij gromes...................... j person for the haulle at xxvjs. viijd. per annum...................	ij tallwood shides, viij candeles of whitelighte

(xxv)

Celare	j sergeaunte.................... j gentilman pro regina........... v yomen....................... iij gromes......................	iij tallwood shides, j lb. of whitelight'

(xxvi)

Buttery	ij yomen........................ ij gromes	ij tallwood shides, j lb. of whitelight'

[f. 19b] (xxvii)

Ale takers	j yoman .... ij gromes	nichil

(xxviii)

Picherhouse ⎰ iiij yomen .... ⎱ For thoffice,
⎱ iij gromes...................... ⎰ ij tallwood,
vj candeles
whitelight'

(xxix)

Spicerye ⎧ j chief clerc .... ⎫ For thoffice j
⎨ j vnderclerc.................... ⎬ tallwood shide,
⎩ j yoman pouderbeter .... ⎭ iiij candeles
whitelight'

(xxx)

Confeccionarye ⎰ ij yomen...................... ⎱ Demi bundle
⎱ j grome...................... ⎰ carbone, iij
candles of
whitelight'

(xxxi)

Waferye ⎰ j yoman .... ⎱ Demi bundle
⎱ ij gromes .... ⎰ coles, when
they wyrk,
iij candeles
whitelight'

(xxxii)

Chaunderye ⎰ ij yomen...................... ⎱ For thoffice,
⎱ ij gromes .... ⎰ j shide demi
tallwood, and
coles, whan
they wyrk as
shall suffice;
iiij candeles
whitelight'

(xxxiii)

Ewerye ⎧ j sergeaunt................... ⎫ j shide demi
⎨ iiij yomen .... ⎬ tallwood,
⎩ iij gromes..................... ⎭ vj candeles
whitelight'

(xxxiv)

Laundrye ⎰ ij yomen...................... ⎱ Wode for to
⎱ ij gromes .... ⎰ wasshe as
shall' suffice,
j lb. candeles

[f. 20a] (xxxv)

Kechyn[55] ⎧ j chief clerc .... ⎫
⎪ ij vnder clerkes .... ⎪ Noo wode
⎨ iiij maister cokes .... ⎬ ne candele
⎪ vij yomen .... ⎪ for thoffice
⎩ viij gromes................... ⎭

(xxxvi)

Lardere

- j sergeaunte . . . . } No wode.
- iij yomen . . . . } j lb. candeles
- iiij gromes . . . . } for kechyn
- j clerc in stede of the iiijth yoman } and larder

(xxxvii)

Boylers[56]

- j yoman . . . . } iij candeles whitelight' to bren in the mornyng in wynter tyme
- ij gromes . . . . }

(xxxviii)

Skaldinghous[57]

- j yoman . . . . } Wood as shall' suffice, and iij candeles
- ij gromes . . . . }

(xxxix)

Pulletrie

- j sergeaunt . . . . }
- j clerc . . . . } j shide tallwood,
- iij yoman puruyours . . . . } ij candeles of
- ij gromes . . . . } whitelight'
- j cariage man . . . . }

[f. 20b] (xl)

Accaterye

- j sergeaunte
- j clerc
- vij yomen, wherof ij yomen for the mouth', ij yomen puruyours, ij yomen bochours, j talowe man.[58]
- ij gromes
- ij herdes
- j yoman pigtaker

(xli)

Squillery

- j sergeaunt . . . . }
- j clerc . . . . } j bundle cooles,
- vj yomen . . . . } x candeles
- iij gromes . . . . } Whitelight'
- ij children . . . . }

(xlii)

Salserye[59]

- j sergeaunte . . . . }
- j clerc . . . . }
- iij yomen . . . . } vj candeles of
- ij gromes . . . . } whitelight'
- iij children . . . . }

(xliii)

Haulle[60]

- vj maresshalles
- j sergeaunte
- j clerc
- iiij yomen
- iiij gromes

ESTIMATE OF THE YEARLY EXPENSES OF THE ROYAL HOUSE-HOLD IN THE TIME OF KING HENRY VII

Exchequer (QR), Accounts Various (E. 101), Bundle 416, No. 10

. . . of the Rolle of King Henry the Vijth

<table>
<tr><td rowspan="9">Summ of the ffore said dyettes by estimacion for one hole yere (dra)weth to</td><td>The king by estimacion . . . . v^ciiij iiij li. vjd</td></tr>
</table>

Summ of the ffore said dyettes by estimacion for one hole yere (dra)weth to	The king by estimacion . . . . v^ciiij ^{xx}iiij li. vjd
	The quene by estimacion . . v^clxvj li. xiijs. iiijd.
	The kinges borde . . . . Ciiij^{xx}ij li. viijs. viijd.
	The quenes borde . . . . nihil
	The kinges chamber . . . . viij^cxxxvij li. xiiijs. xd.
	The quenes chamber . . . . . . ix^ciiij^{xx}xj li. xiijs. xjd.
	The hall and lyueres . . . . . MMMv^ciiij iij li. iiijs. viijd.
	Summa vj^mvij^cxlv li. xvs. xjd.

Other necessaries and fforen charges within the kinges housholde over and aboue the said dayly dyettes of vytaylles by estimacion in the yere as ffoloweth.

The wages of the kinges housholde over and aboue the wages of hys stable in the yere . . . . .MMCCxxiiij li.

The charges of his stable draweth to in the yere with the wages of the officers of the said stable . . . . .vij^cxxiiij li.

The prouysion of spyces in the yere . . . . .iiij^clx li.

The prouision of wex by the yere . . . . .iiij^cl li.

The prouision of tallwodd and ffaggottes in the yere . . . . .iiij^cxx li.

The prouision of coles in the yere . . . . .CCl li.

The kinges dayly aulmes at iiijs. by the day . . . . .lxxiij li.

The prouision of asshen cuppes . . . . .lxvj li.

The prouision of dyaper and lynnen clothes by the yere . . . . .C li.

Apurus ordenarius[1] geuyn to officers by the yere . . . . .lxx li.

Caryage of wyne and ale by the yere . . . . .C li.

Cowperage off the same wyne and ale by the yere . . . . .xxvij li.

Caryage of pultry stuff by the yere . . . . .xl li.

Wages oute of courte to officers being in prouision and other towching the householde . . . . .iiij^{xx} li.

Cariage of the householde stuff at the kinges remeuynges . . . . . .Ciiij^{xx} li.

Pastures hyred, dryuyng of oxen, pewter vesselles, pottes, pannes, broches, and all other necessaries belongyng to the householde by estimacion in the yere . . . . .CCCxliiij li.

The offerynges to the deane of the chapell . . . . .xij li. xiijs. viijd.
Summ of the said fforen charges and all other necessaries in the kinges
housholde ouer and aboue the dayly dyettes. . v^m vj^c xix li. xiiijs.viijd.

Item, xiiij ordenary brekefastes to lordes, ladys, and other in the
kinges housholde by the day, draweth to by the yere, by esti- _{xx}
macion . . . . .iiij li.
Item, for all lyueres at afternone and for all nyght, as bred and wyne to
lordes chambers, ladys, officers, and other ordenary lodged in the
kinges house, draweth to by estimacion in the yere . . . . .v^c li.
Item, for bred, ale, and wyne geuyn at the barres of the pantre, buttre,
and celler thourough oute the yere after xiijs. iiijd. by the day, by
estimacion draweth to in the yere . . . . .ccxx li.
Item, for the enlarging of the iiij principall ffeastes and other feastes in
the yere after the olde ordenary, to be added to the dyettes. .cccc li.
Item, for commyng of all ambassatours and other strangeours to the
courte thorow the yere by estimacion . . . . .iiij^c li.
Item, for the waste and commaundementes of the kinges house
thourough the yere by estimacion . . . . .iiij^c li.
Summ of the foresaide charges by estimacion in the yere . . . . . .MM li.
Summ totall of the forsaid charges, aswell the dayly dyettes as all other
fforen charges belongyng to the kynges housholde, draweth to by
estimacion in the yere. . . . . .xiiij^miij^clxv li. xs. vijd.[2]

ABBREVIATIONS USED IN THE NOTES TO THE TEXTS

B.B. = The Black Book of the Household of Edward IV.

B.I.H.R. = *Bulletin of the Institute of Historical Research.*

B.J.R.L. = *Bulletin of the John Rylands Library.*

C.Ch.R. = *Calendar of Charter Rolls.*

C.C.R. = *Calendar of Close Rolls.*

C.F.R. = *Calendar of Fine Rolls.*

Complete Peerage = G. E. Cokayne, *The Complete Peerage*, revised by V. Gibbs, H. A. Gibbs, H. A. Doubleday, etc.

C.P.R. = *Calendar of Patent Rolls.*

Derby Household Books = *The Household Books of Edward and Henry, Earls of Derby, 1561–90* (Chetham Soc., 1953).

D.N.B. = *Dictionary of National Biography.*

Edward II = T. F. Tout, *The Place of the Reign of Edward II in English History* (2nd ed., Manchester, 1936).

E.H.R. = *English Historical Review.*

Foedera = T. Rymer, *Foedera* (Hague ed., 1737–45).

Great Chronicle = *The Great Chronicle of London*, ed. A. H. Thomas and I. D. Thornley (London, 1938).

Household Ordinances = *A Collection of Ordinances and Regulations for the Government of the Royal Household* (London, 1790).

Migne, P. L. = J. P. Migne, *Patrologia Latina.*

Nicolas = *Proceedings and Ordinances of the Privy Council of England*, ed. N. H. Nicolas, Vol. VI (London, 1837).

Northumberland Household Book = *The Regulations and Establishments of the Household of Henry Algernon Percy, 5th Earl of Northumberland*, ed. Bishop Percy (2nd ed., London, 1827).

O 1318, O 1223 = The Ordinances of 1318 and 1323, printed in *Edward II.*

O 1445 = The Ordinance of 1445, printed above.

O 1454 = The Ordinance of 1454, printed in *Nicolas.*

O 1471, O 1478 = The Ordinances of 1471 and 1478, printed above.

O 1493, O 1526, O 1540, O 1601 = The Ordinances of 1493, 1526, 1540, 1601, printed in *Household Ordinances.*

Paston Letters = *The Paston Letters*, ed. J. Gairdner (4 vols., Edinburgh, 1910).

P.C.C. = Prerogative Court of Canterbury. Wills now kept in Somerset House.

Ritter- Hof- und Pilger-Reise = *Des böhmischen Herrn Leos von Rozmittal Ritter-, Hof-, und Pilger-Reise durch die Abendlande, 1465–67* (Stuttgart, 1844).

R.P. = *Rotuli Parliamentorum.*

Scofield = C. L. Scofield, *Life and Reign of Edward IV* (2 vols., London, 1923).

Somerville = R. Somerville, *The Duchy of Lancaster*, Vol. I, 1265–1603 (London, 1953).

Tout, Chapters = T. F. Tout, *Chapters in the Administrative History of Medieval England* (6 vols., Manchester, 1920–33).

NOTES TO THE FOREGOING TEXTS

THE ORDINANCE OF 1445

[1] For the date (23 Hy. VI), cf. above, p. 51.

[2] Cf. B.B., §78 (viii).

[3] Repd. in O 1478, §22.

[4] Cf. B.B., §62.

[5] Repd. in subst. in O 1478, §23.

[6] Repd. in O 1478, §24.

[7] Repd. in O 1478, §§29, 30.

[8] Repd. in subst. in O 1478, §31.

[9] Repd. in O 1478, §§32, 34, 35, 36.

[10] Repd. in O 1478, §§37, 39 (where, surprisingly, arrangement is more generous).

[11] Repd. in O 1478, §35.

[12] Cf. B.B., §78 (vi).

[13] Repd. in subst. in O 1478, §57.

[14] This order was not repeated in 1478, and was not in fact observed. Thus in account of treas. of household for 25–26 Hy. VI (E 101/409/16), grants of wine to religious houses are entered under 'Oblaciones et Elemosina', to various officials under 'Dona', and wages of mews under 'Vadia falconiariorum'. Same arrangement occurs in surviving controllers' accounts for this reign (e.g. E 101/408/24, E 101/409/9 and 11, E 101/410/6), and in household treasurers' accounts for 30–31 Hy. VI (E 101/410/9) and in the reign of Edward IV (E 101/411/13, 15; E 101/412/2, 10, 11).

[15] Repd. in O 1478, §56.

[16] Repd. in subst. in O 1478, §48.

[17] Repd. in subst. in O 1478, §§11, 12.

[18] Cf. O 1318 in *Edward II*, p. 245: 'Item vn countreroullour, qi doit countrerouller au tresourier de la garderobe toutz les receitez et issues touchantz mesme le garderobe.'

[19] Repd. in O 1478, §51.

[20] Payments to squires and yeomen recorded in Harl. MS. 433 (register of crown grants under Ed. V and Rich. III) usually less than this. John Mortimer, squire for the body, received £40 annuity during nonage of Edward, Earl of Warwick (f. 85a), but more usual rate 50 marks (e.g. *ibid.*, ff. 38b, 77b) and sometimes less (e.g. to Thomas Blount, squire for the body, 20 marks annuity paid, f. 85a). Usual rate in Harl. MS. 433 for yeomen of the crown was 6d. a day, an annual rate of £9 2s. 6d. or under 14 marks. Amount of king's gift often imprecise, for these gifts often took form, not of definite sum of money, but of whole or part of issues or profits of some office or estate.

[21] Clear from Black Book that check-roll kept in countinghouse, (§§22, 37, 62) used to check attendances (§§37, 43, 45, 50) in order to control payment of wages (e.g. §§33, 38, 43 (*bis*), 45, 62, 71, 73, 77 (*bis*), 79, 83). Cf. above, p. xlvi, pp. 23–4.

[22] Repd. in subst. in O 1478, §44.

[23] Repd. in subst. in O 1478, §54, with addition of controller.

[24] Repd. in subst. in O 1478, §58, with additions.

[25] Repd. in subst. in O 1478, §19.

[26] Repd. in O 1478, §61.

[27] Probably the basis of O 1478, §66.

[28] Repd. in subst. in O 1478, §§62, 63.

[29] Repd. in O 1478, §67.

[30] *R.P.*, V. 13–14.

[31] No. of attendants and livery allowed for the night greater than for duke and duchess in O 1478, §68 (ii).

[32] O 1454 allows confessor 2 squires, 2 yeomen, 2 'chamberlains' (= servants) (*Nicolas*, VI. 222).

[33] Cf. O 1478, §68 (xi).

[34] Cf. O 1478, §68 (vi).

[35] Cf. O 1454 (*Nicolas*, VI. 222); O 1478, §68 (xiv).

[36] Cf. notes to §30 of B.B.

[37] Cf. O 1454 (*Nicolas*, VI. 223); O 1478, §68 (xi); below, App. I, List M.

[38] Cf. O 1478, §68 (x).

[39] Cf. B.B., §56.

[40] Cf. O 1454 (*Nicolas*, VI. 223); B.B., §§57, 59, 62.

[41] Cf. O 1471, §§6, 7.

[42] O 1454 names only 8 yeomen of the chamber, and B.B. only 4; but Parl. Rolls refer to 11 for reign of Edward IV (*R.P.*, V. 537, 539, 592, 593, 609; VI. 86, 93, 94), and names of 24 drawn from Patent Rolls of Ed. IV by Mr. E. J. Fox in thesis on 'Members of the Household of Edward IV', (Hons. B.A., Univ. of Liverpool, 1954), p. 81.

[43] Cf. O 1454 (*Nicolas*, VI. 225).

[44] Cf. O 1454 (*Nicolas*, VI. 223); B.B., §48.

[45] The account books of this period do not record payment of wages to more than 3 yeomen falconers (e.g. E 101/409, 11, f. 41a), and they received only 3d. a day—though in Ed. IV's reign 6d. a day was paid (e.g. E 101/412/2, f. 39b). No. of grooms to whom payment recorded in the accounts was greater —5 or 6.

[46] Cf. with more precise orders in O 1478, §68 (vii, viii, ix).

[47] Cf. O 1454 (*Nicolas*, VI. 226); O 1478, §68 (xxii).

[48] Cf. O 1454 (*Nicolas*, VI. 233), where no. of staff prescribed for queen's household was 120.

[49] Cf. B.B., §§80, 81; O 1478, §68 (xxiv, xxxi).

[50] Cf. B.B., §79; O 1478, §68 (xxiii).

[51] Cf. B.B., §§84, 88, 90; O 1478, §68 (xxv, xxix, xxxii).

[52] Cf. O 1478, §68 (xxxv, xxxvi, xl).

[53] Cf. O 1478, §68 (xxxix, xli, xlii).

[54] Cf. B.B., §§91, 92; O 1478, §68 (xxxiii, xxxiv).

[55] Cf. O 1478, §68 (xxxviii).

THE BLACK BOOK OF THE HOUSEHOLD OF EDWARD IV

[1] Cf. Prov. xxiv. 3: 'Sapientia aedificabitur domus.' Most biblical references are not exactly reproduced.

[2] Cf. Ecclus. x. 2: 'Qualis rector est ciuitatis, tales et inhabitantes in ea.'

[3] Ecclus. iv. 35.

[4] Publilius Syrus, *Sententiae*, 322 (commonly attributed to Seneca in the middle ages).

[5] Source unknown; probably from vast penumbra of pseudo-Aristotelian writings created in medieval Europe.

[6] Ecclus. xxxiii. 31.

[7] From De cura et modo rei familiaris vtilius gubernande (i.e. Le Regisme de Mesnaige, *c.* 1130, often wrongly attributed to St. Bernard of Clairvaux or

Bernard Silvestris: cf. M. Manitius, *Geschichte der Lateinischen Literatur des Mittelalters*, III (Munich, 1931), p. 209).

[8] It was common for treatises on law and administration to describe weights and measures (cf. *Fleta*, ed. J. Selden (London, 1685), II. 12, pp. 72–5); and it is typical of fifteenth century to give elaborate allegorical meaning to workaday phenomenon. Cf. Lev. xix. 35 and 1 Chron. xxiii. 29 (Vulgate, 1 Par. xxiii. 29); in connection with shew-bread there were in worship of synagogue Jewish canticles celebrating bountifulness of God; Dr. H. Liebeschütz has suggested that this passage in 1 Chron. may be direct or indirect inspiration of 'lectio prima' of B.B.

[9] Source untraced. Dr. R. W. Hunt has suggested that possible source of this and 'domus regis edificatur sapientia' is liturgy, in various parts of which non-Vulgate texts appear. Cf. M. B. Ogle, 'Bible Text or Liturgy', *Harvard Theological Review*, xxxiii (1940), 191–224, which illustrates from Walter Map's De Nugis Curialium this kind of problem.

[10] 1 Timothy vi. 17.

[11] Source unknown.

[12] 2 Cor. ix. 7.

[13] Gualtiero de Castellione, *Alexandreis sive Gesta Alexandri Magni*, in Migne, *P.L.*, CCIX, col. 467.

[14] Similar expressions occur in voluminous letters of Cassiodorus; but exact source of this not traced; and it may come from corpus of pseudo-Cassiodorian writings popular in middle ages.

[15] *De. Civ. Dei*, IV. 4.

[16] Source not traced.

[17] Cf. St. Thomas Aquinas, *Summa Theologiae*, II. 2. q. 148, art. 5. No such ref. in I. 2, as stated in text.

[18] This misunderstanding of what Epicurus had taught was a commonplace in middle ages.

[19] Cf. 3. Reg. (1 Kings) x. 1–10.

[20] Cf. Jacopo da Voragine, *Legenda aurea* (Caxton's edition of *Golden Legend*, Kelmscott Press repr. 1892, I. 212).

[21] A Hebrew or Phoenician measure of capacity; cf. *ibid.*: 'Salomon had dayly for the mete of hys houshold xxx mesures named chores of corn, and lx of mele.'

[22] Huguccio, noted canonist and tutor to Innocent III (died 1210), and William Briton or Breton, a Franciscan or Cistercian (died 1356) (cf. Manitius, *op. cit.*, III. 191 and *D.N.B.*). In fact Briton's definition in his Vocabularium (e.g. Bodl. Rawl. MS. C 896, f. 63a) is derived verbatim from Huguccio's Liber Derivationum (e.g. Bodl. Laud MS. Misc. 626, f. 33b).

[23] Ruth ii. 17–18.

[24] Used to render Latin bubalus, with meaning of antelope, buffalo, or ox. Cf. *Golden Legend*, I. 212.

[25] From twelfth-century poem edited by W. W. Wattenbach (*Neues Archiv der Gesellschaft für ältere deutsche Geschichtskunde*, I (Hanover, 1876), 600–4, and supposed by him to be work of Henry of Blois, Bishop of Winchester but in fact composed by Richard of Poitiers, monk of Cluny (cf. L. Delisle, *Bibliothèque de l'École des Chartes*, XXXVII (1876), 443–4), author of a chronicle and student of poetry (*Recueil des historiens de la France; Histoire littéraire de la France*, XII (1763, reprinted 1865), 480; *Le Débat des Hérauts d'Armes de France et d'Angleterre* (ed. L. Pannier and P. Meyer, Paris, 1877), p. xiv). It was frequently quoted in fourteenth and fifteenth centuries. (Fourteenth century: (*a*) R. Higden, *Polychronicon*, II (Rolls Series, 1869), 18–20; (*b*) *The Great Chartulary of Glastonbury*, ed. Dom Aelred Watkin, II (Somerset Record Society), 1; (*c*) John of Trevisa's translation of Bartholomew Anglicus, *De*

proprietatibus rerum (Wynkyn de Worde, 1495), XV. 14. Fifteenth century:
(*a*) B.M. Cottonian MS. Julius A 8; (*b*) B.M. Harl. MS. 3643; (*c*) *Duo Rerum Anglicarum Scriptores Veteres*, viz., *Thomas Otterbourne et Johannes Whetham-stede* (ed. T. Hearne, 1732), p. 6, from B.M. Cottonian MS. Vitellius F IX. All three are manuscripts of Otterbourne's Chronicle; (*d*) MSS. Cott. Nero C VI, Bodley 585, Caius 230/116, manuscripts containing extracts from John of Whethamstede's Granarium; I owe these three references to Dr. R. W. Hunt.) Version current in fifteenth century differs considerably from single known twelfth-century copy.

²⁶ Cf. Geoffrey of Monmouth, *Hist. Regum Brittaniae*, ed. A. Griscom (London, 1929), p. 301.

²⁷ Cf. *op. cit.*, p. 313.

²⁸ Cf. Henry of Huntingdon's *Historia Anglorum* (Rolls Series, 1879), p. 190.

²⁹ Comparison and verse originally applied to King Edgar (cf. *ibid.*, p. 166 and Higden, *op. cit.*, VII. 22).

³⁰ Cf. Appendix II, The Lost Ordinance of Edward III, and Introduction, p. 19.

³¹ Not included in O 1318 and O 1323; perhaps part of lost Ordinance of Woodstock (*Edward II*, p. 243; Tout, *Chapters*, II. 248).

³² Unless Ed. III's household ordinance was made early in his reign, keeper of privy seal and his staff must have been already out of court before it was published (Tout, *Chapters*, I. 60, V. 30–1, *et passim*). Whereas O 1279 places two marshals immediately after stewards, O 1318 does not mention marshal, though chief clerk of marshalsea still in royal household (Tout, *Chapters*, II. 158, 162; *Edward II*, p. 266). By Ed. IV's reign marshalsea prison was fixed in Southwark (*R.P.*, VI. 50a). Drift of great wardrobe out of court was practically complete by end of Edward IV's reign (Tout, *Chapters*, IV. 399–401, 406–7). Keeper of great wardrobe called 'le clerk purueour de la graunde garderobe' in O 1318 (*Edward II*, p. 247).

Though B.B. describes countinghouse as 'the grete warderober' and household treasurer as 'custos magne garderobe hospicij', this confusion in terminology was shared by official records and popular usage both before and afterwards. (Tout, *Chapters*, IV. 407–9; e.g. E 101/412/2 (Account of John Fogge, household treasurer, 6–7 Ed. IV, f. 36a) describes Fogge as 'custos magne garderobe hospicij domini regis'; and same privy seal letter can refer to Sir John Elrington as 'tresourer of our houshold' and 'keper of our grete wardrobe of our houshold' (K.R. Memoranda Roll, 22 Ed. IV. Brev. dir. Bar., Easter Term, m. 6a–E 159/259).)

³³ Cf. *Edward II*, pp. 256, 267; B.B., §80.

³⁴ Butler, usually London merchant, had not been resident member of royal household long before Ed. III's reign. In O 1279 butlers receive no allowances of wages or robes (Tout, *Chapters*, II. 159), O 1318 makes it clear that butler is not expected to be resident (*Edward II*, pp. 272–3), and by 1327 great merchant like Richard de la Pole could be made king's butler (*C.F.R.*, IV. 33).

³⁵ outward = outside the household. Offices and rewards for laymen are all mentioned in Fortescue, *op. cit.*, esp. cap. x, xvii, xviii, xix. For offices and rewards given to clerics, cf. J. Otway-Ruthven, *The King's Secretary*, pp. 160–189.

³⁶ In great households of fifteenth century unusual to have more than 3 courses, even at feasts, so that 4 or 5 represented luxury. Each course in royal household consisted of many dishes; cf. O 1526 (*Household Ordinances*, p. 174).

³⁷ Source of this elegiac couplet unknown.

³⁸ Ultimately based on Aristotle's exposition of magnificence in his Nico-machean Ethics, IV. ii. 2 (hence banna vsus is a corrupt transliteration of A.'s

'Βαναυσος'), this passage is probably drawn from Aegidio Colonna's *De Regimine Principum Libri Tres*, II pars, Liber I, cap. XXI.

[39] Introduction, pp. 29–31.

[40] This apparently strange chronology is yet another indication of author's familiarity with royal household accounts. These normally covered year beginning 1 October and ending 30 September of following year, a period rarely starting on Sunday; and weeks were grouped into lunar months. Hence a year in royal household 'dieta' normally comprised twelve lunar months, three weeks, and odd days (making up eight days in all) at beginning and end of year.

[41] Total given for diets generous compared with usual expenditure in earlier years of Ed. IV and later years of Hy. VI, especially as 'dieta' of household accounts include normal wages and alms, and this estimate does not. For extant accounts providing totals of 'dieta', or from which totals of dieta can be worked out, figures are as follows (to nearest pound).

E 101/409/9	20–21 Hy. VI	£10,135
E 101/409/11	22–23 Hy. VI	£9,978
E 101/409/16	15 Nov. 25 Hy. VI–30 Sept. 26 Hy. VI	£10,487
E 101/410/1	26 Nov. 26 Hy. VI–30 Sept. 27 Hy. VI	£9,412
E 101/410/6	29–30 Hy. VI	£10,177
E 101/410/9	30–31 Hy. VI	£9,301
E 101/410/13	3–4 Ed. IV	£8,187
E 101/411/15	5–6 Ed. IV	£9,502
E 101/412/2	6–7 Ed. IV	£9,897.

[42] Five principal feasts, apart from feast of St. George, for which increased diet normally provided, were All Hallows, Christmas Day, Candlemas, Easter Day, and Whitsunday (e.g. E 101/412/10, ff. 7a–33a).

[43] It was not at all unusual for king to keep smaller household when riding about country. In ordinance probably of Ed. IV's reign (Harl. MS. 642, 195b–6a) we read: 'Nor comprised in the number none such officers as shall like the lordes heereafter to appoint to serve the kinges estate more largely with commers and goers to his court, nor for the kinges ryding household with him, aswell as for his abyding household.' A smaller riding household necessary when king travelled so much; household accounts for 18–19 Ed. IV (E 101/412/10), for example, show that king changed his night's lodging about 60 times during that 12 months. Cf. Introduction, p. 21. Assignments of revenue to value of £10,574 6s. 8d. were made by Richard III for upkeep of royal household, but only 2,000 marks and 500 marks per annum were assigned for expenses of his households at Sandal and Carlisle (Harl. MS. 433, ff. 290b, 269b, 120a).

[44] Total receipts for royal household for each year of Ed. IV's reign for which figures have survived are as follows (to nearest pound):

E 101/411/11	4 Mar.–30 Sept. Ed. IV	£8,579
E 101/411/13	3–4 Ed. IV	£8,907
E 101/411/14	3–6 Ed. IV	£23,978
E 101/411/15	5–6 Ed. IV	£6,631
E 101/412/2	6–7 Ed. IV	£12,904
E 101/412/10	18–19 Ed. IV	£14,910
E 101/412/11	19–20 Ed. IV	£10,953

It is therefore possible that when Black Book was made, income of £13,000 could reasonably be envisaged.

[45] Cf. diets ordained for king and queen in 1526 (*Household Ordinances*,

pp. 174-6). Though the two scales are not easy to compare, that of Black Book appears to be smaller.

⁴⁶ If these 8 dishes were for whole meal, it was very economical arrangement compared with that recommended by Humphrey, Duke of Gloucester's usher and marshall, John Russell (*Babees Bk.*, I. 164-8), or compared with diet prescribed for Hy. VIII and his queen in 1526 (*Household Ordinances*, p. 174).

⁴⁷ Probably refers to refreshments provided just before king retired to bed, at ceremony of 'All Night'. There would be bed-making at this time since pallet-beds or truckle-beds would now be pulled out for squires of the body on duty to undress king and sleep in his bedchamber. Cf. reference to All-Night in George, Duke of Clarence's Ordinance of 1468 (*Household Ordinances*, p. 90), description of All-Night at Charles II's Court (*ibid.*, p. 374), and account of All-Night by Ferdinando Marsham, Esquire of the Body to Charles I and Charles II (Pegge, *Curialia*, I. 19-23).

⁴⁸ Chamber was not yet officially sub-divided into Outer or Presence Chamber, Privy Chamber, and Bed-Chamber of Henry VIII's day, still less into elaborate divisions of late eighteenth century—Great Chamber, Presence Chamber, Privy Chamber, Withdrawing Room, and Bed Chamber (Pegge, *Curialia*, II. 68); but there was already distinction in fact between great chamber, which was presence or audience chamber, privy chamber, and bed-chamber. Cf. B.B., §27 and O 1471, §15.

⁴⁹ For difficult and responsible duties of usher of the chamber, see *Babees Bk.*, I. 185-9.

⁵⁰ This corresponds to sums recorded in household accounts of Ed. IV's reign (e.g. E 101/412/2, f. 33b, E 101/412/11, f. 34a).

⁵¹ Cf. B.B., note 32.

⁵² This catalogue agrees with list of holy days for which larger offerings usually recorded in household account books for this reign, except that St. George's Day usually appears instead of Michaelmas Day, and there is added Feast of Relics on 3rd Sunday after 24 June (cf. C. R. Cheney, *Handbook of Dates* (London, 1945), p. 59). Household accounts also show daily offering as a 'great penny', worth 7d. and record 25s. spent on cramp rings (e.g. E 101/412/10, f. 33b; E 101/412/11, f. 33b). It was evidently an old tradition; cf. O 1323 (*Edward II*, p. 283). It will be observed that only 16 festivals are mentioned, not 17.

⁵³ This was worthy of mention because it was relaxation of strictest rules of etiquette. Cf. *Babees Bk.*, I. 188.

⁵⁴ *Babees Bk.*, I. 285.

⁵⁵ O 1445 (§35) and O 1453 (*Nicolas*, VI. 222-3) both list chamberlain and confessor above secretary; and O 1478 (§68), which does not list confessor by name, assigns chamberlain to separate and higher mess than secretary.

⁵⁶ Probably to be identified with those later described in B.B. as bannerets or bachelor knights (§28), especially as bachelor knights included carvers and cupbearers as well as 'knights of the chamber', and O 1478 (§68 (xiv)) groups knights for the body, carvers and cupbearers in same mess.

⁵⁷ Cf. Harl. MS. 642, f. 205, for 'The Order of the estates of the blood royall', which deals with nice points such as whether younger son of royal duke takes precedence over baron, and how one deals with lady of royal blood married to mere knight. Cf. also *Babees Bk.*, I. 185-94.

⁵⁸ Queen Elizabeth's only surviving account-book (E 36/207) does not make it clear whether she contributed towards diets of herself and her staff when she was at court; but sole surviving household account of Queen Margaret shows (D.L. 28/5/8, f. 21a) that she paid for herself and her staff when she was

in king's household £7 a day, which is at same rate as figure of £2,555 for annual cost of queen's household given in Black Book.

⁵⁹ There are many references in both E 36/207 and D.L. 28/5/8 to members of queen's council and to meetings of queen's councillors.

⁶⁰ In D.L. 28/5/8 payments to about 130 members of queen's household are recorded, and O 1454 allowed 120 officials for queen's household (*Nicolas*, VI. 233).

⁶¹ Note in B.M. Cottonian MS. Vespasian C XIV, f. 272b: 'A remembraunce that oure souueraigne lorde King Edward assigned to the Quenes goode grace the XVth yere of his reigne for thexpenses of his honourable houshold, in the tyme of oure said souueraigne lordes absence and being beyond the see for an hole yere, the summe of MMCC. li.'

⁶² 'Service' was food served for a meal, hence allowance or portion of food and drink; cf. next sentence. Hence 'with double service' means 'allowed two courses of food'. Cf. O 1526 (*Household Ordinances*, pp. 174–94), which shows that all important persons at court were entitled to two courses (each, of course, containing many dishes), whereas lesser folk had only one course, on ordinary days.

⁶³ At Westminster there was a building called prince's palace (cf. *C.P.R.*, *1461–7*, pp. 16, 111).

⁶⁴ O 1454 allows 39 officials for prince's household (*Nicolas*, VI. 233).

⁶⁵ Cf. *Babees Bk.*, I. 285.

⁶⁶ Cf. B.B., note 120, and for towel worn by sewer (as mark of respect for his lord), see *Household Ordinances*, p. 118, and *Babees Bk.*, I. 270.

⁶⁷ This is more than had been allowed by O 1445 (§35 (i)), or was to be prescribed by O 1478 (§68 (ii)), which limited numbers to 8 and 6 respectively.

⁶⁸ B.M. Add. MS. 34,213, household account of Anne, Duchess of Buckingham for year 31 March 1465 to 31 March 1466 records total expenditure as £606 6s. 2½d. A more comparable figure, however, is that given in 1468 for annual expenditure of Duke of Clarence's household; this figure of £4,505 15s. 10¾d. (*Household Ordinances*, p. 105, makes estimate of £4,000 seem reasonable.)

⁶⁹ Estimates here given are lower than those allowed for Duke of Clarence's household in 1468 (*Household Ordinances*, pp. 101–2).

⁷⁰ Clarence had 299 in his household in 1468 (*ibid.*, p. 105); but John Howard, Duke of Norfolk, paid wages in 1483 to only 65 servants, and total number of persons in his establishment does not seem to have exceeded 100 (*Howard Household Books*, pp. 468–70).

⁷¹ Cf. O 1493, which establishes elaborate graded tariff of payments to bearers of New Year gifts to king and queen (*Household Ordinances*, p. 120); and monarch was expected to present New Year gifts throughout court. Cf. elaborate lists of New Year gifts surviving from Queen Elizabeth I's day (e.g. C 47/3/38), carefully recording name of recipient, description of gift, and weight or value of it. Until nineteenth century presents were given at New Year rather than at Christmas.

⁷² Cf. B.B., note 53.

⁷³ This is same number of servants as O 1478 was to allow (O 1478, §68 (iii)).

⁷⁴ The total expenditure of Richard Beauchamp, Earl of Warwick, from 14 March 1431 to 18 March 1432, had been £1,316 19s. 10¼d. (f. 183b) for household which had travelled from Rouen to Warwick. (Account-book now in possession of Corporation of Warwick which kindly made it available to me through Warwickshire County Record Office.)

Cf. order made by Cardinal Wolsey for regulation of household of young Earl of Oxford and his wife in 15 Henry VIII (*Archaeologia*, XIX (1821), p. 64), for servants appointed.

⁷⁵ Cf. numbers in Earl of Northumberland's chapel in 1512 (*Northumberland Household Book*, p. 44).

⁷⁶ 'Domestici' seem to be all inmates of household on establishment rather than merely 'domestics' in our sense. 'Vacans' may, perhaps, mean 'free from other obligations', hence 'whole-time member of the household'. Number of persons on strength of Northumberland household in 1512 was 166 (*ibid.*, p. 45), and Earl of Derby had in 1587 118 persons in daily attendance upon him (*Derby Household Books*, pp. 23–57).

⁷⁷ This is same number of servants as allowed in 1445 (O 1445, §35 (ii)), and less than in 1454 (*Nicolas*, VI. 222).

⁷⁸ O 1318 details confessor's allowances and specifies three grooms (*Edward II*, p. 250).

⁷⁹ Cf. B.B., note 32.

⁸⁰ Perhaps allowances for confessor's horses were influenced by military activities of fourteenth-century confessors (Tout, *Chapters*, iii. 120).

⁸¹ Cf. B.B., §64.

⁸² This statement is borne out by household accounts of this reign (e.g. E 101/412/11, f. 34b).

⁸³ Household roll contained names of all who had official connexion with royal household; check roll kept record of officials actually working there. This distinction still maintained in later years of Hy. VIII. Cf. *Household Ordinances*, p. 230 and 'Rotulus nominum officiariorum omnium hospitij domini regis Henrici VIIIʰⁱ' for *c.* 1544–5 in L.C. 5/178.

⁸⁴ These statements can be verified from household accounts of this reign, e.g. E 101/412/2, f. 36a, E 101/412/11, f. 34b.

⁸⁵ O 1454 allowed Viscount Bourchier 1 chaplain, 1 squire, 3 yeomen (*Nicolas*, VI. 222).

⁸⁶ Sum estimated for lord and (or) his lady on average, sometimes excepting dinner and (or) supper on account of public prayers, fasting, vows, or devotions.

⁸⁷ Cf. *Babees Bk.*, I. 285, and a list of precedence of 30 Eliz. I (B.M. Add. MS. 6032, f. 127b).

⁸⁸ Probably keeper of great wardrobe, in this case.

⁸⁹ Cf. *Paston Letters*, III. 52, No. 700.

⁹⁰ Questionable whether chamberlain always had time to carry out these functions in person. Chamberlain throughout this reign was William Lord Hastings, except for re-adeption of Henry VI, 1470–1; and Hastings was, *inter alia*, Master of the Mint from 1461 (*C.P.R.*, *1461–7*, p. 130, *C.P.R.*, *1476–85*, p. 10), Chamberlain of North Wales from 1461 (*C.P.R.*, *1461–7*, p. 26), administrator of lands of Edward, Prince of Wales and one of his tutors and councillors (*C.P.R.*, *1467–77*, pp. 283, 366), constable of Harlech and Beaumaris castles and various castles in England (*Complete Peerage*, revd. Gibbs and Doubleday, VI. 370–4 and *C.P.R.*, *1467–77*, p. 165), justice of the peace in shires of Derby, Leicester, Northampton, Nottingham, Rutland, Sussex, Huntingdon, Yorkshire, Stafford, Warwick, Lincoln (*C.P.R.*, *1461–7*, p. 562 *et passim*; *C.P.R.*, *1467–77*, p. 617 *et passim*; *C.P.R.*, *1476–85*, p. 557 *et passim*), member of a large number of commissions, including over twenty of 'oyer et terminer' (*C.P.R.*, *1461–7*, p. 132 *et passim*; *C.P.R.*, *1467–77*, p. 55 *et passim*; *C.P.R.*, *1476–85*, p. 112 *et passim*) and was prominent in Edward's parliaments as a trier of petitions (*R.P.*, V. 461b, 496b, 571b). He was also used to negotiate with Scots, Burgundians, French, and Bretons (*Paston Letters*, II. 110, No. 459; Scofield, *op. cit.*, I. 378–80; *Foedera*, V. ii. 138, 143, 149); and from 1471 he was Lieutenant of Calais, which he visited on various occasions (*Complete Peerage*, *op. et loc.*

cit.; *Paston Letters*, III. 173, No. 786; Scofield, *op. cit.*, ii. 279; *C.P.R.*, *1476–85*, pp. 205, 214). No mention of a vice-chamberlain, as in Ordinance of Eltham of 1526; in chamberlain's absence some of his more routine duties may have fallen on gentlemen ushers of the chamber (B.B., §36).

[91] Cf. O 1478, §68 (vi).

[92] In household treasurer's accounts for 3–4 and 6–7 Ed. IV chamberlain received only 106s. 8d. (8 marks) for robes at Christmas and Whitsuntide (E 101/411/13, f. 36a, E 101/412/2, f. 36a), but he also drew fee of £6 13s. 4d. (10 marks) in equal instalments at Easter and Michaelmas (*ibid.*).

[93] Cf. note 48.

[94] Cf. *Babees Bk.*, I. 132–3 and *Household Ordinances*, p. 119.

[95] Of 14 bannerets whose names are recorded in roll of French expedition of 1475, at least 9 are identifiable as members of royal household (F. P. Barnard, *Edward IV's French Expedition of 1475* (Oxford, 1925), ff. 2v, 3r). Use of term 'banneret' may be due to conservatism of Black Book; for 'banneret of the household' had still been official position in Edward III's time (Tout, *Chapters*, III. 120; IV. 134). Strictly speaking, bannerets were of slightly higher rank than knights bachelors, but latter were of higher rank than knights 'sans phrase' (*Babees Bk.*, I. 186, 284).

[96] Cf. *Babees Bk.*, I. 140–8.

[97] O 1478 groups carvers and cupbearers with 'knights for the body' (§68 (xiv)); and 'knight for (or of) the body' was much more usual, in patent rolls and elsewhere, than either 'knight of the chamber' or 'banneret'. Various men were promoted from 'king's knight' to more intimate and honourable rank of 'knight of the body' (e.g. Sir William Norris, *C.P.R.*, *1467–77*, pp. 178, 488). But carvers could be chosen from king's knights as well as from knights of the body; Sir Thomas Montgomery and Sir William Stanley, already carvers by 1461 and 1462 (*C.P.R.*, *1461–7*, pp. 125, 198), were still described as king's knights in 1468 and 1470 (*C.P.R.*, *1467–77*, pp. 112, 183), and are first called knight of the body, so far as is known, in 1469 and 1475 respectively (*ibid.*, pp. 173, 556). Number of knights of the body, carvers, and cupbearers in practice exceeded the number here given (cf. *Letters and Papers illustrative of the reigns of Richard III and Henry VII*, ed. J. Gairdner (Rolls Series, 1861), I. 5, 8; O 1471, §7; B.B., note 99).

[98] Cf. *Paston Letters*, III. 262, No. 846.

[99] These statements are borne out by entries in household accounts of this reign (e.g. E 101/411/13, f. 36a; E 101/412/2, f. 36a). As with other officers, these might be only minimum fees. For example, James Radclyf, one of the king's carvers, was granted in 1479 an annuity of £20 (*C.P.R.*, *1467–77*, p. 159).

[100] Cf. O 1445, §35 (v); O 1478, §68 (xiv).

[101] Cf. *Edward II*, p. 252.

[102] Cf. *Babees Bk.*, I. 325.

[103] Just as contemporary chancery enrolments spoke of 'knight of the body' rather than 'knight of the chamber' or 'banneret', so they preferred 'king's knight' to 'knight of the household'.

[104] Cf. O 1478, §68 (xv), knights waiters; and intimacy of duties demanded agrees with appointment of trusted followers to position of king's knight, e.g. John Howard, William Herbert, and William Stanley (*C.P.R.*, *1461–7*, pp. 10, 119, 198; *C.P.R.*, *1467–77*, pp. 41, 183). William Herbert evidently deemed it an honour to be described as king's knight after he had been made a baron (*C.P.R.*, *1461–7*, pp. 114, 119).

[105] Cf. O 1478, §68 (xv).

[106] Contrast with 'thesaurere of houshold' indicates that keeper of the great wardrobe is meant; cf. B.B., notes 32, 112, 132.

107 Cf. Otway-Ruthven, *op. cit.*, p. 110, which describes this paragraph as 'the first clear description of the signet office'.

108 Cf. O 1445, §35 (vi).

109 Cf. Otway-Ruthven, *op. cit.*, p. 111. She explains number of only 2 clerks in O 1454 as result of council's endeavour to reduce size of household to minimum during Henry VI's madness; but O 1445 also allows only 2 clerks. As she points out (*ibid.*, p. 112) that in 1444 5 persons received liveries from great wardrobe as signet clerks, perhaps figure in 1445 is to be explained as goal meant to be achieved but not attained.

110 Cf. *ibid.*, pp. 114–23, esp. p. 116.

111 Professor Otway-Ruthven considers these three men to have been 'almost certainly apprentice clerks' (*ibid.*, p. 113).

112 The great wardrobe.

113 Cf. O 1445, §35 (iii); O 1454 (*Nicolas*, VI. 222–3).

114 Entitled to draw clothing from great wardrobe only if their names are on check-roll, i.e. only if on active strength of household establishment.

115 Usually more than this; six in office simultaneously in 1460's (*C.P.R., 1461–7*, pp. 17, 86, 186, 210, 430; *C.P.R., 1467–77*, pp. 20, 59, 106, 182, 276; *R.P.*, V. 534, 587), nine from Nov. 1471 to Feb. 1472 (O 1471, §§6, 7), and fourteen at Ed. IV's funeral (Gairdner, *op. cit.*, I. 5, 8). Four may, however, be number normally in residence at court at once (O 1445, §35 (xii); O 1454— *Nicolas*, VI. 223; O 1471, §7; H. Spelman, *Glossarium* (London, 1687), p. 43). Cf. Pegge, *Curialia*, Part I, pp. 37–8, for numbers and history of esquires of the body from reign of Mary I to that of William III and Mary II, when this office expired.

116 For duties of esquires of the body in reigns of Henry VIII, Charles I, and Charles II, see *Household Ordinances*, pp. 151–2, 356–7, and Pegge, *op. cit.*, pp. 19–23.

117 Cf. *C.P.R., 1461–7*, p. 380.

118 Merely a basic rate; usual annual reward seems to have been 50 marks a year (e.g. *R.P.*, V. 534; Harleian MS. 433, f. 77b), though there could be variation either way (e.g. Harl. MS. 433 shows one or two such squires receiving 10 marks and 20 marks (ff. 84b, 85a) and at least one getting £40 (f. 85a); cf. list of fees to Edward IV's officials, Harl. MS. 433, ff. 310a–16a.)

119 Cf. O 1478, §68 (xv).

120 Cf. O 1445, §35 (xiv); Nicolas, VI. 232; O 1478, §68 (xvi). For duties of this official, see *Babees Bk.*, I. 162–3; *Archaeologia*, XIII, pp. 321 ff.; *Miscellanea Antiqua Anglicana*, pp. 22–4, *Sussex Archaeological Collections*, VII. 195–6. There may have been two sewers, at least sometimes during this reign; cf. *R.P.*, V. 535, *C.P.R., 1461–7*, p. 379; *C.P.R., 1476–85*, pp. 159, 218; O 1471, §7. There were to be three sewers in 1526 (*Household Ordinances*, p. 165.)

121 In fifteenth century sauces numerous and highly spiced; cf. *Babees Bk.*, I. 151–3, 172–5, 273–4, 277–8.

122 Probably especially New Year gifts, but possibly also presents expected from important guests and suitors. Cf. H. C. Maxwell-Lyte, *The Great Seal of England* (H.M.S.O., 1926), p. 352.

123 O 1445 agrees (§37 (xiv)): O 1478 equates livery of sewers with that of gentlemen ushers (§68 (xvi)).

124 Cf. *Babees Bk.*, I. 271. Apparently fruits served baked were accompanied by bread.

125 Books of etiquette of this period give impression that 'voiding [clearing] of the board' took place after sweet wines had been served (cf. *Babees Bk.*, I. 166, 168, 171, 271).

126 Spices were commonly served with comfits (sugar-plums) and wine after

a feast or before departure of guests or before retiring to bed. For details of serving such a collation, called a void, see Ordinance of Henry VII made in 1493, preserved in Harl. MS. 642 and printed (though wrongly dated as 1494) in *Household Ordinances*, pp. 109, 110, 113.

[127] This account goes back to Florence of Worcester (*Florentii Wigorniensis Monachi Chronicon ex Chronicis*, ed. B. Thorpe (English Historical Society), 1848, I. 134).

[128] Officer who superintended preparation and serving of food. Cf. *Babees Bk.*, I. 317. Ordinances of 1445, 1454, and 1471 allowed one surveyor (O 1445, §35 (xiv); *Nicolas*, VI. 232; O 1471, §7); O 1478 is silent on this point. O 1526 allowed two (*Household Ordinances*, p. 165).

[129] Cf. *Babees Bk.*, I. 326, 372.

[130] Evidently sewer and squires of the body. Cf. O 1445, §35 (xiv).

[131] Cf. Tout, *Chapters*, IV. 407. Although B.B. may be wrong in time it assigns for separation of great wardrobe from royal household, its use of term 'wardrobe' to describe great wardrobe is in keeping with contemporary usage since days of Edward III (Tout, *op. cit.*, III. 179). For other instances of confusion between great wardrobe and wardrobe of the household see B.B., note 32.

[132] Cf. *Edward II*, p. 247.

[133] Cf. *Red Book of the Exchequer*, ed. H. Hall (Rolls Series, 1896), pp. 911–12.

[134] For duties of an usher, cf. accounts given in *Babees Bk.*, I. 185–94, 314–16, and *Sussex Archaeological Collections*, VII (1854), 193–5. O 1445, O 1454 and O 1471 specified four gentlemen ushers for the chamber (O 1445, §35 (xiii); *Nicolas*, VI. 223; O 1471, §7), and seven gentlemen ushers are named as taking part in Edward IV's funeral (Gairdner, *Letters*, I. 8). Difficult to check from patent rolls of Edward IV's reign how many gentlemen ushers were in office at once, since both gentlemen ushers and yeomen ushers are described as 'ushers of the privy chamber' and four 'gentlemen ushers daily waiters' (*Household Ordinances*, p. 165).

[135] Cf. O 1478, §15.

[136] Cf. O 1471, §18; Draft O 1478, §19; O 1478, §22; *Paston Letters*, No. 411, where Clement Paston declares in 1461 that 'the sewer wyll not take no men no dyschys till they be comawndyd by the counterroller'.

[137] Cf. *Babees Bk.*, I. 185–94 for complexity of this task.

[138] Cf. O 1445, §35 (xiii).

[139] Usual sense is 'capable of being ordained, or directed to an end'; but here meaning seems more active one of 'capable of ordaining' and whole phrase appears to mean 'as he may order at his discretion'.

[140] Inside and outside court.

[141] Usual reward of ushers of chamber seems to have been £20 a year (e.g. *R.P.*, V. 535a and b).

[142] For ceremony and 'estate' of laying surnape, see B.B., note 94.

[143] Cf. O 1478, §68 (xvii).

[144] Cf. *Household Ordinances*, p. 148.

[145] Terence's *Adelphoe*, III. 3, 77.

[146] Usually more than this. Acts of resumption in Edward IV's first four parliaments record exemptions for 24, 29, 28, and 29 (*R.P.*, V. 474, 536, 594; VI. 87); and there were probably others for whom no exemption was needed. Account-books of household treasurer for 3–4 and 6–7 Ed. IV record 'Feoda et Roba' to 67 and 69 'valecti camerarie' respectively (E 101/411/13, f. 37a and b; E 101/412/2, f. 37a and b); but it is not certain that they were all yeomen of the crown. Cf. 24 'valletz pur la chambre' in O 1445, §35 (xiv), and 23 yeomen of the crown in O 1454 (*Nicolas*, VI. 224). Perhaps 24 was number required to be in actual attendance at court; for yeomen of the crown were frequently used

for all kinds of missions out of court. They might be sent out as ambassadors (e.g. Scofield, *op. cit.*, II. 232, 254, 281), to seize ships and inquire into insurrections (e.g. *C.P.R.*, *1467–66*, p. 54), or to help in arresting a defeated claimant to an abbacy and his accomplices (*ibid.*, pp. 403–4).

147 Cf. *R.P.*, V. 588, 594; VI. 87 for yeomen of the robes; *R.P.*, V. 537 for yeomen of the wardrobe of beds.

148 Probably a small domestic pet, such as a dog or a monkey. A squire of the body, Ralph Hastings, was keeper of king's beasts, such as lions, lionesses, and leopards, in Tower of London, from 1461 until after 1473 (*R.P.*, V. 475, 516, 533, 598, 624; VI. 81); Thomas Wintreshull, esquire, was serjeant of harthounds in 1467–8 (*ibid.*, V. 600); in 1474 Sir John Audley was made master of king's hounds with 5 yeomen and 2 grooms under him (*C.P.R.*, *1467–77*, p. 444). One of these yeomen may have been responsible for a pet dog.

149 Probably means 'as the gentleman usher shall direct'; cf. B.B., §36.

150 Cf. below, last sentence of this section, §37, and also Appendix XXI, 'Yeomen of the Crown (1400–1600)', by Maurice Church, in R. Hennell's *History of the King's Body Guard* (Westminster, 1904), pp. 302–4.

151 Judging by daily expenditure recorded in household accounts of this reign, five great feasts seem to have been All Hallows, Christmas Day, Easter, St. George's Day, and Whitsunday.

152 Cf. O 1478, §68 (xxi).

153 We find entries in household accounts of Edward IV's reign, under 'Feoda et Roba', such as 'valectis camerarie . . . dicti domini regis cuilibet eorum pro robis et calciaturis suis, xviij s.' (e.g. E 101/412/2, Account-book of household treasurer, 6–7 Ed. IV, f. 38a).

154 Cf. *Edward II*, p. 242.

155 Cf. O 1445, §35 (xiv), and O 1454 (*Nicolas*, VI. 2); latter specifies four yeomen (plus yeoman surgeon, listed later in B.B.). As with other offices, sometimes more holders of post than numbers specified in B.B.; e.g. in 1467–8 five yeomen of the chamber are named (*R.P.*, V. 592, 593, 609).

156 For instance of yeomen of the chamber 'going messages', cf. *Paston Letters*, II. 53, No. 417. Doubtful whether yeomen of the chamber always occupied with domestic functions here described. Thomas Grayston, Grayson, or Greyson, groom of the chamber in 1476, and yeoman of the chamber by 1478, was granted a licence to trade abroad in 1479, and was in 1482 a collector of customs in Exeter and Dartmouth, although apparently still a yeoman of the chamber (*C.P.R.*, *1467–77*, p. 595; *1476–85*, pp. 97, 168, 177, 325). Cf. also confirmation of annuity of £10 to Rauf Vestynden 'oon of the Yemen of oure Chambre . . . for the goode and aggreable service which he did unto us, in beryng and holdyng of our Standard of the Blakbull in the Battaill of Towton on Palme Sonday' (*R.P.*, VI. 93).

157 Cf. O 1478, §68 (xxi); usual annual fee for yeomen of the chamber seems to have been £10 at this time (e.g. *R.P.*, VI. 936).

158 Cf. *Edward II*, p. 253.

159 Cf. O 1454 (*Nicolas*, VI. 225) and B.B., §45.

160 Yeoman of the chamber and of the crown were closely linked in general esteem; Avery Cornburgh was described as a yeoman of the chamber (*Paston Letters*, II. 107, No. 456) when he was already a yeoman of the crown (*R.P.*, V. 474). It was, however, a rise in status for a yeoman of the chamber to be made a yeoman of the crown (e.g. Richard Apryce, *R.P.*, V. 593; VI. 87, or John Forster, *C.P.R.*, *1476–85*, pp. 90, 212, 221).

161 Cf. O 1445, §35 (xiv) and O 1454 (which allowed 1 yeoman, 1 groom, and 1 page, *Nicolas*, VI. 224–5).

162 Cf. *Nicolas*, VI. 224.

[163] Although Tout speaks of pages in connexion with O 1318 (*Chapters*, II. 256; Edward II, pp. 253, 275, 276), there does not seem to be any mention of pages by name in this Ordinance except to forbid any yeoman to have one, save in kitchen (*Edward II*, p. 276).

[164] See Introduction, p. 17.

[165] One yeoman for the beds allowed in O 1445 (§35 (xiv)), O 1454 (*Nicolas*, VI. 224), and O 1526 (*Household Ordinances*, p. 166).

[166] O 1454 shows yeomen of beds as one of yeomen of chamber (*Nicolas*, VI. 224); but in 1464 was keeper of king's beds in palace of Westminster when he was also yeoman of crown (*R.P.*, V. 537).

[167] Two in O 1445 (§35 (xiv)) and O 1526 (*Household Ordinances*, p. 166); one in O 1454 (*Nicolas*, VI. 225).

[168] One in O 1445, but two in O 1526.

[169] Cf. O 1478, §68 (xxi); higher rate of pay in O 1478 may be due to inclusion of an allowance for clothing.

[170] Probably a guard, or small body of soldiers used as a guard, to protect possessions of office.

[171] O 1445 specifies 6 (§35 (xiv)), O 1454 prescribes 9 (*Nicolas*, VI. 225), and O 1526 says 5 (*Household Ordinances*, p. 166). Payments of 'Dona' to 49 'garciones camerarie', however, recorded in E 101/412/10, f. 36b; perhaps most of them non-resident.

[172] Cf. O 1478, §22. Probably check made by comparing lights which gentleman usher swore had been used the previous day (B.B., §36) with tallies of issues submitted by yeoman of chandlery (B.B., §90).

[173] Cf. B.B., note 48.

[174] Cf. O 1445, §35 (xiv), O 1454 (*Nicolas*, VI. 225).

[175] B.B., §45 envisages possibility of him not being a groom of the chamber.

[176] This borne out by household accounts of this reign, e.g. E 101/412/10, f. 36a. Contrast between 'clothing with the household' and 'watching clothing of the wardrobe' suggests contrast between grooms in residence and those given leave of absence from court. E 101/412/10 records wages of 6s. 8d. to each of 5 men who may be grooms of the chamber. O 1478 prescribes 40s. a year (§68 (xxi)), but this may include allowance for clothing.

[177] O 1445 prescribes 3 (§35 (xiv)), and O 1454 allows two, including one 'for the robes' (*Nicolas*, VI. 225).

[178] Keeper of jewel-house often a layman as long ago as reign of Richard II (Tout, *Chapters*, IV. 334–7); and in reign of Edward IV, whatever may have been status of obscure William Port, keeper from at least 1462 to 1464 (*C.P.R.*, *1461–7*, p. 326; *1467–77*, p. 186), his successor was a layman. This was celebrated Thomas Vaughan, chamberlain and councillor to Prince Edward, keeper of jewel-house from 1465 to 1483 (*C.P.R.*, *1461–7*, p. 459; *1476–85*, pp. 561, 569), sheriff of Surrey and Sussex in 1466–7 (*C.F.R.*, *1461–71*, p. 191), knighted in 1475 (Shaw, *Knights of England*, I. 137), member of parliament for Cornwall in 1478 (Wedgwood, *Biographies*, p. 902), justice of the peace in various shires (*Patent Rolls*, *passim*) and member of numerous other commissions (*ibid.*). Perhaps, however, clerk is here used in sense of officer in charge of accounts, regardless of whether he was in holy orders.

[179] Cf. Richardson, *Tudor Chamber Administration*, pp. 87 ff., 110, 111. Tout notes that term 'receiver of the chamber' was beginning to be replaced by 'treasurer of the chamber' as early as reign of Richard II (*Chapters*, IV. 336–7); by beginning of Henry VI's reign usage was well-established (cf. *R.P.*, IV. 293).

[180] O 1454 notes staff of 4 for jewel-house only 'at the principall festes in the yere' (*Nicolas*, VI. 225). There were clerks of the jewel-house in Edward IV's

reign—Richard Lawrence in 1473 and 1475, Roland Forster in 1475, William Daubeney in 1480 and 1482 (*R.P.*, VI. 98; *C.P.R.*, *1467-77*, p. 496; *1476-85*, pp. 76, 223, 258; E 403/845, E 403/848—Issue Rolls, 18 Ed. IV, Easter and Trinity, Michaelmas and Hilary Terms); though Richard Lawrence is called 'yeoman of the king's jewel-house' in August 1478 (*C.P.R.*, *1476-85*, p. 122). E 403/848 probably clarifies position when it calls Daubeney 'clerk of the jewels' and Lawrence and Forster his 'valecti'.

[181] Cf. O 1478, §68 (xxi).

[182] Payments of 18s. each to yeomen of the chamber for clothes and shoes are recorded in household accounts of Edward IV's reign (e.g. E 101/412/2, f. 37b).

[183] Cf. B.B., §14, and table of contents of B.B. on page 77

[184] Cf. petition in parliament in 1425 (*R.P.*, IV. 293): 'les quelles Tresorers & Resceivours (de Chambre), come bien est conuz, n'ount este devaunt ces heures accomptablez au ascuny, forsque tant soulement au Roy'.

[185] Perhaps this passage means that only one physician was to be on duty at once, for there were usually more than one physician in office in this reign. In 1468 three king's physicians acted together to certify that they had found a woman free from leprosy (*C.C.R.*, *1468-76*, p. 30); perhaps one was senior to the others. There had been 3 'physicians and surgeons' in 1445 (§35 (vii)), and 2 physicians and possibly 4 surgeons in 1454 (*Nicolas*, VI. 223).

[186] Perhaps due to widespread concern with dietetics in this age, as evidenced by numerous books of health dealing with properties of different foods, and by fear that, as John Russell's Boke of Nurture had said, cooks invent new dishes that tempt people and endanger their lives (*Babees Bk.*, I. 149). It may owe something to Edward's need for medical attention from early years of his reign. On 9 May 1464, very large sum of £87 18s. 7½d. was paid to John Clerk, king's apothecary, 'for certain physic supplied for the said King's use, and administered to him under the advice of the said King's physicians' (Devon, *Issues of the Exchequer*, p. 488).

[187] Cf. O 1478, §68 (xi), (xv).

[188] Account-book of household treasurer for 6-7 Ed. IV records payment of 40s. to James Friiz for winter and summer clothing, same payment made to squires of the household (E 101/412/2, f. 36b). James Friiz here included among chaplains and clerks of chapel; but likely to be James Friis who was one of king's physicians at this time and for nearly whole reign (*C.P.R.*, *1461-7*, p. 79; *1467-77*, p. 396; *1476-85*, p. 251). Although wages said to be same for physicians as for squires of the household, latter allowed only 7½d. a day (B.B., §53), whereas James Fryse had 2s. a day in 1475 during French expedition (*Foedera*, V. ii. 58). Probably 7½d. only a basic wage, as with other officials. See B.B., note 18.

[189] O 1454 specifies 1 sergeant surgeon, 1 yeoman surgeon (*Nicolas*, VI. 232); but under Edward IV at least 2 surgeons held office simultaneously (see Appendix I (N)). In 1475 William Hobbys is referred to as both 'Phisicus & Cirurgicus pro Corpore Regis'; and seven other surgeons are named as accompanying king to France (*Foedera*, V. iii. 58). In keeping with this superior status, a proviso to an act of resumption in 1473 saved to 'William Hobbys, Cirurgion for oure body' an annuity of 40 marks (*R.P.*, VI. 83b).

[190] Same livery of food, but less lighting (cf. B.B., §29).

[191] Wage and allowance for medicines still same as in O 1318; but clothing allowance now only 40s. instead of former 8 marks (*Edward II*, p. 252). Rate in 1475 was 12d. a day for seven surgeons who accompanied Edward IV's expedition to France (*Foedera*, V. iii. 58). William Hobbys, as both physician and surgeon, drew 18d. a day.

R

[192] Cf. O 1454 for John Marshall, yeoman surgeon who was also yeoman of the chamber (*Nicolas*, VI. 225).

[193] This sum confirmed by household accounts of Ed. IV's reign (e.g. E 101/412/2, f. 38a).

[194] Cf. O 1526 (*Household Ordinances*, p. 166).

[195] Cf. B.B., note 186.

[196] 14 barbers authorized in 1526 (*Household Ordinances*, pp. 169–70).

[197] Cf. B.B., §91.

[198] Cf. O 1478, §22.

[199] Henchmen were squires or pages of honour who walked or rode beside king in processions, progresses, etc.; office abolished by Elizabeth I in 1565 (E. Lodge, *Illustrations of British History* (London, 1791), I. 358). O 1445 had specified 6 henchmen for king (§35 (xiv)), O 1454 allowed only 3 (*Nicolas*, VI. 223). Usual number of henchmen under Edward IV and Richard III seems to have been 7 for king (Nicolas, Great Wardrobe Account of 1480, in *Privy Purse Expenses of Elizabeth of York*, p. 167; F. Grose, *Antiquarian Repertory* (London, 1779), II. 254). Richard's Queen Anne had 5 for her coronation (Grose, *op. cit.*, II. 258); often 3 in a noble household (e.g. *Northumberland Household Book*, p. 254, and *Manners and Household Expenses*, p. 234).

[200] Cf. Nicholas, *op. cit.*, p. 167.

[201] Whereas Mr. E. J. Fox, in thesis mentioned above (O 1445, note 42), has often found references to more holders of an office than Black Book states (e.g. 59 yeomen of the crown), he has discovered mention of only 26 squires of the household, even if one includes under this title 14 'king's squires' who probably held same office. As, however, squires of the household not so prominent as squires of the body, there may have been some of whom it is very difficult to find a trace in royal records now extant. Moreover, as Black Book avowedly based on previous practice, probably influenced by enormous numbers of squires on household establishment in Henry VI's reign. Thus in controller's account for 20–21 Hy. VI we find 'Feoda et Roba' given to 224 'scutiferi aule et camere' (E 101/409/11) and treasurer's account for 25–26 Hy. VI records payments to even more squires—258 (E 101/409/16).

[202] King's squires usually sheriffs, justices of the peace, and commissioners in shires where their influence greatest, and were drawn from very many different shires (e.g. Wedgwood, *Biographies*, pp. 69, 229, 318, 349, 474, 591–2, 838, 933, 946, etc.).

[203] Number of squires here specified may be greater than actual number. O 1445 had allowed only 8 'escuiers pur la chambre' (§35 (xiv)); and as these are contrasted with 'escuiers pur la corps', they may be regarded as squires of the household. O 1454 permitted only 12 'squires of attendaunce' (*Nicolas*, VI. 223–4); but cf. O 1478, §25, which insisted on attendance of 24 squires each day. If Pegge was right in equating squires of the household of Yorkist courts with gentlemen of the privy chamber in Henry VIII's household, then it is relevant to mention that 18 such gentlemen were allowed in 1526, only 6 of whom were to be on duty at once (*Household Ordinances*, pp. 154, 165, 169). At Edward IV's funeral 5 squires of the household were present (Gairdner, *Letters*, I. 8).

[204] Cf. B.B., §74.

[205] These 20 may have been treated as supernumeraries as Sir John Paston was in 1461 (*Paston Letters*, ii. 43, No. 411). This would explain latter part of sentence—happy combination of increased magnificence, greater economy, and relief to squires concerned in not being required at court the whole year.

[206] Cf. O 1478, §68 (xxi); 7½d. only a basic rate—see B.B., §118. 40s. for

clothing agrees with sums allowed in household accounts of this reign (e.g. E 101/411/13, f. 37a; E 101/412/2, f. 37a).

[207] Squires serving in king's household had probably worn his livery since at least Edward I's days. (J. E. Morris, *The Welsh Wars of Edward I* (Oxford, 1901), p. 85). Cf. H. Johnstone, *The Letters of Edward, Prince of Wales, 1304-05*, pp. 62 and xxvi.

[208] By strict rule of household, so that first week's expenditure would serve as guide for whole year following.

[209] Cheese of four varieties suitable either for scooping or gratering.

[210] Cf. B.B., note 151.

[211] Cf. *Babees Bk.*, I. 311. The editor was wrong in saying in footnote to this page that 'The Liber Niger of Edward IV assigns this duty to one of the Gentylmen Usshers'; gentlemen ushers, as usual in royal or seignorial household, supervised seating, not in hall, but in chamber. Cf. B.B., §36.

[212] Cf. Tetzel's account of distribution of largesse at Queen Elizabeth's churching (*Ritter-, Hof-, und Pilger-Reise*, etc., p. 156).

[213] One would expect record of such fees to appear after a section on knights rather than after one on squires; but there is no mention of such fees in either place, though there are references in §§54, 56 of Black Book to fees for waits and deans of chapel royal at making of Knights of the Bath. Cf. description of fees of heralds in Cottonian MS. Nero C IX (*c.* Henry VI's reign), printed in J. Anstis, *Observations upon the Knighthood of the Bath* (London, 1725), p. 105.

[214] Very small number compared with number of serjeants appointed by Edward IV. In 1467 exemption made from act of resumption for 21 serjeants-at-arms (all squires) (*R.P.*, V. 593-4); and Mr. E. J. Fox, in thesis cited above (note 42) has identified another 30 for this reign. Perhaps only a few serjeants were employed on duties in royal household; others may have been used extensively outside household, for arresting persons, and holding inquiries into matters like piracy or smuggling; cf. many recorded commissions of this kind (*C.P.R., 1461-7*, pp. 234, 301, 302, 303; *1467-77*, pp. 28, 286, 319; *1476-85*, p. 347). O 1318 records that of 30 serjeants-at-arms then authorized, four whom king named would be in attendance every day to help usher of chamber (*Edward II*, p. 254).

[215] Act of resumption of 1467-8 stated wage of 21 serjeants-at-arms then named to be 12d. a day (*R.P.*, V. 593-4; cf. Chancery, Parl. & Council Proc. 36/1). This evidently usual rate, as attested by numerous letters patent of appointment of serjeants-at-arms.

[216] Cf. O 1478, §68 (xiii).

[217] Cf. *Edward II*, p. 253.

[218] O 1445 specifies 12 minstrels, with wait (§35 (xiv)). O 1454 allows 4 minstrels, presumably every day, and 9 more at principal feasts (*Nicolas*, VI. 225). In practice number varied: payments to 16 and 19 minstrels are recorded in household accounts of 3-4, 6-7 Ed. IV (E 101/411/13, f. 37a; E 101/412/2), accounts of 3-4, 6-7 Ed. IV (E 101/411/13, f. 37a; E 101/412/2, f. 37a); great wardrobe account of 1483 records deliveries of 2 yards of red cloth to each of 16 minstrels (Grose, *op. cit.*, I. 54).

[219] Probably, as usual, a basic wage; for usual reward seems to have been 10 marks a year (cf. *R.P.*, V. 538, 600; VI. 87, 89).

[220] Household account-books of this reign record payments of 20s. each for winter and summer clothing to minstrels (E 101/411/13, f. 37a; E 101/412/2, f. 37a).

[221] Cf. Ranulph Higden's *Polychronicon*, VII (Rolls Series, 1879), 141-2. Probably itself source of passage in Black Book, for numeration of Emperors

Henry II, III, IV, V, as Henry I, II, III, IV was peculiar to Higden, who was himself dubious about this numbering (*ibid.*, VIII. 84).

²²² Cf. O 1445, §35 (xiv).

²²³ Cottonian MS. Nero C IX said that wait was to have as his fee only 'the grey cope . . . or a noble for it' (Anstis, *op. cit.*, p. 105). For other fees payable at this ceremony, see *Household Ordinances*, p. 124.

²²⁴ O 1445 authorized 3 messengers, O 1318 allowed 12 with 3d. a day, 1 mark a year for clothing, and 4s. 8d. for shoes (Edward II, p. 272). Cf. B.B., §37 and O 1478, §68 (xxi) for wages of yeomen.

²²⁵ Aprons of linen were evidently widely worn to protect clothes from dirt or injury—a very wise precaution in an age when so many fabrics, and liveries into which they were made, were so hard to wash. Linen cloth usually distributed from office of spicery at four principal feasts (probably All Hallows, Christmas, Easter, and Whitsuntide). Even steward, treasurer, controller, and cofferer entitled to allowances of linen in this way (B.B., §§68, 69, 71, 73); and although this allowance not specified as for aprons, linen allowance was for aprons in case of clerks of greencloth and serjeant usher of countinghouse (§§74, 77), who do not appear to have especially needed protective clothing.

²²⁶ Edward IV showed himself mindful of the privileges of his chapels royal. Cf. *C.P.R.*, *1461–7*, p. 487; *1476–85*, p. 341).

²²⁷ Cf. B.B., §14.

²²⁸ Payment of 8 marks to dean of chapel for winter and summer clothing, at Christmas and Whitsuntide, is recorded in household accounts of this reign (e.g. E 101/412/2, f. 36a).

²²⁹ O 1454 also allows dean a yeoman (*Nicolas*, VI. 223).

²³⁰ Cf. Anstis, *op. cit.*, p. 64; also *ibid.*, pp. 44, 73, 103.

²³¹ In spite of prolonged search, source of this passage in Latin not found. Professor E. F. Jacob kindly writes: 'I am afraid that I cannot throw any light upon the passages about the households of Henry III and Henry V, except that the one which . . . refers to Henry V finds very clear illustration in the *Gesta Henrici Quinti*, pp. 89 ff., where the king is acting as Ordinary in his own chapel. Henry went very carefully into the ritual of the office and increased the usual prayers both by psalms and responses, which had to be said by the clerks of the chapel. So it is quite clear that he was capable of committing the 'rule of his chapel' to anybody whom he wanted.' Cf. Introduction, p. 34, n. 10, for possibility that this passage is derived from long account of chapel royal written by its dean under Henry VI and Edward IV, William Say, for King of Portugal.

²³² O 1445 specifies 20 chaplains and clerks of chapel (§35 (x)) as does also O 1454 (*Nicolas*, VI. 223). In practice numbers greater than these. For years 25–26 Hy. VI., 3–4 Ed. IV., 6–7 Ed. IV payments made to 24, 24, and 34 chaplains and clerks of the chapel respectively (E 101/409/16, f. 34a; E 101/411/13, f. 37a; E 101/412/2, f. 37a).

²³³ Not in modern meaning, but descant in one of older senses, i.e. either melody or counterpoint sung above plainsong of tenor or else art of composing or singing part-music. 'Many composers were . . . Gentlemen of the Chapel Royal' (E. K. Chambers, *English Literature at the Close of the Middle Ages*, p. 100).

²³⁴ Probably allowances of food and drink for 'all-night', which would be more conveniently distributed if chaplains and clerks all lodged together.

²³⁵ Household accounts for 3–4 and 6–7 Ed. IV record payment of 40s. each to chaplains and clerks of king's chapel for winter and summer clothing (E 101/411/13, f. 36b; E 101/412/2, f. 36b).

²³⁶ Cf. O 1478, §68 (xi).

[237] Grants of prebends and churches to king's clerks too numerous and familiar to need illustration. Example of grant of a hospital is confirmation for life in 1461 of St. Anthony's hospital, London, to William Say, dean of king's chapel (*C.P.R., 1461–7*, p. 11; cf. *R.P.*, V. 520b).

[238] Cf. *Edward II*, p. 450.

[239] Cf. previous section for reference to 'deanes bourde' in hall, at which all chaplains & clerks sat together.

[240] O 1454 allows seven children of chapel (*Nicolas*, VI. 223). When Henry Abingdon put in charge of boys of king's chapel in 1455, there were ten children (*ibid.*, p. 256). In 1512 Earl of Northumberland had six children in his chapel choir (*Northumberland Household Book*, p. 257).

[241] There seems to have been revival in prestige of chapel royal under Edward IV (cf. J. Harvey, *Gothic England*, pp. 114–15); in 1471 the Duke of Milan addressed a letter to Edward IV, to ask him to help Master of Milanese Chapel (named Rayner) during his visit to England to obtain good English singers and musicians for Milan (*Cal. of State Papers and Manuscripts . . . of Milan*, I, ed. A. B. Hinds, H.M.S.O., 1912, 161). In 1479 famous Gilbert Banaster, who had succeeded Henry Abingdon in 1478, was granted, as Abingdon had been in 1465, 40 marks a year 'for the exhibition, instruction and governance of the Childer of oure Chapell' (*R.P.*, VI. 200, 86).

[242] 'To take their allowances to their quarters.'

[243] O 1454 has one (*Nicolas*, VI. 246), O 1478 has two (§68 (xix)).

[244] As with household officials, office of master of grammar is also to be found in noble households of fifteenth century and sixteenth century (e.g. *Northumberland Household Book*, pp. 44, 47, 97, 100, 254, 323).

[245] Although both O 1454 and O 1526 name yeomen of vestry, they do not mention serjeant (*Nicolas*, VI. 223; *Household Ordinances*, p. 170). He is not mentioned in patent rolls or household accounts of this reign. Cf. note 246.

[246] Probably 20s. on each occasion; for chaplains and clerks of chapel received 40s. a year for clothing (E 101/411/13, f. 36b; E 101/412/2, f. 36b). Perhaps this serjeant is concealed in household accounts as a clerk of the chapel.

[247] O 1445 prescribes 2 (§35 (x)), O 1454 allows 1 (*Nicolas*, VI. 223), O 1526 specifies 2 (*Household Ordinances*, p. 170).

[248] David Chirke or Cherk, yeoman of vestry in 1466 (*C.P.R., 1461–7*, p. 526) received 18s. for winter and summer clothing with other yeomen of household for years 6–7 Ed. IV (E 101/412/2, f. 37b). To act of resumption of 1467–8 proviso made in his favour for grant of 3d. a day from fee-farm of Windsor (*R.P.*, V. 596b).

[249] O 1454 allows one groom (*Nicolas*, VI. 223).

[250] In fourteenth and fifteenth centuries there were 2 clerks of crown in chancery (H. C. Maxwell-Lyte, *The Great Seal of England* (H.M.S.O., 1926), p. 272, and note 4).

[251] Clerks of crown also received clothing from great wardrobe. For typical entry in patent rolls, see *C.P.R., 1461–7*, p. 53.

[252] Gilbert Debenham appointed in 1461 by warrant of privy seal (*C.P.R., 1461–7*, p. 8), and William Tyler appointed in 1471 by king's word of mouth (*C.P.R., 1467–77*, p. 239); cf. terms of appointment in 1484 (*C.P.R., 1476–85*, p. 436).

[253] Perhaps a distorted reminiscence of O 1318 (*Edward II*, p. 252).

[254] Cf. duties of clerk of market as stated in O 1526 (*Household Ordinances*, p. 150).

[255] This passage is taken from Matthew Paris, *Chronica Majora* (Rolls Series,

ed. H. R. Luard), II. 480–1, sub anno 1202, with only two slight differences; the unintelligible 'lora' is taken from Paris.

²⁵⁶ Cf. O 1318 in *Edward II*, p. 352, esp. lines 24–30.

²⁵⁷ Gilbert Debenham, the younger, appointed clerk of market in March 1461 was in October 1461 described as esquire (*C.P.R.*, *1461–7*, pp. 8, 52). William Tyler, appointed clerk in March 1471, was knighted in 1485 by Henry Tudor (*C.P.R.*, *1467–77*, p. 239; Shaw, *Knights*, II. 22). In 1486 he was made keeper of king's jewels and king's knight, and in 1487 promoted to knight of the body (*C.P.R.*, *1485–94*, pp. 110, 126, 172).

²⁵⁸ No parallel in extant ordinances of Edward II. No doubt clerk of works was prominent in household of Edward III, who spent lavishly on building (cf. Tout, *Chapters*, IV. 176).

²⁵⁹ For expenditure of Edward IV on building, see *Scofield*, II. 429–30, and references there given.

²⁶⁰ Except for references to king's privy coffers and jewel-house, this statement is fairly close to that on royal wards in O 1318 (*Edward II*, p. 252).

²⁶¹ This passage mostly taken from St. Thomas Aquinas: *Summa Theologiae*, II. ii. qu. 49, art. VI, 'Utrum providentia debeat poni pars prudentiae'. Aristotle does not appear to have uttered precise form of words in last sentence, though much of their spirit is evident in Nicomachean Ethics, esp. Books II and VI. Notion of end of providence, or prudence, being love seems Augustinian rather than Aristotelian; cf. St. Augustine, De Moribus Ecclesiae Catholicae, I. 15, in Migne, *P.L.*, XXXII. 1322.

²⁶² This less important than it had been in Edward II's time, when chief clerk of marshalsea had had to account once a week before steward and marshal (*Edward II*, pp. 266–7). For statutes limiting jurisdiction of marshalsea in reigns of Edward I, Richard II, and Henry VI, see W. S. Holdsworth, *A History of English Law*, I (3rd ed.), 208. By Edward IV's reign much of its former jurisdiction had passed to king's bench; though steward sometimes still made judgements of life and limb. Cf. *C.P.R.*, *1461–7*, p. 380; and John Davy, who lost a hand in 1462 for striking a man in king's palace of Westminster (*Great Chronicle*, p. 198), was probably condemned in same way.

²⁶³ Stewards of Edward IV's reign not as continually resident in court as this definition of their functions implies. William Neville, Earl of Kent, steward from beginning of reign (E 101/411/14), was serving much in north in early years of reign (*Scofield*, I. 166–7, 177, 204, 243, 264; *C.P.R.*, *1461–7*, pp. 30, 66). In July 1462 he was made admiral of England (*Foedera*, V. ii. 110; *C.P.R.*, *1461–7*, p. 195); as there was serious danger of attack by Queen Margaret on Calais this summer, he spent much time with fleet assembled at Sandwich and in August 1462 raided French coast (Kingsford, *Chronicles of London*, p. 177).

John Tiptoft, Earl of Worcester, steward of household from 1463 to 1467, seems to have been even more active outside household than his predecessor. Treasurer of England until June, 1463 (*C.P.R.*, *1461–7*, p. 286), he remained Constable of the Tower and Chief Justice of North Wales (*ibid.*, pp. 61, 62, 271, 529), was justice of peace various times in nine shires (*ibid.*, pp. 560–72, *C.P.R.*, *1467–77*, pp. 609–36), and commissioner in various counties (*C.P.R.*, *1461–7*, pp. 281, 303, 304, 346). In 1463 king made him admiral at sea (*ibid.*, p. 282) 'to go on his service at sea for defence against his enemies for a certain term of years' and he showed activity in this capacity in following months (*Scofield*, I. 302, 311). Made Constable of England in 1462 (*C.P.R.*, *1461–7*, p. 74), in this capacity he won notoriety for severity in the north in 1464 (*Scofield*, I. 334, 337); but as Edward was also in north at this time, Tiptoft could perhaps have been attending to some of his duties as steward of the household during this period. But soon afterwards we find him engaged in activities which took him far away from royal household; for example, on embassies abroad and commissions of truce between England and Brittany (*Foedera*, V. ii. 126; *C.P.R.*, *1461–7*, p. 450).

His successors in stewardship do not seem to have been so heavily involved in outside activities. Henry Bourchier, Earl of Essex, steward from 1467 to probably 1471, was justice of peace in only threes shires—Essex, Norfolk, Suffolk (*ibid.*, pp. 564, 568, 573; *C.P.R.*, *1467–77*, pp. 613, 622, 630)—during his stewardship, and apparently was not used in varied capacities that Tiptoft had been. Thomas, Lord Stanley, steward probably from 1471 to 1483, also seems to have been relatively inconspicuous in royal service outside household. Although justice of peace in nine shires during this period, it was never for very long in more than one shire (*C.P.R.*, *1467–77*, pp. 612–13, 615, 629, 634–6; *C.P.R.*, *1476–85*, pp. 562, 574). In latter part of reign Black Book's description of duties of a steward may therefore have been closer to reality; perhaps this development reflects influence of Black Book and O 1478.

[264] To have one's cup served with a cover was mark of high rank. Cf. *Babees Bk.*, I. 67, 325.

[265] See B.B., note 62.

[266] This is borne out by reference in parliament rolls. By time of Edward IV tendency to growing terseness in describing opening of parliament precluded any mention of checking of attendances. During first decade of reign of Richard II this checking regularly recorded (*R.P.*, III. 55, 71, 88, 98, 122, 132, 144, 149, 184, 203), but without naming the checker. Then, perhaps because of excitements of parliaments of 1386 and 1388, this custom was dropped. In 1401 and 1402 references reappear, perhaps because checking in these years done in unusual spot—Chancery in Westminster Hall (*R.P.*, III, 454, 647); in 1401 it was said to be in presence of chancellor and steward of the household. In 1411 reference reappears, for last time, in these words: ' . . . le primer jour de Parlement, les chivalers des Countees d'Engleterre, & les Citeins & Bourgeoises des Citees & Burghs, somons au Parlement par Brief du Roy, feurent proclamez al house del Chambre de Peinte deins le Palois de Westm', en presence del seneschall de l'Ostel du Roy, come le manere est'.

The 'certificate' mentioned in line 4 is sheriff's return, by which steward checked attendance of knight or burgesses.

[267] Cf. account of funeral of Edward IV, when steward, chamberlain, treasurer, and controller threw their staves into open grave, as token that their commissions were ended (Gairdner, *Letters*, I. xvii).

[268] Cf. similar wording in O 1445, §35 (xv).

[269] O 1454 allows 7 servants (*Nicolas*, VI. 226), O 1478 prescribes only 5 (§68 (vii)).

[270] Cf. *Babees Bk.*, I. 180, 343.

[271] These figures evidently totals for both feasts in question; for year 6–7 Edward IV John Tiptoft, Earl of Worcester, who was steward at Christmas, received £5 6s. 8d. (8 marks); and Henry Bourchier, Earl of Essex, who succeeded him as steward before Easter, received £5 6s. 8d. for Whitsuntide fee and £13 6s. 8d. (20 marks) for Easter and Michaelmas combined (E 101/412/2, f. 36a).

[272] O 1454 allowed 7 attendants for an earl (*Nicolas*, VI. 222); O 1478 allowed only 5 for both earl and steward (§68 (iii) and (vii)). But as steward already allowed 1 chaplain, 2 esquires, 4 yeomen, these 10 persons may have been menials.

[273] Cf. Ecclesiasticus, x. 2: 'et qualis rector est ciuitatis, tales et habitantes in ea'.

[274] Ecclus. iv. 35.

[275] This had not occurred since earliest days of Edward III (Tout, *Chapters*, III. 18; VI. 42–5). After that time office seems to have been thought too dignified for anyone of lower rank than knight, and sometimes even earls had held it (e.g. Thomas Percy, Earl of Worcester, in reigns of Richard II and Henry IV, and William de la Pole, Earl of Suffolk, in reign of Henry VI).

[276] 'With' can, of course, mean 'against', 'in opposition to', a connotation it has borne since Anglo-Saxon times (cf. German wider). Hence most likely sense of this passage is: 'and against (= to prevent) outward (= open, public) menacing or threatenings, especially amongst officials of the household'. I am grateful to Mr. E. Colledge for his help in elucidating this passage.

[277] Cf. O 1478, §68 (viii).

[278] This is confirmed by household accounts of this reign, e.g. E 101/412/2, f. 36a.

[279] 'Of this memoranda and his longest periods of residence.'

[280] Cf. B.B., note 32.

[281] Cf. B.B., note 62.

[282] Treasurers of this reign seem, on the whole, to have given rather more personal attention to their household duties than did either chamberlain or stewards. During his tenure of office Sir John Fogge seems to have held no offices which need have taken him away from household for long, except for visit to Burgundy in last year of his treasurership, 1467 (*Foedera*, V. ii. 143).

Sir John Howard seems to have been away more often, as ambassador to Burgundy in 1468 and as admiral in 1470 (*Scofield*, I. 455, 509, 519–20). After Edward's restoration in 1471, Lord Howard (as he had become) was appointed deputy to Lord Hastings as lieutenant of Calais, and was there in Aug. 1471 and Sept. 1472, and in May 1473 he was appointed envoy to negotiate with Burgundy and Hanseatic League (*ibid.*, II. 11, 37, 64–9). Moreover, he was justice of peace in four shires during his term as treasurer, whereas Fogge was J.P. only in Kent (*C.P.R., 1461–7*, pp. 608, 613, 622, 631; *1467–77*, p. 566).

Howard's successor, Sir John Elrington, seems to have been assiduous in his household duties. Such duties as he was assigned outside household may have been connected with his office (e.g. auditing accounts of lands of George, late Duke of Clarence (*C.P.R., 1476–85*, p. 64) or acting on various commissions concerned with raising revenue for king (*ibid., 1467–77*, p. 463; *1476–85*, pp. 22, 23, 51, 144, 215, 344). As treasurer of war for campaign in France in 1475 (*Foedera*, V. iii. 56) and again for Scottish campaign of 1482 (*ibid.*, p. 121 and *Scofield*, II. 318, 344, 349; Devon, *Issues*, pp. 501–2), he must, however, have been drawn away from attendance to his routine duties in royal household.

[283] O 1478 allows only 6 months (§65).

[284] 'The stock-in-hand must be checked', so that appropriate official might be held responsible for it.

[285] Treasurer of household always a clerk until appointment of Sir John Tiptoft in 1406 (Tout, *Chapters*, IV. 201–2), and first squire-treasurer appeared a quarter-century later. John Hotoft still an esquire in Feb. 1431, though already treasurer of household since at least 8–9 Hy. VI (E 101/408/9; *C.P.R., 1429–36*, pp. 101, 102). Later in same reign another squire, John Brekenok, was appointed treasurer (E 101/410/15; *C.R.P., 1452–61*, p. 295).

[286] John Buckingham was never called treasurer of the household though he was for four years treasurer or keeper of wardrobe; but he held this office 1353–7 (Tout, *Chapters*, VI. 27), he was Bishop of Lincoln 1363–98, and died in March 1399 (F. M. Powicke, *Handbook of British Chronology* (London, 1939), p. 156). He therefore could neither have compiled his survey of household expenses in reign of Henry VI nor have presented it to Henry Beaufort as Bishop of Winchester, still less as Cardinal. But on f. 2a of Lord Steward's Dept. Misc.

Book 278 in P.R.O. is note: 'There was in Mr. Scot's Library sold in 1682 Jo. Buckingham Bp. of Lincoln and Treasurer of the King's household of the ordering thereof MS. in fol.' Black Book thus justified in referring to such a survey, in spite of erroneous chronology. Fifteenth-century writers lacked our ready access to books of reference; if a London citizen, probably an alderman, could make numerous mistakes about events in his own lifetime in his own city (*Great Chronicle*, esp. pp. 227–8), scarcely surprising that compilers of draft of Black Book should be wrong in chronology in dealing with possibly undated manuscript of a remoter past.

[287] Served with only one course; by 1526 controller promoted to two courses at both dinner and supper (*Household Ordinances*, pp. 188–9).

[288] Sir John Scott, first controller of this reign, must often have failed to do this if he attended personally to commissions and offices showered on him (*C.P.R.*, *1461–7*, pp. 11, 63, 79, 102, 129, 133, 177, 215, 217, 229, 281, 301, 303, 343, 346, 370, 429, 453, 465, 530, 544, 566; *1467–77*, pp. 55, 70, 127, 195, 196, 199, 219, 221, 283, 285, 288). In 1467 and 1468 he was sent to Burgundy in connexion with marriage of Lady Margaret, and remained there from May 1469 to Feb. 1470 to see to treaty with Hanseatic League (*Scofield*, I. 430, 455, 485–6).

His successor, Sir William Parr, was sent on embassies to Scots in Aug. 1471, April 1472, and Aug. 1473 (*Foedera*, V. iii. 6–7, 18, 29); in April 1472 sent to seize Archbishop Neville's manor of Moor Park into king's hands (*Warkworth's Chronicle*, p. 25). Perhaps partly because of his knowledge of Scottish affairs that he was made controller again when Wingfield died, when trouble with Scotland already blowing up again; in Feb. 1483 appointed one of three ambassadors to treat with Scots (*Foedera*, V. viii. 127).

In contrast Sir Robert Wingfield, controller 1475 to 1481, apparently confined himself largely to household duties; one of few occasions when we find him outside household is as member of commission to examine account books (*C.P.R.*, *1476–85*, p. 64).

[289] Cf. O 1478, §68 (ix).

[290] Cf. O 1318 in *Edward II*, p. 245. In 1466 Sir John Scott noted in his memorandum book that he had received from cofferer for his wages in court before 1 April 1466 £3 16s. 3d. (*Archaeologia Cantiana*, X (1876), 255). If this was from 25 Dec. 1465 (and section is headed: 'recepciones . . . Johannis Scotte post festum natalis domini anno regis quinto') it was less than 15d. a day, if he had been in continual attendance. In any case trusted and important household official usually received many lucrative grants by king's favour, as Scott did (*C.P.R.*, *1461–7*, pp. 105, 187, 221, 329, 423).

[291] Allowance for robes to controller not recorded in the extant accounts of Edward IV's reign which give 'Feoda et Roba', but no reason to suppose that this allowance had changed since Henry VI's reign, when it had been 8 marks (e.g. E 101/409/16, f. 33a (25–26 Hy. VI)).

[292] Under 'Necessaria' E 101/412/2, f. 33a allows to Sir John Scott 13s. 4d. a day for his wages out of court on king's business. (Entry disallowed by auditors but that does not affect its value as illustrating this rule.)

[293] Probably this phrase should be interpreted in senses indicated in O 1478, §63, i.e. 'provisions outward' concern dealings with king's subjects outside household, towards whom he must behave justly, 'provisions inward' have to do with delivery into household of goods 'belonging to his accate or purveyance' and this he must do honestly.

[294] 'The precise amounts of liveries due.'

[295] 'Shall take stock and check this against the accounts in the offices.'

[296] Cf. O 1318 in *Edward II*, p. 282.

[297] To do this cofferer would have to be less burdened with duties outside household than his superiors in household hierarchy; and this seems to have been so. First holder of this office in Edward IV's reign, John Kendale, was from 1462 controller of king's works; but this need not have prevented him from attending assiduously to household duties, for office seems to have been a sinecure. Granted in 1466 for his good service to king's father and to king, it was confirmed in 1475 and 1481 for additional reason that he has now come to old age and debility (*C.P.R., 1461–7*, p. 75; *1467–77*, p. 544; *1476–85*, p. 275).

His successor, John Elrington, was made justice of peace for Middlesex in 1472 and clerk of hanaper of chancery in 1473 (*C.P.R., 1467–77*, pp. 622, 396); but these offices need not have interfered much with household duties. Nor need commissions in various shires from 1468 onwards to 1474 (*ibid.*, pp. 127, 352, 405, 408, 463); for either they may have been connected with household's interests (e.g. 'inquisitio post mortem' he was ordered to hold in Staffordshire, p. 408) or may not have necessitated much (or any) absence from household (e.g. commissions to inquire into theft of swans, cygnets, and swan's eggs, pp. 127, 352).

[298] Cf. O 1478, §68 (xii).

[299] 'To pure the jornall' probably refers to preparation of journal or day-book, in which were noted daily, as they occurred, expenses of principal accounting officers of royal household. Cf. *Northumberland Household Book*, p. 61.

'To joyne doggettes' refers to duty of countinghouse to compile a summary of daily expenditure of various departments of household from minutes provided daily by clerks of departments concerned. Cf. O 1540 in *Household Ordinances*, pp. 229, 234. Essential basis of this procedure continued until 1782; cf. L13/193 in P.R.O., 'Rules for the Household of George III', signed by King, which orders (ff. 1b–4b) that accounts of pantry, buttery, cellar, and spicery were to be delivered to board of greenecloth daily and weekly. Docket books included summaries of wages and rewards; cf. Brit. Mus. MS. Vespasian C XIV, f. 272b (note of allowance to Queen during Ed. IV's absence in France in 1475). 'To make the mensall' refers to monthly summary of expenditure in various departments of household during past month. Cf. O 1540 in *Household Ordinances*, p. 220. From these departmental mensals cofferer's underclerk could make mensal for whole household. Cf. *Northumberland Household Book*, pp. 180–9, esp. 187.

[300] As four of five known cofferers of Ed. IV's reign were esquires during their period of office (*C.P.R., 1461–7*, p. 75; *1467–77*, pp. 297, 396, 489; E 101/412/10, ff. 2a–3b), they drew basic pay of esquire, which, as O 1478 tells us (§68 (xxi)) was 7½d. a day; and household accounts confirm that annual fee for robes for cofferer was 8 marks (e.g. E 101/412/2, f. 36a).

[301] Particularly impressive-looking kind of salt-cellar usually made in shape of 'nef' or ship. Right to such a salt-cellar was mark of importance, and even setting of it on table had quite a ceremonial attached to it. Cf. *Babees Bk.*, I. 368.

[302] Cf. O 1478, §68 (ix).

[303] Probably board or table of chamber-servants.

[304] Cf. O 1318 in *Edward II*, p. 246.

[305] 'They are to scrutinize carefully the controlment-books and other records of all allowances, to see whether they are asked for and supplied in accordance with the rules.'

[306] 'For every matter, both particular (small) and great (general).'

[307] Again, merely a basic rate; for the draft of O 1478, §30 refers to yearly reward of £20.

308 This is confirmed by household accounts of Edward IV, e.g. E 101/411/13, f. 36a, E 101/412/2, f. 36a–b.

309 This is confirmed by E 101/412/2, f. 33a, where John Parke was allowed 3s. 4d. a day for four days for riding from Windsor to London to 'take the remanentes' in various offices of the household. Although Black Book says that clerk controller is to join in taking 'remanentes' (6 lines below), allowance of 3s. 4d. a day for 20 days to Richard Bindewyn, clerk controller, who went out on same errand, was disallowed (E 101/412/2, f. 33a). Perhaps he took too long.

310 By O 1540 this task of apposal or inspection, audit, was left to clerk controller (*Household Ordinances*, pp. 229–30).

311 Preparation of journal was duty of cofferer's clerk (B.B., §73). Only cofferer's journal of this reign still extant is that of John Elrington for 1 Nov. 13 Ed. IV to 30 Sept. 14 Ed. IV (E 101/412/5).

312 'Memorande' probably payments by various departments of household for which they had given, not cash, but tallies or bills, returnable into counting-house. Cf. B.B., §82. In Ed. II's day these had been entered in book of *Unde Respondebit* or imprests against charge of officer concerned, and when cancelled sometimes marked: 'Quia computavit in libro memorandorum anni.' MS. Nero C VIII in Brit. Mus. entitled 'Liber de Compotis Diversorum' is referred to as 'Liber memorandorum' in E 101/374/5 (J. H. Johnson, 'The System of Accounting in the Wardrobe of Edward II' in *T.R.H.S.*, 4th Series, XII. 96).

313 'Under' probably refers to foot of indenture which might be made by official of one of departments (e.g. below, §83). Cf. O 1540 in *Household Ordinances*, pp. 229–30 for entering of such indentures into ledger 'called the Booke of Foote of Parcells'. Cf. B.B., §78 (iv).

314 Under-clerk of cofferer would have joined together summary of expenditure from each dept. concerned with supply of food to hall and chamber (B.B., §73); now clerks of greencloth were to help to join these daily totals into lists of expenditure on 'Dieta' for each week and month, as they appear in accounts of treasurer and controller preserved among Exchequer records. Cf. B.B., §84. For 'helpe make the mensale' see B.B., note 299.

315 'The book recording stock-in-hand in each dept. at end of financial year; an abstract of this appears under heading of 'Remanencia' in royal household accounts.

316 Cf. E 101/412/2, f. 33a for example of this—John Parke, clerk of green-cloth, rode from Windsor to London for this purpose during year 6–7 Ed. IV.

317 Cf. O 1478, §68 (xii), (xiv) and B.B., §28.

318 Cf. O 1318 in *Edward II*, p. 246.

319 Cf. *ibid.*, p. 245 for briefer treatment of most of these duties. Clerk controller had to be present at division of fish bought for household to see that proper proportions, according to rule, went to various messes of hall and chambers.

320 Clerks of greencloth evidently helped clerk controller to make book of 'remanentes' (B.B., note 315). As so many household officials were entitled to liveries of wine, not to speak of liveries made to guests, quite essential that strict check be kept in wine-book on arrivals and departures of guests, and absences of officials on leave.

321 Clerk controller had to see that no member of household had more gear carried at king's cost than his own proper clothing, though amount of this would vary according to his office and rank.

322 Clerk controller had to take note from whose pastures and hunting grounds cattle and sheep were obtained, so that payment might be made accordingly. Cf. O 1526 in *Household Ordinances*, p. 196.

[323] Cf. O 1478, §68 (xxii).

[324] Serjeants of those offices where accountant was a serjeant, as in bake-house, pantry, cellar, and ewry (B.B., §§79, 80, 84, 91; O 1478, §68 (xxiii), (xxiv), (xxv), (xxvi), (xxxiii), (xxxvi), (xxxix), (xl), (xli), (xlii)).

[325] Instead of having to make do with trenchers of bread already put out for him on table, he was served personally with a trencher, to ensure that it was clean and had it changed when it became wet or soiled (cf. *Babees Bk.*, I. 67, 138).

[326] Under-clerk may have reputable child to serve him in this court, but child may not draw any livery from kitchen, and is permitted in court only if king is frequently dividing his household into three; otherwise there is need only for one under-clerk.

[327] *Infra* was residue of wax, in form of various kinds of candles, which had to be returned to chandlery every morning and recorded (B.B., §90). Cf. O 1478, §47 for description of checking *infra* of wax. *Extra* was wax which was issued from chandlery and was recorded, both by number of candles and by weight (B.B., §88). By comparing issues and receipts of wax, amount expended, the *expenduntur* could be calculated. Cf. O 1540 in *Household Ordinances*, p. 231.

[328] This phrase does not occur in O 1318 and seems to be one of few added by Ordinance of Edward III.

[329] O 1445 and O 1454 allowed same junior staff to countinghouse (O 1445, §35 (xv); *Nicolas*, VI. 226); but O 1478 reduced junior staff to 1 yeoman and 1 groom (O 1478, §68 (xxii)).

[330] Cf. O 1318 in *Edward II*, p. 348.

[331] Extant versions of Constitutio Domus Regis of Henry I do not seem to have any bearing on this point; but we are dependent for our knowledge of Constitutio on two thirteenth-century versions, both faulty, so that it may easily have contained other material now lost.

[332] Cf. O 1318 in *Edward II*, pp. 248–9.

[333] O 1318 had allowed only 2d. a day as basic wage, and 2d. when sent on messages; allowances for clothing and shoes (payable in two parts, at Christmas and Whitsuntide) were same as here (*Edward II*, p. 249). Four principal feasts of year for distribution of napery were Christmas, Easter, Whitsuntide, and Michaelmas. MS. H here reads 'chauces' instead of usual 'chaunces', which suggests that original text had spelling of 'chauces' and that this was misunderstood by transcribers.

[334] Some general gifts were gratuities expected of departing guests and successful suitors; some gratuities eventually hardened into definite fees (cf. Maxwell-Lyte, *op. cit.*, p. 352).

[335] No mention of pages of countinghouse in O 1318; cf. B.B., §39 and note 163.

[336] Cf. O 1445, §35 (xxxvii).

[337] Presumably such parts of Constitutio Domus Regis as were deemed to be still applicable.

[338] Cf. O 1478, §18.

[339] Cf. O 1318 in *Edward II*, p. 274; cf. also O 1478, §3.

[340] Cf. O 1478, §50.

[341] These were returns from which book of foot of parcells was engrossed (cf. B.B., note 313).

[342] Officials whose work lay outside household, such as keeper of great wardrobe. Cf. O 1478, §65.

[343] Cf. O 1445, §12.

[344] Cf. O 1323 in *Edward II*, p. 282.

³⁴⁵ Cf. O 1478, §§45, 15; O 1318 in *Edward II*, p. 275.

³⁴⁶ Cf. O 1318 and O 1323 in *ibid.*, pp. 276, 282; O 1478, §40; and *Household Ordinances*, p. 90, where it is enacted that no liveries to be made in Duke of Clarence's household after 7 p.m.

³⁴⁷ Cf. O 1445, §31 and O 1478, §63.

³⁴⁸ Cf. O 1318 in *Edward II*, p. 276.

³⁴⁹ Cf. B.B., notes 4 and 7.

³⁵⁰ Cf. B.B., note 262, and case in 1465, where king had, in consideration of good service, pardoned Thomas Seintlegier, an esquire of the body, who had been condemned by Earl of Worcester, as steward of household, to lose his right hand because he had quarrelled with and wounded within palace of Westminster Stephen Cristmasse, esquire, a marshal of king's hall (*C.P.R., 1461–7*, p. 380).

³⁵¹ In view of text dealt with in note 354 one might have supposed that this, too, would be from Vulgate; but it is not.

³⁵² Broken recognizances to be sent into chancery and there dealt with as though deed had been made there and not in countinghouse.

³⁵³ Cf. O 1318 in *Edward II*, p. 274, for similar rules.

³⁵⁴ Ecclus. xxiii. 12, which in Vulgate reads: 'Vir multum jurans implebitur iniquitate.'

³⁵⁵ Higher estimate than that given above (§10), where daily consumption of wheat is estimated at 3 quarters 4 bushels.

³⁵⁶ 'Not to sift it too coarsely to retain the coarse meal'.

³⁵⁷ Evidently some loaves were rectangular and some were round.

³⁵⁸ 'The risk of sullying'.

³⁵⁹ 'Levelled with the strickle' which was a straight piece of wood for striking off surplus grain level with the rim of the measure.

³⁶⁰ John Rokeley, serjeant of bakehouse in 3–4 Ed. IV (E 101/410/13, f. 40a) received 46s. 8d. for his winter and summer clothing (*ibid.*, f. 36a). Cf. also E 101/412/2, ff. 40a, 36a.

³⁶¹ Bread was delivered to avenery and pantry (above, §79, below, §80), and flour was carried to wafery (§81), transactions being recorded on tallies.

³⁶² Confirmed by E 101/412/2, f. 38a.

³⁶³ O 1445 allowed only 2 (§35 (xx)), O 1454 permitted only one (*Nicolas*, VI. 226). O 1478 names only 4 yeomen in all (§68 (xxiii)).

³⁶⁴ They are to receive their 3d. a day only if serjeant or clerk records that they are occupied on king's business.

³⁶⁵ O 1445 allowed only 3 bolters (§35 (xx)), but O 1454 specified 6 groom bolters (*Nicolas*, VI. 226). Cf. O 1478 (§68 (xxiii)).

³⁶⁶ These labourers were given cash instead of clothing.

³⁶⁷ Perhaps this was one of few changes made by Ordinance of Edward III. O 1318 distinguishes between chief clerks of pantry and of kitchen (*Edward II*, pp. 256, 261), besides mentioning serjeant chief pantrer, who received bread by view of chief clerk or under-clerk of pantry. In O 1445, O 1454, and O 1478 there is, however, no mention of chief clerk of pantry but only of serjeant of pantry (O 1445, §35 (xviii); *Nicolas*, VI. 226; O 1478, §68 (xxiv)). Tudor household offices employing clerks besides kitchen, avenery, and spicery were bakehouse, acatry, poultry, pastry, scullery, and woodyard (A. P. Newton in *Tudor Studies*, p. 255).

³⁶⁷ᵃ William Solyngbourne, serjeant of pantry in 3–4 and 6–7 Ed. IV received 46s. 8d. as one of serjeants of household for these years (E 101/411/13, ff. 36a, 40a; E 101/412/2, ff. 36a, 40a).

³⁶⁸ See B.B., note 301; cf. *Babees Bk.*, I. 322 for panter's duties in bringing in covered salt-cellar and spoon for his lord.

[369] For use of neck-towel in ceremonious laying of table, see *Babees Bk.*, I. 129, 367. For use of neck-towel in serving of meals see also 'Breviate' in *Archaeologia*, XIII (1800), 332. For illustrations of neck-towels, one of which appears to be not 'pleyne' but a towel 'of worke fynne,' see miniature for January in Calendar of *Très Riches Heures* of Duc de Berri.

[370] 'And he sets the king's salt-cellar with the required ceremony.' See B.B., note 369 and *Babees Bk.*, I. 368. Even a man of Sir John Fastolf's rank owned 6 great salt-cellars, one of which, in gilt, with a cover, weighed 37 ounces (Inventory of effects in *Archaeologia*, XXI (1827), 247).

[371] Bread had to be pared of its crusts before it was served at king's table.

[372] Whereas yeomen for mouth saw to service of king's person, including setting of his salt-cellar, groom looked after service of king's chamber.

[373] This also may be one of additions made by Edward III, for there appears to be no reference to this rule in extant ordinances of Edward II.

[374] Cf. O 1318 in *Edward II*, p. 257.

[375] William Spen and John Kirkadam, yeomen of pantry in 1464 and 1465 (*R.P.*, V. 537; *C.P.R., 1461-7*, p. 426), received 18s. for clothing and footwear for 6–7 Ed. IV (E 101/412/2, f. 37b).

[376] As this yeoman and yeoman for the mouth took chippings or crusts of bread as perquisites, there might be temptation to them to cut crusts so thick that they wasted 'crumb' or inner part of loaf.

[377] This would make 5 yeomen in all for this office; whereas O 1445, O 1454, O 1478 specified 4, 3 and 6 respectively (§35 (xviii); *Nicolas*, VI. 226; §68 (xxiv)).

[378] 'Or persons of estate in their chambers.'

[379] For deliveries in the hall marshal's orders sufficient; for supplies to chambers tally or other form of receipt necessary, to satisfy yeomen brever and chief clerk of kitchen.

[380] O 1445, O 1454, and O 1478 allowed 2, 3 and 3 grooms respectively, 2 pages, 1 page, and 1 page respectively (O 1445, §35 (xviii); *Nicolas*, VI. 226; O 1478, §68 (xxiv)).

[381] At some of the palaces to which court might move, chamber allotted to pantry staff might not have chimney.

[382] This yeoman is allowed surplus food (e.g. wafers) but must not for that reason deliberately be extravagant, and controller is to watch this point, as he does in case of pantry (§80).

[383] Cf. O 1318 in *Edward II*, p. 257, which allotted to the waferer 7½d. wages a day, 2 robes or 40s. a year, and for livery when he was sick 'j dare de pain, j galoun de seruoise, de la cuisine j messe de rost'. This gave him greater wages and clothing than in Edward IV's day, but not more livery. Yeoman brever of pantry, to whom waferer conformed in allowances for wages and clothing, drew, according to Black Book, only 3d. a day and 20s. a year for clothing; latter figure is confirmed by E 101/412/2, f. 37b.

[384] O 1445 has 2 waferers and 1 groom (§35 (xix)), O 1454 had 1 yeoman and 1 groom (*Nicolas*, VI. 231), and O 1478 had 1 yeoman and 2 grooms (§68 (xxxi)).

[385] Entry of gifts of wine to houses of religion is regular feature of household accounts, under heading of 'Oblaciones et Elemosina' (e.g. E 101/412/10, f. 34a).

[386] houndes = hondes, hands. Hence passage means that butler must make indenture with treasurer of household for any wines which he takes out of king's castle or palace.

[387] Cf. O 1318 in *Edward II*, p. 259.

[388] I.e. to avoid all suspicion that wine was not good or had been secretly consumed.

³⁸⁹ All these offices are mentioned as part of household in O 1318, except clerk of crown and clerk of works (*Edward II*, pp. 246, 247, 248, 252, 266, 283). For reference to clerk of works from statutes of Edward III, see B.B., note 258.

³⁹⁰ 'Which relieves the household, not to its detriment but much to its advantage, and will prove to increase the king's dignity.'

³⁹¹ Besides gifts of wine which appear regularly in household accounts under heading of 'Oblaciones et Elemosina' (cf. B.B., note 385), there are also numerous gifts of wine, under heading of 'Dona', to members of royal household, royal officials outside household such as chief justices, or influential persons such as Duchess of Burgundy or Bishop of Salisbury (E 101/412/11, f. 35a). Casual gifts outside household said to be 'per breve domini regis de priuato sigillo', as stated here.

³⁹² See *P.R.O. Lists and Indexes XXV. Various Accounts, Butlerage*, esp. p. 76 for annual accounts of Edward IV's butlers.

³⁹³ 'And all other devices for drawing off wine from the lees, counterfeiting, subtracting, and saving of wines' (to king's loss and in fraudulent manner).

³⁹⁴ Patent rolls record appointment of yeomen purveyors of wines (e.g. *C.P.R., 1461–7*, p. 14); but O 1445, O 1454, and O 1478 do not list them separately. O 1445 allows cellar and buttery together 9 yeomen (§35 (xxi)), O 1454 allows 1 yeoman for buttery (*Nicolas*, VI. 227), and O 1478 has 2 yeomen for buttery (§68 (xxvi)).

³⁹⁵ Cf. B.B., note 313; also O 1318 in *Edward II*, pp. 272, 273, which enacts that three parts should remain in hands of butler purveyor, serjeant butler, and clerk of buttery.

³⁹⁶ O 1445 (§35 (xxi)), O 1454 (*Nicolas*, VI. 227), and O 1478 (§68 (xxv)) all specify a serjeant of cellar.

³⁹⁷ 'Account of the stock-in-hand.'

³⁹⁸ None of Ordinances of 1445, 1454, and 1478 speak of under-clerks of green-cloth; all three refer to under-clerks of kitchen (§35 (xxiv); *Nicolas*, VI. 228; §68 (xxxv)).

³⁹⁹ O 1445 allowed 2 sumpter horses for cellar and buttery (§35 (xxxvii)).

⁴⁰⁰ O 1445 speaks of 'vallet pur la royne' (§35 (xxi)) and O 1478 allows 'j gentilman pro regina' (§68 (xxv)), an official who was evidently 'for the queen's mouth'; no mention in either ordinance or in O 1454, of yeoman for king's mouth.

⁴⁰¹ For cup-board or side-table laid for meal-times in dining-chamber and another laid for 'all-night' in bed-chamber, see *Babees Bk.*, I. 66, 69. For orders for serving of wines on days of estate in hall at court of Henry VII, with elaborate instructions as to use of cupboard, see *Household Ordinances*, p. 110.

Bar is place at which wines, beer, and ale were served out from cellar and buttery to various departments. Cf. B.B., §84 (*bis*), §85 (*bis*), §87, and cf. estimate of yearly expenses of Henry VII's household: 'bred, ale, and wyen geuyn at the barres of the pantre, buttre, and cellar'. Cf. such bars still *in situ* at Hampton Court.

⁴⁰² With 2 grooms mentioned below, office of cellar is allowed 3 grooms. O 1454 allows 2 (*Nicolas*, VI. 227), and O 1478 specifies 3 (§68 (xxv)).

⁴⁰³ Not clear what this means; but as portion of A containing this passage is lost, and H has different reading, it cannot be checked.

⁴⁰⁴ Wines condemned as unfit for drinking.

⁴⁰⁵ Any man or child servant kept by two grooms must not be allowed in cellar. O 1454 had allowed page for cellar (*Nicolas*, VI. 227), but O 1478 does not mention one (§68 (xxv)).

⁴⁰⁶ Serjeant of cellar and possibly clerk of kitchen.

[407] This may have been one of additions of Ed. III's reign; no reference to this matter in O 1318 or O 1323.

[408] As yeoman trayer was drawer or tapster, cokers may have been wine necessarily dropped when cock or tap inserted into barrel or turned off. These droppings would be considerable in a household so big as king's. It is stated earlier in this section that droppings, spillings, 'kokyrs', and lees were part of fee of yeoman trayer.

[409] O 1454 allows 1 yeoman (Nicolas, VI. 227); O 1478 allows 2 (§68 (xxvi)).

[410] Yeoman is to prefer serving important strangers (though with economy) to issuing usual allowances of ale.

[411] As allowances of ale normally in gallons and half-gallons, less chance of corruption or waste if liveries made in gallons or half-gallons instead of piece-meal in small, odd amounts.

[412] Possibly to lessen risk of damage to ale, but probably a precaution against theft or illicit disposal of ale.

[413] Both O 1454 and O 1478 specify 2 grooms (Nicolas, VI. 227; §68 (xxvi)).

[414] O 1454 allowed for 1 page; O 1478 allows none. For cellar, pitcherhouse, buttery, and aletakers combined O 1445 and O 1454 permitted 4 pages, as in Black Book (§35 (xxi); Nicolas, VI. 227); O 1478 economizes by having none at all (§68 (xxv–xxviii)).

[415] There was in palace of Westminster a little house called 'le Pycherhous' 10 ft. long by 7 ft. broad, but in June 1463, it was granted to tenant, John Randolf, along with other tenements in palace (C.P.R., 1461–7, p. 273). O 1454 allowed only 3 yeomen (Nicolas, VI. 227), O 1478 permitted 4 (§68 (xxviii)).

[416] O 1454 allowed only 2 grooms (Nicolas, VI. 227), but O 1478 permitted 3 (§68 (xxviii)).

[417] Wine and ale might be put out for service of hall and of strangers and left untouched; such drinks to be collected and returned to store.

[418] O 1454 and O 1478 also allow 1 yeoman (Nicolas, VI. 227; §68 (xxviii)).

[419] 'The value of the ale assessed.'

[420] Two methods of payment—either clerk of buttery (i.e. clerk of kitchen (§85)) could make out credit note and creditor could present it for payment at countinghouse, where tallies would be cancelled, or clerk could pay forthwith. In latter case he would need to be credited with this payment, and would have to show tallies as his vouchers.

[421] Hence to refuse payment to person who had supplied bad ale.

[422] Cf. O 1318 in Edward II, p. 260.

[423] He applies to be allowed cost of hooping, and other expenses in making barrels, in books of clerk of controlment and clerk of kitchen.

[424] Appointment of purveyors always done by letters patent under great seal, and bill of household treasurer quoted always as warrant (e.g. three such appointments in 1469, C.P.R., 1467–77, p. 156).

[425] O 1454 allows 1 groom and 1 page (Nicolas, VI. 227); O 1478 permits 2 grooms, but no pages (§68 (xxvii)).

[426] O 1445, O 1454, and O 1478 all mention chief clerk; O 1445 and O 1478 allow only 1 under-clerk (§35 (xxii); §68 (xxix)), whereas O 1454, like Black Book, permits 2 (Nicolas, VI. 227).

[427] In Northumberland Household Book, p. 393, clerk of spicery directed to supervise issue of meat and drink as well.

[428] Cf. O 1478, §68 (xii).

[429] Cf. O 1318 in Edward II, p. 247.

[430] Cf. O 1540 in Household Ordinances, p. 235.

[431] Records of materials coming into offices of spicery, confectionary, chandlery, and napery. Cf. first sentence of this section, §88.

⁴³² Cf. B.B., note 327, and O 1318 in *Edward II*, p. 247.

⁴³³ Cf. O 1445, §35 (xxii).

⁴³⁴ O 1445 permitted 3 yeomen, 2 pages (§35 (xxii)); O 1454 and O 1478 allowed 1 yeoman powder-beater, but no groom nor page (*Nicolas*, VI. 227; §68 (xxix)).

⁴³⁵ O 1445 omits office of confectionary, O 1454 allows 1 serjeant, O 1478 does not (*Nicolas*, VI. 228; §68 (xxx)).

⁴³⁶ 'Plaates' were confections of spices served on a plate. Cf. *Household Ordinances*, pp. 110–13. Cf. various spices bought for household of George, Duke of Clarence, many of which could be classified as 'seeds' (*ibid.*, p. 103).

⁴³⁷ Presumably distinction between pears worth classifying as warden pears, and pears which are only ordinary.

⁴³⁸ After = 'appropriate to'. Richer-looking spice plate for important occasions would be drawn from jewel-house. For serving of spices on days of estate, see *ibid.*, p. 110.

⁴³⁹ 'And to account for the foodstuffs passing through his hands by noting their weights and by recording whether they were delivered to someone inside or outside the office.'

⁴⁴⁰ O 1445 allows 2 grooms and 2 pages for spicery, which probably includes confectionary; O 1454 specifies 1 groom and 1 page; O 1478 permits only 1 groom and no page (§35 (xxii); *Nicolas*, VI. 228; §68 (xxx)).

⁴⁴¹ 'This office is allowed one sumpter man and horse for the conveyance of its proper goods, chargeable to the account of the treasurer of the household and supervised by the countinghouse.'

⁴⁴² O 1445 had also prescribed serjeant as head of chandlery (§35, (xxiii)); but O 1454 and O 1478 allowed it only 2 yeomen as highest officers (*Nicolas*, VI. 228; §68 (xxxii)).

⁴⁴³ Lights fixed on stands made either of silver (for important persons) or of trenchers of bread (for ordinary folk). Cf. note 447.

⁴⁴⁴ Before clerks of greencloth and one of clerks of controlment. Cf. B.B., §§74, 75.

⁴⁴⁵ Yearly allowance for clothing to serjeants of various offices was 46s. 8d. each (e.g. E 101/411/13, f. 36a; E 101/412/2, f. 36b).

⁴⁴⁶ O 1445 allows only 2 yeomen besides serjeant, and O 1454 and O 1478 permit only 2 yeomen without serjeant.

⁴⁴⁷ Loaves cut up into trenchers to serve as candle-stands.

⁴⁴⁸ 'And to bring back to the chandlery any unspent candles, and candle-ends of any size'. This was part of 'infra' of wax (B.B., note 327).

⁴⁴⁹ O 1445, O 1454, O 1478 allow 4, 2, and 2 grooms respectively, and 2 pages, 1 page, and 1 page respectively (§35 (xxiii); *Nicolas*, VI. 228; §68 (xxxii)).

⁴⁵⁰ 'King's chamber, and other men's chambers.'

⁴⁵¹ O 1445, O 1454, O 1478 all allowed 1 serjeant (§35 (xxxii); *Nicolas*, VI. 230; §68 (xxxiii)).

⁴⁵² Christmas, Easter, Whitsuntide, and Michaelmas (e.g. E 101/409/16, f. 33a).

⁴⁵³ Presumably silver and gilt trays. 'Napkin' already in use, but meaning a little table-cloth (*Babees Bk.*, I. 120, 321); earliest example of use of term 'napkin-ring' in *N.E.D.* (Supplement) is 1686.

⁴⁵⁴ Surnape was towel or cloth on which master of house wiped his hands after washing them when meal was done; sewer brought it when meal was finished (cf. *Household Ordinances*, p. 119; *Babees Bk.*, I. 132, 136). Foot-cloth was probably foot-sheet spread before fire in lord's chamber when he retired, dressed, or had a bath (*ibid.*, I. 177, 181, 183, 315).

⁴⁵⁵ Prolonged search has failed to reveal source of this passage.

S

[456] O 1445 allows 2 sumpter horses for this office (§35 (xxxvii)).

[457] Cf. O 1478, §68 (xxxiii), which allows less fuel and light.

[458] With 2 other yeomen and 2 other grooms mentioned in this section, there are 3 yeomen and 3 grooms for this office. O 1445 had 3 and 4, O 1454 specified 3 and 2, O 1478 permitted 4 and 3 (§35 (xxxii); *Nicolas*, VI. 230–3; §68 (xxxiii)).

[459] Groom for king's mouth to be responsible for all cloths in care of this office, checked both by number and by length of each piece.

[460] 'At one of the sittings.' Cf. O 1478, §8.

[461] O 1445 and O 1454 each allowed 2 pages; O 1478 permitted none.

[462] O 1445 and O 1454 permit only 1 yeoman (§35 (xxxiii); *Nicolas*, VI. 231); O 1478 allow 2 (§68 (xxxiv)).

[463] Office in question could give a receipt for laundry either by delivering tally received when articles taken to be washed or by making distinctive mark on sheet of paper or parchment brought by yeoman of laundry for this purpose.

[464] These vestments would need fairly frequent washing, as they all touched neck of wearer.

[465] O 1445 allows 1 groom, 2 pages (§35 (xxxiii)); O 1454 prescribes 2 grooms, 1 page (*Nicolas*, VI. 231); O 1478 permits 2 grooms, no pages (§68 (xxxiv)).

THE ORDINANCE OF 1471

(See Introduction, p. 31)

[1] The material so far is clearly a transcript of first two paragraphs of O 1478.

[2] Cf. O 1478, §46.

[3] Sir Thomas Montgomery was already king's carver in 1461 (*C.P.R.*, *1461–7*, p. 125) and remained knight of body until at least 1482 (*C.P.R.*, *1476–85*, p. 310).

Sir John Dune, Doune, Downe, or Donne was described as one of the esquires of the body in 1469 (*C.P.R.*, *1467–77*, p. 175), was knighted at Tewkesbury (W. Shaw, *Knights of England*, II. 14), and was still alive in Richard III's reign (*C.P.R.*, *1476–85*, pp. 395, 399, 554). Under Edward IV he received a fee of £39 18s. 9d. as keeper of King's armory in Tower of London (Harl. MS. 433, f. 310a).

'Sir Thomas Brought' may be same man as Sir Thomas Borough or Burgh who was squire of body in 1461 and 1462 (*C.P.R.*, *1461–7*, pp. 34, 41, 197), but knighted by Sept. 1463 (*ibid.*, p. 281), knight of chamber by 3–4 Ed. IV (E 101/411/13, f. 36a), and still knight of body in 1484 (*C.P.R.*, *1476–85*, p. 424); also Master of King's Horse, 1465–83 (Wedgwood, *Biographies*, p. 136).

Only 'Sir William Parre' of whom anything is known at this time is controller of household, but unlikely that he would be serving at same time as knight of body. Perhaps name is an error for that of his younger brother Sir John Parr, who was a 'king's esquire' as early as 1461 (*C.P.R.*, *1461–7*, p. 86) and is named among 'scutiferi aule et camere' in 6–7 Ed. IV (E 101/412/2, f. 37a); he was knighted at Tewkesbury (Shaw, *op. cit.*, II. 14).

'Sir John Pollington' seems most likely to be error in transcription for Sir John Pilkington, who was appointed one of squires of body as early as July 1461 (*C.P.R.*, *1461–7*, p. 17; cf. B.B., note 115). Knighted at Tewkesbury (Shaw, *op. et loc. cit.*) he was described as 'king's knight' in Aug. 1471 (*C.P.R.*, *1467–77*, p. 279) and 'knight of the body' in Jan. 1472 (*ibid.*, p. 307).

'Sir Roger Ray' is Sir Roger Ree, senior, made usher of king's chamber in 1461 (*C.P.R.*, *1461–7*, p. 139). Knighted at Tewkesbury (Shaw, *op. cit.*, II. 15), he died in year 15 Ed. IV (*Cal. Inq. Post Mortem* (Record Commission, 1828),

IV. 371). In Wedgwood's *Biographies* he is confused with his son (another Roger) who in fact died before his father (*C.P.R.*, *1467–77*, p. 531).

[4] Thomas Howard, later steward of household to Richard III, Earl of Surrey (1483) and Duke of Norfolk (1514), became squire of body in early 1470's, but year not known. J. Weever, in *Ancient Funerall Monuments* (London, 1631), p. 834, gives from duke's epitaph at Thetford following information: 'And after the warres doon betwyxt the seid kynge Lewes, and the seid Duke Charles, Than the seid Thomas Howard returned in to Englond vn to kynge Edward hys souerayn Lord: And he made hym immedyatly Esquyer for his body. And he was aboute hym at hys makynge redy bothe evenyng and mornyng.' This seems to mean that Howard was made squire of body after Nov. 1472, but he may have come home after first truce between Louis XI and Charles the Bold in Oct. 1471.

'John Chany' (John Cheyne), 'Thomas Porte' (Thomas Prout), 'John Sapecote' (John Sapcote), and John Wykes had all been named as 'scutiferi aule et camere' in household treasurer's account for 6–7 Ed. IV (E 101/412/2, f. 36b). All four mentioned as squires for body in or before 1472 (*C.P.R.*, *1467–77*, p. 305; *R.P.*, V. 534, 587; *Foedera*, V. iii. 23).

[5] For Sir John Parr and Sir Roger Ree, see note 3.

Ralph Hastings appointed squire of body as early as July 1461 (*C.P R.*, *1461–7*, p. 21), and still one of 'scutiferi' of household in 6–7 Ed. IV (E 101/ 412/2, f. 36b). Knighted at Tewkesbury (Shaw, *op. cit.*, II. 14), he is described in patent rolls as knight of body from 1474 onwards (*C.P.R.*, *1467–77*, p. 440).

Maurice Berkeley called one of 'scutiferi aule et camere' in 6–7 Ed. IV (E 101/412/2, f. 36b); also knighted at Tewkesbury (Shaw, *op. et loc. cit.*), described as king's knight by Feb. 1472, and as knight of body by April 1473, he died 27 Mar. 1474 (Wedgwood, *Biographies*, p. 68).

Thomas Gray or Grey was squire of body by 1462 (*C.P.R.*, *1461–7*, p. 186); (reference quoted by Wedgwood for 1461 refers only to 'Thomas Gray, esquire' (Wedgwood, *op. cit.*, p. 47). Knighted at Tewkesbury, he is called knight of body in patent rolls in 1475 (*C.P.R.*, *1467–77*, p. 569). See also B.B., note 115.

[6] It has not been possible to identify Humphrey Shalford or Thomas Bagham (unless latter be Thomas Byngham—*C.P.R.*, *1467–77*, p. 441). Thomas Salinger is Thomas St. Leger, who is once called 'Selyngere' in patent rolls (*C.P.R.*, *1476–85*, p. 168). Squire of body by Feb. 1463 (*C.P.R.*, *1461–7*, p. 208), knighted in 1478 (Shaw, *op. cit.*, I. 138) he is named as knight of body in April 1478 (*C.P.R.*, *1476–85*, p. 91). 'John Blonte' may be error for William Blount, one of 'scutiferi aule et camere' in 6–7 Ed. IV. (E 101/412/2, f. 36b), or John Blount, one of squires of body of Ed. IV (Wedgwood, *op. cit.*, p. 84). After all, even patent rolls could make mistakes in names—cf. Richard Hastynges instead of Ralph Hastynges in pardon of 1472 (*C.P.R.*, *1467–77*, p. 309).

[7] Sir Henry Ferrers, knighted at Tewkesbury (Shaw, *op. cit.*, II. 14) was named as one of 'scutiferi aule et camere' in 6–7 Ed. IV (E 101/412/2, f. 36b), and as one of household knights at funeral of Edward IV (Gairdner, *op. cit.*, I. 8).

John Strangways, esquire, is named as one of king's sewers in 1479 (*C.P.R.*, *1476–85*, p. 159).

[8] Thomas Teryngham or Tyringham is named as one of 'scutiferi aule et camere' in 6–7 Edward IV (E 101/412/2, f. 36b), and exemptions were made to acts of resumption in his favour in parliaments of 1467–8 and 1472–5 (*R.P.*, V. 590b, VI. 85a) as to 'oure seruaunt'.

[9] It has not been possible to identify Richard Pomeroy or John Alton or to associate either with service of household.

[10] Sir Gilbert Debenham, Sir William Norys or Norris, and Sir John Fiennes

were already 'milites camere et trencheatores domini regis' in 6–7 Ed. IV (E 101/412/2, f. 36a).

[11] Several John Youngs of note at this time. Wedgwood includes biographies of three, none of whom seems to have been a royal household official. In household treasurer's account for 6–7 Ed. IV a John Young is included among 'valecti camere' (E 101/412/2, f. 37a). Grants made to John Young, yeoman of crown, were repeatedly safeguarded in acts of resumption of this reign (*R.P.*, V. 474b, 536a, 592a, 594a); and it may be same John Young who had risen in world by 1472 and is described as 'John Yonge Squyer' in act of resumption of parliament of 1472–5 (*ibid.*, VI. 60b).

John Harvey is described as 'late one of the ushers of the king's chamber' in grant to this widow of custody of lands of their infant son, a grant dated 11 Sept. 1475 (*C.P.R.*, *1467–77*, p. 559).

Brian Talbot, whose name frequently appears in grants and commissions in patent rolls of this reign (e.g. *C.P.R.*, *1461–7*, pp. 12, 86, 457, 491; *C.P.R.*, *1467–77*, pp. 285, 352, 619, 626) is described as 'Esquyer for oure Body' in 1473 (*R.P.*, VI. 83b).

Robert Ratcliffe was already one of 'scutiferi aule et camere' in 6–7 Ed. IV (E 101/412/2, f. 36b) and was a squire of body in 1475 (*Foedera*, V. iii. 56).

[12] Hugh Shirley was yeoman of crown from 1461 until at least 1477 (*C.P.R.*, *1461–7*, p. 26; *1476–85*, p. 14).

It has not been possible to identify Bryan Middleton: William Middleton or Myddelton was one of esquires of household by 1479 (*C.P.R.*, *1476–85*, p. 157) and was one of gentlemen ushers at funeral of Ed. IV (Gairdner, *op. cit.*, I. 8).

Edward Argill or Hardgill was already yeoman of crown in Nov. 1460 (*C.P.R.*, *1452–61*, p. 645), was continued in this office by Edward IV (*C.P.R.*, *1461–7*, pp. 24, 48, 72, 522), and was still yeoman of crown in May 1475 (*C.P.R.*, *1467–77*, p. 519). In May 1476 he is described as 'esquire, one of the ushers of the king's chamber' (*ibid.*, p. 586), a post which he still held at funeral of Edward IV (Gairdner, *op. cit.*, I. 8). It therefore looks as though he became a gentleman usher in 1475 or 1476, and that he was a yeoman usher for several years before that date.

Robert Burton was already yeoman of crown in 1461 (*R.P.*, V. 474b) and was still yeoman of crown in 1473 (*ibid.*, p. 87b).

From above notes on officials mentioned in these lists it will be apparent that although one or two of them remain obscure, none of the details creates any difficulties about the dating of the list to 'the eleauenth yeare of our raigne', and that one or two of the officials here mentioned were dead before 1478.

[13] Cf. B.B., note 401.

[14] Cf. O 1478, §§15, 27; B.B., §78 (ix).

[15] Cf. O 1526 for similar rule, referring to privy chamber (*Household Ordinances*, p. 154).

[16] This arrangement more precise than those of Black Book, which often merely specify that officer in question shall sit at meals with person of like service. Same arrangements given in some undated orders to be found in Harl. MS. 642, f. 204b (N).

[17] Cf. this rule with O 1478, §22; both derive from O 1445, §2. Perhaps idea of time-limit drawn from Black Book (B.B., §36).

THE DRAFT OF THE ORDINANCE OF 1478

[1] Cf. B.B., §9.

[2] Repd. in O 1478, §5.

³ Repd. in subst. in O 1478, §§7, 8, 9.

⁴ It is hard to see what this book can be except Black Book. If it is, then here we have confirmation that Black Book was made before O 1478 was attempted.

⁵ Not included in O 1478; but cf. B.B., §78 (xxii) and O 1526 (*Household Ordinances*, pp. 148–9).

⁶ Repd. in O 1478, §6, but with omission of controller and addition of cofferer, clerks of greencloth, as officials authorized to admit persons to breakfasts in absence of steward or treasurer. Probably realized on reflexion that rule as first formulated would work very awkwardly when steward and treasurer were away from court.

⁷ Repd. in O 1478, §§40, 41, but rearranged so as not to break up section on serving of meals in hall.

⁸ Repd. in O 1478, §38, but more succinctly worded there.

⁹ Repd. in O 1478, §39, but with addition of 3 lines adapted from O 1445, §10.

¹⁰ Repd. in O 1478, §10.

¹¹ Repd. in O 1478, §11, but with additions.

¹² Repd. in O 1478, §13.

¹³ Repd. in O 1478, §14, with addition of exemption for great household officers.

¹⁴ Repd. in O 1478, §28, but more neatly worded there.

¹⁵ Repd. in O 1478, §25, but more crisply worded there, and with additions.

¹⁶ Repd. in O 1478, §21, but with extension of rule to marshal as well as usher, and omission of last sentence (adopted from O 1471, §15) which is not in sequence with preceding rule.

¹⁷ Cf. O 1478, §§22, 23, which are longer and limited to ushers of chamber and marshals of hall. As expenditure of chamber and hall could never be precisely forecast, because of possibilities of fluctuating number of guests and other visitors, there was all the more need for daily accounting in their case.

¹⁸ Not included in O 1478, which, however, orders similar procedure at higher level (O 1478, §2). Cf. O 1478, §3.

¹⁹ Repd. in O 1478, §42, but with stiffer penalty for second offence.

²⁰ Repd. in O 1478, §43.

²¹ Latter part of this paragraph is included in O 1478, §§3, 4, but more neatly and clearly. 'Great ledger' of cofferer, dealt with in first part of this paragraph, and possibly referred to in O 1478, §2, appears again in O 1540 (*Household Ordinances*, pp. 228–9). Specimen of such ledger survives from this reign, in journal of John Elrington, cofferer, for 13–14 Ed. IV (E 101/412/5); receipts totalled £7,475 4s. 5½d., payments £6,486 4s. 11½d.

²² Much expanded in O 1478, §59.

²³ Repd. in O 1478, §20, but with addition of cofferers, clerks of greencloth, and clerk controllers, as authorized deputies for treasurer and controller, and with omission of last sentence, which is merely an expression of apprehension, not an order.

²⁴ Repd. in O 1478, §19, but with clarifying addition.

²⁵ Repd. in O 1478, §§45, 46, but more neatly and sternly worded there.

²⁶ Repd. in O 1478, §§47, 50, but with addition of words 'Sondayes and solemne festes excepte' and omission of last sentence. Here again O 1478 is more logically arranged than this preliminary version.

²⁷ In its ruling on 'fees of office' O 1478, §34, returned more nearly to form used in O 1445, §8.

²⁸ Cf. O 1478, §65, which substituted more reasonable limit of 6 months within which treasurer must present his account to exchequer. Even this was

hard to attain; cf. O 1478, note 49. Between 'followeing' and 'the', near end of §30 of draft O 1478, word 'know' obviously omitted.

²⁹ Not included in O 1478. It is an interesting anticipation of methods of Henry VII.

³⁰ Repd. in O 1478, §49.

³¹ Repd. in O 1478, §52, which is, however, more explicit in its wording.

³² Repd. in O 1478, §53, where, however, penalty is much reduced. Cf. B.B., §50.

³³ As O 1478 shows in many ways realization that steward and treasurer might often be absent, hardly likely to include such a stringent rule; so it merely includes a very general order (§7).

³⁴ Unsuitable for public promulgation and omitted from O 1478. Cf. B.B., §§81, 89.

³⁵ Cf. O 1478, §44.

³⁶ Not included in O 1478; but cf. B.B., §78 (xxiii).

³⁷ Marginal notes almost certainly later—probably those of Sir Simonds d'Ewes who also supplied marginal references to his copy of Black Book. Hence not clear whether this last rule was made in Edward IV's reign, along with rest, and merely reiterated by Sir Robert Willoughby, lord of Broke, steward of Henry VII's household (possibly from 1496 to 1502: *C.P.R., 1494–1509*, pp. 72, 315), or whether it was first conceived by Willoughby.

THE ORDINANCE OF 1478

¹ Cf. Aristotle, *Nicomachean Ethics*, IV. 1.

² *Ibid.*, II. 7; IV. 1. Cf. also Aegidio Colonna, *De Regimine Principum*, II. i. 21: 'Nam sicut liberalitas, quae est media inter auaritias et prodigalitates, ideo est virtus quaedam reprimens auaritias, et moderans prodigalitates.'

³ These indentures would enable countinghouse officers to know how much money they had to their credit, and also to check handlers of such moneys (of whom there were many, as is indicated by extant household accounts of this reign), to see whether sums were all paid into countinghouse. Danger that they might not is implied in last sentence of this paragraph.

⁴ Sir John Elrington may have acted as cofferer as well as treasurer between 1471 and 1478, possibly in order to save expense. See below, under sections C and E of 'List of principal officials of royal household during reigns of Yorkist kings'.

⁵ Only controlment book of Edward IV's reign which survives begins the year after the making of this ordinance (E 101/412/11). O 1540 had to insist that clerks of controlment should make a controlment book every year (*Household Ordinances*, p. 231).

⁶ Cf. B.B., §§15, 78 (ii).

⁷ Cf. B.B., §§15, 78 (viii, xxiii).

⁸ Cf. Clarence's Ordinance of 1468 (*Household Ordinances*, p. 89).

⁹ This links up with §7 above. No one, except those on duty, was to have allowances of meat and drink at meal times outside the hall.

¹⁰ Cf. Clarence's Ordinance (*ibid.*, pp. 89–90).

¹¹ This paragraph comes between two on almoner's duties because, as O 1445 and O 1468 make clear, almoner had duty to see that those who ate in hall were served with their proper allowances of food (O 1445, §18; *Household Ordinances*, p. 90). Allowances granted are generous compared with those of O 1445 and O 1468.

¹² 'Adequately marked out and liberally supplied.'

¹³ Cf. O 1468, *Household Ordinances*, p. 91.

[14] If all supernumeraries were struck off these quarterly check-rolls, or made to perform their duties in person, there might have been considerable saving. For example, only 24 squires of household authorized in 1478 (§68 (xx)), yet many more had been employed by Edward IV (e.g. 78 in 6–7 Ed. IV, E 101/412/2, f. 37a) and, still more, Henry VI (cf. B.B., note 201). Cf. *Northumberland Household Book*, p. 50, which says that new check-roll for wages was to begin every quarter.

[15] Cf. B.B., §68.

[16] Cf. B.B., note 263; possibly reference in this paragraph to Black Book, §78.

[17] Repd. from O 1445, §28.

[18] Cf. B.B., §78 (ii), and Clarence's Ordinance (*Household Ordinances*, p. 93).

[19] Repd. in subst. from O 1445, §2; cf. B.B., §36.

[20] Repd. from O 1445, §5.

[21] Cf. O 1445, §35 (xiv).

[22] Cf. B.B., §50.

[23] Cf. B.B., §27 and note 90; also O 1471, §§6, 7.

[24] In these days of affinities, it was fitting that all men of rank in king's household should wear Yorkist badge of rising sun or white rose, just as Lancastrian adherents had worn collar of SS.

[25] O 1478, §§29, 30, 31, 32 repd. from O 1445, §§6, 7, 8.

[26] Kitchen cooking choicer dishes for chamber and kitchen preparing commoner fare for hall.

[27] O 1478, §§34, 35, 36 repd. in subst. from O 1445, §8, but O 1478 stricter and more precise. For use of term 'fee' in §34, cf. use of 'fees' in O 1445, §10; and Clarence's Ordinance in *Household Ordinances*, p. 92.

[28] This provision is more generous and yet stricter than O 1445, §10; hence perhaps an attempt to carry principle laid down in preamble to O 1478, of combining liberality with economy.

[29] Cf. B.B., §78 (xii) and Clarence's Ordinance in *Household Ordinances*, p. 90.

[30] Cf. B.B., §78 (xxvi) and *Edward II*, p. 274.

[31] Repd. in subst. from O 1445, §24, which had 'page' instead of 'officer', thus showing that type of officer forbidden was 'laddes and other raskalls' denounced by O 1526 (*Household Ordinances*, p. 148) or 'prenticez, renners about, pykers' rejected by Black Book (§78 (xxiii)).

[32] Cf. B.B., §78 (viii, xxiii).

[33] Cf. weaker rule of B.B., §90. For infra see B.B., note 327. For 'the statutes aforesaid', cf. §46; both may refer to B.B., §78 (xxvi).

[34] Repd. in subst. from O 1445, §17.

[35] This addition to rule taken from O 1445 seems to indicate greater efficiency and resolution of Edward IV's government.

[36] Cf. B.B., §78 (iii).

[37] Repd. from O 1445, §22.

[38] Cf. B.B., §78 (xi).

[39] Cf. B.B., §78 (ix).

[40] Repd. in subst. from O 1445, §26.

[41] Repd. from O 1445, §11.

[42] Based on O 1445, §14. Temptation to have one's own goods carried at king's cost so widespread that practice often forbidden, e.g. Clarence's Ordinance (*Household Ordinances*, p. 95).

[43] Cf. similar arrangement in O 1445, where second section (§§27–34) is concerned with payments and purveyance.

[44] Repd. from O 1445, §27, with additions of prohibition of assignments and

inclusion of clerk controller; latter probably necessitated by frequent absences of steward and controller (B.B., notes 263, 288).

[45] Cf. B.B., §75. As this clerk had great powers of supervision of delivery of goods, very fitting that his concurrence should be necessary for payment of debts by cofferer and clerks of greencloth.

[46] Repd. from O 1445, §29. If creditors kept waiting for payment, perhaps tempted to sell their tallies, etc., at discount for ready cash; and if corrupt accounting officers delayed payment, they might buy these tallies, bills, etc., at a discount and then obtain payment in full by manipulation of king's moneys passing through their hands. Such an abuse would speedily discredit royal household with king's subjects and needed to be strongly forbidden.

[47] Repd. from O 1445, §31. Edward's awareness of importance of avoiding popular discontent because of abuses of purveyance can be seen from his proclamations on this subject (London Letter Book L, ff. 61b, 170a; London Journal 8, f. 260a, in Guildhall Library).

[48] A precaution not included in O 1445. Cf. *Northumberland Household Book*, p. 116.

[49] Black Book had allowed treasurer 2 years in which to present his account ((§70). Not enough evidence to show whether this stricter rule effectively observed; but unlikely, to judge from performance of controllers, who had chronic difficulty in presenting accounts promptly. One of Henry VI's controllers, John Feriby, presented his account (for 15–17 Hy. VI) to exchequer in less than 6 months (7 Feb. 17 Hy. VI) (E 101/408/24, f. 44b); but delay usually greater than this, sometimes more than a year. For example, controller's account for 20–21 Hy. VI handed into exchequer on 14 May 21 Hy. VI (E 101/409/9, f. 40b) and controller's account for 29–30 Hy. VI reached exchequer only on 28 April 31 Hy. VI. But in earlier years of Edward IV delay sometimes worse than this. In K.R. Memoranda Roll for 12 Ed. IV (E 159/249), Easter Term, Brevia directa baronibus, m. 4a, John Scott, formerly controller of household, and Richard Bindewyn and Richard Jeny, formerly clerks of controlment, were granted expenses for years 3–8 Ed. IV which had been previously disallowed because books of controlment for years in question had not been delivered to exchequer. By later years of Edward IV there had been improvement in this as in other aspects of financial administration, and controller's account for 19–20 Ed. IV was presented to exchequer on 18 July 21 Ed. IV (E 101/412/11, f. 37a), a delay of 9½ months. Henry VII's reign saw no marked improvement; cofferer's account for 8–9 Hy. VII was delivered to exchequer on 13 June 9 Hy. VII (E 101/413/8, f. 36b), 8½ months after close of financial year.

[50] Based on O 1445, §30, which, however, does not mention clerks of various departments and time limit for their delivery into countinghouse of lists of creditors. Evidently not easy for treasurer and controller to collect from departments of household particulars of outstanding debts; and even when these were obtained, some time might elapse before they could be settled. Cf. list of creditors of various household departments for five years 15–20 Ed. IV (E 101/412/1), for total sum of £2501 9s. 1¼d. Perhaps this list and this order both resulted from same financial reforms.

[51] Repd. from O 1445, §32.

[52] Comparison of most of these allowances with those of Black Book and O 1445 will be found above, in notes to those two documents. Generally speaking, allowances in 1478 are smaller than in 1445 or in B.B.

[53] Richard, Duke of York, probably nearly 5 years old when this Ordinance was made, having probably been born on 17 Aug. 1473 (*Scofield*, II. 60). His

brother Edward, Prince of Wales, had been at Ludlow since winter of 1472–3 (*ibid.*, II. 54), and so did not need provision made for him.

[54] Cf. B.B., note 104.

[55] Departments which follow, from kitchen to hall, not dealt with in Black Book, which is obviously incomplete.

[56] Boiling of meat is meant. Cf. O 1540 and O 1601 (*Household Ordinances*, pp. 237, 288).

[57] Scaldinghouse not only 'scalded' or cooked poultry, but did plucking, drawing, etc.; it was under control of office of poultry.

[58] Tallow-man would look after grease collected from animals killed for office of acatry, so that tallow could be used to make candles.

[59] Department of saucery worked closely with office of pastry, as most of pastry was made for meat pies which, to taste of fifteenth and sixteenth centuries, needed plenty of highly-spiced sauces. Cf. O 1601 on duties of offices of pastry and saucery (*Household Ordinances*, p. 291).

[60] Even O 1478 fails to deal with some household departments, e.g. woodyard and stables.

ESTIMATE OF THE YEARLY EXPENSES OF THE ROYAL HOUSEHOLD IN THE TIME OF KING HENRY VII

[1] An 'apurus' is a liquidation of debts, but as this is such a small amount in relation to total budget of household, it seems likely to represent only petty cash payments, not foreseen in advances by countinghouse to various departments.

[2] Cf. estimate of £13,000 in Black Book (§10) and estimate of £26,750 in 1532–3 (Elton, *Tudor Revolution in Government*, p. 399). Cf. also assignment by act of parliament in 1485 of over £14,000 a year for expenses of royal household, with over £2,100 for cost of great wardrobe (*R.P.*, VI. 299a–304b). In 1495 fresh assignments were made to value of just over £13,000 for upkeep of royal household (*ibid.*, VI. 497a–502a). For comparison of actual expense of Edward IV's household, see Introduction, pp. 45–6.

SELECT GLOSSARY

With each word is given a reference to an example of its use

1. ENGLISH

abrooche = broach, pierce a cask, O 1445, §6.

abyde = to wait for, B.B., §84.

acatour = purchaser of provisions, purveyor, O 1445, §31.

accates, achates = purchases, provisions, O 1445, §31.

according = fitting, appropriate, B.B., §49.

affermed = confirmed, B.B., §45.

anempst = anent with respect to, over against (warrant for engrossing, O 1478).

appose = to audit, B.B., §74.

apposyle = apposal, the interrogation of accountants, the audit of accounts, B.B., §74.

apron, napron = an article of dress (usually of linen in the fifteenth century) worn in front of the body to protect the clothes from dirt or injury, B.B., §53.

architectour = one who has chief control; a superintendent, B.B., §43.

assaye = the act of tasting the food or drink intended for a king or other important person before presenting it, B.B., §17. Cf. *Babees Bk.*, I. 324.

assewer = sewer (q.v.), O 1445, §35 (xiv).

asshin cuppis = cups made of ash-wood, B.B., §86.

assithing, assiethyng = assything, satisfying, compensating, O 1445, §31.

avener = a chief officer of the stable, who had charge of the provender of horses, B.B., §79.

aventure = risk, B.B., §79.

avery, averey = avenery, the office of the avener, B.B., §79.

avoydez = void, the withdrawal of dishes after meals; also the drink served with spices, comfits, etc., when the table had been cleared, before retiring to rest, or before the departure of guests, B.B., §33. Cf. *Babees Bk.*, I. 166, 168, 171, 271.

awbe = alb, B.B., §92.

awmery = almonry, the office of the almoner, B.B., §61.

bacheler knyztes = probably here meaning young knights rather than the seventeenth-century sense of knights of the lowest but most ancient order, B.B., §28.

banneret = originally a knight able and entitled to bring a company of vassals into the field under his own banner, and ranking below a baron but above other knights; here used in a less exact sense of a knight of military distinction (who would probably have led a contingent of an indentured retinue) or of good family, B.B., §28.

beam, fees of the = perquisites of the unconsumed remnants of lighted candles placed before the rood, B.B., §56.

berm = barm, leaven, yeast, B.B., §79.

beves = cattle, B.B., §7.

blaundrel = blaundrell, a kind of white apple, much in repute at this time, B.B., §89.

bolte = to bolt, sift the bran from the flour, B.B., §79.

bon gayte = good walk, regular and speedy perambulations, B.B., §54.

bouche, bouge of court = court rations, allowances to those on the household establishment, O 1445, §22.

brefmentes, brevementes = entries in books, especially account-books, B.B., §84.

breve = to render an account, B.B., §52.

brever = book-keeper, ledger-clerk, B.B., §80.

bubale = used to render Latin bubalus with the meaning of antelope, buffalo, or ox, B.B., §2.

bulter = bolter, a piece of cloth used for sifting out the bran; a sieve, strainer, B.B., §79.

can = ken, to know, B.B., §61.

capitle = chapter, B.B., §43.

capon = castrated cock, a fat and succulent bird, B.B., §29.

carbone = charbon, charcoal, B.B., §29.

cast of brede = the quantity of bread made at one time, B.B., §37.

casueltie = casualty, casual source of income, O 1445, §33.

chaffers, chauffers, chaufirs = braziers, chafing-dishes, vessels for heating something, B.B., §91.

chamberlayn = 1. chief officer of the chamber, O 1445, §35. 2. chamber-servant equivalent to a groom in rank, O 1445, §18. Cf. *Babees Bk.*, I. 282–3, and Edward II, p. 247.

chardquinces, cardqwyns = chare de quince, preserve made of the pulp of quinces, B.B., §89.

charyott = cart, B.B., §43.

chase = a hunting-ground, unenclosed park-land, B.B., §78 (vi).

chaumbre dekens = chamber deacons, servants or attendants who kept the chambers of noblemen and others attending court, B.B., §36.

chaunces = chauces, chausses, footwear, shoes, boots, B.B., §37.

chaundelers = chandlers, chandeliers, candle-sticks; probably also candles suitable for chandlers, B.B., §80.

chaundry = the office of chandlery, B.B., §90.

chawcers = chaussures, shoes, boots, B.B., §28.

chekker-rolle = check-roll, the roll by which the attendances in court of the household officials were checked, O 1445, §23.

chete-loffe = cheat-loaf, wheaten bread of the second quality, made of flour more coarsely sifted than that used for manchet, the finest quality, B.B., §32.

chevage, chyvyage = capitation or poll-money paid to a lord or superior, B.B., §14.

choore, chooris = cor, a Hebrew and Phoenician measure of capacity, about 9½ bushels (liquid) and 8 bushels (dry) measure, B.B., §2.

clystryng = treatment with clysters, enemas or suppositories, B.B., §29.

coining = fabrication, counterfeiting, invention, B.B., §83.

coker = caulker, a dram, B.B., §84.

comfit = a sweetmeat made of some fruit, root, etc., preserved with sugar; a sugar-plum, B.B., §33.

commune = the commonalty, the common people as distinguished from those of rank or dignity, B.B., §92.

competent = suitable, appropriate, B.B., §48.

conduyte = conduit, conductor, one who conveys or carries goods; a porter or carrier, B.B., §73.

conged = licensed, permitted to be absent, B.B., §7.

contentacion = compensation, payment in satisfaction, O 1478, §1.

controller, countroller = 1. one who keeps a counter-roll so as to check a treasurer or person in charge of accounts, B.B., §27. 2. a customs-officer, douanier, B.B., §20.

conveaunce = conduct, management, B.B., §34

convenable = suitable, appropriate, B.B., §82.

convenite = meeting, assembly, B.B., §48.

copage = cooperage, the making or preparing of casks, tubs, B.B., §83.

corps = probably a guard, or small body of soldiers used as a guard, to protect the possessions of the office, B.B., §40.

correction = disciplinary punishment; chastisement, B.B., §49.

corrody = pension, annuity, provision for food and accommodation made by religious houses in return for a lump sum paid down at the outset, B.B., §7.

cotydyan = quotidian, daily, B.B., §74.

country = neighbourhood, men of the neighbourhood, B.B., §73.

cowperage, coperage = money payable to a cooper for his services, B.B., §87.

crakyng = cracking, damaging of reputation, B.B., §79.

crauing = demanding, begging, B.B., §79.

crome = the inner part of the loaf, opposed to the crust, B.B., §80.

cubbard, cupbourde = cupboard, the side table or dresser on which cups and other vessels were set and from which the drinks were served, B.B., §13.

cunter-clerkes = counter-clerks, reckoning-clerks, B.B., §82.

cuntriez = people of the countryside round the household, B.B., §73.

custellers = ? custodians, B.B., §88.

customer = customs-house officer, B.B., §19.

dampned = condemned as unfit to drink, B.B., §75.

dapsilite = bounty, from the Latin *daps* = feast, banquet, B.B., §2.

dease = dais, in the more usual fifteenth-century sense of the raised table at which distinguished persons sat at feasts; the high table, B.B., §86.

debentours = vouchers given for goods supplied, O 1478, §59.

defuse = diffuse, difficult, doubtful, B.B., §74.

demerites = merits, deserts, B.B., §50.

devoir = duty, O 1478, §23.

dight = order, appoint, B.B., §33.

disclaundryd = slandered, brought into opprobrium, B.B., §79.

distaynyng = distaining, defiling, sullying, B.B., §79.

doctryne = doctrine, discipline, correction, punishment, B.B., §85.

dogette = docket, abstract, digest, minute, B.B., §73.

dolium = in Roman antiquity a large earthenware jar, more or less spherical, for holding wine, oil, or dry commodities; hence, in English usage, a cask, B.B., §82.

doom = judgement, B.B., §68.

dyettes = totals of daily expenditure for the chief departments of the household, B.B., §74.

edyfye = edify, make, B.B., §68

elle = ell. The English ell was 45 in., the Scottish 37·2, the Flemish 27, B.B., §28.

endrayzt = endroit, quality, species, B.B., §33.

erthe = earthenware, B.B., §72.

eschetour = escheator, an officer appointed yearly by the lord treasurer to take notice of the escheats of the shire to which he was appointed and to certify them into the exchequer, B.B., §20.

ewen herbage = common herbs (ewe-bramble = common bramble, ewe-gowan = common daisy), B.B., §50.

expenduntur = net consumption of wax each day, B.B., §75.

extra = issue of wax from the chandlery, B.B., §75.

facet = the book *Facetus de Moribus* (by some attributed to John Garland) which was used in schools as a book of instruction in behaviour, B.B., §59.

falace = filace, file, B.B., §30.

fates = vats, B.B., §75.

faucetes = faucets, taps for drawing liquor from a barrel, B.B., §85.

feryall = ferial, week-day as distinguished from a festival day; an ordinary day, B.B., §13.

fett = fet, an obsolete verb meaning to fetch; O 1445, §2.

fferrers, fferys = barrel-ferrers, vessels (casks, jars, or leather bottles) in which water or wine was carried on horseback on a journey or military expedition, B.B., §84.

forborn = done without, dispensed with, spared, B.B., §70.

foreine officers = officials outside the household establishment, O 1445, §22.

forwached = wearied with waking or watching, B.B., §32.

foyllys = foils, counterfoils, B.B., §84.

fugacion = a chase, privilege of hunting, B.B., §75

fumigacion = the act of perfuming with aromatic herbs, rather than the modern sense of disinfecting by smoke; perfuming of this kind was believed to ward off disease, B.B., §39.

furnour = baker, B.B., §79.

fysycean = physician, B.B., §46.

gardeviandes = meat-safes, food-containers, B.B., §80.

gawge = to gauge, ascertain the capacity of a cask by combined measurement and calculation, B.B., §85.

gladly = aptly, usually, B.B., §47.

gospeler = one who reads the Gospel in the mass, B.B., §57.

graciers = cattle, for grazing, cattle to feed on pasture, B.B., §78 (xxvii).

greete = grate, grater. See 'payle' below.

greete meate = great meat; the flesh of large animals; the principal dish of the meal; boiled meat in contrast to roast, B.B., §18.

grene cofyrs = green coffers, strong boxes covered with green cloth, or the coffers of the greencloth, the countinghouse, B.B., §77.

grene feald = the greencloth of the countinghouse, B.B., §59.

groom, garnetour = the superintendent of a granary, B.B., §79.

groose = gross, sum, sum total, B.B., §71.

gros chare, gros meat = greete meate (q.v.).

gurgeons = coarse meal, coarse refuse from flour, pollards, B.B., §79.

harneys = apparel, B.B., §49; gear, B.B., §75.

henxman, henchman = a squire or page of honour, B.B., §48.

herbiger, herbyiour = harbinger, one who was sent on before to purvey lodgings for the royal household, B.B., §20.

herborow = to assign lodgings, to billet, B.B., §27.

herbygage = lodging, B.B., §77.

herdes = herdsmen, O 1478, §68 (xl).

hogges = hogsheads, large casks of liquor, B.B., §75.

hogman = bread for the king's horses made from the bran of a bushel of flour, B.B., §79.

holy-bred = ordinary leavened bread which was blessed after the Eucharist and distributed to those who had not communicated, B.B., §62.

housellyng = communion, B.B., §60.

huisshers = ushers (q.v.).

huntys = huntsmen, O 1445, §21. Cf. *Babees Bk.*, I. 320.

husbandry = management, economical ordering, B.B., §50.

inch = a very small amount (not necessarily an exact measurement), B.B., §84.

incontinent = forthwith, O 1478, §2.

infra = within, hence the entries of wax returned to the chandlery every morning from the various offices, B.B., §75.

inned = included, brought in, B.B., §36.

intaile with = receive tallies from, B.B., §86.

invention = inventory, B.B., §84.

journey, wex of = daily wax, ordinary issues of wax, B.B., §90.

kersse = crease, fold, B.B., §62.

kokyrs = caulkers, drops, B.B., §84.

lavers = jugs, B.B., §84.

lenton wardens = a kind of pear, B.B., §89.

lett = let, hinder, prevent, stop, B.B., §72.

levable = leveable, credible, trustworthy, B.B., §83.

lityll, to lityll = to diminish, reduce, B.B., §36.

lyes = lees, sediment deposited in vessel containing wine, B.B., §84.

lymitted = limited, defined, assigned, specified, O 1445, §26.

magry = maugre, ill-will, displeasure, spite, B.B., §70.

maine flour = flour of the finest quality, B.B., §79.

mal engyne = malengin, fraud, deceit, guile, O 1445, §31.

male = mail, bag, pack, travelling-bag, B.B., §40.

marciable = merciable, merciful, compassionate, laudable, B.B., §50.

maunchette = manchet, a small loaf or roll of the finest kind of wheaten bread, B.B., §13.

maynie, meyne, meynie, meinie = family or household, body of retainers, attendants, followers, retinue, train, B.B., §16.

melewell = a kind of small cod-fish, B.B., §26.

mene ale = light, weak, small ale, B.B., §50. Cf. *English Gilds*, (E.E.T.S., 1870), p. 382.

mensall = monthly account, B.B., §73.

merchandise = the act of trading as well as the goods traded, O 1478, §60.

messe, mess = 1. company of persons sitting together for a meal

usually four together, O 1445, §18 (cf. *Babees Bk.*, I. 188).
2. portion of food, prepared food, B.B., §13.

messe gros de cusyn = a portion or helping of the principal dish, or a portion of boiled meat as distinct from roast, B.B., §13.

mess gros chare = a portion of 'great meat'. See *greete meate*, above.

moder, modyr = to regulate, settle, B.B., §74.

morter = a bowl of wax or oil with a floating wick; also a kind of thick candle, used especially as a night-light, B.B., §13. Cf. *Babees Bk.*, I. 315.

motones = sheep, B.B., §7.

mustrid = displayed, exhibited, B.B., §36.

mwe = mew, a cage for hawks while mewing or moulting; hence the department which looked after the hawks, O 1445, §15.

napors = linen for aprons, B.B., §80.

o = one, B.B., §28.

officyaship = the post of an ecclesiastical official, B.B., §19.

opposer = apposer, questioner, auditor, B.B., §60.

or = before, in preparation for, B.B., §40.

ordinance = order, regulation, management, meeting for making orders, B.B., §§2, 34.

ordinate maistyrs = appointed teachers, B.B., §61.

ostries = hostries, hostelries, hostels, inns, B.B., §82.

out-take = except, B.B., §20.

panter = the head of the office of the pantry, or one of his staff, B.B., §80.

part with = share in, B.B., §74.

partycion = department, B.B., §77.

pavilloner = pavilioner, tent-maker, B.B., §82.

payle = pale, a cheese scoop; hence 'chese of iiij kyndes to the payle or greete' = cheese of four varieties, suitable either for scooping or gratering, B.B., §50.

payling = broaching, tapping, B.B., §82.

payn = a loaf of fine quality, B.B., §13.

payne de mayne = pain-demaine, panis dominicus, lord's bread, a loaf or cake of white bread of the finest quality, B.B., §13.

pease = appease, pacify, B.B., §68.

peele = pell, parchment skin or roll on which accounts were written, hence account roll, B.B., §82.

pejon = pigeon, B.B., §50.

pellys = ? pails, B.B., §86.

percher = a tall candle of wax or tallow, B.B., §13. Cf. *Babees Bk.*, I. 182.

peric' candelle = paris candle, a kind of large wax candle, B.B., §18.

perker = parker, a park-keeper, B.B., §20.

perused = used up, worn out by use, B.B., §7.

peysed = pondered, considered, estimated, B.B., §9.

pikers = pickers, thieves, B.B., §54.

pisteller = epistler, one who reads the epistle at the mass, B.B., §58.

pistrin, pistrine = bakehouse, B.B., §79.

plaate = plate, dish or course, B.B., §89.

podage, potage = pottage, a dish made of vegetables alone, or with
    meat, boiled to softness in water, and appropriately seasoned;
    a thick soup, O 1471, §15.

poll = unit of numbering chattels, B.B., §84.

polycyes = conduct of public affairs, acts of statecraft, diplomacy,
    B.B., §50.

portatiffes = trays or other carrying utensils, B.B., §84.

potell, pottle = a measure of capacity for liquids, equal to 2 quarts or
    half a gallon; a pot or vessel containing a pottle, B.B., §84.

powdred = salt or pickled, B.B., §50.

praysyd = appraised, assessed, B.B., §85.

prest = advance of money, a loan, O 1445, §23.

pricket, prikett = a candle or taper such as was stuck on a pricket
    candlestick, B.B., §13.

prise = 1. purchase at a price fixed by royal officials, O 1445, §7.
    2. appraisal, test, B.B., §72.

prof = proof, testing, inspection, B.B., §87.

propyrties = properties, attributes, characters, qualities, B.B., §68.

pryse, preyse = see 'praysyd'.

pullayle = poultry, B.B., §4.

pulter = poulterer, official who attended to the purchase of poultry
    and other provisions, B.B., §41.

pure = to pare, prepare, make ready, B.B., §73.

purveyance = direction, government; also the requisitioning or com-
    pulsory purchase of goods for the king's use, B.B., §75.

pyles = piles, stores of goods, B.B., §39.

quadran = quadrant, farthing, B.B., §85.

racking = drawing off wine, cider, etc., from the lees, B.B., §83.

raunger = a forest official, gamekeeper, B.B., §19.

raveyn, raven = the taking away of goods by force, B.B., §75.

ray hoodes = hoods made of striped cloth, B.B., §77.

rebating = reduction, lessening, subtraction, B.B., §83.

relysed = probably from relish = to sing, to warble, to be practised
    in singing, B.B., §57.

renned = supplied, from the verb 'to rein', B.B., §3.

renomed = renowned, B.B., §2.

reward = remuneration, also an extra supply or allowance of food,
    an extra dish, B.B., §39.

rundelettes = runlets, casks, or vessels of varying capacity; large runlets appear usually to have varied between 12 and 18 gallons, small ones between a pint or a quart and 3 or 4 gallons, B.B., §75.

rynes = raines; cloth of raines was a kind of fine linen or lawn originally made at Rennes in Brittany, B.B., §80.

sad = serious, earnest, B.B., §69.

saler = salt-cellar, B.B., §73.

saler, to make the = to set the salt-cellar on the table in the ceremonious manner then required, B.B., §80.

salvacion = saving, peculation, B.B., §83.

saultre = saltire (her.), an ordinary in the form of a St. Andrew's cross, B.B., §76.

saye = assay (q.v.), B.B., §33.

sepulcre = a structure prepared in a church for the dramatic burial of the reserved sacrament (sometimes also the cross) on Good Friday, B.B., §62.

sergeantries = spending departments, under care of sergeants, such as the bakehouse, the pantry, the cellar, the poultry, the acatry, O 1445, §28.

serviture = servitor, servant, B.B., §61.

servoice = cervoise, barley-beer, ale, B.B., §27.

sewer, shewer = an attendant at the meal who superintended the arrangements of the table, especially the high table, and the tasting and serving of the dishes, B.B., §18.

sextary = sester, liquid measure for beer, wine etc., B.B., §84.

shaftmount = shaftment, the distance from the end of the extended thumb to the other side of the hand, used as a measure and usually about 6 inches, B.B., §56.

shalmus = shawms, musical instruments of the oboe class, having a double reed enclosed in a globular mouthpiece, B.B., §53.

Shere Thursday = Thursday in Holy Week, B.B., §54.

shides, shydez = billets of firewood, B.B., §13.

shreves = sheriffs, B.B., §20.

singing-bred = the wafer used in the celebration of the mass, B.B., §62.

sise, size, syze = 1. a kind of large candle used especially at court and in churches, B.B., §13. 2. assize, ordinance, regulation fixing the standard of quality or quantity for food, drink, and other commodities, B.B., §64.

soden = sodden, boiled, from the verb 'to seethe', B.B., §33.

sompter = sumpter, pack-horse, baggage-horse, B.B., §60.

soote = sweet, B.B., §87.

soveraignes, souveraignes = sovereigns, chief officers of the household, O 1445, §4. Cf. B.B., §74.

staken out = steeken out, garnished, O 1478, §12.

stokfishe = stockfish, salted and dried cod, etc., B.B., §29. See notes in *Babees Bk.*, I. 155, 214.

stole = stool, commode, privy, B.B., §37.

strengmen = stringmen, players on stringed instruments (probably viols), B.B., §53.

streng minstrelles = viol players, B.B., §53.

stuffed = supplied, equipped, armed, B.B., §3.

suffraunce = sufferance, allowance, B.B., §73.

suggeoure = sojourn, place of temporary stay, B.B., §21.

sure = to secure, B.B., §62.

surnape = a towel or napkin provided at table for use when washing the hands, B.B., §36.

surveour, surveyor = 1. an officer of the royal or other great household who superintended the preparation and service of the food, B.B., §34. 2. a tax-collector, the administrator of an office, B.B., §19.

syowed = showed, shown, i.e. produced for inspection, B.B., §70.

taille, in = by tally, on credit, O 1445, §27.

tailles foylls = tally-foils, B.B., §85.

tallwood = cut or chopped wood, for fuel (from *tailler*, to cut), B.B., §18.

tayle = tally, O 1445, §28. To damn tallies (B.B., §87) = to cancel tallies.

tayle, by = by tale, by counting individually, B.B., §79.

tight = term appended to 'ton' and 'dolium' as measures of capacity, B.B., §82. Cf. *R.P.*, IV. 365.

tortayis = tortis, a kind of very large wax candle, B.B., §13.

towell, at the = the time towards the end of the first sitting of meals when water and towels were brought for the higher ranks to wash their hands, and the lower ranks could begin their meal, B.B., §79. Cf. B.B., §50.

towell of work = worked towel, ornamented cloth, B.B., §60.

travers = traverse, a small compartment shut off or enclosed by a curtain or screen in a church, house, etc; also the curtain used for this purpose, B.B., §60; Cf. *Household Ordinances*, p. *28.

trayour = drawer, tapster, B.B., §84. Cf. *Household Ordinances*, p. 234.

tree, cup of = wooden cup, B.B., §71.

trencher = slice of bread used instead of a plate, B.B., §13; (trenchers were sometimes made of wood, cf. *Babees Bk.*, I. 367).

truss, trusse = to bundle, pack, stow, load, B.B., §43.

vnder, the vnder = the foot of the indenture which might be made by an official for the supply of provisions to the household, B.B., §74.

unray = undress, B.B., §32.

vssher, usher = in general, a door-keeper; but the ushers of the chamber were important officials of gentle birth who regulated the seating of the courtiers and guests there according to their rank, and were responsible for preventing in the great chamber any commotion, confusion, breach of etiquette, waste or theft, B.B., §36.

vtterance = issue, supply, B.B., §70.

venus = venues, imports, arrivals, B.B., §82.

verder = verderer, a judicial officer of the king's forest, sworn to maintain the assizes of the forest, and to enroll all the attachments and presentments of all manner of trespasses of the forest of vert and venison, B.B., §19.

verger = an official who carried a rod or similar symbol of office before the dignitaries of a cathedral or other great church, B.B., §19.

vergeouse = verjuice, the acid juice of green or unripe grapes, crab-apples, or other sour fruit, pressed out and formed into a liquor; much used in cooking as a condiment and valued for medicinal purposes, B.B., §50.

veriger = see B.B., §53 for definition.

vestyary = office of vestiary, O 1445, §3.

viander = host or entertainer, B.B., §3.

waching clothing = official clothing, uniform on duty, B.B., §41.

wafer = a very light thin crisp cake baked between wafer-irons, formerly often eaten with wine, B.B., §80.

warderober of chamber, kinges warderober, warderober private = treasurer of the chamber, B.B., §26; B.B., §29; B.B., §21.

wardrobez = dressing-rooms, store-rooms, private chambers, B.B., §39.

warener, waryner = an official employed to watch over the game in a park, preserve or warren, B.B., §7.

wareynes = warrens, pieces of land enclosed and preserved for breeding game, and especially appropriated for breeding rabbits, B.B., §78 (vi).

wedring = weathering, suitable weather, B.B., §91.

weeke = wick, wicking, B.B., §75.

white swordes = burnished and shining swords, without colouring or stain, B.B., §56.

with = against, B.B., §68.

withdrawzt = retreat, private chamber, closet, B.B., §15.

wykely, wikely = weekly, B.B., §49.

ypocras = hippocras, a cordial drink made of wine flavoured with spices, so called from the Hippocrates sleeve or bag through which it was filtered, B.B., §33.

zyma = fermentum, leaven, B.B., §56.

2. LATIN

allec = herring, B.B., §10.

ancer = *anser*, goose, B.B., §29.

apurus = liquidation of debts (estimate of yearly expenses of royal household, temp. Hy. VII).

aquaria = office of ewry, B.B., Tabula.

aula et camera = hall and chamber, B.B., §10.

baconus = salted carcase of a hog, B.B., §29.

banna vsus = *banausus*, from βαναυσος, coarse, gross, boorish, B.B., §8.

bannerettus = *bannerettus*, knight-banneret, B.B., Tabula.

bartagium = ? grooming of horses, B.B., §26; fee for this.

boucherus = butcher, B.B., §29.

brasium = malt, B.B., §50.

brennium = bran, B.B., §64.

buletellum = sieve; bran; the refuse of meal after it is dressed by the baker, B.B., §64.

butelleria = buttery, office of the butler or bottles, B.B., §10.

cantans = singer, B.B., §25.

capella = hat, B.B., §19.

carrectata = *carectata*, cart-load, B.B., §29.

cenapium = *senapium, sinapium*, mustard, B.B., §29.

cepa, cepum = *sebum*, tallow, grease, B.B., §18.

cervisia = ale, B.B., Tabula.

charreta = *carreta*, cart, B.B., §10.

cipha = sieve, measure or about 5 quarters, B.B., §10.

cirpi = rushes, B.B., §29.

cisera = *sicera*, cider, B.B., §29.

clericus panni viridis = clerk of the greencloth, B.B., Tabula.

cocus = *coquus*, cook, B.B., §29.

colistriagialis = *collistriagialis*, of or pertaining to the pillory, B.B., §64.

comes = earl, B.B., Tabula.

contrarotulator = controller, B.B., Tabula.

coquina = kitchen, B.B., §10.

cuniculus = rabbit, rabbit-skin, B.B., §18.

dama, damus = doe or buck, B.B., §18.

dapifer = steward of the household; also a sewer, B.B., §1 (i).

dapsilitas = bounty, generosity, B.B., §1 (ii).

decima = tithe, B.B., §56.

depositarius ciborum camere regis = usher of the king's chamber, B.B., Tabula.

depositor mense regis = king's sewer, B.B., Tabula.

dispensaria = office of store-keeper; the spence, B.B., §10.

elemosina = alms, B.B., §10.

equisequelus = henchman, B.B., Tabula.

equus gylding = gelding, B.B., §26.

escambia, excambia = exchange, B.B., §28.

estivalis = of or for summer, B.B., §18.

falcacio = mowing, B.B., §50

falconaria = falconry, B.B., §10

furnarius = baker, B.B., §64.

galona = gallon, B.B., §29.

garcio = groom, B.B., §18.

garderoba = wardrobe, B.B., §10

magna garderoba hospicij = wardrobe of the household, not the great wardrobe of clothes and bulky articles, B.B., §7.

herba = hay or herb, B.B., §29.

hernesium = *harnesium*, harness, B.B., §29.

iactus pani equini = cast of horse bread, B.B., §26.

imposicio = storing, stowing, stacking, B.B., §50.

lardenarius = larderer, B.B., §29.

ledit = ? rises (ledo = tide), B.B., §2.

liberata = gift, livery, B.B., §28.

litera, litterium = litter, straw, B.B., §10.

lucrari = to make a profit of, on, from, B.B., §64.

mapparia = linen, napery, B.B., §10.

marca = mark (13s. 4d.), B.B., §18.

marchio = marquis, B.B., Tabula.

mortuarium = mortuary-due, B.B., §56.

morum = *morua*, codfish, B.B., §25.

multo = sheep, wether, B.B., §18.

muta = mew or cage for hawks, B.B., §10.

nisus = bird, fish-hawk, sparrow-hawk, B.B., §50.

oblacio = oblation, offering, B.B., Tabula.

obolus = halfpenny, B.B., §18.

ortus = *hortus*, garden, orchard, B.B., §29.

ostria = *ostrea*, oyster, B.B., §29.

pagettus = page (servant), B.B., §18.

panetria = *panetaria*, pantry, B.B., Tabula.

panis de quadrante = quartern loaf, B.B., §64.
paraclytus = comforter, B.B., §1 (i).
peruificentia, paruificentia = parsimony, miserliness, B.B., §8.
pincerna = butler, B.B., Tabula.
pingu(r)do = abundance, B.B., §1 (i).
pipa = pipe of wine, two hogsheads, B.B., §29.
pistrina = bakehouse, B.B., Tabula.
policiam, per policiam = by strict rule of the household, B.B., §50.
pulcinus = chicken, B.B., §29.
pulletria = office of poultry; poultry, B.B., §10.
pullina = pullet, B.B., §18.
quarta, quarteria = farthing, B.B., §26.
quarterium = quarter of grain, B.B., §10.
recens = fresh-killed, B.B., §18.
receptor = receiver, B.B., §29.
regardum = reward, payment, B.B., §18.
rogaciones = public prayers or processions, B.B., §25.
sal album = sea salt, fine salt, B.B., §29. Cf. A. R. Bridbury, *England
        and the Salt-Trade in the Later Middle Ages*, pp. 10, 52, note
        4, *et alia.*
sal grossum = salt in large crystals or lumps, coarse salt, B.B., §29.
salseria = saucery, office of the royal household, B.B., §10.
scutilleria = scullery, B.B., §10.
senescallus = steward, B.B., Tabula.
servicia = cervisia, ale, B.B., Tabula.
sextarium = sester, dry or liquid measure, B.B., §10.
signus = cygnus, swan, B.B., §29.
sitiarum = ? of places, sites, B.B., §2.
somerarius, somarius = sumpter, sumpter-horse, B.B., §10.
sqyllourius = squelarius, scullion, B.B., §29.
stagnum, stancum = pond, B.B., 29.
staurum = stock, B.B., §29.
superveniens = visitor, B.B., §18.
tela = cloth, B.B., §10.
vadia = wages, B.B., §10.
valectus = vallettus, yeoman, B.B., §19.
vergerus = vergutum, verjuice, B.B., §29.
vesperae = vespers, evensong, B.B., §25.
vicecomes = sheriff; also viscount, B.B., Tabula.
vigilia noctuali = wait, B.B., Tabula.
vinacrum = vinegar, B.B., §29.
vitulus = calf, B.B., §18
yemalis = of or for winter, B.B., §18.

3. FRENCH

All the references in this glossary are to the Ordinance of 1445

afferant = assignment, allowance, §35 (xii).

arcus = bows, §35 (xiv).

asmoigner = almoner, §35 (viii).

assewer = sewer, an attendant at the meal who superintended the arrangements of the table, especially the high table, and the tasting and serving of the dishes, §35 (xiv).

aveigner = avener, supplier of oats or fodder, §35 (xxxvii).

bastardz = cross-bred horses, §35 (xxxvii).

bouchours = butchers, §35 (xxvi).

boulters = those who sifted out the bran from the flour, §35 (xx).

caterie = the office of the royal household which provided meat, §35 (xxvi).

chambrer = chamber-servant, §35 (xvii).

cheens = *chiens*, dogs, §35 (vix).

chevalier herberciour = knight harbinger, §35 (xiv).

chivacher = *chevaucher*, to ride, §35 (xiv).

contrebener = perhaps berner, keeper of dogs (cf. bernarius), §35 (xiv).

dauncelle = lady-in-waiting, waiting-woman, §35 (xvii).

dextrer = *destrier*, charger, battle-steed, §35 (xxxvii).

escuier = squire, §35 (i).

ferour = blacksmith, ironsmith: an official of the royal household who had care of the horses, §35 (xxxvii).

gaite = *guette*, watch or wait, §35 (xiv).

garceon, garcion = groom, §35 (xiv).

haberger = to lodge, accommodate, §35 (xii).

herberiours = harbingers, §35 (xxxv).

herlaultz = heralds, §35 (xiv).

lauender = laundress, washerwoman, §35 (xxxiii).

lectes, litez = beds, §35 (xiv).

memstrealx = minstrels, §35 (xiv).

pastour = shepherd, §35 (xxvi).

pelter = skinner, §35 (xiv).

pik = pike or pick, §35 (xxvi)

pistour = baker, §35 (xx).

pistrine = bakehouse, §35 (xx).

portones = porters, §35 (xxx).

salcerie = saucery, §35 (xxxi).

seruoise = *ceruoise*, ale, barley-beer, §35 (i).

someres = pack-horses, §35 (xxxvii).

soutremen = sumptermen, men who looked after pack-horses, §35 (xxix).

squillerie = scullery, §35 (xxx).

surueour = an officer of the royal household who superintended the preparation and serving of food, §35 (xiv).

valet, vallet = yeoman, §35 (i).

vestiaire = vestiary, vestry, §35 (x).

wheller = wheel-wright or wheel-maker, §35 (xxxvii).

APPENDIX I

Lists of Principal Officials of the Royal Household during the Reigns of the Yorkist Kings of England

The following lists are obviously incomplete; to make an adequate investigation into the careers of the household officials of this period would be a considerable study in itself. But it seemed worth while to include these lists, as those given in Vol. 2 (Register) of the *History of Parliament 1439–1509* (henceforth referred to as *H.P.* II) were found on inspection to contain many errors, inconsistencies with the biographies given in Vol. I, and dates which the present writer has been unable to verify. R. L. Storey's 'English Officers of State, 1399–1485', in *B.I.H.R.*, XXXI (1958), 84–92 (hereafter cited as *Storey*) has valuable lists of household stewards and treasurers, the only household officials with which it deals.

Where dates of office seem likely but cannot be precisely substantiated, they are enclosed in brackets.

A. *Stewards of the Household*

William Neville, Earl of Kent   1461–1463

Created Earl of Kent 1 Nov. 1461, he was steward from beginning of reign (E 101/411/11) until his death in Jan. 1463 (*C.P.*, V. 285 — 9 Jan. 1463).

John Tiptoft, Earl of Worcester   1463–1467

He held this office by 24 July 1463 (*Storey*, p. 89); he probably became steward soon after ceasing to be treasurer of England on 24 June 1463 (*ibid.*, pp. 308, 326), perhaps even in Feb. 1463 (*ibid.*, p. 217). Patent roll still speaks of him as steward on 30 July 1467 (*C.P.R.*, *1467–77*, p. 23), but close roll refers to Henry, Earl of Essex, as steward on 8 June 1467 (*C.C.R.*, *1461–68*, p. 456). Probably close roll is correct, for E 101/412/2, f. 36b, states that Tiptoft was steward at Christmas 1466, and that Bourchier had succeeded by Easter 1467.

Henry Bourchier, Earl of Essex   1467–(1471)

C.P., V. 138 says that he was steward 1463–71, but this cannot be true. Certainly steward by 8 Sept. 1468 (*Report from the Lords Committees touching the Dignity of a Peer of the Realm*, V (1829), 374–5), and was still steward on 22 May 1469 (*C.P.R.*, *1467–77*,

p. 170). He may have vacated this post before he was made treasurer of England on 22 April 1471 (*C.P.R., 1467–77*, p. 258).

Thomas, Lord Stanley (1471–1483)

H.P., p. xli, states that he became steward on 14 Aug. 1471 but gives no reference. He was steward by 25 March 1472 (*Report on Dignity of a Peer*, V. 390) and still held this office on 10 Feb. 1483 (*Storey*, p. 89) (*C.P.R., 1476–85*, p. 230). In Feb. 1483 he was steward of household of Edward, Prince of Wales (Sloane MS. 3479).

Thomas Howard, Earl of Surrey 1483–(1485)

Thomas Stanley is stated by J. Gairdner (*Richard the Third*, rev. edn., 1898, p. 100) and J. Tait (*D.N.B.*) to have been steward of the household at Richard III's coronation, but they give no evidence for this. It seems unlikely in view of Richard's very recent arrest of Stanley. Gairdner's statement is to be found in J. Stow's *Annales of England* (1631 edition, p. 458), and he claims to have taken it from Sir Thomas More, as does G. Buc in his *Life and Reign of King Richard III* (London, 1647), p. 26; but it appears in neither Latin nor English version of More's work. Hall's *Chronicle* (ed. H. Ellis, 1809), p. 376, says that at Richard's coronation Stanley was 'lorde Stewarde'; but may he not have meant that Stanley had received a temporary commission as Lord High Steward of England? Bishop Mandel Creighton stated (*D.N.B.*) that Richard III in 1483 made Earl of Surrey steward of household; and this is borne out by contemporary account of Richard's coronation (not mentioned by Creighton), printed by S. Bentley, in *Excerpta Historica*, p. 382. *C.P.*, IX. 613 says that Surrey was steward 1483–4; but no reference is given, and it is hard to see why he did not continue to hold this office until Richard's death.

B. *Chamberlains of the Household*

William, Lord Hastings Before 31 July 1461–29 Sept. 1470

C.P.R., 1461–7, p. 26. He fled to Holland on 29 Sept. 1470 with Edward IV (*Warkworth's Chronicle* (Camden Soc., 1839), p. 11).

Sir Richard Tunstall 23 Oct. 1470–11 April 1471

C.P.R., 1467–77, p. 227. On 11 April 1471 Edward IV entered London (*Historie of the Arrivall of Edward IV in England* (Camden Soc., 1838), p. 17).

William, Lord Hastings April 1471–13 June 1483

Presumably he resumed his duties as chamberlain, without

formality, immediately after Edward's entry into London, since Tunstall's appointment was, from Yorkist point of view, null and void. Sir Clements R. Markham argued in his *Richard III* (London, 1906), p. 99, that Hastings was executed on 20 June, but Dr. J. Gairdner's arguments for traditional date of 13 June (*E.H.R.*, VI. 454–5) seem to be clinched by reference in official and contemporary Inquisitiones post Mortem (*C.P.*, VI. 373 (f)).

Francis, Viscount Lovell   Before 14 Aug. 1483–22 Aug. 1485

At Richard III's coronation (Bentley, *Excerpta Historica*, p. 382). He was, of course, a fugitive after the battle of Bosworth and was attainted in Nov. 1485 (*R.P.*, VI. 276a).

C. *Treasurers of the Household*

Sir John Fogge   March 1461–(1467)

Already treasurer in March 1461 (E 101/411/11), E 101/412/2 shows that he was still treasurer on 30 Sept. 1467. This account-book proves that *H.P.* II. 474, must be wrong when it makes Howard already treasurer in 1466.

Sir John Howard   (1467)–1474
(Lord Howard, 1470)
(Duke of Norfolk, 1483)

Already treasurer on 25 Oct. 1468 (*C.P.R., 1467–77*, p. 98). Still treasurer on 15 Feb. 1474 (*Storey*, p. 92).

Sir John Elrington   Sept. 1474–(Feb. 1483)

E 101/412/5 shows that he was cofferer until 30 Sept. 1474, and E 101/412/3, which records payments of household debts for years 11–14 Edward IV, describes Elrington as 'nuper coferarius hospicij domini regis Edwardi quarti'. Already treasurer by 8 Dec. 1474 (*C.P.R., 1467–77*, p. 477) he was still 'tresorer of the kinges house' when he made his will at Newcastle on 11 July 1482. His will was proved at Lambeth on 5 Feb. 1483 (P.C.C. 8 Logge).

Richard, Lord Beauchamp of Powick, 1483

Acting on 4 June 1483 (*Storey*, p. 92).

Sir William Hopton   1483

A contemporary account of Richard III's coronation names his household treasurer as Sir William Hampton (*Excerpta Historica*, p. 382). Hopton was appointed 4 July 1483 and died 7 Feb. 1484 (*Storey*, p. 92).

Sir Richard Croft   ? 1484–1485

See *Storey*, p. 92, for references to him as treasurer in Receipt Rolls on 13 May 1484 and 20 May 1485. *H.P.*, II. xliii, includes Edmund Chaderton among household treasurers; but this is due to a confusion between treasurers of the household and treasurers of the chamber of the household (see List F, below). Cf. *C.P.R., 1485–94*, p. 474, for reference to him as 'late treasurer of the household of the present king and of Richard III'.

D. *Controllers of the Household*

Sir John Scott   1461–(1470)

Already controller in March 1461 (E 101/411/11) and still holding this office on 12 May 1469 (*Foedera*, V, Part 2, p. 170).

Sir William Parr   (1471)–(1475)

D.N.B. says that 'when Edward IV returned from exile in 1471 Parr met him at Nottingham, and was rewarded with the controllership of the household, which he held till Edward's death'; but this ignores Wingfield's tenure of the office. Parr must have been out of office by 14 April 1475, when Wingfield is described in a charter as controller of the household (*C. Ch. R., 1427–1516*, p. 243).

Sir Robert Wingfield   (1475)–1481

Still controller in Sept. 1480 (E 101/412/11), he was described on 13 Nov. 1481 as deceased (*C.P.R., 1476–85*, p. 285).

Sir William Parr   1481–1483

Still controller on 17 April 1483 (*Letters and Papers . . . of Richard III and Henry VII* (ed. J. Gairdner, Rolls Series), I. 5). *H.P.*, II. xlii states that he held office 'till death Aug./Nov. 1483' whereas *H.P.*, I. 664 says that he was controller until May 1483. Patent roll records him as deceased by 26 Feb. 1484 (*C.P.R., 1476–85*, p. 409).

Sir Robert Percy   1483–1485

Controller by 23 March 1484 (*ibid.*, p. 434). Markham, *op. cit.*, p. 145, says that he was of Scotton, near Knaresborough, and was slain at Bosworth; but in March 1488 a general pardon and restitution of goods was granted to Robert Percy, late of Scotton, co. York (*C.P.R., 1485–94*, p. 222). Markham makes John Buck succeed Percy as controller and hold office at time of Bosworth; but he gives no references for these assertions (pp. 145, 246), and usually reliable Croyland Chronicle, in telling of Percy's flight from Bosworth Field, calls him 'contrarotulator hospitii Regii' (*Croyland Chron.*, p. 574).

Contemporary account of Richard's coronation gives name of then controller as Sir *Thomas* Percy (*Excerpta Historica*, p. 382); but this is doubtless a slip.

E. *Cofferers of the Household*

John Kendale   1461–(1470)

This John Kendale was not the man who was later secretary to Richard III, as stated by J. Otway-Ruthven (*op. cit.*, p. 79), R. Davies (York Records (London, 1843), pp. 164–5), and B. P. Wolffe (*E.H.R.*, LXXI (1956), 27); for in 1475 he was already described as 'come to old age and debility' (*C.P.R., 1467–77*, p. 544), and in 1482 'because he has come to old age and debility' was given a place as one of knights of king's alms in college of St. George's at Windsor (*C.P.R., 1476–85*, p. 296). By May 1483 Richard Tilles, clerk controller of Richard III's household could, in petition to king, refer to 'the deth of Sir John Kendale, late one of the almesse knightes within your collage of Wyndesore' (Nichols, *Grants of Edward V*, p. 50). There seem to have been, in fact, at least four John Kendales who appear in royal records of Yorkist period—(*a*) cofferer of Edward IV, (*b*) secretary to Richard III (as duke and then as king), (*c*) brother of Order of St. John of Jerusalem (e.g. *C.P.R., 1467–77*, p. 506), and (*d*) yeoman of crown under Richard III (*C.P.R., 1476–85*, pp. 367, 525, 546). The John Kendale described as 'notary alias scryvener, alias yoman, alias late of York, clerk', to whom general pardon was granted in 1474 (*C.P.R., 1467–77*, p. 440) may be a fifth, and the John Kendal, citizen and pewterer of City of London, whose will was proved at Lambeth on 23 July 1468 may be a sixth (P.C.C. 24 Godyn).

The John Kendale who was cofferer was already holding this office in 1461 (E 101/411/11) and was still cofferer at Michaelmas 1468 (E 101/412/2, f. 36a).

John Elrington   1471–1474

E 101/412/3 (account book of cofferer, 11–14 Ed. IV) makes it clear that he was cofferer from at least May 1471. This account, compiled after Sept. 1474, refers to him as 'nuper coferarius hospicij domini regis Edwardi quarti'; and it appears from E 101/412/5 that he was cofferer until 30 Sept. 1474. He remained an esquire until after he became treasurer (*C.P.R., 1467–77*, pp. 489, 596).

Richard Jeny   1479
James Blundell   1479–1481

E 101/412/10, ff. 2a–3b. This is account-book of Sir John Elrington, treasurer of the household, for 18–19 Ed. IV. Some receipts are stated to have been given to Richard Jeny as cofferer, and still more to Jacques or James Blundell as cofferer; so presumably one succeeded other in office during year. Blundell was native of Normandy who acquired letters of denization in 1471 (*C.P.R.*, *1467–77*, p. 297). He is also stated to be cofferer in E 101/412/12, an indenture as to delivery of money by treasurer of exchequer to treasurer of household, 20–21 Ed. IV.

John Belle 1483–(1485)

Named as 'coferer of the kyngs hous' in Great Wardrobe account for 1483 (F. Grose, *The Antiquarian Repertory*, I. 53).

F. *Treasurers of the Chamber and Keepers of the King's Jewels*

William Porte 1461–(1465)

E 101/411/11. Still in office in April 1464 (*C.P.R.*, *1461–7*, p. 326) and may have continued to hold office until 1465.

Thomas Vaughan 29 June 1465–(1483)

Ibid., p. 459. He is still called treasurer of chamber on 27 May 1482, in commission of peace for Hertfordshire; but he is described merely as knight on 18 Feb. 1483 in commission of peace for Oxfordshire, although in July 1481 he had still been called treasurer of chamber in commission for same shire (*C.P.R.*, *1476–85*, pp. 561, 569).

Edmund Chaderton 26 April 1484–1485

Ibid., p. 449. Keepership of king's jewels may have been separated from treasurership of chamber after Vaughan's execution; for whereas Vaughan's patent of appointment had made him 'treasurer of the king's chamber and master of the king's jewels', Chaderton received appointment only as 'treasurer and receiver of the king's chamber'. *H.P.*, II. xlii includes him among household treasurers. On 14 Nov. 1485 general pardon was granted to him as 'late treasurer of the chamber to Richard III' (*C.P.R.*, *1485–94*, p. 41). He lived until 1499 (R. Newcourt, *Repertorium Ecclesiasticum Parochiale Londinense*, I (1708), 131.

G. *Deans of the Chapel*

William Say 1461–1468

C.P.R., *1461–7*, p. 11; still dean at Michaelmas, 1467 (E 101/412/2, f. 36a). Dean of St. Paul's since 1457, he was dead by 7 Dec. 1468 (P.C.C. 26 Godyn; C.N.L. Brooke, 'The Deans of St. Paul's, *c.* 1090–1499', *B.I.H.R.*, XXIX (1956), 243).

Thomas Bonyfaunt (1468)–(1470)

Described as dean of king's chapel on 23 Feb. 1469 (*C.C.R.*, *1468–76*, p. 51). Dead by 16 Nov. 1470 (P.C.C. 31 Godyn; cf. Brooke, *A History of St. Paul's Cathedral* (ed. W. R. Matthews and W. M. Atkins, 1957), p. 94.

William Dudley (1470)–(1476)

Referred to as 'dean of the king's chapel' on 10 July 1471 and 16 May 1476 (*C.P.R.*, *1467–77*, pp. 276, 583). He resigned archdeaconry of Middlesex before 30 Oct. 1476, when he became Bishop of Durham (J. Le Neve, *Fasti Ecclesiae Anglicanae* (corrected by T. D. Hardy), I (1854), 313), so presumably he resigned deanery of royal chapel at same time.

John Gunthorpe (1476)–1483

Previously king's almoner (see List H, below). Still dean on 28 Feb. 1483 (*C.P.R.*, *1476–85*, p. 341), appointed keeper of privy seal on 27 June 1483 (*ibid.*, p. 480).

William Chauntre 16 May 1483–(June 1483)

On 16 May 1483 grant for life was made to William Chauntre of 'the deanery of the free chapel royal of the household, on the demise of John Gunthorpe, late dean' (*ibid.*, p. 348). As, however, by 11 Oct. 1483 William Beverley was described as dean of king's chapel (*ibid.*, p. 373), it looks as though William Chauntre lost his office in revolution of 1483, probably in June or July.

William Beverley (July 1483)–1485

Still dean on 30 Jan. 1485 (*ibid.*, p. 509).

H. *King's Almoners*

Thomas Wilford 1461–(1466)

E 101/411/11.

Thomas Bonyfaunt (1466)–1468

In E 101/412/2, f. 36a (account-book of treasurer of household, 6–7 Ed. IV), Thomas Bonyfaunt is described as 'clericus elemosinarum hospicij dicti domini regis'. He was made dean of chapel royal in succession to William Say, who died before 7 Dec. 1468.

John Gunthorpe 1468–1476

Referred to as king's almoner as early as 9 Dec. 1468 and as late as 17 Sept. 1476 (*C.P.R.*, *1467–77*, pp. 120, 597).

Thomas Danet   1476–1483

Referred to as king's almoner as early as 15 Nov. 1476 (*ibid.*, p. 604) and as late as 16 Feb. 1483 (*C.P.R.*, *1476–85*, p. 342). He died on 18 Sept. 1483 (Newcourt, *op. cit.*, I. 106).

Walter Felde   1483

Like William Chauntre, Walter Felde received a grant for life of his office in May 1483 (*ibid.*, p. 349) and like him must have fallen victim to revolution of this year; for by 4 Dec. 1483 we find John Taillour named as king's almoner (*ibid.*, p. 374).

John Taillour   1483–1485

Still in favour in Jan. 1485, when he received canonry and prebend in Salisbury Cathedral (*ibid.*, p. 509), and probably remained king's almoner until Richard's downfall.

I. *King's Secretaries*

(Cf. the valuable list of secretaries supplied by Professor Otway-Ruthven in *The King's Secretary and the Signet Office in the XVth Century* (henceforth referred to as *Otway-Ruthven*) pp. 153–5, which has been drawn on here.)

John Bothe   (1462)–(1465)

Cal. Papal Registers, Vol. XI (1455–64), ed. J. A. Twemlow, (H.M.S.O., 1921), p. 630, notes John Bothe as a secretary of Edward IV on 18 Aug. 1462; *Otway-Ruthven*, p. 155, gives Bothe's final date as 1464, but he was still secretary in Jan. 1465 (*C.C.R.*, *1461–8*, p. 307). Cf. A. H. Thompson's article on Bothe in *Diction-naire d'Histoire et de Géographie Ecclésiastiques*, IX. col. 1164.

William Hatteclyffe   (Before 1466)–(1480)

On 1 Sept. 1464 he is described as 'unus secretariorum nostrorum' (*Foedera*, V, Part II, p. 126); but between 1466 and 1480 he is usually described as 'the king's secretary' (*C.P.R.*, *1461–7*, p. 476; *C.P.R.*, *1476–85*, p. 208). Last will proved on 6 Nov. 1480 (P.C.C. 2 Logge).

Peter Courtenay   1470; (1472)–(1474)

C.P.R., *1467–77*, pp. 228, 330, 439.

William Slefeld   1474

Otway-Ruthven, pp. 136, 155.

U

Oliver King   1480–1483

    C.P.R., 1476–85, pp. 196, 208, 367.

John Kendale   1483–1485

    Ibid., p. 367: attainted in Nov. 1485 (*R.P.*, VI. 276a). For the various John Kendals of this period see the first note in List E. It seems very doubtful whether J. G. Nichols was correct (*Grants of Edward V*, pp. xxix–xxx, footnote) in identifying this secretary with Turcopolier of Rhodes who later became Grand Prior of Order of St. John of Jerusalem in England. Often said that John Kendall, the secretary, was killed at Bosworth Field (e.g. Markham, *op. cit.*, p. 145; Davies, *op. cit.*, p. 165); but Croyland Chronicler states that he was one of those who fled from battle (*Croyland Chron.*, p. 574). Quite clear that J. Otway-Ruthven, R. Davies, and B. P. Wolffe were mistaken in supposing that John Kendale, the secretary, had previously been cofferer of household of Edward IV (see above, List E), though Miss Otway-Ruthven and Dr. Wolffe were right in saying that he had previously been secretary to Richard III when he was Duke of Gloucester (*The Stonor Letters and Papers*, ed. C. L. Kingsford, Camden Soc., 1919, II. 82).

J. Keepers of the Great Wardrobe

George Darell   17 April 1461–1465

    C.P.R., 1461–7, pp. 17, 436.

Robert Cousin   4 April 1465–(Sept. 1470)

    Ibid., p. 436, for appointment; he is likely to have lost his office when Edward IV fled to Holland in Sept. 1470, in view of appointment of Sir John Plummer in his stead.

Sir John Plummer   28 Nov. 1470–(April 1471)

    C.P.R., 1467–77, p. 228, for appointment; still keeper in Feb. 1471 (*ibid.*, p. 237) and seems likely to have remained so until Edward IV re-entered London in April 1471.

Robert Cousin   (April 1471)–1476

    Ibid., p. 597.

Sir John Say   13 Oct. 1476–April 1478

    Ibid., p. 597, for appointment; died after 10 April 1478 (P.C.C. 35 Wattys; will made 10 April 1478 but no record of probate). Brother of William Say, dean of chapel royal.

Peter Curteys   11 Oct. 1480–Michaelmas 1483

He was given custody of great wardrobe from 12 April 1478 until his formal appointment as keeper on 11 Oct. 1480 (*C.P.R., 1476–85,* pp. 198, 222). He lost his office at Michaelmas 1483 (*ibid.,* pp. 438, 513).

Robert Appulby   Michaelmas 1483–(1485)

Office to which Robert Appulby was appointed on 23 June 1484, as from Michaelmas 1483, was not described as that of 'keeper of the great wardrobe' as that of Darell, Cousin, Plummer, Say, and Curteys had been, but was said to be 'custody of the king's wardrobe within the palace of Westminster' (*C.P.R., 1476–85,* p. 438); and in a confirmation of 3 Dec. 1484 this office is given as 'keeper of the king's beds and clothes within the palace there' (*sc.* of Westminster), (*ibid.,* p. 513). However, it seems likely that Robert Appulby or Appleby did succeed Peter Curteys as keeper of great wardrobe, as he undoubtedly followed Curteys as keeper of palace of Westminster, and as Curteys had to be reappointed keeper of great wardrobe in 1487 (*C.P.R., 1485–94,* p. 176).

K. *Clerks of the Greencloth*

John Parke   (1466–1467)

E 101/412/2, f. 33a.

Peter Beaupie   1471–(1480)

H.P., I. 59; *C.P.R., 1476–85,* p. 64. Will proved 5 Aug. 1480 (P.C.C. 38 Wattys).

John Belle   (1482)

C.P.R., 1476–85, p. 298.

L. *Clerks of Controlment*

Richard Bindewyn   (1463)–(1468)

Brevia directa Baronibus on K.R. Memoranda Roll for Easter Term, 11 Ed. IV, m. 4a, record allowances of expenses incurred by Richard Bindewyn and Richard Jeny in carrying out duties of clerks of controlment during period 3–8 Ed. IV (E 159/249).

Richard Jeny   (1463)–(1468)

See previous note. Richard Jeny's will was proved on 16 April 1481 (P.C.C. 3 Logge).

Peter Beaupie   Before 1471

H.P., op. et loc. cit.

Richard Tilles   (1483)

Nichols, *Grants of Edward V*, p. 50. His will was proved at Knole
on 26 Feb. 1485 (P.C.C. 21 Logge).

M. *King's Physicians*

Clear that although Black Book tells us of one physician there
were in fact usually more than one at a time. In 1468 we find three
king's physicians—William Hatteclyffe, Roger Marchall, and
Dominic de Serego—acting together, to certify a woman free of
leprosy (*C.C.R.,1468–76,*p. 30); and in 1482 James Fryse is described
as 'one of the king's physicians'. Perhaps only one was usually
resident at court at any one time.

James Fryse, Friis, or Frus   1461–1482

C.P.R., 1461–7, p. 79; *C.P.R., 1476–85*, p. 251. In 1473 letters
of denization were granted to 'James Friis, doctor in medicine, the
king's physician, born in the parts of Friesland' (*C.P.R., 1467–77*,
p. 396).

William Hatteclyffe   4 March 1461–1465

C.P.R., 1461–7, pp. 82, 444; by 1466 he had made very unusual
transition to office of king's secretary (*ibid.*, p. 476).

Roger Marchall   (1468)

C.C.R., 1468–76, p. 30. Some of the books he owned still survive
in various libraries (M. R. James, *Catalogue of MSS. in Pembroke
College, Cambridge*, p. 204).

Dominic de Serego   (1468)–(1475)

Ibid.; C.P.R., 1467–77, p. 555.

Edmund Albon   (1479)

C.P.R., 1476–85, p. 163. Died before 4 Oct. 1485 (*C.P.R.,
1485–94*, p. 12); will proved on 22 Nov. 1485 (P.C.C. 19 Logge).

William Hobbys   (1483)

C.P.R., 1476–85, p. 374; also *C.C.R., 1476–85*, p. 315. Will proved
on 17 Oct. 1488 (P.C.C. 16 Milles).

N. *King's Surgeons*

William Hobbys (1462)–(1475)

Referred to as king's surgeon as early as April 1462 (*C.P.R.*, *1461–7*, p. 182), he was described as 'principal surgeon of the body' by July 1470 (*C.P.R.*, *1467–77*, p. 211). By 1476 he was both surgeon and physician to king (*Foedera*, V, Part 3, p. 58). In view of customary inferiority of surgeons to physicians at this period, and usual difference in training, this rise from surgeon to physician is remarkable.

Richard Felde (1463)–(1475)

R.P., V. 529–30; Rymer, *op. et loc. cit.*

APPENDIX II

The Lost Ordinance of Edward III

It looks as though the Ordinance of Edward III was in the main a re-enactment of those of Edward II; perhaps that is why it was not worth preserving in later years. If a comparison be made of the numerous references in the Black Book to the statutes of Edward III with the Ordinances of Edward II, as printed in T. F. Tout's *The Place of Edward II in English History* (2nd edition, 1936), it will be seen that a close parallel can be found for the overwhelming majority of them. The following table of references will bring out this point.

Black Book, section number in this edition	Brief reference to subject matter	Tout, page number
§7	keeper of the privy seal	246
7	clerk purveyor	247
7	clerks of the marshalsea	267
7	clerks of the kitchen and the pantry	Separate in Edward II's time—256, 267
7	24 archers	272
7	liveries for horses	269
7	Number of courses at meals	276
14	Offerings	283
21	King's confessor	250
28	Squires as carvers and cupbearers	252–3
33	Sewers to serve all the dishes	255–6
35	Wardrober called 'clerk purueour', etc.	247
36	usher of the chamber purveyor for wood, litter and rushes	253
37	24 archers	272
38	allowance out of court to yeomen of the chamber	253
39	pages of the chamber not officers in Edward III's day	No mention of pages on 253
42	grooms take allowances in kind	253
50	duties of yeomen of the household	No. ref.
52	30 serjeants-at-arms	253
55	12 messengers	272

57	6 priests and their wages	272
57	clerks singers and their wages	250
64	duties of clerk of the marshalsea	252
65	clerk of works	No ref.
69	Description of treasurer of the household	No ref.
71	Wages of the controller	245
73	Payment of purveyors by the cofferer	282
74	Description of the clerks of the green-cloth	246
75	clerk controller and clerks of the green-cloth work together in the wardrobe	246
76	Description of the countinghouse	No mention
77	Duties of serjeant usher of the counting-house	248
77	Pages not officers in the countinghouse	249
78 (ii)	Daily attendance of steward, etc.	274
78 (vii)	Accountants in arrears to be committed to the marshalsea	282
80	Clerk of the kitchen also clerk of the pantry since Edward III's day	Separate in Edward II's time—256, 267
80	No groom to approach the king's table	No mention
84	King may buy wine from the yeoman trayer	No mention
87	Wages of ale-taker	260
88	Description of chief clerk of the spicery	247

BIBLIOGRAPHY

The follov ring l'st of manuscripts, books, and articles does not by any means incluae all which have been used, but only those most important for the subject. Full references are given in the introduction to the books cited there.

I. ORIGINAL SOURCES

A. MANUSCRIPTS

(1) *Library of the Society of Antiquaries, London*

MS. 118. Ordinances for the government and ordering of the household of James I.

MS. 211. The Black Book of the household of Edward IV.

(2) *The British Museum*

Harleian MSS. 293, 369, 610, 642; Add. MS. 21,993. The Black Book of the household of Edward IV.

Lansdowne MS. 1. Provisions made for the regulation of the household of Henry VI, in the 23rd year.

Add. MS. 46,354, ff. 56a–57a. Household ordinance of Edward IV, possibly 1471–2.

Harleian MS. 433, f. 269a. The Ordinance made by Richard III for his household in the north, in the 2nd year of his reign.

Sloane MS. 3479. Ordinance made for the household of Edward, Prince of Wales, in 1483.

Add. MS. 14,289. Ordinance made for the household of Edward, Prince of Wales, in 1483.

Harleian MS. 2210. Ordinances made for the household of Henry VII.

Add. MS. 17,721. Account of the great wardrobe, 13–14 Henry VI.

Add MS. 23,938. Expenses of Queen Margaret coming into England, 22 Henry VI.

Harleian MS. 4780. Account of the great wardrobe, 20 Edward IV.

Cottonian MS. Nero C VIII. Liber de compotis diversis diversorum reddituum in garderoba regis, anno quarto regis Edwardi secundi incipiente.

Add. MS. 34,122A. Household accounts of Lady Isabella of Morley, 1463–4.

Add. MS. 34,213. Household book of Anne, Duchess of Buckingham, 1465–6.

Cottonian MS. Vespasian C XIV. Expenses for the king's table, June–Sept. 1475; also the allowances for the Queen and the Prince of Wales in that year.

Add. MS. 21,480. Household book of Henry VII as kept by John Heron, Treasurer of the Chamber, 1499–1505.

Add. MS. 21,481. Household book of Henry VIII, 1509–18.

Add. MS. 35,182. Household book for year ending 30th Sept., 24 Henry VIII, as kept by Edmund Peckham, Cofferer of the household.

Egerton MS. 2604. Wages of the household of Henry VIII, 17 Henry VIII.

Harleian MS. 279, Stowe MS. 1055. Account of dishes, etc., served at various royal and other banquets in the fifteenth century.

Lansdowne MS. 59. The difference of the daily charge of the household in the reigns of Henry VII, Henry VIII, Edward VI, and Mary.

Lansdowne MS. 118. Provisions for a household in victuals, and the ancient prices thereof, temp. Henry VII.

Lansdowne MS. 86. Memorial of Gregory Lovell, former clerk of the avery (or avenery) to Lord Treasurer Burleigh on the system of promotion by seniority in the household.

Add. MS. 6032. Officials and service appropriate to various ranks of the nobility, temp. Elizabeth I.

Stowe MS. 571. Lists of officials of the royal administration (including the royal household) in the time of Edward VI and Elizabeth I.

(3) *The Public Record Office*

Wardrobe and Household Accounts (E 101 class) for the reigns of Henry VI, Edward IV (none for Edward V and Richard III), and Henry VII (E 101/408/9–E 101/415/4).

Enrolled Wardrobe and Household Accounts (E 361 class).

Exchequer Treasury of the Receipt, Miscellaneous books (E 36 class), especially No. 206, The Ordinances of 1478; No. 207, Account of the receiver-general of Elizabeth, Queen of Edward IV, 1466–7; Nos. 208–14, royal household accounts of the reign of Henry VII; No. 230, the Black Book of the household of Edward IV; No. 232, Wages for the Household in 12 Henry VIII; and No. 233, Diets of the Household, temp. Henry VIII.

Lord Steward's Department, Miscellaneous Books (L 13 class), especially No. 6, Check-roll of James I, Nos. 193 and 194, Rules for the households of George III and George IV, No. 278, The Black Book of the household of Edward IV.

Chancery Warrants under the Signet (C 81 class).

Issue and Receipt Rolls (E 403 and E 401 classes).

Duchy of Lancaster Accounts Various (D.L. 28 class); includes household accounts such as D.L. 28/1/1, 2, 3, 9, 10; 28/5/8.

King's Remembrancer's Memoranda Rolls (E 159 class), especially the Brevia directa Baronibus.

Chancery Miscellanea (C 47 class), especially Bundle 3/36, a mid-fifteenth-century copy of the Ordinance of 1445, and Bundle 4/8 A & B, Accounts of Dame Alice Bryene for 12 Henry IV–1 Henry V.

U*

Lord Chamberlain's Department, Miscellanea, No. 178, Ordinances of
    1526 and 1540 including the unprinted Roll of names of household
    officials.

(4) *The Bodleian Library, Oxford*

MS. Ashmole. 1147; MS. Dugdale 8. The Black Book of the household of
    Edward IV.
Rawlinson MS. B 47. Articles ordained by Henry VII for the regulation
    of his household.
Laud MS. Misc. 597. The Ordinances of 1526 (fine copy, possibly an
    official one).
MS. Eng. hist. b.136. The Establishment of the Household of George II,
    1727.

(5) *College of Arms, London*

Arundel MS. XVII. The Black Book of the household of Edward IV.

(6) *Guildhall Library, London*

London Letter Book L; London Journal 8. Proclamations against abuses
    of purveyance, made in 1469 and 1481.

(7) *Westminster Abbey Muniments*

No. 12158. Revenues of Richard, Duke of York, for unspecified year.
    (The revenues listed total £2,590 15s. 8¾d.)

(8) *Somerset House, London*

Wills from the Prerogative Court of Canterbury.

(9) *Muniment Room, Guildford, Surrey*

Loseley MSS. Household Accounts. Class 1087. Temp. Eliz. I–eighteenth
    century.

(10) *County Record Office, Warwick*

Household Account of Richard Beauchamp, Earl of Warwick, 1431–2.

B. PRINTED SOURCES

(i) *Ordinances and Regulations*

(a) *Royal Household*

Constitutio Domus Regis (*c.* A.D. 1136) in *Dialogus de Scaccario*, ed. C.
    Johnson (Nelson's Medieval Classics, 1950), pp. 128–35.
The Household Ordinance of 1279, in T. F. Tout, *Chapters in the Ad-
    ministrative History of Medieval England*, Vol. II (Manchester,
    1920), pp. 158–63.
The Household Ordinances of Edward II, 1318 and 1323, in T. F. Tout,
    The Place of the Reign of Edward II in English History (2nd
    edition, Manchester, 1936), pp. 244–84.

A Collection of Ordinances and Regulations for the Government of the Royal Household made in divers reigns from King Edward III to King William and Queen Mary: Also Receipts in Ancient Cookery (London, 1790, printed for the Society of Antiquaries).

The Household Ordinance of 1454, in *Proceedings and Ordinances of the Privy Council of England*, Vol. VI (ed. N. H. Nicolas, London, 1837), pp. 220 ff.

William Cecil, Lord Burghley: Queen Elizabeth's Annual Expence, Civil and Military. Part II, The Offices, Salaries, Fees, and Perquisits of Her Majesties Houshould, in F. Peck, *Desiderata Curiosa*, Vol. I (London, 1779), pp. 58–61.

A true collection as well of all the Kinges Majesties Offices and Fees in any of the Courtes at Westminster, as of all the Offices and Fees of his Majesties honorable Houshould (Anno 1606), in *Archaeologia*, Vol XV (1806), pp. 72–91.

(b) *Seignorial Households*

The Regulations and Establishment of the Household of Henry Algernon Percy, 5th Earl of Northumberland, begun 1512 (ed. T. Percy, 2nd edition, 1827). Often cited as 'The Northumberland Household Book'.

Thomas Wolsey, An Order . . . to lymitt John Earle of Oxenford in the orderinge of his Expences of Household, A.D. 1524, ed. Sir Henry Ellis in *Archaeologia*, Vol. XIX (1821), pp. 62–5.

The Household Regulations of Edward, 3rd Earl of Derby, and of Henry, 4th Earl of Derby, ed. F. R. Raines, in *Stanley Papers*, Part II (Chetham Society, Manchester, 1853), pp. 8–10, 20–2.

A Book of Orders and Rules of Anthony, Viscount Montague, in 1595, ed. S. B. D. Scott, in *Sussex Archaeological Collections*, Vol. VII (London, 1854), pp. 173–212.

A Breviate touching the Order and Governments of a Nobleman's house, with the Officers, theire places and chardge, as perticularly apearethe (1605), ed. Sir Joseph Banks, in *Archaeologia*, Vol. XIII (1800), pp. 315–89.

Instructions by Henry Percy, 9th Earl of Northumberland, touching the management of his estate, officers, etc., A.D. 1609, ed. J. H. Markland in *Archaeologia*, Vol. XXVII (1838), pp. 306–58.

Richard Braithwait: *Some rules and orders for the government of the House of an Earle set down by Richard Braithwait*, printed in the collection entitled *Miscellanea Antiqua Anglicana* (London, 1821).

(ii) *Accounts and Payments*

(a) *Royal Household*

Liber Quotidianus Contrarotulatoris Garderobae Anno Regni Regis Edwardi Primi Vicesimo Octavo (London, Society of Antiquaries, 1787).

The Account-book of Joan of Navarre (widow of Henry IV) at Leeds Castle, Kent, 1420–1, summarized, with passages in extenso, by

A. R. Myers, from the John Rylands Library MS. 238, in 'The Captivity of a Royal Witch', in the *Bulletin of the John Rylands Library*, Vol. 24 (1940), pp. 263–84.

Privy Purse Expenses of Elizabeth of York: Wardrobe Accounts of Edward IV (Abridged edition of Harleian MS. 4780, account of the great wardrobe for 20 Edward IV) (London, 1830).

Extracts from the Privy Purse Expenses of King Henry the Seventh, 1491–1505, printed by S. Bentley in *Excerpta Historica* (London, 1831), pp. 85–133.

Privy Purse Expenses of Henry VIII, 1529–32, ed. N. H. Nicolas (London, 1827).

Household Expenses of the princess Elizabeth during her residence at Hatfield, 1551–2, ed. P. C. S. Smythe, Viscount Strangford, in *Camden Miscellany*, II (1853).

The Antiquary, Vols. VI, VIII, X, XIV, XVI, XVIII contain abstracts of the accounts of Henry IV to Richard III, by Sir J. H. Ramsay (London, 1882–8).

J. P. Collier: On a State Manuscript of the Reign of Henry VIII: the property of Sir Walter Calverley Trevelyan, bart., in *Archaeologia*, XXXVI (1855), pp. 14–22. A royal household account, 1528–31.

Extracts from the Wardrobe Account of Prince Henry, eldest son of King James I, ed. W. Bray, in *Archaeologia*, XI (1794), pp. 88–96.

Inventories of the wardrobes, plate, chapel stuff, etc., of Henry Fitzroy, duke of Richmond and Katharine, princess dowager: ed. J. G. Nichols, in *Camden Miscellany*, III (1855).

Inventory of Apparel, Stuffs, &c provided for the Coronation of Richard III and his Queen, in *The Antiquarian Repertory*, ed. F. Grose & T. Astle (4 vols, 2nd edition, 1807), Vol. I, pp. 28–63.

(b) *Seignorial Households*

Les Comptes de l'Hotel du Duc de Berry, 1370–1413, in *Mémoires de la Société des Antiquaires du Centre*, Vol. 17 (1889–90) (Bourges, 1890).

E. Petit: *Itinéraires de Philippe le Hardi et de Jean sans Peur, Ducs de Bourgogne, 1363–1419* (Paris, 1888), in 'Collections de documents inédits sur l'histoire de France'.

The Household Book of Dame Alice de Bryene, Sept. 1412–Sept. 1413 (Suffolk Institute of Archaeology and Natural History, Ipswich, 1931).

Illustrations of the Manners and Expences of Antient Times in England in the 15th, 16th, and 17th centuries, printed by John Nichols for the Society of Antiquaries in 1797.

Accounts and Memoranda of John Howard, 1st Duke of Norfolk, A.D. 1462–71, ed. T. Hudson Turner, in *Manners and Household Expenses of England*, pp. lxxxv–xciii (Roxburghe Club, London, 1841).

Household Books of John, Duke of Norfolk, and Thomas, Earl of Surrey, temp. 1481–90, ed. J. P. Collier (Roxburghe Club, London, 1844.)

Extracts from the Household Books of Edward, Duke of Buckingham, by John Gage, in *Archaeologia*, Vol. XXV (1834), pp. 311–41.

Selections from the Household Accounts of Sir Thomas Lovell (1523–4) and of the Earls of Rutland (1524–1700), ed. Sir Henry Maxwell-Lyte and W. H. Stevenson in *The Duke of Rutland MSS.*, Vol. 4 (Historical Manuscripts Commission, 17th Report, London, 1905), pp. 260–558, with Appendix, pp. 559–73.

Extracts from the Household Books of the Willoughbys of Wallaton, ed. W. H. Stevenson, in *The Middleton MSS.* (Hist. MSS. Comm., 1911), pp. 324–624.

Extracts from the household accounts of Richard Bertie, Lord Willoughby, 1560–2, ed. Mrs. S. C. Lomas, in *Historical Manuscripts Commission, 13th Report* (London, 1893), Appendix, Part VI, pp. 256–61 and *The Earl of Ancaster MSS* (Hist. MSS. Comm., 1907), pp. 459–73.

Household Accounts of Edward and Henry, Earls of Derby, 1561–90, by the Comptroller William ffarington, Esq., ed. Rev. F. R. Raines (Chetham Society, Manchester, 1853).

Selections from the household books of Sir William Fairfax, ed. by Mrs. S. C. Lomas, in *Historical MSS. Commission, Report on the MSS. in Various Collections*, Vol. 2 (1903), pp. 67–86.

The Booke of the Howsold Charges and other Paiments laid out by the Lord North and his commandement, 1575–81, ed. W. Stevenson, in *Archaeologia*, Vol. XIX (1821), pp. 283–301.

Extracts from the Household Book of Thomas Cony of Basingthorpe, co. Lincoln, 1549–99, by Edmund Turner, in *Archaeologia*, Vol. XI (1794), pp. 22–33.

Selections from the household books of Lord William Howard of Naworth Castle, 1612–40, ed. Rev. George Ornsby (Surtees Society, Vol. 68, 1878).

(iii) *General*

Bentley, S.: *Excerpta Historica* (London, 1833), for various documents but especially accounts of the marriage of Princess Margaret to Charles the Bold in 1468 and of the coronation of Richard III.

Brooke, Mr.: The Ceremonial of Making the King's Bed, temp. Henry VIII, in *Archaeologia*, Vol. IV (1777), pp. 311–14.

Calendars of Patent Rolls, especially for Henry VI, Edward IV, Edward V, Richard III, and Henry VII (H.M.S.O., 1903–16).

Calendars of Close Rolls for Henry VI and Edward IV (H.M.S.O., 1933–54).

Calendars of Fine Rolls for Henry VI and Edward IV (to 1471) (H.M.S.O., 1935–49).

Chambers, R. W. (ed.): *A Fifteenth Century Courtesy Book* (E.E.T.S., 1914, Original Series, No. 148).

Fortescue, Sir John: *The Governance of England*, ed. C. Plummer (Oxford, 1885).

Furnivall, F. J. (ed.): *The Babees Book* and other works on etiquette (E.E.T.S., 1868, Original Series, No. 32).

Italian Relation. *A relation, or rather a true account, of the island of England, c.* 1500. Translated from the Italian by C. A. Sneyd (Camden Society, London, 1847).

La Marche, Olivier de: *L'État de la Maison du Duc Charles de Bourgogne dict le Hardy*, ed. H. Beaune and J. d'Arbaumont, Vol. 3 (Librairie Renouard, 1885) of his *Mémoires* (3 vols. 1883–8), which contain a long account of the festivities (organized by him) on the occasion of the marriage of Charles the Bold to Margaret of York.

Leland. *Joannis Lelandi Antiquarii De Rebus Britannicis Collectanea*, Vol. VI (London, 1774), contains 'The Inthronization of Archbishops Nevill and Warham'.

Newton, A. P.: A list of Records of the Greencloth extant in 1610, in *English Historical Review*, Vol. XXXIV (1919), pp. 237–41.

Noblesse, The Boke of (ed. J. G. Nichols, Roxburghe Club, 1860).

Paston Letters, ed. J. Gairdner (4 vols. Edinburgh, 1910).

Rotuli Parliamentorum, Vols. 5 and 6 (London, n.d.).

Rozmittal. *Des böhmischen Herrn Leos von Rozmittal Ritter-, Hof- und Pilger-Reise durch die Abendlande, 1465–7* (Stuttgart, 1844).

Rymer, T.: *Foedera, Conventiones, Literae, etc.* (10 vols. Hague edition, 1737–45), especially Vol. 5.

Thomas, A. H. and I. D. Thornley (eds.): *The Great Chronicle of London* (London, 1938).

Whethamstede: *Registrum Abbatiae Johannis Whethamstede Abbatis Monasterii Sancti Albani*, ed. H. T. Riley (2 vols., Rolls Series, 1872–3).

Wood-Legh, K. L. (ed.): *A Small Household of the XVth century* (Manchester, 1956).

II. SECONDARY WORKS

Barnard, F. P.: *Edward IV's French Expedition of 1475* (Oxford, 1925).

Bray, W.: An account of the obsolete office of purveyor to the king's household, in *Archaeologia*, Vol. VIII (1787), pp. 328–62.

Cartellieri, O.: *The Court of Burgundy* (London, 1929).

Chambers, E. K.: *The Elizabethan Stage* (Oxford, 1923), Vol, I. chapter 2.

Drummond, J. C., and Wilbraham, A.: *The Englishman's Food* (London, 1939).

Dietz, F. C.: *English Government Finance, 1485–1558* (Urbana, 1920).

Elton, G. R.: *The Tudor Revolution in Government* (Cambridge, 1953).

Fox, E. J.: *Members of the Household of Edward IV*. Thesis presented for the degree of B.A. in the University of Liverpool in May, 1954.

Gairdner, J.: *History of the Life and Reign of Richard III* (New edition, Cambridge, 1898).

History of Parliament, 1439–1509, ed. Wedgwood, J. C. Vol. 1, *Biographies of the members of the Commons House, 1439–1509* (London, 1936), Vol. II, *Register of the Ministers and of the Members of both Houses, 1439–1509* (H.M.S.O., 1938).

Johnson, C.: The System of Account in the Wardrobe of Edward I, in *Transactions of the Royal Historical Society*, 4th Series, Vol. VI (1923), pp. 50–72.

Johnson, J. H.: The System of Account in the Wardrobe of Edward II, in *T.R.H.S.*, 4th Series, Vol. XII (1929), pp. 75–104.

Johnson, J. H.: The King's Wardrobe and Household, in *The English Government at Work, 1327–36*, ed. Willard, J. F. and Morris, W. A., Vol. I (Cambridge, Massachusetts, 1940).

Jolliffe, J. E. A.: *Angevin Kingship* (London, 1955).

Jones, D. H.: *A Household Account of Queen Elizabeth Woodville*. Thesis presented for the degree of B.A. in the University of Liverpool in May, 1949.

Jones, P. V. B.: *The Household of a Tudor Nobleman* (University of Illinois Studies, Vol. VI, 1918).

Lander, J. R.: Edward IV. The Modern Legend and a Revision, in *History*, Vol. XLI (1956), pp. 38–52.

Lander, J. R.: The Yorkist Council and Administration, 1461–85, in *English Historical Review*, Vol. LXXIII (1958), pp. 27–46.

Newton, A. P.: The King's Chamber under the Early Tudors, in *English Historical Review*, Vol. XXXII (1917), pp. 348–72.

Newton, A. P.: Tudor Reforms in the Royal Household, in *Tudor Studies presented to A. F. Pollard*, ed. Seton-Watson, R. W. (London, 1924).

Otway-Ruthven, J.: *The King's Secretary and the Signet Office in the XVth Century* (Cambridge, 1939).

Parker, J. H.: *Some Account of the Domestic Architecture in England from Richard II to Henry VIII* (2 vols., Oxford, 1859).

Pegge, S.: *Curialia* (London, 1782).

Pegge, S.: *Curialia Miscellanea* (London, 1818), especially pp. 1–70 on the royal household, William I to Edward IV.

Ramsay, J. H.: *Lancaster and York* (2 vols., Oxford, 1892).

Richardson, W. C.: *Tudor Chamber Administration, 1485–1547* (University of Louisiana State Press, Baton Rouge, 1952).

Scofield, C. L.: *Life and Reign of Edward the Fourth* (2 vols., London, 1923).

Somerville, R.: *The Duchy of Lancaster, Vol. I, 1265–1603* (London, 1953).

Steel, A.: *The Receipt of the Exchequer, 1377–1485* (C.U.P., 1954).

Stretton, G.: The Travelling Household of the Middle Ages, in *Journal of the British Archaeological Association* (London, 1935), New Series, Vol., 40, pp. 75–103.

Thompson, G. S.: *Two Centuries of Family History* (London, 1930).

Tout, T. F.: *Chapters in the Administrative History of Medieval England* (6 vols., Manchester, 1920–33).

Warner, R.: *Antiquitates Culinariae* (London, 1791).

Wright, T.: *History of Domestic Manners and Sentiments in England during the Middle Ages* (London, 1862).

INDEX

(Figures in bold type indicate the more important references)

Abingdon, Henry, 249
Acatours, 67, 221, 222
Acatry, catery, 17, 39, 59, 73, 164, **228,** 257, 269
Aegidio Colonna, 236
Albon, Edmund, 296
Ale-takers, 15, 23, **184-6, 226,** 260
All-night, ceremony of, 237, 248, 259
Almoner, 17, 65, **70,** 106, 150, 205, 214, 215, 218, **224,** 225, **292-3**
Almonry, 138, 193, 205, 214, 215
Alton, John, 199, 263
Anne, Queen, 246
Anstis, John, 55
Apothecary, 16, 118, 125, 245
Appulby, Robert, 295
Aprons, 133, 248
Apryce, Richard, 243
Aquinas, St. Thomas, 16, 250
Argill (Hardgill), Edward, 200, 264
Aristotle, 13, 27, 34, 39, 76, 80, 86, 233, 235, 250, 266
Armory, 71, 116, 121, 176
Audley, Sir John, 243
Augustine, 13, 80, 250
Avenar, 65, 166, 193
Avenery, 39, 167, 257

Bagham, Thomas, 199, 263
Bakehouse, 15, 23, 39, 59, 72, 164, **165-9,** 173, **226,** 256, 257
Banaster, Gilbert, 249
Banneret, 89, 106-8, 237, 240
Bar (of Cellar and Buttery), 259
Barber, 16, 125
Barkly, Sir Maurice (see Berkeley, Sir Maurice)
Baron, 72, 89, 91, 95, 98, **103-4,** 133, 147, 151, 153, 165, **224,** 237, 240
Bartholomew Anglicus, 234
Beauchamp, Richard Lord Beauchamp of Powick, 288
Beaufort, Henry, Bishop of Winchester, 252
Beaupie, Peter, 33, 295, 296
Beds, Yeomen of, 71, 119, 244
Belle, John, 291, 295
Berkeley (Barkly), Sir Maurice, 32, 199, 263

Bernard, St., of Clairvaux, 18, 76, 163, 233
Beverley, William, 292
Bible, 13, 16, 19, 34, 76, 87, 144, 165, 233, 234, 251, 257
Bindewyn, Richard, 33, 268, 295
Bishop, 96, **100,** 189, 203, **224**
Black Book of the Household of Edward IV, 4, 9, 12, **13-34,** 35, 38, 39, 40, 41, 42, 44, 49, 50, **51-6,** 59, **76-197,** 232, **233-62,** 264, 269
Blonte (Blount), John, 199, 263
Blount, Thomas, 232
Blundell, James, 43, 290, 291
Boiling-house, 17, 228
Bolters, 72, 257
Bonyfaunt, Thomas, 292
Borough, Sir Thomas (see Brought, Sir Thomas)
Bothe, John, 293
Bourchier, Henry, Earl of Essex, 251, 286-7
Bourchier, Thomas, Cardinal, Archbishop of Canterbury, 15, 29, 30, 86
Bourchier, Viscount, 239
Bows, Yeomen of the, 116
Bray, William, Clerk of the Board of Greencloth, 52, 55
Brekenok (Brecknock), John, 252
Briton, William, 81, 234
Brought (Borough, Burgh), Sir Thomas, 199, 262
Buckingham, Anne, Duchesse of, 238
Buckingham, Duke of, 5
Buckingham, John, Bishop of Lincoln, Treasurer of the Household, 17, 147, 252
Burgh, Sir Thomas (see Brought, Sir Thomas)
Burgundy, Court of, 3, 4, 18, 32, 252, 253, 259
Burke, Edmund, 49
Burton, Robert, 200, 264
Butler, 165, 235, 258
Butler, Chief, 15, 59, 87, 101, **174-6**
Buttery, 15, 23, 63, 64, 71, 164, 178, **181-3,** 184, 185, 186, 202, 206, 208, 216, 217, 220, **226,** 230, 254, 259, 260

309

Cardinal of Canterbury (see Bourchier, Thomas, Cardinal, Archbishop of Canterbury)
Carver, 2, 32, 34, 41, 42, **69, 106, 107,** 112, 147, 201, 215, 217, **225,** 237, **240**
Cassibellan (see Cassivellaunus)
Cassiodorus, 13, 56, 80, 234
Cassivellaunus, King, 14, 18, 83
Castellione, Gualtiero de, 234
Catery (see Acatry)
Cellar, 15, 63, 64, 73, 164, 175, 176, **177–81,** 184, 187, 202, 206, 208, 216, 217, 220, **226,** 230, 254, 256, 259, 260
Chaderton, Edmund, 289
Chamber, Bed, 14, 201, 237
Chamber, Great, 2, 14, 15, 90, 106, 120, 201, 237
Chamber, Grooms of the, 16, 65, 120–121, 200, 201, 243
Chamber, King's, 16, 26, 27, 35, 59, 65, **90–3,** 94, 100, 101, 103, 104, 106, 108, 110, 111, 112, 114, 115, 116, 117, 119, 120, 121, 122, 125, 128, 134, 135, 144, 150, 152, 154, 155, 159, 170, 175, 179, 180, 182, 184, 189, 190, 191, 194, 197, 201, 202, 203, 205, 209, 214, 218, 220, 229, 247, 255, 261, 265
Chamber, Knights of the, 16, 125, 240, 262
Chamber, pages of the, 71, 121, 200
Chamber, privy, 14, 106, 201, 234, 242, 264
Chamber, Treasurer of the, 22, 49, 103, 121, 122, 124, 244, 245, 291
Chamber, Treasury of the, 22, 23, 39, 105, 116, 117, **121–3,** 125, 131, 133, 138, 139, 158, 178, 190, 192
Chamber, Yeomen of the, 22, 70, **117,** 118, 120, 126, 200, 201, 226, 233, 243, 244, 245
Chamberlain, Great, 16, 21, 101, 114, 117
Chamberlain, King's, 22, 23, 32, 39, 42, **69,** 89, 90, 91, **104–6,** 111, 114, 116, 117, 118, 119, 120, 121, 122, 123, 125, 126, 127, 130, 131, 133, 137, 138, 139, 162, 200, 201, 202, 204, 215, 218, **224,** 237, **239–40,** 251, 252
Chancellor, 16, 21, 96, **100–1,** 163
Chancery, 164, 251, 254, 257
Chandlery, 15, 63, 73, 132, 156, 186, 187, **190–2,** 194, 208, 216, 219, **227,** 244, 260, 261
Chany, John, 199, 263
Chapel, Children of the, **136–7,** 138, 249

Chapel, Dean of the, 16, **70,** 91, **133–5,** 138, 139, 203, 213, **224,** 230, 248, **291–2,** 294
Chapel, Yeomen of the, **136,** 139
Chaplains, 2, 16, 41, **69,** 70, 91, 111, 133, 134, **135–6,** 137, 201, 210, 215, 223, 224, **225,** 248, 249
Charles I, 237, 241
Charles II, 237, 241
Chauntre, William, 292
Check-Rolls, **23, 24,** 41, 66, 101, 111, 113, 115, 116, 117, 122, 124, 128, 132, 133, 135, 137, 138, 139, 148, 151, 153, 158, 159, 177, 185, 232, 239, 241, 267
Cheyne, John (see Chany, John)
Chirke, Cherk, David, 249
Clarence, George, Duke of, 12, 15, 20, 21, 23, 29, 30, 31, 35, 37, 41, 53, 86, 237, 238, 257, 266, 267
Clerk, John, 245
Closet, Clerk of the, 39, **137,** 138, **225,** 249
Cofferer of the Household, 15, 22, 24, 25, 29, 33, 34, 39, 42, 43, 44, 49, 67, 71, 142, 146, **150–2,** 153, 156, 161, 163, 173, 177, 198, 207, 209, 213, 215, 221, 223, **224,** 226, 253, 254, 255, 265, 266, 268, **290–1**
Cofferer's Clerk, 39, 255
Common Pleas, Chief Justice of the, 16, 21, 69, 101
Common Pleas, Court of, 163
Confectionary, 15, 186, **188–90,** 191, 196, **227,** 260, 261
Confessor, King's, **69,** 91, **100,** 133, 201, 233, 237, 239
Controller of the Household, 15, 24, 25, 29, 33, 39, 43, 64, 66, 67, 71, 87, 89, 90, 111, 112, 117, 119, 121, 125, 127, 130, 131, 132, 134, **136,** 137, 138, 139, 142, 143, 144, 145, **147–52,** 155, 156, 161, 162, 163, 171, 173, 174, 175, 176, 177, 178, 179, 183, 185, 192, 193, 198, 204, 205, 207, 209, 215, 218, 220, 221, 223, **224,** 232, 242, 246, 251, 252, 253, 258, 262, 265, 268, **289–90**
Controlment, Clerk of the, 24, 25, 29, 33, 39, 42, 43, 48, 49, 64, 71, 112, 142, 146, 153, **154–6,** 158, 161, 177, 178, 179, 188, 189, 204, 208, 213, 215, 217, 218, 219, 223, **225,** 226, 255, 256, 260, 261, 268, **295–6**
Cook, 123, 217, **226,** 227
Cornbrugh, Avery, 243
Council, King's, 27, 28, 127, 201, 202, 203, 211, 241
Countinghouse, 21, 22, 23, 24, 25, 26, 27, 28, 29, 33, 41, 43, 48, 49, 57, 63,

Countinghouse—*cont.*
64, 66, 67, 68, **71,** 85, 89, 90, 91, 92,
93, 101, 102, 104, 105, 113, 114, 115,
116, 117, 118, 120, 121, 122, 125,
127, 128, 130, 133, 134, 135, 138,
139, 140, 143, 144, 145, 147, 148,
149, 150, 151, 152, 154, **156–65,** 167,
169, 170, 171, 172, 173, 174, 175,
176, 177, 178, 179, 180, 181, 182,
183, 184, 185, 186, 187, 188, 189,
190, 191, 192, 194, 196, 198, 202,
203, 204, 206, 207, 208, 209, 213,
215, 216, 218, 219, 220, 221, 222,
223, **226,** 235, 248, 254, 256, 257,
261, 268
Courtenay, Peter, 293
Cousin, Robert, 294
Cristmasse, Stephen, 257
Croft, Sir Richard, 289
Cromwell, Thomas, 48, 49
Crown, Clerk of the, 16, **139,** 163, 176,
177, 249, 259
Crown, Yeomen of the, 22, **116,** 117,
119, 210, 226, 242, 243, 244
Cupbearer, 2, 32, 41, 42, **69, 106,** 107,
112, 201, 215, 217, **225,** 237, 240
Cup-house, 15
Curteys, Peter, 46, 47, 295

Danet, Thomas, 293
Darell, George, 294
Daubeney, William, 245
Davy, John, 250
Debeny, Sir Gilbert (Debenham), 200,
249, 250, 263
De la Pole, Richard, 235
De la Pole, William, Earl of Suffolk,
252
Dennis, Sir William, 200
Derby, Henry, Earl of (A.D. 1587), 1,
239
D'Ewes, Sir Simonds, 17, 27, 32, 53,
54, 57, 58, 59, 60, 266
Domus Providencie, 17, 24, **141–2**
Domus Regie Magnificencie, 15, **86**
Dudley, William, 292
Dugdale, Sir William, 55
Duke, **69,** 89, **94–6,** 173, 189, 203,
223, 233, 237
Dune, Doune, Donne, Sir John, 199,
262

Earl, 71, 89, 91, 96, **98–100,** 144, 173,
189, **224**
Edgar, King, 235
Edmund, King, 113
Edward I, 247, 250
Edward II, King, 8, 19, 38, 84, 235,
250, 298

Edward III, King, 14, 16, 17, 19, 25,
38, **84–6,** 100, 118, 121, 131, 133,
136, 146, 148, 150, 154, 158, 160,
161, 169, 170, 171, 173, 175, 181,
185, 187, 235, 240, 242, 250, 252,
256, 257, 260, **298–9**
Edward IV, King, 4, 8, 9, 10, 11, 12,
13, 18, 21, 22, 29, 30, 31, 32, 33, 35,
36, 37, 38, 41, 43, 44, 45, 46, 47, 48,
54, 55, 57, 198, 211, 232, 236, 240,
241, 242, 243, 244, 245, 246, 247,
248, 249, 250, 251, 253, 259, 262,
265, 266, 267, 268, 269, 287, 288,
289, 290, 294, 295
Edward V, 10, 11, 39, 239, 244, 269,
287
Elizabeth I, Queen, 238, 239
Elizabeth Wydeville, Queen, 21, 28,
38, 237, 247
Elrington, John, 33, 34, 35, 36, 37, 42,
43, 252, 254, 265, 266, 288, 290
Epicurus, 81, 234
Etiquette, 2, 3
Ewry, Yeoman of the, 2
Ewry and Napery, 15, 74, 124, 125,
181, 186, **192–5,** 196, **227,** 256, 260.

Falconers, 71, 233
Fastolf, Sir John, 258
Felde, Richard, 297
Felde, Walter, 293
Feriby, John, 268
Feris, Sir Henry (Ferrers, Sir Henry),
199, 263
Fiennes, Sir John (see Fynes, Sir
John)
Fogge, Sir John, 235, 252, 288
Forster, John, 243
Forster, Roland, 245
Friiz (Fryse, Frus), James, 245, 296
Fynes, Sir John, 200, 263

Gate, 74, 160, 203, 204, 214
Geoffrey of Monmouth, 235
George II, King, 50
George III, King, 254
Grammar, Master of, 137, 249
Gray (Grey), Sir Thomas, 199, 263
Grayston, Grayson, Greyson, Thomas,
243
Greencloth, Board of, 52
Greencloth, Clerks of the, 24, 25, 29,
33, 39, 42, 43, 44, 48, 49, 67, 142,
146, 150, 151, **152–4,** 156, 161, 177,
178, 186, 206, 208, 213, 215, 221,
223, **225,** 226, 248, 254, 255, 259,
261, 265, 268, **295**
Gruthuyse, Louis de, 4
Gunthorpe, John, 292

Hall, 2, 15, 27, 39, 63, 65, 66, **71,** 90,
91, 93, 94, 100, 101, 103, 106, 108,
110, 111, 112, 115, 116, 119, 122,
123, 125, 126, 128, 130, 131, 133,
134, 135, 137, 139, 143, 144, 145,
150, 151, 152, 154, 155, 159, 165,
166, 168, 169, 171, 173, 175, 177,
179, 180, 182, 184, 187, 189, 190,
191, 194, 195, 196, 197, 203, 204,
205, 209, 210, 214, 216, 217, 218,
220, 221, 223, 224, 225, 226, **228,**
229, 247, 255, 265
Hall, Marshalls and Ushers of the, 17,
63, 64, 71, 91, 106, 117, 122, 134,
143, 145, 153, 156, 165, 171, 179,
191, 195, 204, 210, 214, 258
Harbingers, 17, 71, 74, 95, 98, 100,
105, 111, 115, 116, 117, 118, 121,
123, 124, 127, 128, 130, 137, 138,
152, 158, 170, 187, 193, **226**
Hardgill, Edward (see Argill, Edward)
Hare, Robert, 55
Harthacnut, King, 14, 83
Harvey, John (see Heruie, John)
Hastings, Sir Raphe (Hastings, Sir
Ralph), 199, 243, 262
Hastings, William, Lord Hastings,
32, 239, 240, 287
Hatteclyffe, William, 293, 296
Haward, Thomas (see Howard,
Thomas)
Henchmen, 71, **126,** 127, 138, 246
Henchmen, Master of, 126
Henry I, King, 25, **83,** 158, 160, 256
Henry III, King, 248
Henry IV, King, 7, 252
Henry V, King, 6, 134, 248
Henry VI, King, 5, 6, 7, 8, 9, 10, 17,
21, 35, 44, 45, 46, 47, 50, 51, 63,
232, 236, 241, 244, 248, 250, 252,
253, 267, 268
Henry VII, King, 4, 8, 20, 22, 45, 46,
47, 48, 49, 54, 58, **229–30,** 250, 259,
266, 268, 269
Henry VIII, King, 8, 53, 54, 237, 239,
241
Henry of Blois, Bishop of Winchester,
234
Henry of Huntingdon, 235
Henry, Prince of Wales, son of James
I, 54
Heralds (Kings of Arms and Pur-
suivants), 48, 70, 130
Herbert, Sir William, 240
Heruie (Harvey), John, 32, 200,
264
Higden, Ranulph, 234, 235, 247
Hobbys, William, 245, 296, 297
Hopton, Sir William, 288
Hotoft, John, 252

Howard, Sir John, later Duke of
Norfolk, 34, 238, 240, 252, 288
Howard, Thomas, Earl of Surrey, 199,
263, 287
Huguccio, 81, 234
Humphrey, Duke of Gloucester, 237

James I, 27, 53
Jeny, Richard, 33, 43, 268, 290, 295
Jewel-house (see Chamber, Treasury of
the)

Kendale, John, 254, 290, 294
King, Oliver, 294
Kitchen, 17, 39, 64, 73, 85, 100, 112,
113, 154, 155, 167, 169, 177, 178,
179, 180, 182, 183, 185, 187, 188,
196, 205, 208, 217, 218, **225, 227,**
257, 258, 259, 260

Langton, Thomas, 57, 211
Larder, 17, 39, 73, **228**
Laundry, 15, 17, 74, **195–7, 227,** 262
Lawrence, Richard, 245
Lincoln, Bishop of, Chancellor
(Thomas Rotherham), 211
Lovell, Francis, Viscount Lovell, 288
Lud, King, 14, 18, 82

Map, Walter, 234
Marchall, Roger, 296
Margaret, Queen, 7, 9, 10, 20, 24, 38,
51, 237
Market, Clerk of the, 100, 102, **140–1,**
154, 176, 182, 249
Marquis, 89, 96
Marshal, 2, 63, 64, 85, 115, 203, 204,
210, 216, **225,** 235, 257, 265
Marshall, John, 246
Marshalsea, 23, 24, 85, 141, 142, 161,
163, 176, 235, 250
Mary I, Queen, 241
Mary II, Queen, 241
Messengers, 70, 133, 248
Mews, 65, 71
Middleton, Bryan, 200, 264
Middleton, William, 264
Milan, Duke of, 249
Minstrels, 16, 48, 71, **131–2,** 247
Mongomery (Montgomery), Sir
Thomas, 199, 240, 262
Morreis (Norris), Sir William, 200, 240,
263
Mortimer, John, 232

Neville, George, Archbishop of York,
2, 253
Neville, Richard (see Warwick)
Neville, William, Earl of Kent, 286

Northumberland, Earl of (Henry Algernon Percy, 5th Earl, Household Book, 1512), 1, 21, 60, 239, 249, 254, 260, 267, 268
Norys (Norris), Sir William (see Morreis, Sir William)

Ordinances of 1318 and 1323, 20, 232, 235, 237, 239, 244, 256, 257, 259, 260, 261
Ordinance of 1445, 7, 8, 9, 22, 27, 40, 41, 42, 43, 50, 51, **63–75, 232–62,** 264, 266, 267, 268
Ordinance of 1454, 27, 41, 51, 233, 237, 239, 241, 242, 243, 244, 245
Ordinance of 1471, 32, **198–202,** 233, 242, 267
Ordinance of 1478, 13, 19, 20, 22, 27, 29, 30, 32, **39–44,** 47, 49, 50, **56–9,** 198, **203–10, 211–28,** 232–69
Ordinance of 1493, 58
Ordinance of Eltham, 1526, 31, 235, 236, 238, 242, 244, 245, 249, 253, 267
Ordinance of 1539–40, 48, 49, 266, 269
Ordinance of 1601, 269
Ordinance of 1727, 50
Oxford, Earl of, 239

Pantler, 2, 257
Pantry, 15, 23, 63, 64, 72, 85, 131, 162, 167, **169–74,** 177, 178, 180, 181, 183, 184, 190, 191, 195, 196, 202, 206, 208, 216, 217, 218, 220, **226,** 230, 254, 256, 257, 258
Paris, Matthew, 249
Parke, John, 255, 295
Parker, 66, 85, 220
Parliament, 8, 63, 66, 142, 251
Parre, Sir John, 199, 262
Parre, Sir William, 199, 253, 262, 289
Paston, Sir John, 246
Pastry, 17, 257, 269
Percy, Sir Robert, 289, 290
Percy, Thomas, Earl of Worcester, 252
Physicians, **70,** 91, 106, **123–4,** 125, **225,** 245, 296
Pitcher-House and Cuphouse, 15, 63, 64, 181, **183–4,** 186, 193, **227,** 260
Plummer, Sir John, 294
Pollington (Pilkington), Sir John, 199, 262
Pomery, Richard, 199, 263
Port (Porte), William, 244, 291
Porte (Prout), Thomas, 199, 263
Porters, 17, 64, 65, 71, 121, 160, 201, 202, 203, 204, 205, 214, 218, 220
Poultry, 17, 39, 74, **228,** 257, 269

Prince, 89, 93, 96, 159, 163, 238
Pulter, 121
Purveyance, 67, 102, 103, 144, 147, 149, 153, 154, 165, 168, 174, 176, 185, 187, 222
Purveyors, 65, 67, 97, 98, 102, 140, 149, 165, 168, 181, 189, 221, 222, 253, 260
Purveyors of Wines, 15, **177–8, 259**

Queen, 71, 72, **92–3,** 96, 129, 159, 163, 197, 204, 206, 207, 209, 213, 214, 218, 220, 225, 226, 233, 238, 259

Radclyf, James, 240
Randolf, John, 260
Ratcliffe, Robert, 200, 264
Ray (Ree), Sir Roger, 32, 199, 262
Richard II, King, 250, 252
Richard III, King, 12, 15, 29, 30, 86, 232, 236, 246, 262, 287, 288, 289, 290, 291, 293, 294
Richard of Poitiers, 234
Robes, Yeomen of the, 71, 116
Roger of Waltham, Keeper of the Wardrobe to Edward II, 21
Rokeley, John, 257
Rozmittal, Leo, Lord of, Brother of the Queen of Bohemia, 47
Russell, John, 1st Earl of Bedford, 20
Russell, John, Usher and Marshall to Humphrey, Duke of Gloucester, 237, 245

Salinger (St. Leger, Seintlegier), Thomas, 199, 257, 263
Salt-cellar, 254, 257, 258
Sapecote (Sapcote), John, 199, 263
Saucery, 39, 64, 74, 167, 181, 187, **228,** 269
Say, Sir John, 294
Say, William, 248, 249, 291
Scalding-House, 17, 74, **228,** 269
Scott, Sir John, 253, 289
Scullery, 17, 39, 59, 64, 74, 181, 193, **228,** 257
Seal, Privy, 66, 85, 103, 133, 174, 176, 235, 249, 292
Seal, Signet, 56, 110, 211
Secretary, 22, **69,** 91, **110–11,** 133, 201, **224,** 237, **293–4**
Seintlegier, Thomas (see Salinger, Thomas)
Seneca, 18, 76, 163
Serego, Dominic de, 296
Sergeants, 64, 66, 68, 204, 206, 218, 219, 223, 225, 256, 257, 261
Serjeants-at-Arms, 17, 85, **131,** 247
Serjeants-at-Law, 69

Sewer, 2, 32, **70,** 71, 92, 93, 94, 106,
  112–13, 123, 127, 201, 209, 217, 220,
  225, 238, 241, 261
Shalford, Humphrey, 199, 263
Sherley, Hughe (Shirley, Hugh), 200,
  264
Signet Warrants, 29, 56, 211
Slefeld, William, 293
Solomon, King, 14, 79, **81–2,** 83, 84, 234
Spicery, 15, 39, 59, 63, 64, 73, 100,
  110, 113, 137, 144, 145, 149, 151,
  156, 159, 17**1,** 173, **186–8,** 189, 190,
  191, 196, 216, 217, 220, **225, 227,**
  254, 257, 260, 261
Squires, 64, 65, 66, 89, 147, 209, 220,
  226, 232, 246, 247, 254
Squires for the Body, 17, 32, 41, 42,
  70, 91, 106, **111–12,** 113, 115, 123,
  200, 201, 205, 206, 215, 217, **225,**
  232, 241, 242, 246, 262
Squires of the Household, 16, 41, 63,
  124, **127–30,** 131, 141, 205, 206, 210,
  215, 216, 217, 245, 246, 267
Stable, 17, 23, 59, 65, 74, 75, 221, 229,
  269
Stanley, Thomas, Lord Stanley, 251,
  287
Stanley, Sir William, 240
Steward of the Household, 15, 24, 25,
  26, 29, 39, 43, 66, 67, 68, 71, 87, 89,
  90, 105, 112, 123, 126, 127, 128,
  129, 130, 131, 132, 133, 134, 136,
  137, 139, 141, **142–4,** 145, 148, 149,
  150, 152, 154, 155, 156, 160, 161,
  162, 163, 173, 174, 176, 177, 198,
  204, 205, 207, 209, 213, 215, 219,
  220, 221, 223, **224,** 235, 250, 251,
  252, 257, 265, 268, **286–7**
Stool, Yeoman of the, 116
Strangwis, John, 199, 263
Sumpter-Horses, 75, 121, 137, 172,
  178, 191, 193, 261, 262
Surgeon, 16, **70,** 91, 117, 121, **124–5,**
  243, 245, 297
Surveyor, 32, **70,** 71, 112, **113–14,** 242
Syon Monastery, 211

Taillour, John, 293
Talbot, Brian, 200, 264
Terence, 242
Teringham (Tyringham), Thomas,
  199, 263
Tilles, Richard, 290, 296
Tiptoft, John, Earl of Worcester
  (d. 1470), 32, 250, 251, 257, 286
Tiptoft, Sir John (d. 1443), 252
Towels, 258, 261
Trayer, Yeoman, 260
Treasurer of the Chamber (see
  Chamber, Treasurer of the)

Treasurer of the Household, 15, 17,
  24, 25, 26, 29, 34, 35, 39, 42, 43, 65,
  66, 67, 68, 71, 85, 87, 89, 92, 93, 94,
  105, 112, 114, 118, 119, 122, 123,
  126, 127, 128, 130, 131, 132, 133,
  136, 137, 138, 139, 141, 142, 143,
  144–7, 148, 149, 150, 151, 152, 153,
  154, 155, 156, 158, 160, 161, 162,
  163, 172, 173, 174, 176, 177, 187,
  190, 193, 204, 205, 207, 208, 209,
  213, 215, 220, 221, 223, **224,** 232,
  235, 240, 242, 243, 245, 250, 251,
  252, 260, 265, 266, 268, **288–9,** 290,
  291
Trevisa, John of, 235
Tunstall, Sir Richard, 288
Tyler, William, 249, 250

Usher, Gentleman, 2, 20, 22, 32, 41,
  42, 63, 64, **70,** 90, 91, 92, 105, 106,
  114–15, 120, 133, 191, 194, 200, 201,
  202, 206, 215, 216, **225,** 237, 240,
  241, 242, 243, 244, 247, 262, 265
Usher, Yeoman, 32, 70, 200, 201, 202

Vaughan, Sir Thomas, Treasurer of
  the Chamber, 22, 38, 244, 291
Vestiary, 63, 137, 138, **138–9,** 196,
  221, 249
Vestynden, Rauf, 243
Viscount, 101–3
Voragine, Jacopo de, 234

Wafery 15, 72, 167, **172–4,** 181, 187,
  209, **227,** 258
Waiters, 91, 201, **225,** 240, 242
Waits, 16, 71, **132–3,** 247, 248
Wardrobe, 23, 63, 85, 100, 105, 111,
  118, 120, 138, 221, 232, 235, 242
Wardrobe, Great, 17, 45, 47, 85, 111,
  112, 114, 117, 121, 135, 176, 235,
  239, 240, 241, 242, 247, 249, 256,
  291, 294
Wardrobe of Beds, 23, 116, **119–20,**
  196
Wardrobe of Robes, 17, **117–18,** 196
Wards Royal, 17, 21, 68, 126, **141,** 250
Warrant, 56, 66, 103, 210
Warwick, Edward, Earl of, 232
Warwick, Richard Neville, Earl of, 2,
  5, 21, 30, 238
Whethamstede, John of, Abbot of
  St. Albans, 5, 235
Wilford, Thomas, 292
Williamson, Sir Joseph, 57
Willoughby, Sir Robert, Steward of
  Henry VII's Household, 266
Wingfield, Sir Robert, 37, 253, 289
Wintreshull, Thomas, Serjeant of
  Harthounds, 243

Wolsey, Thomas, Cardinal, 238
Woodyard, 17, 257, 269
Works, Clerk of, 16, 141, 176, 259
Wydeville, Elizabeth (see Elizabeth
    Wydeville)

Wykes, John, 199, 263

York, Cecily, Duchess of, 11
York, Richard, Duke of, 223, 268
Younge (Young), John, 200, 264